# Instability and Change
## in the
## World Economy

# Instability and Change in the World Economy

### edited by
### Arthur MacEwan and William K. Tabb

Ⓜ
Monthly Review Press
New York

Copyright © 1989 by Arthur MacEwan and William K. Tabb

**Library of Congress Cataloging-in-Publication Data**

Instability and change in the world economy / edited by Arthur MacEwan
and William K. Tabb.
    p.  cm.
    Bibliography: p.
    Includes index.
    ISBN 0-85345-782-4 : $36.00—ISBN 0-85345-783-2 (pbk.) : $18.00
    1. Economic history—1971–    2. Capitalism.  3. Business cycles.
4. International economic relations.  I. MacEwan, Arthur.
II. Tabb, William K.
HC59.I4966  1989
330.9′04—dc20
                                          89-9373
                                          CIP

Monthly Review Press
122 West 27th Street, New York, N.Y. 10001

Manufactured in the U.S.A.

10 9 8 7 6 5 4 3 2 1

# Contents

## 6  Contents

## Part III
### The Lasting Crisis: Constraints and Opportunities

# Introduction

## *Arthur MacEwan and William K. Tabb*

The Exploratorium in San Francisco is a "hands-on" science museum where visitors are encouraged to learn by doing. The centerpiece of one of the participatory exhibits is a pendulum, a cement cylinder encased in steel, weighing about three hundred pounds and suspended by a cable from the ceiling high above. A low fence forms a circle, perhaps twenty feet in diameter, around the slowly swinging pendulum. Several small magnets, the type one might use to attach a note to the refrigerator, are tied to the fence with long pieces of string. The participant-visitor is supposed to toss a magnet so that it adheres to the steel case of the pendulum. Then, using this rather tenuous connection, she or he is supposed to take up the string and redirect the motion of the pendulum.

Attempting to execute this seemingly prosaic task, one quickly learns some important lessons about the problem of using such a limited device for affecting the direction of a large mass that is already moving with considerable inertia. If one is careful, determines just how the pendulum is already moving, and uses the string-magnet connection to alter that motion bit by bit, a considerable effect can be achieved in a reasonably short time. If, however, one ignores the motion of the pendulum and attempts immediately to alter its direction to some other path, magnet and string will fall to the floor, and the pendulum will continue on its slow, steady, predetermined course.

History, the economy, and social relations are not subject to the well-defined laws of pendular motion. Yet if we want to be effective political actors and have an impact upon the direction of history, we had better figure out how history is moving. If we act on our ideals per se—that is, if we simply demand that society be altered to conform to our goals—we will achieve little. If, however, we give some attention to the way history is moving, ascertain the particular changes that are already taking place in our society, and then attempt to affect the course of history, we might achieve a considerable effect.

This book of essays grew out of our desire to figure out how history is moving in order that we might help the development of progressive, oppositional political forces in the United States and elsewhere. We have focused on international economic affairs because during the current era instability and change in the international economy play such an important role in our political lives. Indeed, an increasingly worldwide system of production dominates peoples' lives as at no other time in history.

People attempting to bring about change through popular political action are often caught in a dilemma. On the one hand, political affairs are organized on a national basis; frequently, in fact, popular political activity is best organized on the local level of the community or the workplace. On the other hand, our economy is international; economic events which affect the local environment have their roots in geographically distant occurrences, and their evolution is conditioned by an array of interdependencies operating in a worldwide system. There is no easy resolution for this political-economic dilemma. It seems clear, however, that people attempting to bring about progressive social change must give a good deal of attention to the world economy and to the interactions and tensions that connect local, national, and international affairs.

Of course, we are by no means the first to recognize the importance of these issues, and, even among progressives, there are many competing interpretations of the changing organization of international production and exchange. The essays in this book contribute to the discussions and debates by examining the interaction between the national and international aspects of the world economy. Recognizing that the world economy is in the midst of a period of dramatic and far-reaching change, the authors of these essays have attempted to figure out how particular parts of the system are changing, and how the changes of the parts relate to the change of the whole. Also, although the focus of our essays is economic and social change, we have examined related political issues, attempting to offer some help in resolving the political-economic dilemma faced by progressive forces.

We think that our book may provide a partial antidote to problems that have plagued oppositional action and analysis. In the realm of action, many people have responded to the internationalization of economic life by turning inward and concentrating simply on local work. When facing problems with an obvious international dimension, political activists have sometimes responded with nationalist solutions that ignore change in the world economy; reiteration of traditional sorts of protectionist programs is an example.

Many analysts have reacted to localist and nationalist political tendencies by giving extreme emphasis to the increasing importance of the international, or "global," aspects of economic relations. This work has given rise to the idea that the force of the world economy is sweeping aside national boundaries. The writings of Immanuel Wallerstein (1979 and 1983, for example) have had an important impact, establishing the vision of a single "world system" since the sixteenth century, sweeping aside all else. In the globalist perspective, the great mobility of capital and a "new international division of labor" render national policies and local politics ineffective (Frobel et al. 1980). Many of the broad analytic and empirical generalizations of the "globalists" have been called into question (Gordon 1988), but it would be folly to argue that nothing new is happening in the world economy, that policy and politics at the national and local level can be unaffected by the changes that have been taking place.

The dichotomy between globalists and localists is to some degree, as we have suggested, a dichotomy between theorists and activists. The former tend to develop grand historical visions, while the latter tend to focus on practical, immediate tasks. Yet effective political work needs both the grand vision and the practical focus, as is summed up in the slogan of the popular bumper sticker: "Think Globally, Act Locally." For the slogan to be put into practice, connections need to be drawn between the global and the local so that concrete political action can be conceived in the broader context.

The essays in this book are important because they move beyond the simple dichotomy between globalist and nationalist (or localist) approaches. We begin our work with a recognition of the central importance of the world economy in affecting national (and local) developments. Yet we also maintain that the national events retain considerable importance and that, in particular, the nation-state is a key unit of analysis. In spite of the increasing internationalization of economic affairs, there is an interaction—a dialectic—between the national and world economies. The particular aspects of this interaction deserve attention if we are to figure out how things are developing and find openings for progressive political action.

In asking various authors to contribute to this project, we requested essays that would provide concrete analyses of particular aspects of the instability and change in the world economy. We asked them to consider their topics in relation to the evolution of the national-international tension that is so important in shaping current events. Thus these essays—on oil and agriculture, debt and macropolicy, the organization of work and the changing position of women—give us useful insights on the particular topics they address and on the larger issue of the evolution of the world economy.

### Issues and Arguments

During the last two decades, the world economy has been enmeshed in a crisis. Slow economic growth, or stagnation, has been the most obvious symptom of the crisis, and, from the point of view of capital, the difficulties are summed up in the dramatic decline in profit rates at the end of the 1960s and their poor performance in subsequent years. While profits rose in the late 1980s, the improvement was based on a one-time distributional gain at the expense of labor and on an extreme debt build-up, not on any firm foundation for long-run expansion. For people, the crisis appears in high unemployment rates, inflation, worsening income distribution, rapid dislocation of industry, general economic insecurity, and, especially in the 1980s, the worsening conditions of life in much of the third world. Despite the expansion of new technologies and growth in some regions and sectors, the current era is one of relative stagnation and generally poor economic performance.

Yet an economic crisis does not simply mean bad times. More important, a crisis means change, the destruction of the old bases on which the system operated and the creation of new relationships. New structures of power and new forms of economic organization will be created if international capitalism is going to maintain itself. And in this process of change, there are various opportunities for progressive forces.

At the center of the crisis is the disarray of international affairs which has altered relations between national events and developments in the larger world economy. In our own essay, "Instability and Change in the World Economy," the first in Part I, we give considerable attention to the connection between the world economy and the national economy, pointing out that capitalist development is based on a complex international-national duality. In order to understand the world economy and, particularly, to understand the political implications of economic affairs, one must give attention to the international operation of capitalism, its national foundations, and the interaction between the two. We also examine the connections between stagnation and international instability, arguing that there is a reciprocal interaction by which stagnation causes international instability and international instability exacerbates stagnation. We develop our arguments by examining problems of debt and the international reorganization of production.

James Petras and Morris Morley take up an especially important part of the international-national interaction in "The Imperial State in the Rise and Fall of U.S. Imperialism." Recognizing that the decline of U.S. power has been a major feature affecting the emergence of stagnation and instability, they examine the particular contradictions that have undermined the U.S. state relative to its Japanese and West German rivals. Positing that the state must play major economic roles in the maintenance of capitalist expansion, Petras and Morley then explain why those branches of the U.S. state which perform directly economic functions have been weakened.

In "British Capitalism in a Changing Global Economy" Hugo Radice challenges views put forth by some of us who have developed our analyses more on the basis of the U.S. experience. Radice's argument suggests that British capital's international resurgence in recent years indicates the power of private business independent of the state support seen as so essential by Petras and Morley. Also, as compared with some of the other analyses in this book, Radice would place a much greater emphasis on the international or "global" as opposed to the national realm of events. He does not, however, ignore the importance of the national; for example, he writes of "British capital" as an entity and describes its particular strategy and practices. Radice's views force us to avoid an excessive emphasis on the U.S. experience in shaping our concepts about the world economy.

The essays by James Crotty and Gerald Epstein—"The Limits of Keynesian Macroeconomic Policy in the Age of the Global Marketplace" and "Financial Instability and the Structure of the International Monetary System"—continue the discussion by examining the operation of national economic policies in an internationalized economy. Crotty's essay provides a thorough explanation of the way the Keynesian policy agenda has been eviscerated by the current reality, and Epstein demonstrates how the evolution of the international monetary system has greatly reduced the flexibility and effectiveness of traditional government policy measures. Both analyses give considerable attention to the implications of the increasing size and rapidity of international capital movements, and point out how the mobility of liquid capital would undermine even mildly progressive national policies. Thus their arguments demonstrate that some forms of control on capital movements would be a necessary component of any progressive program.

Robert Pollin's essay "Debt-Dependent Growth and Financial Innovation" examines the relation between the national and the international by focusing on the debt build-up of the last two decades. Pollin traces the debt expansions in both the United States and the third world to common roots in the stagnation of the world economy, though he also points out the important difference between the debts in these two regions. He argues that financial innovation has contributed to the debt build-up, created a very fragile international capital market, and rendered national monetary policies all but ineffective. Pollin concludes that any progressive program cannot rely simply on inhibiting the increasingly powerful international financial markets and, instead, should call for a radical restructuring of those markets.

One theme which continually reemerges in the essays of Part I, and which recurs throughout the book, is that the problems of current-day capitalism cannot be explained as aberrations, as transitory phenomena resulting from "incorrect" policy, bad luck, or "external" events. International instability and stagnation, with the myriad particular difficulties they generate, have their roots in the operation of capitalism as a system. While we offer varying perspectives on the emergence of the current crisis, we share a general agreement that its deep roots are forcing a major restructuring of economic life.

Several of the essays in Part II examine the way restructuring is evolving in particular parts of the economy. In "International Development and Industrial Restructuring" M. Patricia Fernández Kelly uses case studies of the garment and electronics industries in southern California to point out the way the international operation of firms in these industries has lead to a dramatic restructuring—not simply a decline or deindustrialization—within the country. Her study is a powerful antidote to an overly simplified view of the world economy, in which firms' locational decisions are dictated purely by a global search for cheap labor.

The complexities of international restructuring and firms' locational decisions are also evident from Richard Child Hill's essay "Divisions of Labor in Global Manufacturing: The Case of the Automobile Industry." Hill describes and explains the "production systems" in the U.S. and Japanese automobile industries. He demonstrates that labor relations, organizational structure, and locational decisions interact in ways that can only be explained in historically specific terms, and sweeping generalizations about the "inevitable logic" of a new international division of labor are often misleading. In formulating responses to business actions, local communities and labor organizations need to take account of the particular bases of those actions and the nature of the production systems in which they occur.

In "Bound by One Thread: The Restructuring of U.K. Clothing and Textile Multinationals," Diane Elson examines the way strategies of large firms in these industries have been affected by change in the international economy. She points out that while labor cost differentials have been significant, several other factors have also played important roles; moreover, companies' decisions to expand abroad are combined with decisions to restructure production at home. Elson addresses political problems and opportunities raised by these changes, especially for women, who are such a large portion of the labor force in the clothing and textile industries. She suggests that an effective response by labor to the strategies of the multinationals must move beyond the firm and be carried out on the social level, involving the community at large as well as the labor movement.

The continuing instabilities in the international operation of two major sectors are taken up by Jean-Pierre Berlan and Michael Tanzer in their essays "Capital Accumulation, Transformation of Agriculture, and the Agricultural Crisis" and "Growing Instability in the International Oil Industry." Berlan argues that in the 1980s a long-established tendency toward overproduction in U.S. agriculture has reappeared. After explaining the basis of this tendency, he examines future prospects, and, seeing little basis to believe that markets will expand sufficiently to balance growing productive capacity, suggests that agriculture will be a continuing source of international instability. Likewise, Tanzer's examination of international oil leads to the expectation that here too we will see continuing disruption and disarray. Tanzer's analysis provides a clear example of the connections between the international operations of capitalist firms and their reliance on national state power. He describes the way international instability and the fragmentation of power have both contributed to and been affected by the instability of the oil industry.

The final essays in Part II, those by Lourdes Benería and William Tabb, lead toward some important political implications about the current restructuring of the world economy. Benería, in "Gender and the Global Economy," provides an overview of the way the changing nature of international production is affecting women's economic roles. Increasingly, women are being drawn into wage production and experience substantial dislocation from traditional roles. These changes are generating new political initiatives. Progressives will have to adjust, developing new sorts of demands and programs consistent with the changing needs of women, or be left behind. Tabb's essay "Capital Mobility, the Restructuring of Production and the Politics of Labor" also points to the need for new politics for the left. As U.S. capital has become thoroughly international, the basis has been eliminated for the traditional cooperation of the AFL-CIO with business. U.S. workers no longer hold such a special, exceptional position in the world economy, and they must find new ways to respond to the pressures created by restructuring. Tabb notes some new steps that have already been taken by progressive forces in the labor movement, and suggests that with all its negative impacts, restructuring may create positive opportunities.

The essays in Part III offer some further investigation of the opportunities—and the constraints—contained in the ongoing changes of the world economy. John Bellamy Foster, in "The Age of Restructuring," argues that restructuring can be understood as the strategy of capital and the dominant political forces in the advanced capitalist countries, specifically, their effort to both immediately lower costs and shift power in their favor. Foster argues, however, that restructuring is contradictory, and in its very success will spread the conflicts, instabilities, and stagnation of capitalism on a wider and wider scale. He then sees a basis for optimism in the correspondingly wider scale of resistance that restructuring will generate, and he suggests that workers' local resistance to the impacts of restructuring will strengthen progressive forces.

Robert Wood, in "The International Monetary Fund and the World Bank in a Changing World Economy," raises questions about the power of these institutions and, more generally, about the possibilities for third world struggles to overcome constraints imposed by the world economy. Pointing out the way the global recession and debt crisis of the 1980s have vastly expanded the roles of the IMF and the World Bank, Wood nonetheless contends that these two institutions are finding it increasingly difficult to contain the current instabilities and impose their favored "solutions." He argues that their experience reflects a larger issue: while the world economy imposes severe constraints on the viability of progressive forms of development, contradictions in the international system are also undermining those constraints just as the need for alternatives becomes more evident.

Carlos Vilas' "International Constraints on Progressive Change in Peripheral Societies" takes up the recent experience in Nicaragua. Small third world countries attempting a progressive social transformation face severe difficulties in balancing the agro-export orientation which they have inherited with a desire to reorient the economy toward the internal market. One route tends to subordinate social needs to the generation of foreign exchange, while the other may advance social transformation but only at the expense of economic growth. Vilas argues that this dilemma can be overcome only by an infusion of external assistance. To overcome their heritage of underdevelopment and their weak position in the world economy, countries such as Nicaragua, he argues, require some form of substantial foreign funds to transform their societies. Although Vilas sees the external constraints as severe, he also sees possibilities for obtaining the needed assistance and suggests that there are possibilities for the small countries of the periphery.

Clive Thomas also focuses his attention on the periphery in "Restructuring the World Economy and its Political Implications for the Third World." His analysis is directed toward the political conclusion that the left in the third world should more strongly embrace formal democracy as its cause. Thomas sees the current crisis as extremely deep, involving a fundamental disjuncture in the world capitalist economy. He believes that capitalism will be able to emerge from this crisis on new technological and new organizational foundations, but that the depth of the crisis is forcing extensive political changes in the third world. Ruling groups, in order to save their position, will have no choice but to extend the formal processes of democracy. The introduction of democracy, however, can move in varied directions and opens opportunities for either restrictive or progressive social change. Thomas argues that the left can have the most positive impact by supporting democratic change and pushing it as far as possible.

In the book's final essay, "A New Stage of Capitalism Ahead?" Harry Magdoff focuses on the anticipated removal of economic barriers within the European Community, scheduled to take effect in 1992. The vision expressed by Magdoff is very different from that expressed by Thomas in the preceding essay. For Magdoff sees no basis for a capitalist renewal. He argues that more open markets were not the basis of growth during the long post-World War II expansion, and still freer markets will not do the trick at this stage. After World War II, economic expansion was based on major technological innovation which lead to massive investments and on a set of demand factors peculiar to the era. Examining the current period, he sees no parallel set of specific development factors which would precipitate a new era of expansion, regardless of market integration in Europe or elsewhere. Magdoff's analysis carries with it the implication that our era will be one of continuing pressure on labor, and also that there will be continuing change and struggle over the direction of society's development.

## New Themes and Continuing Questions

Most of the authors in this volume took part in a conference during May 1988 at which original drafts of these essays were the basis for discussion. At that conference, several common themes emerged, many of which are not fully and directly raised in the essays in this book.

There was, for example, recognition of a convergence of sorts between the "core" and the "periphery" of the world economy. Of course the income and power distinctions that divide the developed and underdeveloped regions of the world have not been altered. These two broad categories of countries are, however, increasingly facing similar sorts of problems and are being affected by those problems in similar fashions. Internationalization has created common constraints, and, as is brought out by several of the essays (e.g., Crotty, Epstein, Pollin), even the United States and other core nations cannot stand above the international economy.

We also noted that international restructuring has led to a variety of new patterns of labor appropriation and control. "Informalization," where workers are employed temporarily, part time, in their own homes, or "off the books" is one aspect of this process that deserves particular attention. Previously recognized as a significant phenomenon in the third world, informalization, as Fernández Kelly has pointed out, is also playing a major role in the United States. Even while informalization is often developed as a business strategy, it also emerges at times as a defensive strategy initiated by workers (street vendors, small contractors, etc.).

Internationalization of economic activity has spread the social relations of capitalism, and placed workers around the globe in similar positions. One important aspect of this change is increasing involvement of women in wage labor, as is brought out by Elson's examination of the textile industry and as is discussed more generally by Benería. The rapid entrance of women into wage labor has created new social needs as well as new possibilities for progressive action. Also, as internationalization has spread the common conditions of wage labor, the exceptional position of workers in the most advanced countries has been altered. Workers in the United States, for example, are both placed in competition with their counterparts elsewhere and subjected to a common condition. Again, the change creates possibilities for new political initiatives, as Tabb and Foster have both stressed.

The changes in the international economy are placing severe and contradictory pressures on governments. On the one hand, the instabilities and social dislocations created by international change lead to demands that governments provide protection for their own citizens and industries. On the other hand, internationalization has enhanced the power of capital and reinforced the rise of conservative political forces demanding a reduction of government interventions and controls on economic life. Through the 1980s, in countries where political circumstances differ widely, privatization and reductions of social programs have been the common response to international debt problems, increased international competition, and instabilities of international prices and exchange rates. (These matters are touched on by several authors—Wood, Epstein, Pollin.)

In addition to common themes which emerged in our discussions, the conference produced useful disagreements. Some of these come out clearly in the essays themselves, and we have noted them above. Some of the other disagreements that arose among us, however, were not so clear. For example, the papers by Wood, Vilas, and Thomas elicited considerable discussion over the extent to which independent development in the third world is a viable option. The world economy and the power of institutions such as the World Bank and IMF give little leeway to any country which attempts to opt out. At the same time, however, the present organization of economic activity in most of the third world results in considerable waste and underutilization of resources; a radical break might allow growth through more effective resource use.

Our discussion also reached no clear conclusion on the interaction between stagnation and the financial explosion. Pollin's essay provided useful insights, and the work of Harry Magdoff and Paul Sweezy (1987) has been especially important in setting out a broad understanding of the stagnation-finance connection. We agree, it seems, that the financial explosion is in some sense a product of stagnation, yet we do not agree—or perhaps it is better to say we lack clarity—as to the way in which the financial explosion feeds back and affects stagnation. Certainly, a better grasp of this issue would enhance our general analyses.

The conference discussions also made us acutely aware of the many topics which were missing from our essays and which are missing from this book. We had no illusions about the possibility of assembling a comprehensive set of analyses on "instability and change in the world economy," and we are sure that each reader will be able to compile a long list of topics that are missing or receive no thorough treatment: the impact of the current crisis on the environment; the changing role of the "newly industrializing countries" such as Korea and Brazil; economic reforms in the socialist bloc and their relation to the world economy; the particular role of Japan and the connections between the Japanese domestic economy and the world economy; social democratic policy options, as represented by the Brandt Commission studies; and any number of analyses of particular countries or regions in the world economy. Even though some of these matters do receive passing treatment, the omissions are substantial, and we do not wish to pretend otherwise. Still, the essays here provide numerous insights, and together they move us toward a better understanding of how the world economy is currently developing.

### Economic Analysis and Political Program

As we hope will be the case with this book, our essays led to considerable exchange at the conference on the relation between the world economy and possible economic programs for the left. Several of the authors, as we have noted above, directly address political issues in their essays, and the points they raised were thoroughly discussed.

There was, in addition, extensive discussion of the extent to which a progressive program can go beyond defensive demands. All agreed that defense is important. Protecting workers' incomes and rights in the face of international pressures and blocking interventions in countries that have broken with international capitalism are essential parts of any left program.

Yet the question remains as to how far we can go and should go in pushing positive economic demands. Our analyses lead toward conclusions about what can be done, and some argued that we should emphasize the policy implications of our work. We have pointed out above, for example, that the essays by Crotty and Epstein suggest the need for control of international capital movements as a precondition for any progressive macroeconomic policies. The articulation of a progressive economic program, however, often cannot avoid one of two opposite pitfalls. On the one hand, if the program were to provide a real solution to current economic problems, it would be so extensive as to appear thoroughly unrealistic as an intrasystem reform. On the other hand, if the program is "realistic" it may be so timid that it would have no significant progressive impact.

Our conference discussion of left economic programs was, of course, unresolved. Nonetheless, it did bring out some important agreements about the criteria on which progressive programs should be derived from the sorts of analyses represented in these essays. Often progressive analysts fail because the program and demands they suggest have been designed largely on the basis of their practicality—in the sense that they could be implemented without any radical restructuring of political or social relations. Such practical, or "realistic," programs can appear as nothing but an effort to make the system work better, and they may present no challenge to the system itself. We would do well to avoid this tendency and continually raise questions such as: To what extent does this demand or this program contribute to the development of a mass oppositional movement? Is this a "class oriented" program? To what extent do these demands further a socialist agenda?

Moreover, there is an interaction between analysis and political work that needs to be developed as a basis for the formulation of program. A progressive economic agenda cannot be developed as an intellectual exercise. For our work to be useful it needs to be tied to an actual political movement. Community action, labor struggles, anti-intervention efforts—all have provided some context, some connections, for our work. In so far as these sorts of activities coalesce into a substantial political movement in the coming period, work like ours will be all the more meaningful. Perhaps our work can even help development in that direction.

Several people helped make this book possible. The authors of the essays were especially cooperative, and we appreciated their extra efforts at each step of the way. In addition to the authors, Carmen Diana Deere, Fred Deyo, Cheryl Payer, and Paul Sweezy took part in our conference and made numerous valuable contributions. David Hunter and W. H. and Carol Ferry provided support which made the conference and the whole project possible; we are very appreciative. Betty and Herman Liveright and the staff of the Berkshire Forum provided us with the setting and circumstance that allowed us to have a conference that was both effective and enjoyable. At Monthly Review Press, Susan Lowes helped us in developing this project from its first conception and provided important advice along the way; Karen Judd did a fine and much appreciated job of moving the manuscript through to publication. To all of these people, we extend our thanks.

## References

Frobel, Folker, Jurgen Heinrichs, and Otto Kreye. 1980. *The New International Division of Labor*. Cambridge: Cambridge University Press.

Gordon, David. 1988. "The Global Economy: New Edifice or Crumbling Foundation?" *New Left Review*, No. 168, March/April.

Magdoff, Harry and Paul M. Sweezy. 1987. *Stagnation and the Financial Explosion*. New York: Monthly Review Press.

Wallerstein, Immanuel. 1979. *The Capitalist World-Economy*, Cambridge: Cambridge University Press.

———. 1983. "Crisis: The World-Economy, the Movements, and the Ideologies." In Albert Bergesen, ed. *Crisis in the World-System*, Beverly Hills: Sage Publications.

# Part 1
# The Changing World Order and the Limits of State Intervention

# Instability and Change in the World Economy

## Arthur MacEwan and William K. Tabb

The world economy has been in a state of instability and change for many years now. Since roughly the beginning of the 1970s, there has been an almost continual stream of disruptions: oil crises, severe trade imbalances, sharp exchange-rate fluctuations, a huge buildup of debt. These particular phenomena are part of a widespread crisis, a grand disruption that is profoundly altering the structural and institutional relations of international capitalism.

A primary feature of the current international disarray has been a relative decline in the position of the United States. The U.S. government and U.S. corporations have retained great economic and political power in international affairs, and over the 1970s and 1980s their power has by no means moved uniformly downward. Yet the extent and nature of their domination have changed since the 1950s and 1960s, and they are no longer able to set the rules and provide secure stability for international capitalism. Conflicts of the 1950s and 1960s that undermined U.S. hegemony thus weakened the stability of the world economy, ushered in an era of relative stagnation, and set in motion a period of crisis.

The era of U.S. hegemony, which lasted roughly from the end of World War II to the early 1970s, left an extensive legacy in the highly integrated and interdependent world economy. Barriers to the movement of commodities and capital were substantially lowered, and each region of the capitalist world—if not the entire world—is closely connected to and quickly affected by economic events in distant realms. Yet with the decline of U.S. hegemony, there is less basis to regulate this complex international system.

We have thus entered into an era of crisis with a highly interconnected *and* a highly unstable international system. As a consequence, people—especially in the United States—are increasingly aware of the extent to which their lives are affected by events in the larger world economy. The importance of international events in the evolution of capitalism is, however, nothing new. Adam Smith remarked in *The Wealth of Nations:* "The discovery of America, and that of a passage to the East Indies by the Cape of Good Hope, are the two greatest and most important events recorded in the history of mankind . . . [O]ne of the principal effects of those discoveries has been to raise the mercantile system to a degree of splendour and glory which it could never have otherwise attained to" (1937 rep. ed.: 590–91).

Nonetheless, while international events have defined the dynamic of capitalist development, nations have remained principal units of economic organization, providing the social and political foundations for capitalism. The relation between the national and the international, or the "global," has been a theme of recurring debate among people trying to understand how the system is moving. This debate has become particularly acute in the current era, as we have moved into a period of increasing "internationalization." To what extent are we living in a "global economy" or "world system" and to what extent are we living in "national economic systems" with important connections to one another? The answer to this question is significant because it affects how one approaches the formation of political programs to deal with the economic change.

The polar positions in this debate tend to lead toward withdrawal from or unrealistic approaches toward political change. The extreme globalist position often carries the implication that no change is possible except on the international level, and since there is no political mechanism for such change—aside from that of formal relations among governments—oppositional political activity is easily seen as useless. On the other extreme, those who view the national economic system as a viable unit are led to formulate programs that ignore the importance of economic forces which transcend national boundaries. Such an outlook can lead to both unrealistic programs which fail because of capital's international flexibility and implicit alliances with reactionary nationalist groups to advocate, for example, increased "competitiveness."

We think it is possible to overcome the simple dichotomy on which this debate has evolved. In our view, capitalist development—both historically and in the current era—involves an international-national duality. The system has both "global" and "national" characteristics with a complex interaction between the two. It would be equally misleading to obscure the international (global) operations of capitalism, its national foundations, or the interaction between the two.

The complexity and change in the relationship between the international and the national is usefully described by the concept of "combined and uneven development." While developments in many regions of the international economy are unified or "combined" by the international operation of capitalism, they nonetheless proceed in an "uneven" manner because of the multiple national foundations of capitalist activity. Distinct national foundations embody separate social structures, political organization, and historical experiences which yield different responses to economic interdependence. The differences between the unevenly developing parts of the system matter, but those differences always exist and evolve within the interconnections of the entire system.

Moreover, relationships change, not only in the sense that the hierarchical positions of different national units change in relation to one another, but also in the sense that the relative importance of the national as opposed to the international factors changes as well. Even while it is possible to identify a "logic" of capitalist development that drives the system toward an ever greater geographic scope of operation, the process is frequently disrupted and reversed.

In the current period of crisis, economic affairs would appear to be moving us more and more toward a global system. Surely the recent history of financial affairs seems to support the "global system" interpretation, and the global interpretation seems to garner support from the importance of the debt crisis and from the way in which attempts to formulate national economic policy in the United States have been subverted by international movements of capital and commodities. As further evidence of globalization, one could add the evolving practices of multinational firms rationalizing production on a world scale. It would appear that the international economy is becoming more and more "combined."

Yet the extreme globalist interpretation of these occurrences can be sustained only by a thorough separation of economics and politics, a separation which would be damaging to reality. Economic life is necessarily highly political because economic relations in capitalist society (or in any class society, for that matter) involve conflict. The state must be continually involved, and, though one might identify cases of supranational institutions (perhaps the IMF), we still have nothing approaching a supranational state. Politics, and other aspects of national-specific social organization, maintain capitalism's "unevenness."

Attacks on organized labor by the Reagan administration in the United States and by the Thatcher government in Britain have provided examples of the role of the national state in, if we may use the academic euphemism, organizing labor markets. National governments also continue to dominate infrastructure expansion, education, health care, pension policies, subsidies for research, and many other programs that lie at the base of economic development. Of course, all such programs are constrained by global economic forces, just as fiscal and monetary policies are limited in the face of global forces. Yet these programs lie within the realm of politics, and politics remains fundamentally national. If economics and politics are thoroughly intertwined, as they surely are, and if politics is fundamentally national, then, even though the national economy is immersed in a system of global forces, the national economy has crucial importance.

In the remainder of this essay, we are going to elaborate this view—of a "combined and unevenly developing system," of a system of national economies thoroughly immersed in a global economy. Our purpose is to establish elements of a theory—or a general understanding—of the instability and change that is taking place in the world economy, and to provide a basis for determining where those changes may be leading.

## The International-National Duality of Capitalist Development

The international operation of capitalism, of course, neither began nor ended with Adam Smith's "two greatest and most important events recorded in the history of mankind." International trade, from the search for exotic commodities in the Middle Ages to oil shipments in the current period; international investments, from the nineteenth-century railway loans to today's semiconductor plants in East Asia; and international labor migration, from the European movement to the Americas in the sixteenth century onward to the third world movement to North America and Europe today—all have played major roles in driving and shaping capital accumulation. Capitalism is always *international* in its operations.

At the same time, capitalism always develops on *national* foundations. The national state (or "nation state") has performed essential roles in creating, protecting, and extending the social institutions—property rights, factor markets, generalized commodity markets—that are fundamental to the accumulation process. The state's role has been essential because the social relations embodied in these institutions are coercive relations of dominance and subordination, and the state is the instrument of coercion. Yet there is nothing automatic about state policies; they are shaped through struggle. During the formulation of state policies, capitalists in each nation have come together from various sectors of the economy and formed a cohesive political relationship. Capital has thus taken shape as a set of distinct national classes.

The national foundations of capitalism have been essential for the system's operation, including its international operation. Without the national state, "the two greatest and most important events recorded in the history of mankind" would never have occurred. Later, the revolutionary expansion of international trade in the nineteenth century depended not only on the technical advances of the industrial revolution and the economic drive for markets and materials, but also on the sponsorship of powerful national states—particularly the British. Similarly, in the period following World War II, the hegemonic role of the U.S. state was the pillar upon which a new order was constructed, with rapidly growing international trade and investment, and with a concomitant and far-reaching extension of the social relations of capitalism.

Petras and Morley, in their essay for this volume, use the term "the imperial state" to describe the expansion of state power that accompanies the international extension of capitalist operations. Imperial economic activity finds in the imperial state the political power, the coercive force, that it requires. Moreover, unfettered by needs for legitimacy, the imperial state is often extremely and blatantly violent. International operations, which have always been most successful under imperial sponsorship, depend upon a strong and active state—which is to say, international operations depend upon strong national foundations.

Yet within the duality of capitalism's national foundations and international operations there is a contradiction. Although international expansion depends upon national bases of power and can generate an extension and deepening of that power, the very process of successful international expansion also tends to undermine those national bases of power. The way in which success generates failure in the expansion of imperial power takes many forms. Most generally, the spread of economic activity not only spreads the power and domination of the imperial center, it also spreads the social relations of capitalism, disperses the accumulation process, and gives rise to alternative and ultimately contending centers of accumulation.

In the eighteenth and nineteenth centuries, for example, British commercial and financial relations with North America simultaneously strengthened British imperial power and created the basis for the eventual displacement of that power by the United States. In the twentieth century, the international economic network sponsored by the United States has been both a keystone of U.S. imperial power and a foundation for Japanese and European challenges to that power. U.S. firms which, in the 1950s and 1960s, developed strategies without regard for competition from foreign rivals were slow to respond when the challenges from Japan and Europe did become effective. Most recently, the successful internationalization of capitalism has given rise to industrial development in several countries which, while they remain relatively poor and underdeveloped, nonetheless pose challenges to U.S. economic power. The problems surrounding the U.S. trade imbalances with certain East Asian countries and the imports of autos from Mexico and steel from Brazil are examples.

The dissolution of imperial power as a consequence of imperial power also operates in socio-political affairs. The international dispersion of economic activity from a national imperial base can create divisions among contending segments of capital. Financial capital tends to be the most unequivocally international, and within the industrial sector the largest firms are also the most internationally involved. These very powerful interests tend to oppose measures which would use the state's power and resources to preserve the productive capacity of the domestic imperial economy because such actions would conflict with their own international operations. In late-nineteenth-century Britain as in the late-twentieth-century United States, programs of industrial policy made little headway. In addition, imperial power involves military and political burdens. While extensive military spending generates a demand which stimulates economic growth, it also creates a burden, diverting resources from more directly productive uses. At the very least the need for military spending limits the flexibility of state economic policies, and, as the U.S. experience in Vietnam illustrates, military operations can generate political divisions which impinge upon economic affairs.

Nonetheless, through the operation of social institutions and conscious political intervention, the disruptive consequences of capitalism's international-national contradiction can be contained. During most of the nineteenth century, Britain's industrial strength, its naval power, and the gold standard combined to hold the forces of instability at bay and engendered a great surge of international commerce. The period following World War II provides a more immediate example of relative international stability and economic expansion. Even as the war had begun, the U.S. government, working closely with powerful private groups, had moved to establish an institutional framework for extending U.S. power and maintaining the stability of the world economy in the postwar era. As the war ended, these efforts came to fruition in both formal and de facto arrangements: the Bretton Woods monetary system (including the World Bank and the International Monetary Fund), the General Agreement on Tariffs and Trade, the Marshall Plan and a broad system of international aid, regional military alliances (for example, NATO, CENTO, SEATO), decolonization, and a vast U.S. military machine.[1]

As these structural arrangements spread U.S. imperial authority, both economic and political, they served a broader function as well, limiting, or containing, the disruption that would otherwise have been generated by capitalism's systemic international-national contradiction. Most generally, they provided a stable set of rules, allowed a relatively unfettered movement of commodities and capital, and inhibited political and military disruption. The circumstances after World War II were particularly favorable for economic expansion: the tremendous destruction of capital during the Great Depression and World War II established wide opportunities for investment; in much of the world, a large supply of labor was still available outside of modern capitalist activity; the war had set loose a set of technological advances; governments were committed to and capable of providing the demand and allowing the debt expansion which would keep growth going. U.S. imperial authority then established the international stability in which expansion could proceed.

We have already suggested the ways in which these structural arrangements of U.S. hegemony gave rise to a new era of instability. The stability provided by U.S. power created conditions which allowed rapid redevelopment in Europe, especially Germany, and Japan, and which also resulted in significant industrialization and growth in certain regions of the third world. Indeed, U.S. strength in the postwar era depended upon the emergence of strong trading partners and political allies; it also depended upon extensive international investment by U.S. firms. Yet there was no way the emergence of strong partners and the wide movement of investment could take place without ultimately presenting a challenge to U.S. authority.

Similarly in the political realm, the stability provided by U.S. power depended on a growing and more extensive international role for U.S. military forces. The U.S. government moved to replace former colonial authorities with its own presence, and, as U.S. economic and strategic interests became more thoroughly international, the government deepened its involvements around the globe. This creation of a modern and effective imperial state was a necessary foundation of U.S. hegemony. At the same time, it brought the United States into military conflicts which directly threatened that hegemony and which created unmanageable domestic economic and political strains.

Thus we arrive in the current era of crisis. The very nature of capitalist development, its international-national duality, creates a constant pressure toward instability. In the mid-twentieth century this instability was contained for a period by the institutions of U.S. imperial power. The success of this era was remarkable—in terms of the extension of U.S. power, in terms of economic stability and growth, and in terms of the spread of capitalism. By the early 1970s, however, the structural arrangements of the era had been undermined by changes in the international organization of production; U.S. hegemony no longer contained the force of capitalism's fundamental international-national duality; and the world economy entered a new period of disruption and change.

## The Current Era of Instability and Stagnation

U.S. imperial power is still extensive. Even if it is not sufficient to regulate international affairs and thus maintain stability, that power remains a paramount fact of economic and political life at the end of the twentieth century. Moreover, the highly integrated international economy that was so firmly established in the postwar period has not dissolved. In fact, from the perspective of the United States itself, economic integration has increased substantially during the instability that has dominated international affairs since the early 1970s. U.S. foreign trade rose substantially more rapidly than GNP during the 1980s, and the average ratio of trade to GNP in the 1980s was thus roughly double that of the 1960s. U.S.-based international investment, particularly financial investment, also rose dramatically: gross receipts on foreign financial investments climbed from $2.7 billion in 1970 to $32.8 billion in 1980, and peaked at $59.5 billion in 1984.[2]

Increased internationalization of the U.S. economy after 1970 is partially explained as the consequence of the successful elimination of barriers to commerce in the preceding quarter century. In addition, the "communications revolution" and the greatly reduced cost of international travel and transport have allowed U.S. firms to organize production on a much wider geographic scale, gaining direct access to foreign markets and—as we will discuss below—undercutting the domestic labor movement.

The increased immersion of the United States in the world economy also reflects some serious problems and contradictions of international capitalism. One of the fruits of the successful economic expansion of the post-World War II quarter century was intensified competition, arising as old centers of accumulation in Europe and Japan were reestablished and new centers of accumulation emerged in the third world. A result of this successful spread of economic activity was over-accumulation and the appearance of excess capacity on a global scale.[3] In an environment with intensified competition and without the regulation formerly provided by U.S. hegemony, firms struggle to capture one another's markets and governments vie to shift advantage in favor of "their" firms. The consequence is both greater internationalization and greater instability.[4]

*Expansion and Stagnation*

Moreover, the greater instability of the international economy has indirectly produced the rise in international activity. If stability was a foundation for economic growth, instability contributes to stagnation. Stagnation, in turn, forces an intensification of the search for profits, and one facet of this search is its international dimension.

Stagnation is tied to capitalism's great capacity for economic growth, and capitalist growth and stagnation can be understood as two parts of a basic contradictory process. In its tendency for the growth of production to outstrip the capacity of the market to absorb the goods at a profit, capitalist development continually threatens itself with disruption. Historically, disruption has taken the form of sharp downturns, recessions, and depressions. Although damaging both to the system and to people, sharp downturns recreate a basis for expansion. In the modern era, however, when production is dominated by very large corporations and when the state takes an active role in demand manipulation, downturns are at least partially contained and thus cannot fully perform their function of regenerating growth. Yet, while downturns are contained, the basic forces which generate disruption cannot be eliminated. Consequently, the stagnation tendency can become particularly severe; periods of successful expansion are likely to transform themselves into periods of slow and uneven growth.

Of course, capitalism's great capacity for growth often predominates over the tendency toward stagnation, and we have cited above some of the factors that prevented stagnation in the period following World War II. When stagnation does appear, it generates considerable international instability—as we shall explain shortly. Also, international instability contributes to stagnation. In general, the dominance of growth over stagnation requires some bases for a strong rise of investment. Therefore, in today's highly internationalized economic life, one necessary (though not sufficient) condition to prevent stagnation is international stability—stability in the sense of minimal fluctuation in exchange rates, trade balances, and financial movements, and in the government policies which respond to and affect the variation of these interconnected measures of international economic relations. Without stability, the basis for investment is seriously undermined. Sharp fluctuations in exchange rates, trade balances, and financial movements, either directly or through their influence on government policies, are bound to generate periods of rising unemployment, inflation, and slow and unstable economic growth. While the lack of international stability has not been the only factor causing general stagnation in the past two decades, it has certainly been an important factor.[5]

## Debt and Disorder

Causation, however, as we have already suggested, runs in both directions: stagnation is at the root of many of the changes in the international economic relations of the United States. Perhaps most important, stagnation has been a basic cause of the multifaceted buildup of debt. Pollin, in his essay in this volume, has drawn attention to the way in which the debt buildup—by consumers, businesses, and governments—is a response to slow growth. Taking on debt is, first, an attempt to maintain expenditure levels in spite of a decline (or lack of growth) of revenues. Also, stagnation leads to a buildup of debt for speculative activities, as investors, lacking productive opportunities, seek profit through the purchase and resale of existing assets.

During the 1980s, two international aspects of the debt explosion attracted considerable attention, the so-called third world debt crisis and the huge, rapid increase in the foreign debt of the United States. The U.S. government has been no less an actor in the former than in the latter, and each exhibits the way in which national policies operate in the current era to exacerbate international disorder.

The third world debt crisis has roots, of course, in the history of underdevelopment and in the long-established dependence of third world countries on external sources for capital and technology. Yet this dependence took on the form of an international debt buildup largely because of global stagnation and instability. The principal link between these grand phenomena and third world debt was the emergence of the virtually unregulated, dollar-based international money market, the Eurodollar market.

This Eurodollar market is the example *par excellence* of capitalism's international operations, and it represents the extreme success of international integration in the postwar period. Its development was spurred by a series of U.S. government policies which were reactions to international instability and stagnation. In the late 1960s, the supply of dollars held in banks outside the United States grew substantially as the U.S. government generated large dollar surpluses in its efforts to finance international military operations (especially in Indochina) through monetary expansion. Then, in the early 1970s the U.S. government responded to the onset of stagnation by more monetary expansion. The Eurodollar market was given a further boost with the huge dollar surpluses built up by several oil exporting nations; and of course these surpluses were a result of OPEC's growing strength, one of the clearest manifestations of the increasing inability of the United States to impose order on the world economy. Finally, additional growth in this "offshore" supply of dollars came from further U.S. efforts to overcome stagnation by monetary expansion and another round of oil price increases at the end of the decade. All these expansions of their currency base allowed the major internationally operating banks to create a veritable explosion of liquidity.

At the same time as stagnation contributed to this great expansion of the availability of funds, stagnation also meant that these funds could not be absorbed in the central capitalist countries. Because of the drop-off in the growth of income and investment in virtually all the advanced countries, the banks looked elsewhere to market funds. They found their market by pushing loans onto the ready and waiting third world national enterprises and governments.[6]

With the tremendous expansion of debt in the third world during the 1970s, it was only a matter of time until a crisis—in the sense of an inability of the debtors to meet payments while maintaining the normal operation of their economies—would appear. With the 1982 recession and the inability of Mexico to earn sufficient foreign exchange to meet its international debt obligations, the third world debt crisis became an official event. Since 1982, economic growth in many of the debtor countries has come to a virtual halt, and bank lending has been confined almost entirely to new loans to pay off the interest on old loans. The third world is no longer a major outlet for the excess funds which have built up in the world's major financial institutions. The forces which generated the international debt crisis, however, have not gone away. New sorts of policies in the United States have combined with the new circumstances to give those forces a new expression. At the end of the 1980s, the former grand creditor of the world economy, the United States, had become the grand debtor.[7]

As with the third world debt buildup, the expansion of U.S. reliance on foreign debt has been a consequence of stagnation and instability. Also, as the third world debt owed much to the international expression of U.S. macroeconomic policies (monetary expansion), so is the United States debt a consequence of national policies working through an internationally operating system. The first pillar of U.S. macropolicy throughout the Reagan years was the fiscal stimulation of federal deficits. This stimulation was a necessary response to continued stagnation; lacking other bases of growth, the U.S. economy needed the stimulation provided by government demand. In addition, fiscal policies in the Reagan years were in part a response to the decline of U.S. hegemony. In an effort to reestablish U.S. authority, the Reagan administration spent heavily on the military, and rising military spending was a prime factor generating the fiscal deficits.

In the early Reagan years fiscal stimulation was accompanied by monetary restraint (which began, in fact, during 1979). The monetary restraint was implemented to precipitate a recession, curb inflation, shift power and income away from labor toward capital, and bring some stability to domestic and international financial markets. It also established high real interest rates which attracted foreign capital to the United States and sharply raised the value of the dollar. The foreign capital, not incidentally, financed the growing federal deficit. With these tasks accomplished in large measure after the 1982 recession, monetary policy was eased substantially.

In a relatively stagnant world economy, the United States in the 1980s became, through this particular combination of fiscal and monetary policies, a haven for capital. The post-1982 expansion, accompanied by relatively high interest rates, attracted huge amounts of foreign funds. In combination with the curtailment by U.S. banks of their lending to the third world, this inflow of funds led to a huge shift of international financial balances. In 1981, the net international investment position of the United States peaked at $141 billion, but by 1987 it had plummeted to *minus* $403 billion (but see footnote 7). Perhaps more than any other single indicator, this shift shows the continuing instability of the international economic relations of the United States in the 1980s.

Funds which flowed to the United States in the 1980s, however, were not attracted simply by economic growth. That growth was not particularly great by the standards of preceding decades, and in spite of fiscal stimulation and post-1982 monetary ease, the United States remained part of a stagnant world economy. Real investment opportunities in the United States and elsewhere did not provide a sufficiently profitable outlet for the huge buildup of international liquidity; and third world loan pushing was no longer an option. Investors, however, found an outlet in a speculative expansion centered in the United States. Speculation in the 1980s had its most spectacular expression in the huge leveraged buyouts of giant corporations, and the process was encouraged by peculiarities of the tax laws. More basically, however, the speculation results from instability and stagnation, which limit profitable productive investment opportunities, and a world financial system which generates huge amounts of liquidity.

## Trade, Capital Mobility, and Restructuring

Any period of financial speculation may end with disaster, but the rising specter of economic apocalypse is only the most dramatic of the changes taking place. The processes we have described above, the interactions of government policies and events in the wider world economy which lie at the foundation of the speculation, have directly created disruptions in real economic, social, and political relationships. These disruptions and the financial disorder are connected parts of the same set of global changes.

The shifts of U.S. international trade during the 1970s and 1980s have been the most visible expressions of changing relations between the U.S. and world economies. These shifts have involved a rise in the overall importance of trade for the U.S. economy, a change in the pattern of trade, the appearance, for the first time in the twentieth century, of trade deficits during the 1970s, and then the huge trade deficits of the 1980s. With the deficits of the 1980s, workers in many industries lost jobs while the products they formerly produced were supplied from abroad; and there was little compensation through expansion of jobs in export-producing activity.

There are several separate aspects to an explanation of these trade shifts. They were, first of all, set in motion by the success of the postwar era in establishing a highly integrated international economy. Then, as postwar recovery was completed abroad and modern facilities came "on-line" in many countries, firms in the United States began to lose their advantage in mass production activity where labor costs played a relatively important role. An early example was consumer textiles, where the United States switched from being a net exporter to being a net importer in 1955. More widely noticed was the experience with automotive vehicles, parts and engines, of which the United States became a net importer in 1968. (Branson, 1980) The advance of the technology of mass production and, in particular, the deskilling that this technology carries with it began to undermine production in the United States. The methods of production, once well developed, were easily transferable. The advantage of production in the United States, where large amounts of highly educated labor are available, became irrelevant. Production more and more moved abroad.

The trade shifts of the 1970s were not so widespread; the deficits were concentrated in oil and auto trade, and if one excludes these sectors from the calculations, no trend toward a trade deficit is evident until the early 1980s. Nonetheless, the increasing internationalization of the economy did have devastating effects on particular communities and groups of workers and these effects had significant political implications. Poorly paid, relatively unskilled workers in manufacturing were one of the groups on which the impact was most severe. Increasing openness of the U.S. economy and the emergence of mass production facilities elsewhere put these workers in direct competition with even more poorly paid workers abroad. Thus, internationalization contributed to a growing inequality of income. Moreover, a disproportionate number of poorly paid workers are women and members of minority groups. So the impact of internationalization exacerbated race and gender inequalities. It was not, however, simply poorly paid workers who were affected. In certain industries—most notably in auto and steel but also in other sectors of heavy manufacturing—effective unionization and relatively high wages have been attained. Yet partly as a consequence of workers' success in these sectors, the technology of mass production has been relatively well developed, and thus both the motivation and possibility are present for replacing domestic with foreign production. The impact has been felt not only in those unionized industries where imports began to become important in the 1970s. A few examples created a general threat which had a widespread, chilling effect upon workers' demands.

What had been a stream of troubles in the 1970s became a deluge in the 1980s: a huge increase of imports, the stagnation of exports, and a resultant explosion of the trade deficit (now appearing in almost all categories of manufactured goods). The principal forces which effected these developments were the same as those which led to the explosion of the U.S. foreign debt. The debt and the deficit were two sides of the same coin, as the U.S. macropolicies of the 1980s induced foreigners to purchase U.S. assets (real and financial) instead of U.S. goods. The sorts of long run shifts that characterized trade changes in the 1970s were then greatly increased in the 1980s. General stagnation of international economic activity made competition all the more intense, and the pressures that appeared for U.S. workers in the early phase of international instability became more extreme and widespread in the 1980s.

U.S. corporations were also affected by sharp shifts in international trade, and in the 1980s many firms which had relied heavily on exports or which faced import competition suffered substantial losses. Capital, however, is mobile, and an important part of the internationalization of economic life has been the relocation abroad of their operations by many U.S. firms. In the immediate post-World War II period, the U.S. accepted the restrictions which many governments—European and Latin American, for example—imposed upon imports as long as direct foreign investment was unhampered; free trade was limited, but free enterprise flourished. U.S.-based firms then reached the markets of other countries by establishing production facilities in those countries. Investment by U.S. multinationals went primarily to areas where markets were large and rapidly growing, particularly Western Europe and a few third world countries, such as Brazil and Mexico.

In the 1970s and 1980s, as part of the decline of U.S. hegemony, U.S. firms came under more pressure from foreign rivals. Also, U.S. success in the era of hegemony had eliminated a good many of the restrictions on trade. Consequently, U.S.-based firms have given greater attention to cost reductions, and one key mechanism for lowering costs has been to use, directly and indirectly, foreign labor. U.S. auto firms have developed "foreign sourcing" (well beyond their traditional Canadian operations); U.S. producers of consumer electronics, if they have not been displaced by Japanese competition, rely heavily on the Far East for both final products and components; and Mexican plants just south of the U.S. border handle labor-intensive chores in producing apparel, auto parts, electronics. The large multinationals often reduce the risks and disruptions involved in employing unskilled, low-wage labor by sub-contracting. Nonetheless, the large firms are prime movers and marketers in these increasingly international production processes.

By spreading their operations internationally, U.S.-based firms have been able to separate themselves from some of the misfortunes that have fallen on U.S. workers and show up as statistical losses for the U.S. economy. For example, between 1966 and 1984, the U.S. share of world manufactured exports declined from 17.5 percent to 14.0 percent. Yet U.S.-based multinationals' share in world exports actually rose slightly in this period, from 17.7 percent to 18.1 percent; the "parent" firms' declining share was more than balanced by a rising share of their foreign affiliates. (Lipsey and Kravis, 1987: 151) This ability of large multinationals to secure their position through geographic relocation means, of course, that pressures usually described as falling on "the U.S. economy" fall disproportionately on U.S. workers.

Using workers abroad can in fact boost U.S. corporations' profits at home because U.S. workers are forced to make concessions when placed in competition with poorly paid foreign workers. Also, connected to internationalization, U.S. businesses have lowered costs by "informalization," developing small scale, irregular production processes which make heavy use of immigrant labor, often women (Fernández Kelly, in this volume).

The combined result of growing international trade and capital mobility is a "restructuring" of production with considerable social and political consequences. This restructuring on a global level shifts the balance of power between capital and labor within the United States. Although the decline of real wages since the early 1970s and the growing inequality of income distribution have multiple roots, the power shift associated with the international reorganization of production is certainly a major factor. Similarly, the balance of power in struggles over issues of the environment, workplace safety, taxation, and, indeed, the whole gamut of economic issues, has been altered by restructuring.

## Economics and Politics

In reviewing relations between the U.S. and world economies, we have been trying to explain some of the more important aspects of instability and change in the current period. Also, we have been attempting to extend our general understanding—our theory—of international aspects of the current crisis. The national-international duality of capitalist development is illustrated in the way U.S. macroeconomic policy worked through the international system to extend disruption; in the evolution of debt and trade problems; in the thorough connection between international and domestic restructuring.

The points we have touched on are only a part of the story of capitalism's development in the current era, but our discussion suggests some politically useful conclusions. Most generally, the disarray of the last two decades has very deep roots and is likely to continue until some new basis of order is created in the world economy. The powerful tendencies toward international instability were contained by U.S. hegemony. Now, without effective institutions of stability, the world economy is mired in recurring disruption and general stagnation.

As we have noted (and as is elaborated in the essays by Crotty, Epstein, and Pollin in this volume) government policies intended to counter these problems are often ineffective and at times exacerbate or simply change the manifestation of the difficulties. Private sector response to conditions of crisis focus on shifting the burdens of disorder. In the speculative binge, capitalists vie with one another over claims on society's wealth. In restructuring, capitalists generally search for ways to raise their profits at the expense of workers. Both processes only add to the instability of the system as a whole.

In much of the third world, the changes of the current era have had disastrous impacts on living conditions, but they have also created an unmanageable situation for many regimes. Several dictatorial governments have been driven from or ceded power, and the old ruling groups throughout the third world are on the defensive. It is difficult to anticipate the coming changes—the extent to which they will be revolutionary or contained by reform (see Thomas in this volume). Yet because of the endemic instability of underdevelopment and the weakness of the ruling classes in the third world, the changes generated by the current crisis will surely be extensive and dramatic. Without the stability provided by U.S. hegemony, we are again in a situation where "the center cannot hold," and in the periphery "things fall apart."

The structures of social and political stability within the United States (and in other advanced countries) have also been affected by the economic changes that are underway. Simply in creating an environment of continual economic instability, the crisis has weakened the foundation of social and political accommodation. Furthermore, internationalization and restructuring have increased class inequality. The divisions between capital and labor in the United States have become more intense, and the common position of workers in the United States and abroad has become more apparent.

There are, of course, no automatic connections between these material changes and positive political developments in the United States. Yet progressive, oppositional forces are confronting the changing character of capitalism and figuring out new ways to shape demands, programs, and actions. There is, for example, a wide awareness of the need to move beyond traditional protectionism in order to protect jobs, wages, and working conditions. Also, people in the labor movement have begun to challenge the long established practices of the AFL-CIO in supporting the foreign policy—and thus the international economic order—advocated by the government and capital (Tabb, in this volume). International economic change, moreover, has altered gender relationships, placed women in new economic positions, and thus created new political struggles and new possibilities for change (Benería, in this volume).

As internationalization of the U.S. economy generates greater inequality, there are possibilities for U.S. workers to recognize their common interests with foreign workers and even with third world liberation movements (though there are also possibilities for the growth of national chauvinism and racism). In addition, it appears that within the United States the pressure on living standards is creating a more widely shared common experience for the majority of working people; common experience can be the basis for greater solidarity and common programs. In general, the new conditions are undermining the logic of old practices, practices that encouraged the quiescence of labor and its acceptance of status quo arrangements.

Even while the "combined" nature of capitalist development places constraints on national political forces, the "uneven" aspect of that development continually opens up new opportunities for struggle. The instability of the current era obviously creates a danger of war and severe difficulties in the destructive onslaught on living standards and workers' rights. At the same time, it creates opportunities. There is nothing predetermined about the change that comes out of a crisis, and there is considerable room for the impact of popular forces.

## Notes

1. The argument here is akin to that of the "social structures of accumulation" theory developed by Bowles, Gordon, and Weisskopf (1983) and the "regulation" theory put forth by Aglietta (1979). The common theme in these analysis is that capitalism's contradictions are contained or regulated at various times by particular structural institutions. While these institutions are maintained, accumulation can proceed. Hence we can learn a good deal about a particular historical period by analyzing the institutions that buttress the system in that period. Some of these analyses focus on the changes in social and political institutions per se as the causal factors in precipitating a crisis. We, however, emphasize a reciprocal dynamic, in which economic changes (changes in methods of production and exchange) disrupt the operation of political and social institutions, and then, as those institutions can no longer perform their stabilizing role, the economic change is affected, altered, disrupted, and thrown into crisis.
2. Data here are from *Economic Report of the President* (1988) and U.S. Department of Commerce (1987); subsequent data are from these, plus U.S. Department of Commerce (1988), unless otherwise noted.
3. A useful industry-by-industry survey of the early 1987 state of excess capacity in the economy was provided in a March 9, 1987, *Wall Street Journal* article entitled "A Global Overcapacity Hurts Many Industries; No Easy Cure Is Seen." The article describes excess capacity problems in auto, steel, computers, semiconductors, heavy equipment, and textiles, and cites only chemicals and plastics as examples of industries lacking an overcapacity problem.
4. A part of the instability can be traced to widespread adoption of neomercantilist,

export-oriented policies. They are a beggar-thy-neighbor approach to development, leading to direct protectionism, exchange rate manipulation, covert barriers to commerce, and generalized trade conflicts. Mercantilism can certainly work for some nations, as it did historically, but only at the expense of others. Thus both historically and in the current era, it generates conflict.

5. Recent technological developments, computerization and bio-technology, in particular, are often seen as the foundation for a new era of economic expansion (see Thomas, this volume). The nature of capitalism is such, however, that technological advances which enhance society's productive capacity can aggravate rather than alleviate the tendency toward stagnation. If the expansion of productive capacity is not matched by an expansion of markets, it can lead to an increase of excess capacity and thus a worsening of stagnation (see Berlan, this volume).

6. The third world debt story told here is elaborated in MacEwan (1986); the U.S. debt and trade story in MacEwan (1989). As to "loan pushing" by the major banks, the phenomenon is well illustrated by the fact that between 1975 and 1979, on their loans to non-OPEC "less developed countries," the banks were willing to double the average maturity and cut their average margins by 50 percent—and there is no reason to believe that these improved terms reflected any improvement in the economic outlook (Darity 1984).

7. Official statistics that show the United States as having become a large net international debtor are misleading, as official reserve assets held in gold are greatly undervalued, and private assets are listed at their "book value" rather than their current replacement value. If gold and other assets were correctly valued, it is possible that the United States would still be a net international creditor; certainly the net debt of the United States would be much smaller. Nonetheless, the important phenomenon is the *shift* in the U.S. position, which during the 1980s amounted to over half a trillion dollars.

## References

Aglietta, M. 1979. *A Theory of Capitalist Regulation*. London: New Left Books.

Bowles, Samuel, David M. Gordon and Thomas E. Weisskopf. 1983. *Beyond the Wasteland: A Democratic Alternative to American Decline*. Garden City: Doubleday.

Branson, William H. 1980. "Trends in United States International Trade and Investment Since World War II." In M. Feldstein, ed., *The American Economy in Transition*. Chicago: University of Chicago Press.

Darity, William, Jr. September 1984. "Loan Pushing: Doctrine and Theory." *International Finance Discussion Papers,* Number 247, Washington: Board of Governors of the Federal Reserve.

*Economic Report of the President, 1988,* Washington, D.C.

Lipsey, Robert E. and Irving B. Kravis. 1987. "The Competitiveness and Comparative Advantage of U.S. Multinationals, 1957–1984." *Banca Nazionale del Lavoro Quarterly Review,* no. 161.

MacEwan, Arthur. 1986. "International Debt and Banking: Rising Instability within the General Crisis," *Science & Society,* Summer.

Smith, Adam. 1776. *The Wealth of Nations.* New York: Random House, 1937.

———. 1989. "U.S. International Trade and Economic Instability," *Monthly Review.* February.

U.S. Department of Commerce. 1987. *Survey of Current Business,* June.

———. 1988. *Survey of Current Business,* March.

# The Imperial State in the Rise and Fall of U.S. Imperialism

## James F. Petras and Morris H. Morley

No country can rely simply on private initiative or "the magic of the marketplace" to establish its businesses as influential actors in the global economy. The activities which accompany large-scale, long-term international capitalist operations are dependent on the support of the state. Either directly or indirectly, the state must, for example, facilitate financing, assure the sanctity of contracts, maintain social and political stability, support research and development. In international operations, at least as much as in domestic operations, the state provides the matrix which nurtures the expansion of private businesses.

In discussing the United States today, however, we are not dealing simply with the "capitalist state." The capitalist state operates within the bounds of the nation, where it is the only source of sovereign authority. Global economic operations demand something more, an "imperial state." The imperial state exercises its authority across national boundaries, amidst a field of competing and aspiring sovereigns—local authorities, regional powers, and other imperial states. The imperial state is thus the principal actor in international power relations. Accordingly, in understanding changing international power relations—the instability and disarray that has characterized the global economy in recent years—we need to give considerable attention to the imperial state.

The emergence of the United States as a competitive—and subsequently dominant—imperial power within world capitalism is of relatively recent origin. Since the last decade of the nineteenth century, however, no movement of U.S. capital overseas has taken place without the sustained involvement of the U.S. imperial state; such involvement has occurred in the entree, expansion, and survival of this capital in the areas where it has located. The roots of the imperial state are anchored within U.S. society, in the national structures of social power; its branches span the globe. The centrality of internationally oriented capital within U.S. society has defined both the policies and structures of the state, assuring that it would perform its imperial functions.

The U.S. imperial state can be said to be composed of those executive bodies or agencies within "government" that are charged with promoting and protecting the expansion across national boundaries of capital based in the imperial center. Some of these agencies, such as the departments of Commerce and the Treasury, are more directly linked to the U.S. corporate world than are others, but the actions of all are directed toward the goal of facilitating U.S. capital accumulation and reproduction on a worldwide scale. The U.S. imperial state essentially exercises two major coercive functions, one economic and the other political. Although analytically distinct, the economic and political functions combine at the operational level to sustain the conditions for global capital accumulation. During 1959 and 1960, for example, the imperial state mounted an aggressive policy of economic sanctions against the Cuban revolution, and these sanctions helped create the basis for the indirect military intervention of 1961. A more successful example is provided by U.S. operations in the Dominican Republic, where the 1965 military intervention crushed nationalist and working-class forces and was then followed by loans and trade arrangements designed to restore and appropriate a secure milieu for foreign capital accumulation.

While all capitalist countries depend on an imperial state to facilitate expansion in the world economy, not all imperial states are the same. Moreover, the composition and functioning of the different imperial states can have major consequences for the position of each country in the international system and for the overall structure of international power. The focus of this analysis is the current decline of U.S. imperialism and the seminal contribution of the U.S. imperial state to America's deteriorating power and influence within the capitalist world economy. The following propositions serve as a basic guideline to our discussion:

(1) The divergence between the internal components of the imperial state—between military/ideological on the one hand and economic on the other—will have consequences for the overall position of competing imperialist countries in the world economy.

(2) The disproportionate emphasis on military and ideological

components of the U.S. imperial state relative to Japanese and German imperial states has led to a declining capacity of the U.S. state to service overseas capital and has contributed to the relative decline of U.S. global hegemony.

(3) The disproportionate emphasis on economic agencies in the Japanese and German imperial state, relative to the United States, has led to an increasing capacity of these states to service and promote capitalist expansion and contributed to the relative improvement in their position in the world market.

(4) The U.S. emphasis on reversing third world revolutionary upheavals, first in Vietnam and later in Central America, Southern Africa, South Asia, and the Middle East, strengthened the ideological/military components of the imperial state. In the process, Washington sacrificed the kind of restructuring necessary to regain economic leverage and competitiveness within the global economy in the context of growing challenges from principal allies (e.g., West Germany, Japan) and newly industrializing states (e.g., South Korea, Hong Kong).

(5) In the balance, positions within the global economy and hegemonic status are determined by relations and competition among the major capitalist countries, not by ties between core and peripheral economies or conflict between the United States and third world countries.

### Imperial Power and the Structure of the Imperial State

The decline of U.S. imperial power can be understood in relation to its major capitalist competitors, Japan and West Germany. Major shifts in markets, investments, and profits in the contemporary world have been determined primarily by the actions of these competitor powers, not by third world social revolutions which, with the possible exception of Iran, have taken place in nonstrategic areas of capitalist investment. At the same time, while third world revolutions have not undermined the imperial system, they have had a profound effect on imperial countries insofar as they have contributed to the displacement of one imperial power from a dominant position and facilitated the ascent of a competitor capitalist power. The most striking recent case is the massive U.S. financial commitment to prosecute its war against social-revolutionary forces in Vietnam which had a powerful negative impact on the American economy and the imperial state which, in turn, was instrumental in advancing the global economic fortunes of Washington's competitor "allies."

Based on the assumption that the major challenge to U.S. imperial domination is coming from the advanced capitalist countries, it follows that we need to examine the respective imperial states and the state-class relationships to identify the qualitative differences that account for the decline of the United States and the rise of countries such as West Germany and Japan. Our principal argument is that notwithstanding the centrality of military and ideological components, the rise and fall of a country's position within the world economy is dependent on the strategic role of the economic components of its imperial state—more precisely, on the deep structural links between these imperial economic agencies and dynamic productive capital. We further hypothesize that the West German and Japanese imperial states, among others, are constructed and function largely as economic institutions with a high proportion of personnel oriented toward economic roles and functions that benefit imperial capital; whereas the U.S. imperial state is primarily a political-ideological-military-intelligence apparatus with little or no direct relevance to promoting U.S. capital accumulation and expansion in the international marketplace.

A key element in the rise of an imperialist power and, by extension, its decline, is the relationship between the imperial state and the dominant classes. As noted earlier, during the ascending period of U.S. imperialism the imperial state played a central role in creating the conditions for the internationalization of capital. There was a reciprocal relationship between the imperial state and international capital: sustained and comprehensive state activity promoted capital expansion and high rates of return, and low-priced commodities financed the growing power of the state. This reciprocity was accompanied by a dynamic equilibrium between the growth of the two basic components of imperialism. Up to the mid-1960s, the growth and expenditures of the state were commensurate with the growth of international capital. Then, two factors intervened to upset this equilibrium: an overextended imperial state in Vietnam and the relative decline of the American economy due to a combination of excessive military spending and increasing international competition from capitalist economic competitors.

The general disequilibrium between state and capital was exacerbated by a further disequilibrium within the U.S. imperial state between the economic and military-intelligence components, with the latter increasingly eclipsing the former. The relative decline of the economic agencies of the U.S. imperial state occurred precisely at the moment when its principal imperial competitors—especially West Germany and Japan—were constructing imperial apparatuses almost exclusively devoted to economic functions. As the crisis in U.S. state-capital relations deepened, Washington sought to re-establish its formerly dominant position by resort to two major strategies: detente in the early 1970s and military superiority in the 1980s.

Detente was an attempt by Washington to reach an agreement with the Soviet Union to accept the status quo regarding spheres of influence and the arms race, and to cut back military spending in order to recreate an equilibrium between the imperial state and capital. Detente, however, was not accompanied by any serious effort to reform the imperial state apparatus and convert it into an effective instrument of capital expansion. Moreover, neither the Soviet Union nor U.S. regional clients were capable of limiting or containing revolutionary upheavals in the third world. Washington therefore decided to shift to a policy of putting the imperial state in command through an unprecedented strengthening of its military-intelligence and ideological components. The hope was that the imperial state would create a politico-military "shell" for regaining economic losses and reasserting global economic hegemony. But this approach not only failed to gain its stated objective—a new period of global economic dominance—it also exacerbated the problems in the U.S. domestic economy, thus precipitating a further decline in America's worldwide power.

It is important to recognize the primacy of the economic relations between the state and the capitalist class in determining a country's position within the world economy. The long-term functioning of an imperial system is made possible only by the dynamic reproduction of capital. A crisis of capital reproduction has a direct effect on all other aspects of society (ideological, political, etc.). This is not to say that military, cultural, and other factors do not impinge on the reproductive capacities of capitalist classes; it is to argue that these other elements cannot exist or reproduce themselves in the absence of production and exchange. Comparisons of a single country at different periods or of different countries demonstrate the centrality of the economic linkages. The rise and decline of U.S. global hegemony between the 1950s and the 1980s coincides with the subordination of the military-ideological to the economic agencies of the imperial state and vice versa.

Similar outcomes are observable if we compare West Germany and Japanese imperial state-capital relations to those of the United States over the same time period. In both these cases, the expansive and interventionist state in itself is not the decisive factor in maintaining hegemony; rather it is the content of the state and its linkages to the class structure that is decisive in changing the possibilities of global hegemony. "State" or "class-centered" analyses by themselves do not tell us the full story. The interaction between state and class, more precisely the interaction between productive capital and the economic agencies of the state, are central to understanding the creation of global hegemonic powers.

## Imperial Rivalries in the Current Era

Since the Vietnam war period, differences between the United States and competitor imperial states have become more accentuated. Except for the detente interlude of the early and mid 1970s, the United States has steadily expanded the military/intelligence agencies of the imperial state, while the economic agencies have declined in relative and even absolute terms. The Reagan presidency, in its determination to reverse the deteriorating position of the U.S. political economy through a global strategy of military confrontation and overt subversion, offers the most dramatic illustration of this process. In terms of institution building, budget allocations, and personnel recruitment, the Pentagon and the Central Intelligence Agency (CIA) have far outstripped the economic departments of the U.S. imperial state since the end of the Carter years.

Between 1980 and 1987, the U.S. defense budget increased by approximately 50 percent. Military outlays rose from 4.8 percent of Gross National Product (GNP) in 1978 to 6.4 percent in 1987 (Morrison 1987a: 421, 414; 1987b: 3192). According to a joint Commerce-Labor Department study, defense spending between 1980 and 1985 not only increased from 23 percent to 27 percent of the federal budget but also generated approximately 1 million new military-related jobs during this period (Rauch 1987: 3194). The Reagan White House also substantially increased American troops abroad, the army's special counterinsurgency forces, and weapons sales to foreign countries. Exports of military-related goods skyrocketed from

$10.2 billion in 1980 to $24.4 billion in 1984 (Markusen 1986: 499). One authority described the Reagan defense buildup as "an unparalleled six-year era of sustained real growth in defense dollars (Morrison 1987a: 414).

In the intelligence sphere, the Reagan administration presided over a similar upsurge in funds, personnel, and institutions. The overall intelligence budget increased from $10 billion in 1979 to $24 billion in 1986, and between 1981 and 1986 it grew at an even faster rate than the defense budget (Tyler and Ottaway 1986: A14). Under the directorship of William Casey the CIA came "closer to worldwide coverage for the first time" (Woodward 1987: 386). During the Carter years the number of CIA covert operatives declined to approximately 300 and two or three large-scale clandestine programs were mounted annually. Within three years of Reagan's taking office, the number of operatives had risen to 1,000 and the agency was running seven or eight major covert operations around the world (*Newsweek*, October 10, 1983, p. 39). The CIA's annual budget for secret missions reached its highest level since the Vietnam war and in late 1985 or early 1986 the White House established a new secret interagency committee—the "208 Committee"—to oversee the imperial state's proliferating covert operations abroad.

The shift in the structure of the U.S. imperial state is both a cause and consequence of a declining American economy and a shifting corporate orientation from industrial to finance capital. In contrast to Washington's military-intelligence focus, Western Europe and Japan since the mid-1960s have embarked on policies to expand to the maximum the economic agencies, personnel and institutions of their respective imperial states, deepening the integration (interpenetration) of the state and private corporation. This increase in overseas economic activity accompanied the dynamic of accumulation of external private capital; each reinforced the other in an upward spiraling process.

The almost exclusively economic nature of the Japanese imperial state offers a particular contrast to the overdevelopment of the military-clandestine-ideological components of the U.S. imperial state. Over the last quarter-century, big business in Japan has exerted considerable influence over domestic and foreign economic policymaking through its personal and financial relationship to the politically dominant Liberal Democratic Party and its close working ties with the powerful state bureaucracy (Destler, et al. 1976: 50–51).

The key ministries of Foreign Affairs, Finance, and International Trade and Industry (MITI) have collaborated, on an ongoing basis, with Japan's major business organizations and associations, individual corporations, and influential business leaders to devise and pursue policies favorable to the country's outward-oriented (trade and investment) capitalist class. One of the favored means for conducting economic diplomacy abroad has been the economic mission staffed by senior state and business leaders. "Since the mid-1960s," writes one authority, "participation by businessmen in Japanese diplomacy has been considered a constant rather than [as in the United States] an intermittent phenomenon." (Bryant 1975:4). Finally, within the Japanese imperial state, a disproportionate number of bureaucrats with foreign-policy responsibilities are located in the economic agencies (over 7,000 out of 10,000 during the mid-1970s) (Destler et al 1976: 75).

The West European and Japanese imperial states specialized in economic activity because they functioned under the American military umbrella at low, if any, cost. Early on, senior Japanese and West German imperial state officials, in particular, must have recognized the advantages of a militarily strong and economically weak U.S. imperial state and have seen the opportunities that it offered. This resulted in encouragement, promotion, and reinforcement of U.S. cold war military postures as long as they did not curtail or interfere with the pursuit of economic markets. On occasion, of course, conflicts have arisen over U.S. ideological-military policies attempting to restrict Western Europe/Japanese trade relations with the East or South—most notably during the Reagan presidency.

During 1981 and 1982, the U.S. imperial state aggressively campaigned to halt all European capital goods exports and credits allocated to the Soviet Union's natural-gas pipeline project and to force NATO governments to participate in a program of economic sanctions against Poland after General Jaruzelski's declaration of martial law. In both these instances, America's imperial state competitors refused to go along with White House policy because it jeopardized important existing economic ties in the absence of meaningful trade and financial alternatives. In 1980, for instance, according to Commerce Department figures, total two-way trade (exports and imports) between the European Economic Community and Eastern Europe reached approximately $56 billion. Moreover, Soviet natural gas exports to Western Europe had more than tripled since 1975 and the

Bonn-Moscow natural gas agreement signed in November 1981 was the single largest business transaction in East-West history (Graham 1981; Jentleson 1986: 172–214).

Reagan administration efforts to impose global economic sanctions against third world countries—Libya in 1981 and 1986 and Iran in 1987—were also strongly resisted by its West European and Japanese allies. Officials of these imperial states described Washington's call for trade retaliation measures against Libya in January 1986 as "an unsuitable instrument," which was not surprising in view of the fact that European Economic Community exports to Libya in 1984 totaled over $3.8 billion compared with U.S. exports worth a paltry $220 million (*New York Times,* January 12, 1986, p. 21). Refusal to risk a lucrative and economically strategic relationship also shaped Japan's rebuff to Reagan efforts to institute trade sanctions against Iran in 1987. The Middle East country was one of Japan's key oil suppliers (over $1 billion worth of crude petroleum in 1986) and a significant market for machinery and ship sales (total exports valued at $1.4 billion in 1986) (*New York Times,* January 9, 1986).

Beginning in the early and mid 1970s, key U.S. policymakers began to perceive the unequal benefits of a situation in which competitor imperial states pursued economic objectives while Washington paid the military bills. The White House and the State Department argued that allied imperial states, especially West Germany and Japan, should expand their military components and shoulder part of the burden for policing the imperial system. This pressure on NATO countries and Japan to increase their weapons procurement policies, build up their armed forces, and assume an increasing share of the military costs of defending the imperial system reached a peak during the early period of the Reagan administration. "It is essential," Secretary of Defense Weinberger declared in March 1981, "that we develop a more rational 'division of labor,' under which our NATO allies and Japan will be asked to join in contributing more to our common defense" (*New York Times,* March 27, 1981, p. 7). Japan, in particular, was singled out for its failure to devote a greater proportion of the national budget to defense spending. In October, Weinberger raised the issue again, this time in regard to the Persian Gulf: "Western Europe and Japan dare not settle for merely increasing their trade and diplomatic contacts with nations in Southwest Asia as their contribution toward keeping the oil fields out of unfriendly hands" (*Washington Post,* October 23, 1981, p. A26). Nonetheless, despite continuing pressures and threats emanating from the Reagan White House, the disparities in defense spending remained essentially unchanged. In 1987, U.S. imperial state military outlays accounted for 6.7 percent of GNP; the equivalent figures for its two major competitors—West Germany and Japan—were 2.5 percent and just over 1 percent respectively (*Business Week,* November 16, 1987).

As far back as the latter half of the 1970s, however, there were also a few voices raised in support of trimming the military component of the U.S. imperial state and shifting more resources to the economic agencies. That such a potentially important historical debate never took place, or at least never moved to center stage and engaged the executive-branch leadership, requires an explanation. Two primary reasons account for this failure to restructure the U.S. imperial state and, by extension, to redefine the division of labor between military and economic roles among key allies/competitors. First, during the mid and late 1970s, a wave of revolutionary upheavals throughout the third world unraveled longstanding regional client networks. Successful revolutions in Angola, Ethiopia, Zimbabwe, Mozambique, Iran, and Nicaragua displaced strategic U.S. clients who had formerly collaborated in policing these regions and containing local revolutionary forces. The U.S. imperial state lacked a political leadership which could have put these regional "losses" in a broader structural-historical context. Instead, the Carter and Reagan administrations set in motion the bureaucratic, political, and ideological machinery to reconstitute, then expand, the military components of the imperial state.

Second, the nature of U.S. capital—both domestic and overseas—had shifted during the 1970s, decreasing the pressure for an economic activist imperial state. Internally, the shift involved the relative growth of financial transactions to productive activities, graphically revealed in the nature of the U.S. economy's debt explosion. Over the last decade, borrowing in the financial sector has far outstripped borrowing by government, consumers, or nonfinancial businesses. The unparalleled growth in speculative and financial activity has structurally transformed the domestic economy into one where, in the felicitous words of Paul Sweezy and Harry Magdoff (1986) "making money" has become relatively much more important than "making goods." In 1985, the financial sector (finance, real estate, and insurance) accounted for 40 percent of the goods-production sector's contribution to GNP—compared with 21 percent in 1950! Externally, the shift involved the relative growth of financial to capital investments and the subsequent displacement of public loans by private loans. The growth of private overseas lending (finance capital) reduced the role of imperial state financial institutions. Public overseas lending was perceived by the private banking institutions as a potential competitor in the financial markets. This growth and expansion of private finance capital overseas effectively encouraged the relative decline of the economic agencies of the U.S. imperial state and, deliberately or not, furthered the expansion and ascendency of the military instrumentalities. This trend was accelerated during the Reagan presidency, with its emphasis on the free market, political and ideological activism, and military confrontation on a world scale. During the 1980s, the ascendency of finance capital, a weakening of the economic agencies of the imperial state, and the rise to political power of ideological-political rightists espousing global military metaphysics combined to exacerbate the imbalance between the economic and military components of the U.S. imperial state.

The increasing severity of the international debt crisis and global economic recession of the early 1980s, however, began to force this convergence of financial and political-ideological factors into the background and replace it with a conflict of interests. Finance capitalists during the first Reagan administration increasingly sought to bolster the international economic agencies of the imperial state, pressuring them either to provide the necessary economic resources to revive the debtor economies or bail out the overexposed bankers. Nonetheless, the ideological-political power bloc continued to pursue and promote policies based on the primacy of an ever-expanding military structure on the imperial state. Despite rising friction between the dominant economic and political-ideological groups, the continued ascendency of the latter ensured the increasing loss of overseas markets. Between 1981 and 1986, for instance, the value of U.S. exports to the biggest Latin American debtor countries dropped from $32 billion to $22 billion (Clark 1986: 1934).

Meanwhile, the coordination of the private investment/commerce sectors with the economic agencies of the West German and Japanese imperial states facilitated major inroads into former U.S.-controlled overseas markets.

In 1950, the United States produced 40 percent and Western Europe/Japan less than 22 percent of the world's goods and services. By 1980, these figures were reversed to 23 percent and 39 percent respectively (Auerbach and Behr 1907: 6). Between 1960 and 1980, the U.S. share of world trade declined from 16 percent to 11 percent, with the worsening competitive position most marked in manufacturing (market share down from 26 percent to 18 percent) (Ferguson and Rogers 1986: 81). In 1986, for the first time since World War II, the U.S. lost its position as the world's leading exporter—to West Germany, with Japan threatening to topple it from second place. During 1986, West Germany and Japan achieved a combined trade surplus with the United States totaling almost $68 billion (Morse, 1987–88: 5).

The Japanese challenge in the areas of high technology, automobiles, machine tools, and consumer electronics since the 1960s, and especially during the 1980s, has been dramatic. In the high technology field, Japan has already overtaken the United States in the production of computer chips and now supplies "critical" components for U.S. weapons systems. Moreover, in the last decade, Japan's share of the world's semiconductor market has risen from 25 percent to 45 percent while the U.S. share has shrunk from 60 percent to 40 percent (*Far Eastern Economic Review,* November 5, 1987, p. 37). Finally, in 1986 the United States for the first time ran a trade deficit in high-technology products.

At the same time, Japan has also overtaken the United States in the production and export of industrial products. In the early 1960s, the United States produced nearly 90 percent of the world's color television sets, almost half of the world's automobiles, and almost a quarter of the world's machine-tool exports. By 1987, Japan produced more than half of all the color television sets and nearly half of the world's cars, while America's share of the world's machine-tool exports fell to a minuscule 4 percent. In all of these areas, the United States was forced to purchase increasing quantities from abroad, principally from Japan, contributing substantially to the persistent and growing trade deficit. The U.S. trade balance in manufacturing goods, fell from a surplus of $11.8 billion in 1981 to a deficit of $133.4 billion in 1986 (*Business Week,* April 20, 1987, pp. 56, 58).

In Southeast Asia, Japan has supplanted the United States as the dominant external power in the areas of trade, capital flows, and technology transfers. Japanese manufactured exports such as textiles and electronics have displaced U.S. competitors from traditional ASEAN markets. A similar trend is evident in the foreign investment sphere: U.S. direct investments in the ASEAN countries declined during 1985 and 1986 to an estimated $9 billion while Japanese investment soared during this same period, reaching $13.5 billion (*Business Week,* November 3, 1986, p. 42).

Fueled by massive profits from exports and overseas investments topping $80 billion in 1987, and large-scale domestic savings, Japan emerged as a dominant global financial power and capital exporter during the 1980s—exerting an unprecedented impact on the world's financial markets. The country's gross external assets (medium and long term) more than quadrupled from $160 billion in 1980 to $727 billion in 1986. Japanese banks played an important role in this rise to investment preeminence. In 1982, the largest Japanese bank, measured by assets, ranked eighth in the world; by 1988, the world's seven largest private financial institutions were Japanese-owned. (*Far Eastern Economic Review,* December 17, 1987, p. 60). Currently, Japanese banks constitute the largest single group of international bank lenders (25 percent of all loans) and are close to the top in foreign currency lending. In the process, Japan has become an increasingly important source of funds for the two major financial instrumentalities of the Western political economy: the World Bank and the International Monetary Fund (IMF). It has also substantially expanded its lending and investment activities in Latin America, carrying with it the power to pressure the region to increase its purchases of Japanese goods—thereby threatening a new challenge to traditional U.S. markets.

In 1985, Japan became the world's largest creditor nation, based on net overseas assets of $130 billion; by 1987, this figure exceeded $220 billion (*The Economist,* September 19, 1987, p. 76). Paralleling Japan's rise to global lending powerhouse has been the transformation of the United States from the world's biggest creditor to biggest debtor country. In 1985, foreign claims on U.S. assets (direct investments, stocks, bonds, other financial instruments) exceeded similar U.S. claims by approximately $110 billion; one year later, this American foreign debt had risen to almost $264 billion (*Washington Post,* June 24, 1987, p. B1). The global power of the dollar has also slipped dramatically. Since the early 1970s, the number of third world countries that peg their currencies to the U.S. dollar has fallen from three fifths to one quarter. Over the same period, the dollar's share of the world's foreign exchange reserves has fallen from over 80 percent to less than 60 percent while the Deutschemark has risen from 2 percent to 14 percent and the yen from almost zero to 7 percent (*The Economist,* September 19, 1987, p. 76).

Heading into the 1990s, the internal composition of the U.S. imperial state has become increasingly skewed toward the military-intelligence side of operations in contrast to competitor imperial states such as Japan and West Germany that continue to accord priority to economic activities and the requirements of capital and commerce (services, promotions, subsidies, etc.) for entry into new markets or expansion into existing ones.

Under Reagan, the gap between the needs of overseas capital and the operations of the imperial state widened significantly. While rhetoric about the virtues of capitalist enterprise flourished under his administration, the priority concerns (manifested through state action at the international level) focused on increasing the state's military capacities, political intervention, and ideological alignments. Such activities have often had devastating consequences for overseas investors and traders: destabilized political systems, a hostile environment for investors, disrupted markets, and capital flight. The massive Reagan military-ideological-clandestine offensive in Central America is a case in point: the region's economies are at a standstill due to declining terms of trade, a rising foreign debt, billions of dollars in capital flight, falling investments, and huge nonproductive spending by U.S. client regimes. The region's GDP grew at an average annual rate of less than 1 percent between 1980 and 1985. During the same period, regional investment declined by 27 percent and the region's imports plummeted by 28 percent (*Central America Report*, September 19, 1986, p. 283).

Meanwhile, in competitor capitalist countries the integration between state and capital intensified, and the interlock became more pronounced. While the U.S. merchandise trade deficit increased from $27.9 billion in 1981 to an all-time high of $124.4 billion in 1984, the formulation and implementation of long-term, comprehensive export strategies enabled Japan and West Germany to record substantial trade surpluses during the 1980s—in large part at Washington's expense (*National Journal*, December 13, 1986, pp. 2992–93).

Reagan officials remained preoccupied with diverting time, expertise, and massive financial resources into sustaining military-dominated regimes and large-scale counter-terrorist activities throughout the third world. In Central America, more than $1 billion in official military assistance to corrupt and autocratic regimes has been augmented by the provision of hundreds of millions of dollars for the establishment of a permanent U.S. military presence in Honduras, and the channeling of additional hundreds of millions of dollars (overtly and covertly) to fund the contra war against Nicaragua (Morley and Petras 1988). In South Asia, covert military aid to the Afghan rebels between 1984 and 1986 totaled almost $900 million (*New York Times,* November 28, 1984, p. 1). In southern Africa, the Reagan administration began shipping millions of dollars worth of sophisticated weapons, including several hundred Stinger missiles, to Jonas Savimbi's Pretoria-supported UNITA forces in Angola in March 1986 as part of a concerted effort to destabilize that country's established and internationally recognized government. Amid these military-clandestine-terrorist initiatives, the U.S. multibillion trade deficit continued to soar and U.S. export markets in the debt-ridden third world continued to contract at an accelerated rate. But the Reaganites' only response to these crises reflected their priorities: instead of reactivating the economic agencies of the imperial state, improvised proposals such as the "Baker Plan" were periodically floated as long-term solutions to the deepening third world debt crisis.[1]

Left to its own devices, U.S. overseas capital has been no match for its most formidable competitors. Rearguard action such as U.S. exporters denouncing "unfair competition" based on strong state backing for West European and Japanese traders thus became the order of the day. Unable to gain new markets abroad, investors have also sought to protect existing markets at home through resort to protectionism. The rise of protectionist rhetoric is, above all, symptomatic of the declining competitiveness of U.S. capital and the declining overseas capacity of U.S. economic agencies. In the heyday of American overseas expansion, when the economic agencies of the imperial state were promoting capital and commerce in every corner of the globe, free trade was the battle cry of an ascending empire of multinational corporations. Today, the Reaganites' free trade exhortations ring hollow as every major U.S. industry from automobiles to machine tools to computers to semiconductors has lost crucial market shares to West European and Japanese competitors.

As presently constituted, the U.S. imperial state apparatus represents a liability, not an asset, to the expansion of capital. From a narrow cost-benefit analysis, the financial allocations to sustain the overblown military structures far exceed the economic opportunities that are created. Even if cost/benefits are only examined from the point of view of the narrower interests of corporate capitalism, the huge budget deficits ($221 billion in FY 1986) resulting from skyrocketing military expenditures have set in motion long-term economic forces that work against the reproduction of capital. The broader effects of the overdevelopment of the military components of the imperial state are found in the political-social-economic environment for U.S. investment and trade that results from global interventionist policies. Central America has experienced a major decline in trade and massive capital flight with no foreseeable economic recovery as a result of the ascendancy of imperial ideologues, intelligence operatives, and counterinsurgency strategists. The Persian Gulf has become a war zone for large-scale, costly U.S. military maneuvers in place of previously profitable economic endeavors. Symbolic of the change, Japanese and European vessels engage in trade while Washington spends millions of dollars in order that the U.S. Navy can patrol the area and protect oil shipments that probably benefit Japan (specifically, its industrial sector) more than any other country.

The irony is that the self-styled promoters of free markets in Washington—the Reagan administration—have failed to take advantage of the market liberalization processes that have occurred throughout the third world and the Soviet bloc during the 1980s. The primary beneficiaries have been Washington's major economic competitors within the capitalist world, and they remain in the best position to continue to take advantage of further market openings around the globe.

## Conclusion: Can U.S. Imperial Decline Be Reversed?

By any standard measure or relevant index, U.S. imperial capital has lost power in the world economy: its share of global trade and investment has declined over the past thirty years, leading to the transformation of the United States from the world's largest creditor to debtor accumulating unprecedented budget and trade deficits. Are there policy options available to imperial policymakers which can reverse the downward slide of the United States toward the level of mediocrity that characterizes the current British economy? Theoretically, a combination of three levels of reform and restructuring could serve to expand U.S. hegemonic influence.

First, it would require a restructuring of the imperial state in the direction of expanding and upgrading its economic agencies relative to the ossified, overstaffed, and nonproductive ideological-military apparatus. This would necessitate the wholesale replacement of several layers of bureaucratic officials with little, if any, enterprise responsibilities and their replacement by technocratic and entrepreneurial cadres with the expertise to link state programs to overseas investors.

Second, there would be a need to restructure U.S. capital toward productive activity and away from its preoccupation with financial, speculative, and real estate dealings. This could be achieved only through large-scale, long-term state regulation and intervention and a willingness to discipline capital.

Third, the imperial state reformers would have to increase and strengthen the linkages between the economic agencies and productive capital. Such an outcome would depend on the ability to further marginalize Congress' and extra-parliamentary inputs and would require a much greater interlock between industrial capital and the imperial state agencies than presently exists.

These moves to reform the imperial state and restructure capital would unquestionably provoke massive resistance from within the imperial state and the influential higher circles of financial capital—an opposition that, given the current configuration of political forces, is likely to prove insurmountable. The imperial ideologues' and their military counterparts' first line of defense will almost certainly be a resort to "national security"—based on assertions about rising terrorism, untrustworthy Soviets, contra military victories, and the like. However, while it would be folly to underestimate the strength of the Ollie Norths and Elliott Abramses, especially in the context of a complicit mass media always ready to amplify uncritically official propaganda as statements of fact, their position in the imperial system is vulnerable on a number of grounds. First, it is becoming increasingly transparent to some influential sectors of American business that the U.S. economic decline is directly linked to the dominant policy roles played by these ideologues and military strategists.

Second, the military strategy has proven ineffective on its own terms. As a result, the general public that was promised the ideal of becoming "Number One" again—and drawn into the arms build-up under the illusion that the boom times of the 1950s and 1960s would be recreated—has become disillusioned with massive defense outlays. Confronted with the choice of increased military spending and social-sector cuts or a reduction in the military program to protect the "social net," public opinion is now overwhelmingly in favor of the latter.

Third, the Soviet peace initiatives under Gorbachev have contributed mightily to the plummeting popular appeal of the state ideologues and the Pentagon militarists. Finally, the evolution of economic policy in third world revolutionary countries (mixed public and private, market liberalization, etc.) represents an opportunity, not a threat, to the United States, demonstrating that capitalist countries can link up "down the road" with the technological and investment needs of these less-developed countries.

At the same time, a requirement for reestablishing hegemony even more fundamental than reform of the imperial state is the need to restructure capital from financial to productive. Here the obstacles are perhaps most formidable: financial capital in today's United States includes the largest and most influential sectors of the corporate community whose "reach" extends into the government, media, and cultural organs of the society. Any thoroughgoing policy of state regulation will inevitably be portrayed as contravening the basic rules governing the operations of private capitalism in the domestic economy.

To counter the resistance of financial capital, those reformers intent on promoting an imperial revival could offer an effective response: state policy is not anticapitalist but simply a different style of capitalist development (thus disarming charges of "subversion"); financial capital is undermining America's global position and relegating productive capital to a subordinate role within the U.S. economy; and, most pointedly, financial capital is leading the United States to an economic crash for which Black October 1987 was only a dress rehearsal.

Clearly, the ideological-military-financial power bloc became more vulnerable to attack during the second Reagan administration and there is every likelihood that this trend will accelerate, especially if another economic collapse occurs. Yet, the possibility of realizing reforms and reconstructing U.S. hegemonic power is still remote, precisely because there is an absence of any organized constituency in the United States capable of challenging the dominant power bloc. Democrats and Republicans, liberals and conservatives, all share the same basic outlook as the power bloc and none have demonstrated the least inclination to reform the imperial state or restructure capital. U.S. imperialism lacks the political leadership of a Gorbachev who could begin the process of establishing a "foundation" for the renewal of imperial power.

But economic pressures persist, competition continues apace, and the U.S. economy pursues its slide. Between the pressures stemming from the crises of the hegemonic state and absence of political leadership, we can expect marginal shifts in policy: limited arms agreements with the Soviets, caps on military spending, economic summit meetings, and improvised debt agreements accompanied by SDI programs, intensified pressure on the dollar, loss of overseas markets, a likely financial crash, and continued military intervention and funding of surrogate wars in the third world. Marginal shifts in policy toward reforming the state and restructuring capital will not, however, shift the historical downward drift of U.S. capital in the world economy.

The imperial state that was fashioned to promote domestic capital in pursuit of overseas markets and profits has become an albatross undermining overseas opportunities and increasing domestic costs. The final irony: the very imperial state evoked to save capitalism becomes its gravedigger.

### Note

1. The so-called Baker Plan, announced by the Reagan administration in October 1985, urged greater World Bank and private commercial bank lending to third world debtor countries in return for "structural adjustments"—privatizing state enterprises, new "openings" to foreign investment, eased regulations on private banks, etc.—acceptable to the IMF.

### References

Auerbach, Stuart and Peter Behr. 1987. "America Faces a Rude Awakening." *Washington Post National Weekly Edition,* May 4.

Bryant, William E. 1975. *Japanese Private Economic Diplomacy: An Analysis of Business-Government Linkages.* New York: Praeger.

Clark, Thomas B. 1986. "Tackling the Debt Crisis." *National Journal* 18, no. 32 (August 9).

Destler, I. M. et al. 1976. *Managing an Alliance: The Politics of U.S.-Japanese Relations.* Washington, D.C.: The Brookings Institute.

Ferguson, Thomas and Joel Rogers. 1986. *Right Turn: The Decline of the Democrats and the Future of American Politics.* New York: Hill and Wang.

Markusen, Ann. 1986. "The Militarized Economy." *World Policy Journal* 3, no. 3 (Summer).

Morley, Morris H. and James F. Petras. 1988. "The Reagan Administration and Nicaragua: How Washington Constructs its Case for Counterrevolution in Central America." In Morris H. Morley, ed., *Crisis and Confrontation: Ronald Reagan's Foreign Policy.* Totowa, NJ: Rowman and Littlefield.

Morrison, David C. 1987a. "Downhill Slide." *National Journal* 19, no. 8 (February 21).

————. 1987b. "Military Buildown." *National Journal* 19, nos. 51–52 (December 19).

Morse, Ronald A. 1987–88. "Japan's Drive to Pre-eminence." *Foreign Policy* no. 69 (Winter).

Rauch, Jonathan. 1987. "After the Boom." *National Journal* 19, nos. 51–52 (December 19).

Sweezy, Paul and Harry Magdoff. 1986. "The Logic of Stagnation." *Monthly Review* 38, no. 5 (October).

Tyler, Patrick E. and David B. Ottaway. 1986. "Casey Strengthens Role Under 'Reagan Doctrine.'" *Washington Post,* March 31.

Woodward, Bob. 1987. *Veil: The Secret Wars of the CIA 1981–1987.* New York: Simon & Schuster.

# British Capitalism
# in a Changing Global Economy

## *Hugo Radice*

### Introduction

The "British decline" has been going on for a very long time now.
Always a relative decline in most respects, after 1945 it took the form
of a rate of economic growth markedly slower than that of most other
advanced capitalist countries. In the global context of the postwar
boom, the decline was attributed variously to bad economic management, to institutional features of the labor and capital markets or of
the state, and to the unavoidable legacy of imperial rule. Whatever
the reason, the analysis of decline centered on the problem of lack of
international competitiveness, rooted in low and slowly growing
industrial productivity.

This essay is concerned with changes in British capitalism since
the end of the postwar boom. These changes have for the most part
been analyzed in terms of the long battle for political hegemony
between Keynesian social democracy and pre-Keynesian neo-
liberalism, which has seemed to emerge victorious in the Thatcherite
economic policies of the 1980s. In turn, the debates over this process
of change have usually focused on "internal" political, economic,
and social aspects: the Thatcher government's attacks on the labor
movement, privatization and the promotion of "people's capitalism,"
and so on. I believe, however, that these developments can only be
properly understood in the context of changes in global capitalism as
a whole, for throughout the "British decline" Britain has remained a
major imperialist power and a major participant in international
trade and capital flows.

The next section sets out some general hypotheses about the

relationship between "national capitalisms" and the contemporary capitalist world economy. The essay then turns to the British case, focusing on two issues in particular, the nature of Britain's "deindustrialization" and the resurgence of capital export since the 1970s. The conventional view on the left is that these two phenomena are linked together very simply in the continued dominance within British capitalism of a financial sector that is externally oriented; under this hegemony of the City, British capital has invested abroad to escape the low profitability forced upon it by a strong labor movement. This implies an alternative of national industrial reconstruction, based on an alliance of national capital, labor, and the state. I shall argue, instead, that British capital has played and continues to play a leading role in the restructuring of *world capitalism*. In this context, deindustrialization has not in itself been a sign of weakness of British capital, but rather the result of choices made by British capital; and the City and British industry, far from being antagonistic fractions of British capital, have become thoroughly integrated into a more or less classic form of finance capital, whose sphere of operation is the world economy as a whole.

### The Changing Character of the Capitalist World Economy

Traditionally, both orthodox economics and Marxism have viewed the world economy as a set of interacting national economies. For orthodox economics, this goes back to the mercantilist origins of classical political economy, and was already enshrined in Ricardo's theory of comparative advantage. For Marxism, it was Bukharin, in *Imperialism and World Economy,* who provided the most explicit theoretical justification for this approach. He argued that capitalism contained within it lawlike tendencies toward *both* "internationalization" *and* "nationalization." Competition and accumulation drove capitals outward regardless of geographical or political boundaries to form a global capitalist system; but at the same time, the concentration and centralization of capital, engendered by those same drives, both promoted and was structured by the nation-state. In Bukharin's view, the tendency toward "nationalization" became the dominant one, and this gave the process of internationalization its *imperialist* form.

By the 1960s, however, the capitalist world economy was showing signs of transcending this "nation-statist" form of organization. The standard Marxian view of the U.S. imperial hegemony after 1945, and the growing challenge from Europe and Japan in the 1960s, was perfectly consistent with the conventional wisdom: this was inter-imperialist rivalry in essentially the same form as in 1914. Yet this analysis could not easily come to grips with some profound changes in the nature of the internationalization of capital: in particular, the interpenetration of "national capitalisms" through the spread of transnational corporations, and the emergence of unregulated global financial markets beyond the reach of supposedly powerful state authorities.

Although these changes were the subject of vigorous debate (e.g., between Murray 1971 and Warren 1971), they were by no means resolved. In essence, the argument became widely interpreted as being over the "strength" or "capacity" of the nation-state, rather than over its structural role. Both sides tended to argue within the framework of a "nation-statist" conception of the world economy, and the problem was to determine who, or what agency, would carry out those public functions which individual nation-states seemed no longer able to undertake.

Insofar as the debate concerned primarily the advanced industrial states this is not surprising, given that for so long the state had played such a central role in a specifically *national* accumulation process. However, analysts of the third world tended to adopt a very different perspective on the state. For them, the central problem in the postcolonial period was that the nation-state and the national econ-omy were to a great extent structured by the *global* patterns of capitalist competition and accumulation; this structuring being summed up in the concept of dependency. Development strategies pursued by third world ruling groups were jointly determined by "internal" economic and political interests aimed at creating a viable national capitalism on the conventional model, and by "external" forces of world markets and the political/military dispositions of great powers.

From this tradition, therefore, there emerged that view of the capitalist world economy characterized rightly by Gordon (1988) as "globalist" and exemplified by writers such as Wallerstein (1974) or Frobel, Heinrichs, and Kreye (1980). The "globalists" are right to contend that capitalism has always been structured in the first in-stance at the global level. But how nation-states and national econo-mies fit in to this global system remains to be specified for each historical period and each country. It is *not* simply that there are national and international "moments" to capitalist accumulation and reproduction, *nor* that national capitalisms can be more interdependent or "combined." That way of viewing the problem remains itself locked in the conception of the world economy as a set of interacting national economies. It is, if you will, insufficiently globalist.

An alternative view can be briefly sketched out. Within intrinsically global capitalism, national economies crystallized in the eighteenth and nineteenth centuries from the interaction between the dynamics of capitalist competition and accumulation on the one hand, and the preexisting forms of political authority (notably the absolutist state) on the other. Britain emerged as hegemonic within this inter-state system, and British capital dominated and structured worldwide accumulation. In response to this, emergent capitalist classes in the United States, Germany, and other Western countries, promoted an explicitly national form of capitalism in the last third of the nineteenth century, which took on the imperialist form analyzed by Hilferding, Bukharin, and Lenin. Out of the crisis of inter-imperial rivalries there emerged, under American hegemony, the finished form of national capitalism. Mass production and consumption on national norms, an extensive welfare (or welfare/warfare) state, Keynesian macroeconomic intervention, the incorporation or pacification of labor, the liquidation of formal empires: these signaled the institutionalization of an apparently stable "inter-national" order of interacting nation-states and national economies.

My contention is that the end of the postwar boom did not merely lead to the undermining of U.S. hegemony, and hence of the stability of that international order. Rather, the forces that led to economic slowdown and crisis *also undermined the century-old "national" organization of the world economy*. The crisis of world capitalism appeared, *given* that organization, as a crisis of British, American, German, and so on, capitalisms. The response of British, American, or German capitalists was to try to transcend the close limits of national organization—a process that appeared as the "internationalization of capital." Competition between *individual* capitals now played out in a global arena; a process of global concentration and centralization of capital (Andreff 1984) tended to break up the national "coalitions" of capitals which typified the old form of organization of the world economy. The freeing up of large industrial, commercial, and banking capitals from national constraints has led to a general process of *disintegration* (or "disarticulation") of national economies.

In this alternative view, the "inter-national" form taken by the world economy, roughly from 1870 to 1970, was a historically bounded, contingent form, and not an immanent feature of capitalism as such. The emergent "transnational" form has been characterized by Jenkins (1987:114) thus: ". . . The significance of the internationalization of capital is that it creates a world economy in which capitals rather than nation states are the basic units." But further, this transnational integration of economic processes, which goes far beyond that achieved by international trade alone, in turn promotes a globalization of class formation and of the structuring of states in the world economy. The attempts of capitalists to deal with the dual challenge of the 1960s, from organized labor at home, and a rebellious third world abroad, have had the effect of *bringing the third world home*. Economically, this appears in the devastation wrought by global restructuring on old industrial areas and on their labor markets. Politically, the role, institutions and policies of the state are now formed, as in the third world, by the intersection of internal economic and political interests with the "external" world market as bearer of the forces of global competition and accumulation. The state in the advanced capitalist countries is not weakened. Rather, it is turned on its bearings and compelled to "serve two masters": to struggle to reconcile the need to reproduce capitalist class rule within its boundaries, with the demands placed by global capitals seeking to accumulate and reproduce on a worldwide basis.

This is emphatically *not* to suggest that a political strategy of developing a national capitalism, or seeking to direct accumulation to improving "national" competitiveness, is no longer *possible*. Rather, I argue that this is no longer the "natural" pattern. In some countries (e.g., Japan or Sweden) contingent factors ensure that economic and social interests continue to be mobilized around such a project under the hegemony of a national capitalist class. The experience of the NICs (including Spain and Yugoslavia), however, suggests that it is extraordinarily difficult to construct that project and that hegemony, even in relatively industrialized countries outside the ranks of the most developed: what even semiperipheral (let alone peripheral) industrialization has created, as a rule, is islands of industrialization articulated with world markets, rather than the foundations of new national capitalisms.

In my view, the same tendency can be observed among the large advanced capitalist economies also. The next sections look at British capitalism as a case in point, seeking to understand changing patterns of economic activity and economic policy in Britain by placing them in the global context just outlined.

## Deindustrialization and National Decline

In a pioneering article, Singh (1977) defined deindustrialization directly in relation to trade performance:

> Given the normal levels of the other components of the balance of payments, we may define an efficient manufacturing sector as one which, currently as well as potentially, not only satisfies the demands of consumers at home but is also able to sell enough of its products abroad to pay for the nation's import requirements. (Singh 1977:128)

This suggests that we should first look at trends in the United Kingdom's trade before directly assessing the factors behind the decline in manufacturing employment.

Until the devaluation of the pound in 1967, the United Kingdom's postwar balance of payments followed a rather stable pattern. The visible trade account tended to be slightly in deficit; this was not usually offset by a sufficient surplus on invisible trade; and both long- and short-term capital flows were also slightly negative. The overall balance of payments was usually in deficit, and the trend deficit was growing. During this period, the United Kingdom's competitive trade performance in manufacturing was taken to be steadily deteriorating: the United Kingdom's share of world manufacturing exports declined from 25.5 percent in 1950 to 10.8 percent in 1970.[1] As for the invisibles account, here the consistent surplus on private services trade was reduced by a significant deficit on the government account, attributed mostly to the continuing cost of maintaining military forces abroad. Meanwhile, the net outflow of long-term capital remained at a historically low level of 0.5 to 1 percent of GDP: portfolio investment abroad was restricted by exchange controls to reinvestment of profits earned abroad, while direct investment by U.K. companies was offset by foreign (mainly U.S.) direct investment in the United Kingdom.

The devaluation of 1967 led to a considerable improvement in the United Kingdom's current account by 1970, but in the following decade this improvement was swamped by other dramatic changes.

The boom of 1972–3 led, like earlier booms, to a burgeoning trade deficit, and the pound, by then floating, sank like a stone. Inflation that peaked at over 25 percent, the rise in the cost of imported oil, and the effect on U.K. imports of EEC accession all served to plunge the current account into a deficit averaging around 2–3 percent of GDP. The root cause of this was still generally taken to be poor industrial productivity.

Once North Sea oil came on stream in 1979, and Mrs. Thatcher launched her headlong deflation, the current account was transformed, to an annual average surplus of about 1.5 percent of GDP in 1979–84. But the effect of deflation and the high pound on manufacturing employment was catastrophic. It fell from 8.4 million in 1966, to 7.1 million in 1978, 5.9 million in 1981, and 5.3 million in 1987. Trade performance in semimanufactures and manufactures (SITC sections 5–8) also worsened sharply, from a surplus of £5.4 billion in 1980 to a deficit of £5.5 billion in 1986. Imports rose from 21 percent of home demand plus exports in 1979 to 27 percent in 1987, while exports stagnated at around 21–22 percent of domestic sales plus exports.

Figures such as these have been widely regarded as indicating disastrous performance by U.K. manufacturing industry by comparison with other advanced industrial countries. They provide the starting point for a search for causes of poor manufacturing performance. This perspective has been termed by Rowthorn and Wells (1987) the "failure thesis" on deindustrialization. Proponents of this thesis then look for causes in government policies (deflation, lack of industrial policy), in industrial relations (union resistance to change), or in the institutional structures of British capital ("short-termism," external orientation, poor management, lack of finance). However, while other writers offer only various versions of the "failure thesis," Rowthorn and Wells offer two alternatives: the "maturity thesis" and the "specialization thesis."

The maturity thesis argues that a reduction in the share of manufacturing in employment may be an indication of successful economic performance, if it is the joint result of high incomes, a shift in demand therefore toward services, and high industrial productivity which reduces labor demand in the manufacturing sector (Rowthorn and Wells 1987:213). Essentially, the agent of relative deindustrialization is the growth of the service sector.

The specialization thesis, on the other hand, argues that the United Kingdom's decline in manufacturing employment is primarily due to more or less exogenous changes in the United Kingdom's foreign trade. These changes are indicated starkly by Rowthorn and Wells: in 1950–52, the U.K. *surplus on trade in manufactures* averaged 10.5 percent of GDP, while its *deficit on trade in nonmanufactures* was 13.3 percent. By 1981–83, however, the balance of trade in nonmanufactures had shifted dramatically to a *surplus* equivalent to about 1 percent of GDP. This they attribute mainly to a massive growth in domestic food production, reductions in raw materials use, and North Sea oil—with the nongovernment services (including financial services) playing only a modest role. They conclude that as a result, the United Kingdom no longer needs a huge surplus in its manufacturing trade.

This is an important argument, for in terms of Singh's definition of deindustrialization it means that a significant part of at least the *relative* decline in U.K. manufacturing employment should not be seen as a problem. However, Rowthorn and Wells do not thereby conclude that Britain's manufacturing performance was after all satisfactory. If a surplus on manufacturing trade is no longer required, that says little about the absolute level of manufacturing output and employment. Thus in relation to the 1980s experience, the burgeoning North Sea revenues—worth some £10 billion by 1985 before the collapse in oil prices—could have been spent on £10 billion of manufactured imports for immediate consumption, with, *ceteris paribus,* no change in the absolute level of manufacturing output or employment; but alternatively, and particularly in the context of a program of reflation and rising investment in industry, they could have been spent on £10 billion of capital and intermediate goods, with rising consumption met to a much greater extent from domestic sources, and an overall rise in manufacturing output and employment.

Why, then, has this shift in trade structure in fact been accompanied by such a decline in the *absolute* level of manufacturing output and employment? The most common argument is a two-stage one. First, the general crisis of accumulation in the advanced capitalist countries since the late 1960s has opened up a process of capitalist industrialization in certain LDCs, the so-called NICs. Following the analysis of Frobel, Heinrichs, and Kreye (1981), this relocation of industrial production is seen as centering on relatively labor-intensive sectors or production phases, which are moved to low-wage production sites; the process as a whole being very much under the control of advanced-country MNCs through their control of technology and final markets. Secondly, the United Kingdom is seen as coming off particularly badly in this process for several reasons: a relatively poor quality, low-skill labor force is unsuited to the location of high-level productive activities in the United Kingdom; labor costs, taking into account the costs of labor unrest, are perceived to be relatively high; the United Kingdom has a relatively large share of the type of traditional industry most vulnerable to relocation; and it has a disproportionate share of the world's MNC-controlled production.

Although the perspective offered by Rowthorn and Wells is clearly more subtle, most writers have used such arguments to explain deindustrialization as "failure"—and they have attributed the failure to Mrs. Thatcher's policies. On the other hand, the Thatcher policies could be seen as promoting a process of adjustment to "new realities" of international competition. The sustained attack on the unions, for example, opens the way for the installation of Japanese-style ("post-Fordist") management methods, reducing Britain's labor costs and thereby making it relatively attractive as a location for footloose multinationals. At the same time, the sharp rise in personal disposable incomes of those in work—due mainly to the impact of North Sea oil and the booming financial sector—has made Britain a more attractive market, and in many sectors location in or near the target market is still desirable. Evidence for such a view may be found in the recovery of inward direct investment to a level of about £4 billion in 1985 and 1986, with much publicity given to Japanese direct investments in particular. In addition, considering how disastrous U.K. manufacturing performance is supposed to have been, it is striking that exports of manufactures have grown at about 5.5 percent per year in value terms between 1983 and 1987—helping to offset a fall of nearly £8 billion in fuels exports between 1985 and 1987.

In short, Mrs. Thatcher can argue, as she did in the 1987 election campaign, that her policies are working, in the sense that at present the growth in overall U.K. output and employment, and indeed for manufacturing output and exports (if not employment), is comparatively strong. Critics of the government have of course argued that, given the very high degree of openness and internationalization of the U.K. economy, the recovery may be fragile. As North Sea oil earnings decline in the long term, a structural trade deficit will open, and it may be impossible to "reindustrialize" effectively to meet the

"Singh condition." Record trade deficits in late 1988 are thus seen as evidence of a new phase of "failure."

Whichever prognosis turns out to be correct, the huge fall in industrial employment in the Thatcher years is not simply an acceleration of "national economic decline." Rather, in the perspective of the previous section of this essay, it points to an increasing disjuncture between the British *economy* and British *capital*. In the context of a significant decline in import requirements, British-owned MNCs could expand production abroad at a rapid rate; meanwhile, Mrs. Thatcher's assault on the bastions of labor allowed them to restructure their activities at home. The consequence is an industrial structure that is highly disintegrated at regional and national level, with individual branch plants highly dependent on world markets for both supplies and sales, often from and to affiliates of the same MNC (whether British- or foreign-owned). However, to understand fully the nature and significance of this new industrial system, we must now turn to the other key feature of British capital's position in the world economy—the question of capital export and the role of the City.

### Capital Exports and the Role of the City

From 1979, three factors jointly led to a dramatic rise in the export of long-term capital from the United Kingdom: the abolition of all remaining exchange controls; the current account surplus caused by North Sea oil revenues and deflation; and the consequential rise in the value of the pound. The balance on the long-term capital account averaged $-£6.7$ billion in 1979–84, and then soared to $-£15.1$ billion in 1985 and $-£20.4$ billion in 1986; at first, outflows rose while inflows stagnated, but more recently the latter have grown as well. At the same time, the dramatic expansion, or rather renewal, of the City as a world financial center saw a huge rise in short-term capital flows in both directions, with a surplus helping to finance the long-term capital deficit during this period.

Because exchange controls before 1979 chiefly affected portfolio investments, it was these that showed the sharpest rise subsequently. Yet the volume of direct investments was remarkable, especially when placed in an international context. By 1983, U.K. foreign direct investments amounted to 31 percent of total corporate assets, and

23.3 percent of GDP: the latter figure compares to 6.4 percent of GDP for the United States, 9.6 percent for West Germany and 4.2 percent for France (UNCTC 1988). Between 1981 and 1985, U.K.-based firms were responsible for 20.8 percent of total outward FDI, more than the U.S. share of 19 percent, and well over the shares of Japan (11.0 percent) and West Germany (8.6 percent). Interestingly, in 1980–83 52 percent of U.K. outward FDI (excluding oil investments) went to the United States, compared to a meager 4.7 percent to the whole of Western Europe.

The rapid rise in capital exports since 1979 has raised the possibility that British capital is seeking to return to the position of international rentier which it held before 1914. At first sight, it would seem that this is still a very distant prospect. In 1913, net property income from abroad covered fully 25 percent of total import requirements: in 1986, at £5.6 billion, it only covered some 7 percent of imports. The ratio to net national income has equally diminished from around 9 percent to around 2 percent. Nevertheless, given the apparent "export of jobs" by MNCs, the very low level of industrial capital formation in Britain, and the outward flood of portfolio investment, it is not surprising that attention has focused on the relation between industrial decline and the export of capital.

The traditional left argument on this is as follows. Historically, the City has developed as a network of capitalist interests oriented toward world markets for commodities and for money. The precocious development of manufacturing industry in Britain assured industrial capitalists of very high profits, so that their accumulation was largely self-financed, drawing at most on the mobilization of regional savings for short-term finance through the provincial banking system. This meant that London-based merchant and banking capital played virtually no direct role in industrial accumulation; instead, it functioned as commercial and banking capital in worldwide trade and investment. Throughout the decline of the last hundred years, the internationally oriented City has thwarted efforts at industrial renaissance, partly by refusing to supply capital for domestic investment, and partly by successfully controlling government economic policies to ensure that its sectional interests were favored (notably a high value of the pound and minimal controls on capital flows). This, in essence, is the position recently reformulated by Ingham (1984).

This thesis is open to challenge in several respects. First, Fine and Harris (1985:66–71) argue that the City is bound to be concerned about the health of British industry, and indeed the whole British economy, since it is still the ultimate source of most of the City's wealth: it is just that the preferred medicine for the ills of the wider economy is market discipline rather than planned infusions of long-term private or public finance.

Secondly, the City and industrial capital are now intimately related to each other. Throughout the postwar period, but especially since the merger boom of the mid-1960s (repeated notably in the early 1970s and mid-1980s), merchant banks and institutional investors have played a major role in the restructuring of industrial capital. They mobilize long-term finance for accelerating the internal growth of individual firms, and for the centralization of capital through takeovers. Furthermore, since the mid-1970s, and culminating in the "Big Bang" of deregulation in 1986, the boundaries between the different types of City institution have steadily eroded, bringing, for example, even the big clearing banks into the provision of long-term industrial finance.

The City has been still more crucial in assisting in the expansion by British-based MNCs abroad. The unparalleled international reach and flexibility of British banking and finance has offset relative weakness in industrial technology and production, allowing the MNCs to establish powerful bridgeheads first in Western Europe, and more recently in the United States. The internationalization of British banking has also supported the internationalization of British property companies, accountancy firms, advertising agencies, construction companies, and the like.

What about the specific argument that the City's power has diverted investment funds abroad? As Fine and Harris point out, this argument rests on the assumption that the two are substitutes. But all the evidence suggests that British industrial capitalists have themselves been unwilling to invest more in Britain, for their own perfectly good capitalist reasons—notably, low profit prospects. The few demands made by industrial capitalists on the City have been satisfied. Recent evidence suggests that large British industrial firms are today operating with historically low levels of debt (Rodgers and Tran 1988), which also suggests that they are not starved for funds.

There is a further important point about the changing character of the City: it is less and less composed of only British-owned capital. American and more recently European and Japanese banks have been for years deeply involved in the London-based Euromarkets, and in the climate of deregulation they have rapidly spread their interests into securities dealing and all spheres of "domestic" finance. Barratt Brown concludes that "the City of London is no longer a British institution but an international enclave" (1988:50). Fair enough, but an international enclave in *what?* In view of my argument in the previous section on the national disintegration and international integration of British industry, it would be better to say that the City of London *and* industrial capital located in Britain collectively form British-based finance capital, of mixed British and foreign ownership, while British-owned capital has taken full advantage of the international scope of the British financial system to operate increasingly at a global level. The result is that, rather than the City being an international enclave, British capitalism as a whole is thoroughly internationalized.

## Prospects and Alternatives

From a capitalist standpoint, the changes that have taken place in Britain's economic performance since 1979 have undoubtedly been beneficial. The City of London has so far been able to maintain its role in the world's financial markets, with British capitals in this arena being willing to concede substantial participation to foreign financial institutions, but able at the same time to expand abroad. While some of this overseas activity has involved significant risk (e.g., sovereign lending to LDCs), the City's bankers can rest secure in the knowledge that no challenge to their influence over those government policies which are central to their interests is likely to come from within their own class: for British industry, despite occasional huffing and puffing, is now predominantly integrated into the world economy also, and shares the same interests. At the same time, the productive operations of British and foreign-owned capitals within Britain have been ruthlessly restructured to fit into the new international division of labor—broadly in an intermediate position (below Germany or Japan, but above Spain or Brazil), but at a high level in some sectors (armaments, pharmaceuticals, food and drink, retailing, advertising). Stronger British-owned transnational corporations have successfully consolidated their global positions, notably in the important North American market.

The consequences for British workers, however, have been very different. Those in employment have been cushioned from the effects of "restructuring," since they have been allocated a share of the benefits of North Sea oil (e.g., through direct tax cuts), and of the productivity gains. Many have also won windfall capital gains as a result of the rising real price of housing. The losers have been those who have become and remained unemployed and those who have been forced, as they enter or reenter the labor market, into low-paid jobs. Figuring disproportionately among the losers have been women, the young, blacks, those in declining "traditional" industries such as coal, steel, and heavy engineering, and those in peripheral regions such as Northern Ireland and the north and northwest of England.

Other things being equal, in the short term it is quite possible that relatively fast economic growth will continue to push the north/south boundary northward, and to open up islands of prosperity farther north also—notably around large-scale urban redevelopment projects along the lines of the London Docklands renewal. Unequally though the gains of such growth will be distributed, many families will leave the ranks of the losers and gain some relief from the ravages of the past ten years. Among the factors which will make for short-term prosperity will be the continued attractiveness of the United Kingdom as an investment location (weakened and divided unions, cheap labor, political stability) and the potential for productivity growth through catching up with European levels of technique.

What about the longer term? Much has been made of the consequences of the completion of a unified internal market in the European Community in 1992—the usual presumption being that "Britain will lose out" if "we" are unable to match "their" cost levels by that date. However, national disintegration and international integration imply that "we" and "they" can no longer be treated as independent economic abstractions: relative competitiveness is determined more at the *corporate* than at the national level. What matters for workers is how much of British-located labor and physical plant is included, through its corporate ownership, in the upper levels of the global inter-corporate division of labor; and to what extent those assets are securely fixed—through a wide variety of means—to those British locations. So long as a Thatcher, or Thatcherite, government is in power, we can expect the hegemony of private capital over such questions to be unchallenged. Only the most catastrophic circumstances would lead such a government to impose public intervention to protect jobs—and the 1980s tell us that 20 percent unemployment, however distasteful to many, does not spell political catastrophe. Hence, it has been made clear to British workers that their future is in *their* hands: if they accept the rule of capital, the recovery will continue.

This leads to the question of alternatives. Centrist proposals, both within and to the right of the Labour Party, offer a similar objective of enhanced "national competitiveness." They believe that traditional measures of Keynesian demand-management—notably manipulation of the exchange rate and an active fiscal policy—remain effective. They would add a range of "supply-side" measures, especially in education, training, and physical infrastructure. While such a program is widely supported by economists and other intellectuals, its political representatives, especially in the ill-fated Liberal-Social Democratic Party alliance, have signally failed to translate media support into an effective challenge for power.

The left has criticized the Keynesian approach as unrealistic, particularly given the international mobility of capital, and the patent hostility of the ruling class to any renewal of the postwar "Butskellite" consensus. Its alternatives have centered on some variant of national industrial planning (e.g. Cowling and Sugden 1987: ch.6; Rowthorn and Wells 1987:314–16; Gilhespy et al. 1986). The package typically centers on a state-owned investment bank, a hierarchy of public planning agencies, and the reassertion of public ownership in certain sectors. Other elements include the repeal of Thatcher's anti-union measures, a rejuvenation of the welfare state, and strict controls over money capital—especially the reintroduction of foreign exchange controls (Glyn 1986).

Criticism of such proposals *within* the left has tended to focus on the *politics* of winning electoral support and then implementing them. But important questions are also raised by the changed character of British capitalism as described above. Given the high levels of trade and of inward and outward stocks of direct investment, the industrial economy is now highly fragmented. Short of instituting command planning on the Soviet model (not a very popular option at present), it is hard to see what possible system of incentives and controls could ensure a coherence of capitalist interests around a program of national industrial expansion. At the very least, substantial powers would be required to compel MNCs to carry out investments in accordance with a national plan. But in any case, such a program tends to remain locked within the logic of international competition, pitting a newly reintegrated "British manufacturing" against Japanese, American, or German (more realistically, Italian, French, or South Korean) manufacturing.

It is possible, instead, to construct an alternative which takes a more realistic view of the present condition of British capitalism, and in particular the view of its global character set out in this study. Elements of this "internationalist" alternative have been emerging over the last ten years.

First and foremost, national planning should be founded upon an evaluation of social needs, rather than on a drive for manufacturing "success" measured by the criteria of the world market. Since social needs are best defined in the first instance at the level of the local community, it is not suprising that the most fertile and practical proposals have emerged from socialist local governments and trade union bodies (e.g., Wainwright and Elliott 1982, Greater London Council 1985). An approach to planning "from below" rapidly points up the need to redefine the nature of work itself, including the characteristic divisions of labor in the workplace, among sectors, in the household, and in society as a whole, rather than simply seeking to expand employment in its present forms.

Second, to elaborate an alternative solely on an economic terrain means taking on Thatcherism at its strongest point—especially if we wish to turn back the tide of privatization in all its forms. Hence, planning for social need is part of a broader set of policies arising from the traditional socialist (and liberal) objectives of democracy, equality, and community. Social needs drawn most directly from those objectives, in the form of education, health, and welfare provision, absorb a high proportion of labor and other resources. Other needs may be met by some mixture of market and nonmarket provision, but an emphasis on democracy and equality can redefine the scope and forms of private ownership—emphasizing, for example, producer cooperatives and worker participation. The British labor movement has rich but dormant traditions which could be called upon to promote such ideas.

Third, in recognition of the global nature of capitalism today, and the interdependence of all national polities within it, a left alternative has to be *explicitly and firmly internationalist*. In part, this means simply giving far more attention to global issues. For example, we should give positive support to proposals to bring under control the anarchic international financial system—to reconstruct a public regulatory agency that can resolve the burden of indebtedness in the third world, restore some order to foreign exchange markets, and concentrate the attention of governments on the equitable distribution of resources such as food and energy. Given the extent of interest and commitment among the public in Britain on issues such as famine, a clear lead in this area would find a strong echo. But a more important and much more difficult task is to *take global inter-dependence into account* in every field of policy. Any form of national economic planning thus has to include the planned management of trade flows, and hence coordination with private and public decisionmakers in other countries. The harmonization of policies—for example, on labor standards and public support for private investments—is essential if the divide-and-rule policies of MNCs are to be undermined. But equally, local governments and plant-level trade unions have to be aware that the lives of their residents and members are lived out within a world economy: hence the need to support the growth of international links at this level too; for example through the "twinning" of communities and the formation of worldwide rank-and-file union committees in MNCs.

An internationalist program along such lines will seem utopian to many. In my view, at least in Britain, it is the traditional left-nationalist program that is utopian, because it does not take proper account of the global dimensions of the restructuring of British capitalism.

### Note

1. For reasons of space, statistics in the text have not been referenced. Recent figures are taken from current editions of the U.K. Central Statistical Office publications *Economic Trends, Monthly Digest of Statistics* and *U.K. Balance of Payments Pink Book.* Historical data are drawn mostly from Barratt Brown (1970), Blackaby (1979), and Rowthorn and Wells (1987).

### References

Andreff, Wladimir. 1984. "The International Centralization of Capital and the Re-ordering of World Capitalism." *Capital and Class* 22 (Spring): 59–80.

Barratt Brown, Michael. 1970. *After Imperialism.* 2nd ed. London: Merlin Press.

———. 1988. "Away with all Great Arches: Anderson's History of British Capitalism." *New Left Review* 167 (January-February): 22–51.

Blackaby, Frank, ed. 1979. *Deindustrialization.* London: Heinemann.

Cowling, Keith and Roger Sugden. 1987. *Transnational Monopoly Capitalism.* Brighton: Wheatsheaf.

Fine, Ben and Laurence Harris. 1985. *The Peculiarities of the British Economy*. London: Lawrence & Wishart.

Frobel, Folker, Jurgen Heinrichs, and Otto Kreye. 1980. *The New International Division of Labour*. Cambridge: Cambridge University Press.

Gilhespy, Diana et al. 1986. *Socialist Enterprise: Reclaiming the Economy*. London: New Socialist/Spokesman Press.

Glyn, Andrew. 1986. "Capital Flight and Exchange Controls." *New Left Review* 155 (January-February): 37–49.

Gordon, David. 1988. "The Global Economy: New Edifice or Crumbling Foundations?" *New Left Review* 168 (March-April): 24–65.

Greater London Council. 1985. *The London Industrial Strategy*. London: Greater London Council.

Ingham, Geoffrey. 1984. *Capitalism Divided?: The City and Industry in British Social Development*. London: Macmillan.

Jenkins, Rhys. 1987. *Transnational Corporations and Uneven Development*. London: Methuen.

Murray, Robin. 1971. "The Internationalization of Capital and the Nation-state." *New Left Review* 67 (May-June): 84–109.

Radice, Hugo. 1984. "The National Economy—a Keynesian Myth?" *Capital and Class* 22 (Spring): 111–40.

Rodgers, Peter and Mark Tran. 1988. "U.S. Feathers Ruffled at British Invasion." *The Guardian* (U.K.) April 26.

Rowthorn, Robert and John Wells. 1987. *Deindustrialization and Foreign Trade*. Cambridge: Cambridge University Press.

Singh, Ajit. 1977. "UK Industry and the World Economy: a Case of De-industrialisation?" *Cambridge Journal of Economics* 1 no.2: 113–36.

United Nations Commission on Transnational Corporations. 1988. *Transnational Corporations in World Development: Trends and Prospects*. New York: United Nations.

Wainwright, Hilary and David Elliott. 1982. *The Lucas Plan: A New Trade Unionism in the Making*. London: Alison & Busby.

Wallerstein, Immanuel. 1974. "The Rise and Future Demise of the World Capitalist System: Concepts for a Comparative Analysis." *Comparative Studies in Society and History* 16 no.4 (September): 387–415.

Warren, Bill. 1971. "The Internationalization of Capital and the Nation-state: a Comment." *New Left Review* 68 (July–August): 83–88.

# The Limits of Keynesian Macroeconomic Policy in the Age of the Global Marketplace

## *James Crotty*

The United States emerged from World War II as the unchallenged leader of world capitalism, in virtually complete control of its own economic destiny and with the power to establish a new economic order, both domestically and internationally. By the early 1950s, the new economic order was solidly in place. Domestically, we had a Keynesian welfare/warfare state in which fiscal and monetary tools were to be used to guide our capitalist economy toward stable economic growth with full employment. Internationally, we had U.S. hegemony, a degree of military/political and economic dominance in world affairs that would assure relative stability, the free movement of capital across national boundaries, and, eventually, increasingly free movement of merchandise. Domestic growth would provide the economic foundation for international dominance. International dominance would assure the stability and access to markets and resources needed for domestic growth. By 1966, with the U.S. economy in the midst of a decade-long expansion, Keynesian economists celebrated the total victory of the Keynesian regime over the instability and inequality of the laissez-faire capitalism of the prewar era.

Yet just twenty years later, in 1987, Paul Volcker, noting "how vulnerable our own financial markets and our own economy have become to what other people think," warned Americans that "we are obviously in danger of losing control of our own [economic] destiny." And in 1988, Felix Rohatyn declared that Volcker's worst fears were now facts:

> More than two hundred years after the Declaration of Independence, the U.S. has lost its position as an independent power. . . . We now

conform to the classic model of a failing economic power: with increasingly high levels of foreign debt, a constantly depreciating currency, and a continuing negative trade balance, whether the dollar is rising or falling. . . . We are becoming constrained, in some ways, as other large external debtors such as Brazil and Mexico.

Less than one generation ago the United States was prosperous and powerful, the banker to the western world. Today the United States is economically unstable and in hock to its allies, unable even to formulate macropolicy without the consent of its creditors. We've come a long way, baby!

In the body of this essay we attempt to explain why the Keynesian regulatory system was powerful enough to help promote prosperity in the early postwar period yet was too weak to prevent the instability and decline of the past fifteen years. We also investigate the role played by the emerging globalization of the world economy in the rise and fall of the Keynesian state and the loss of U.S. economic independence. We conclude by asking: where do we go from here? Can Keynesian macropolicy recreate prosperity in the coming decades? And if not, what is to be done?

## A Theory of Keynesian Macropolicy

Of course, we cannot address these questions without reference to a *theory* of modern capitalism and a theory of Keynesian regulation that can elaborate the conditions under which macropolicy can effectively promote its advertised goals of high employment, a high rate of growth, and a "fairer" distribution of income.[1]

Keynesian economists have themselves provided one such theory. They acknowledged that the Great Depression proved that capitalism has one *major* structural flaw: it has no internal or endogenous mechanism to keep aggregate demand at the full-employment or market-clearing level. But, they argued, this weakness can be corrected by nonradical government fiscal and monetary policy which will neither usurp nor impede the power and efficiency of capitalist markets. Keynesian regulatory mechanisms were never designed to *directly* control the profit-seeking capitalist processes that determined economic outcomes in our society; their role rather was to influence and guide them to perform in the public interest.

On the other hand, radical critics of mainstream Keynesianism have always argued that the Keynesian theory of macropolicy itself had a *major* structural flaw—its erroneous assumption that once macropolicy was wisely set, profit signals would *automatically* motivate those private enterprises that are in direct control of employment, production, and investment to make decisions supportive of balanced full-employment growth. The relation between macropolicy and economic performance, the radical argument went, is mediated by the character and condition of the institutional and structural determinants of profitability. In the absence of more direct public control over economic outcomes, profit signals can frustrate as easily as facilitate macropolicy effectiveness.

The radical critics were right. The story of the rise and fall of the Keynesian regime is the story of the creation and destruction of the domestic and international institutional foundation of long-term profitability in the postwar U.S. economy. In this section we develop the theoretical background needed to understand this story by discussing the conditions required for macropolicy effectiveness. As a simple matter of logic, two such conditions are needed.

First, policymakers must be able to control the level of aggregate demand.

To control the level of aggregate demand, *policymakers must be free to manipulate policy tools in pursuit of domestic objectives.*[2] They will not be free to do so, however, when international problems dominate domestic objectives. For example, concern over a large trade deficit may rule out fiscal stimulation, or difficulties with an unstable exchange rate may foreclose significant manipulation of interest rates in either direction. Such constraints are especially severe when pursuit of some domestic objective threatens to trigger a "crisis," such as a run on the dollar, major defaults of third world debt, or a panic in financial markets.

Furthermore, *changes in policy tools must be capable of generating significant alterations in the level of aggregate demand,* yet various complications may interfere with the connection between policy change and demand response. For example, the Fed cannot lower the interest rate by expanding the money supply if its expansionary move yields heightened inflationary expectations which push interest rates upward. Also, the Fed cannot adequately control U.S. interest rates and credit availability when financial markets are thoroughly international. The most deeply rooted difficulty of this sort occurs when policymakers try to raise aggregate demand by stimulating investment through tax credits or interest rate reduction (as opposed to stimulating investment by first raising aggregate demand). Such policies may be powerless unless current and expected aggregate demand is already strong enough to press on current and expected capacity—in which case the policies are superfluous.

Second, policy-induced changes in aggregate demand must induce the desired changes in domestic objectives.

For the impact of aggregate demand upon objectives to be effective, *the changes in aggregate demand must yield changes in domestic production, employment, income, and capacity utilization instead of changes in prices and in the demand for imported goods.* The experience of the 1970s and early 1980s made it clear that in an inflationary environment nominal aggregate demand can grow at a rapid rate while domestic production and employment are stagnant or even declining. Events of the mid-1980s showed that the leakage of aggregate demand to the foreign sector can be substantial; in 1986, for example, net imports lowered GNP by about 3.6 percent.

Beyond these short-run factors of inflation and trade leakage, however, there is a long-run issue that is more basic, more suggestive of the extent to which Keynesian theory and Keynesian macropolicy are fundamentally flawed. We have seen that is is not always possible for policymakers to control the level of aggregate demand, either because they cannot alter policy or because aggregate demand does not respond to policy changes. Also, we have seen that even when aggregate demand changes, domestic production and capacity utilization may not fully respond. Yet even if these problems are overcome, to attain the most basic domestic objective of raising the rate of growth of potential output and labor productivity, *an expansion of aggregate demand must raise the pace of capital accumulation.* Macropolicy is at times unable to ensure that this condition holds.

Vigorous and sustained capital accumulation takes place when the representative corporation confidently believes that the average profit rate it expects to receive over the expected life of its potential capital investments significantly exceeds the return it could expect to get on financial assets, and when it feels that its current financial position will permit it to shoulder the risks inevitably associated with capital accumulation.[3]

We know what the determinants of the rate of profit on capital *in place* are. The profit rate on capital in any period will be high if output demand is strong and capacity utilization high, if competitive pressures are not intense so that output price is attractive, if wages are modest in comparison with worker productivity (so that labor's share is modest), and if raw material costs are low. If these conditions hold, and the interest rate is low, corporations will be pleased with the return on domestic capital (provided only that the return on foreign capital is not significantly higher).

Now it is clear that macropolicy may be helpless to create these conditions if they are not present in the economy to begin with. Under the best of circumstances macropolicy can stimulate or retard aggregate demand and affect the rate of interest—that's all. It has no direct power to control capital-labor conflict, rearrange price-cost relations, or change the degree of competition at a given level of aggregate demand.

But the problem is yet more complex because corporations will undertake major new capital spending projects only if they are convinced that the rate of profit on this capital will remain high on average for some ten or twenty years. In other words, in order for macropolicy to be able to stimulate an investment boom, it must be able to create an environment seen by the representative corporation as not just temporally profitable but as stably and predictably profitable over long periods of time. The insights of both Keynes and Marx can help us understand why the recreation of such an environment has been beyond the power of the Keynesian regulatory apparatus for the past two decades.

As Keynes argued so persuasively, the determinants of the future rate of profit are in principle unknowable. His investment theory stressed the instability of expectations formation and the importance of the degree of confidence the typical firm placed in its ability to make meaningful forecasts of future economic conditions. An unstable, unpredictable environment will lead to unstable expectations formation, a collapse in corporate confidence in its ability to forecast, and a preference for the safety of short-term financial assets as opposed to the risk attached to physical capital. Unstable or stagnant investment spending will follow.

Keynes also stressed the potential for extreme instability in unregulated capitalist financial markets, domestic and international. In *The General Theory* he argued that the inherently speculative character of stock and bond markets strongly exacerbated investment instability. The remedy he proposed was not macropolicy manipulation but rather a "comprehensive socialization of investment" with "the state . . . taking an ever greater responsibility for *directly* organizing investment" (emphasis added). His hope was that capital accumulation could be insulated from the irrationality and instability of the private-profit rate and the insanity of unregulated financial markets.

He made an analogous argument in his work on international finance. He believed that *unregulated international capital flows would generate instability in domestic interest rates and in the balance of trade and balance of payments and, therefore, in domestic production, employment and investment.* For the last twenty years of his life Keynes was a strong supporter of strict state controls on the movement of goods and, especially, money across national borders. In the absence of such controls, he believed, effective national economic planning in pursuit of full employment and a more equitable income distribution would not be possible, a point to which we return below. Finally, Keynes also argued that any system of international payments settlement which forced economic stagnation on deficit countries would, under conditions of payments imbalances, drag down the growth rate of the whole world economy, harming the surplus as well as the deficit countries.[4]

Whereas Keynes' theory pointed to unrooted entrepreneurial expectations and speculative financial markets as the Achilles' heel of modern capitalism, Marxian theory has traditionally stressed the contradictory relation between capital accumulation and profitability as the most important impediment to balanced growth in capitalist economies. In Marxian theory, changes in the state of the macroeconomy alter the rate of profit. Changes in the profit rate, in turn, generate alterations in the pace of capital accumulation which, in their turn, affect the state of the macroeconomy and the rate of profit. That is, investment is always responding to trends in profitability that are eventually reversed by its response. Consequently, in Marxian theory there is no counterpart to the early postwar Keynesian tale of the potential for endless prosperity and no foundation for the modern Keynesian theory of macropolicy.

Several interesting Marxian explanations of the crisis that has shaken world capitalism in the past two decades offer two creative variations on the traditional Marxian theory of the dynamics of profit-rate determination. The first recognizes that the high average rate of profit required for long-term prosperity could not be sustained if the economy were composed of the competitive markets of neo-classical theory. Rather, the argument goes, stable prosperity requires an internally coherent and stable set of institutions, structures, practices, and policies that are powerful enough to shore up the profit rate and hold back the onset of crisis over long periods of time.[5] The second variation is that capitalist competition is not only powerful, it is ultimately structurally and institutionally corrosive. Competition provides the coordination that at times characterizes capitalist processes, as well as the disruptive and destructive pressures that produce its bouts of anarchy and crisis. The disruptive power of competition may be stifled for a time by forms of domestic monopoly or by international schemes of market segmentation, but it eventually breaks down all barriers and erodes the institutional status quo.

The general argument used in the most persuasive of Marxian analyses of the outbreak of instability in the past twenty years combines these two innovations in a dialectical way. The prosperity of the early postwar period, it is argued, was made possible by the creation of an effective institutional structure of profitability during and after World War II. But the process of two decades of economic growth and the corrosive forces of competition spawned by that growth caused changes which weakened that structure, ultimately rendering it incapable of sustaining a high profit rate. With the collapse of this institutional and structural guarantor of stability and profitability, the instability and stagnation of the current period emerged.

The important point to note here is that the constellation of institutions and forces that permitted Keynesian macropolicy to be effective in the first half of the postwar period could not reproduce themselves forever. Yet once that eroded, Keynesian regulation would be unable to function effectively. Keynes' theory of financial instability and Marx's theory of profit determination turned out to be right and Keynesian macrotheory wrong. In the next two sections we outline the process through which Keynesian regulation self-destructed, focusing on the role played by the globalization of markets.

### The Decline of the Keynesian Regime and the Internationalization of Production and Finance

Stable secular growth was possible in the 1950s and 1960s because the international and domestic institutional structures of the period kept the average profit rate high and the rate of accumulation strong. The following factors contributed to this prosperity.

First, this was a period of relative stability and predictability in international economic relations because the institutional structures that mediate these relations were stable and effective. The United States used its virtual monopoly of international military, economic, and political power to construct and control these structures of dominance. Under U.S. hegemony, exchange rates were stabilized, national markets were kept open to trade and investment, and the raw materials of the third world remained cheap and abundant. This environment helped sustain a strong trend toward growth in international trade and investment and provided low-cost imported raw materials to the industralized world.

Second, there was relative labor peace. The industrial conflict of the 1930s and 1940s induced capital to enter into an implicit and limited "accord" with labor. Organized labor ended its struggle for greater control of the labor process and for control of corporate investment policy in return for official recognition and acceptance by the country's economic and political elite. Workers in the core of the economy achieved a reasonably high rate of real wage growth in the 1950s and 1960s through struggle within the confines of the accord. For its part, capital achieved stability and predictability in labor relations and a high trend rate of productivity growth through technical progress and labor-saving investment. Thus, high profit margins could be maintained in a noninflationary environment in spite of rising real wages. And capital was free to erode the domain of the accord and reduce union power by investing in the anti-union South and overseas.

Third, under the stimulus of rising real wages and family incomes, demand for domestically produced goods and services grew at a strong average rate. Domestic demand was sustained by the growth of the auto industry, the construction of the highway system, the growth of housing and consumer durables in the process of suburbanization, and by government spending on defense and on social programs. But export markets were also important, especially in the early postwar years.

Fourth, the degree of competition in the core of the economy was stabilized and restricted through the various mechanisms associated with oligopolistic industrial structures and the virtual absence of foreign competition until the late 1960s. This not only supported high profit margins, it gave corporations that confidence in future profitability that is essential for capital accumulation.

Fifth, the corporate and household sectors entered the period free of significant indebtedness and laden with liquid assets accumulated during the war. Investment and consumption decisions were not constrained by financial burdens. The generalized liquidity of the era also contributed to the low interest rates that characterized it.

Sixth, U.S. financial markets were relatively insulated from foreign financial markets throughout most of this period. As a result, through the late 1960s the Fed had reasonably firm control over U.S. interest rates and the rate of growth of domestic money and credit and could use this control to pursue domestic objectives relatively unconstrained by international problems.

In sum, in the first half of the postwar period international as well as domestic institutional structures supported both stability and high profits in the U.S. economy. Positive trade balances, cheap and stable sources of imported raw materials, and the stability and predictability of the fixed exchange rates of the Bretton Woods system all strongly contributed to the maintenance of U.S. markets and U.S. profit margins; this helped make it profitable for firms to respond positively to expansionary macropolicy.

Thus, Keynesian regulation was successful in the 1950s and 1960s in spite of its fundamental structural flaws because the determinants of the profit rate were held in a favorable position for capital accumulation and there were few domestic or international constraints on the use of policy to pursue domestic objectives. However, by 1973 it had become clear that the long phase of stable postwar prosperity had come to an end as the institutions and practices that made it possible crumbled one by one. The effectiveness of macropolicy crumbled with them. Most noteworthy from our perspective is the extent to which the collapse of these institutions and practices and the economic dynamics of the fifteen years which followed were affected by, and in turn affected, the pace and character of the internationalization of production and finance.

First, twenty years of growth and change caused a redistribution of economic and political power among the leading capitalist nations. Inter-nation rivalry in trade, foreign investment, and access to raw materials erupted. With the erosion of U.S. hegemony, the foundation of international institutional stability crumbled. One key manifestation of this change was the collapse of the Bretton Woods system in the early 1970s. From that point on, exchange rates fluctuated wildly, adding a new source of uncertainty and instability to the economy. The proximate cause of the downfall of Bretton Woods was massive speculation against the U.S. dollar in the early 1970s led by U.S. multinational banks and corporations. During 1971 alone, almost $24 billion in private capital fled the United States, most of it headed toward the ever-growing Eurodollar market. After 1970 the pace of the globalization of financial markets accelerated: the Fed's control of domestic interest rates and the supply of credit weakened continuously.

Second, contradictions embedded in the limited capital-labor accord eventually led to its collapse. Capital had undermined the basis for the accord from the beginning by accumulating capital in non-union areas. Then in the late 1960s industrial conflict broke out as low unemployment rates helped spark an upsurge in labor militance that contributed to a significant decline in the profit share trend. Of course capital responded with a multidimensional attack on labor that included support for a high-unemployment macropolicy, union-busting tactics, and labor-saving investment. One important weapon in capital's arsenal was its ability to discipline U.S. labor by threatening to substitute foreign for domestic investment and use foreign rather than domestic components. When key industries like auto and electronics "ran away" on a large scale in the 1970s the entire U.S. labor movement was weakened. By the early 1980s the volume of cheap-labor-seeking foreign investment was substantial.

Thus, the labor militance of the late 1960s and early 1970s eventually accelerated the speed with which U.S. corporations internationalized their operations, a process which in turn helped destroy the power of the U.S. labor movement. Even so, the defeat of U.S. labor was a mixed blessing for U.S. capital. The past fifteen years have seen a low trend rate of productivity growth and stagnation in real wages and median family incomes. In turn, stagnant working-class income contributed to the secular rise in household indebtedness of this period as families struggled to maintain their living standards by borrowing, and it constrained domestic demand, making U.S. industry ever more dependent on foreign profit sources.

Third, the OPEC price increase of 1973–74 inaugurated a fifteen-year period of volatility in petroleum prices and, to a lesser degree, in the price of other raw materials. The end of U.S. hegemony meant the end of guaranteed supplies of cheap imported raw materials.

Fourth, in the 1970s and 1980s both the domestic and the international economies became debt laden and crisis prone. Following each of the two OPEC oil-price hikes in the 1970s the Eurodollar market was flooded with petrodollars just as stagnant economic conditions overtook Europe and North America. With a huge supply of interest-earning deposits and a weak demand for loans in the first world, multinational banks poured money into the third world. By 1982 third world debt was $500 billion; by 1987 it was $1 trillion. Financial fragility not only crippled the third world's ability to buy exports from the developed countries and from its own member nations, it made the solvency of the third world dependent upon the continued existence of a large U.S. trade deficit and low real interest rates.

Domestic financial fragility evolved alongside its international counterpart. The relative indebtedness of nonfinancial corporations grew dramatically from the mid-1960s through 1970 as competitive pressure kept capital accumulation high while the profit rate declined. It held steady at this higher level until the 1980s, then leapt up again in the Reagan years as corporate America engaged in an orgy of leveraged financial speculation. Household indebtedness began its secular ascent after 1975 as families strove to maintain living standards in the face of stagnant or declining real incomes. Meanwhile, financial institutions relied on increasingly speculative short-term sources of funds and used them to support ever-riskier classes of loans. And of course federal government debt exploded under Reagan while the United States emerged as the biggest debtor nation in the world.

Fifth, beginning in the late 1960s the intensity of foreign competition confronting U.S. corporations began a dramatic rise. European, Japanese, and Southeast Asian corporations as well as foreign subsidiaries of U.S. corporations successfully penetrated U.S. markets. The rise in the intensity of competition naturally reduced the domestic rate of profit. Since this was also an era of wildly fluctuating exchange rates, the rate of profit became more unstable even as it declined.

This set of institutional and structural changes drastically eroded the necessary conditions for macropolicy effectiveness. After 1970 the use of policy to pursue domestic objectives would often be constrained by problems in the international sector while the links between policy moves and domestic production and employment became ever more tenuous and uncertain. More important, the trend rate of net capital accumulation was retarded by two aspects of these developments that Keynesian regulation was powerless to control. First, these structural changes lowered the rate of profit. Second, they dramatically increased the degree of uncertainty associated with expectations of future profit rates and simultaneously increased corporate debt burdens; thus, corporate risk tolerance declined just as capital accumulation became riskier.

*Macropolicy Under Reagan: the Collapse of Keynesian Regulation*

Entering 1983, with the unemployment rate close to 11 percent, we could look back at fifteen years of instability and stop-go macropolicy and a decade of low growth, high inflation, high unemployment, and the lowest average rate of net capital accumulation in the postwar period. The Reagan expansion that began that year represents the latest phase in the long process of decline in the potential of macropolicy to achieve its traditional domestic objectives. To be sure, Reaganomics did help achieve an average rate of growth of real GNP of about 4 percent per year for the past five years (and about 3 percent per year since early 1984) in a context of modest inflation. But the means used to generate these results left the U.S. and world economies more unbalanced and financially precarious than at any time since the 1930s and they left macropolicy passive and powerless. The Reagan years have demonstrated that in the present era it takes ever more extreme policies to achieve modest short-term gains, policies that only make our long-term situation more intractable.

Reagan's fiscal policy can be summarized concisely. He raised military spending and cut or restrained social programs (other than social security and medicare), raising federal spending as a share of GNP while skewing its priorities to adhere to his reactionary ideology. Meanwhile, he slashed the tax obligations of the rich and of the corporations they own. These policies led to an explosion of the structural federal budget deficit that began in the second half of 1982 and continues to this day, almost tripling federal debt held by private investors. This orgy of regressive debt-financed fiscal stimulation was the driving force behind the Reagan expansion which accelerated U.S. demand for imports. Simultaneously, the stratospheric real interest rates caused by Volker's monetary repression were attracting financial capital inflows that raised the exchange value of the dollar by some 60 percent (in nominal terms) between 1980 and 1985, making it ever easier for foreign companies to penetrate U.S. markets. (We discuss post-1985 developments below.)

As a result, the U.S. trade deficit, which had averaged about $30 billion a year from 1980 through 1982, accelerated rapidly to about $160 billion in 1987. Meanwhile the inflow of foreign capital that financed these cumulative U.S. trade deficits quickly destroyed the U.S. position as the world's largest creditor nation, a position that had taken many decades to construct. The U.S. net foreign investment position was about +$140 billion in 1981 and 1982; by 1984 it was close to zero; by the end of 1987 we owed the rest of the world about $400 billion. In other words, the macropolicy that helped create the expansion of 1983 through 1988 also made U.S. economic health dependent on foreign capital. The $143 billion of foreign funds that entered the United States in 1986, for example, was far greater than total net business fixed investment that year. The United States now *had to* keep real interest rates high enough (relative to foreign rates) to increase the stock of foreign financial capital in this country.

Since early 1985 the value of the dollar has declined precipitously. This decline initially helped to stabilize the dollar value of the trade deficit, then it contributed to a slow process of decline. Even so, our debt to the rest of the world will continue to grow as negative net investment income flows are added to a long string of foreseeable trade deficits in the $100 billion plus range. It is commonly assumed that U.S. debt will top $1 trillion some time in the early 1990s. As a result, our foreign creditors will soon have virtual veto power over U.S. macropolicy. When they disapprove of our macropolicy, they will withdraw their funds from U.S. markets. This will cause a decline (and could cause a collapse) in U.S. financial markets and in the value of the U.S. dollar. The resulting rise in interest rates and decline in stock, bond, and even real estate prices will ultimately force U.S. officials to adopt macropolicies more to foreign investors' liking. Keep in mind that foreign lenders like high growth, low unemployment and inflation least of all.

Of course the enormous trade deficits and the growth of U.S. dependence on foreign capital are not the only dangerous side effects of Reaganomics. Debt-dependence, financial fragility, poverty, inequality, and the deterioration of our natural environment and our economic infrastructure have all increased in the 1980s. Nevertheless, this brief discussion of policy and performance under Reagan should provide an adequate background from which to undertake an assessment of the prospective state of macropolicy in the next decade.

## *Keynesian Regulation in the 1990s: Prospects and Problems*

Prospects for the effective use of macropolicy in pursuit of traditional domestic economic objectives in the coming decade are so dim as to be almost invisible. The Keynesian regulatory mechanism is feeble, constrained by numerous developments, many of which have their origin in the globalization of the economy. The U.S. economy is now deeply enmeshed with global markets that are literally out of control.

The necessary conditions for the effectiveness of macropolicy discussed at the beginning of this essay will provide the framework for our evaluation of the contradictions confronting policymakers in the current era. The first condition was that policymakers must be free to pursue domestic objectives. Today and for the foreseeable future policy seems constrained from moving very far in *either* direction by international problems or the threat of domestic and international financial crisis.

The structural limitation to expansive policy lies primarily in U.S. dependence on foreign capital and the generally speculative nature of international financial flows. Should monetary policy be used to lower U.S. interest rates, it is feared that a flight from the U.S. dollar will take place, causing a potential collapse in the exchange rate and in U.S. financial markets generally. The potential of a dollar collapse is perhaps greater than is commonly thought. In 1987 private foreign capital flows to the U.S. virtually dried up. According to *The New York Times* (Jan. 1, 1988) "Official intervention to directly support the dollar [in 1987] amounted to between $100 billion and $140 billion or almost all of America's current account deficit." Imagine the U.S. interest rate level that would have been required to have financed the 1987 current account deficit in the absence of central bank intervention. Meanwhile, any hint that the structural budget deficit might be increased in pursuit of growth could cause fear of renewed inflation and balance of trade deterioration, creating panic in financial markets.

But restrictive policy faces a major constraint as well: the precarious condition of domestic and international financial markets. Can our overleveraged corporations, our overindebted households, and our speculatively financed banks withstand a serious recession without triggering a wave of bankruptcies and a financial crisis? Can the debt-laden countries of the world avoid bankruptcy if real interest rates rise dramatically or the U.S. import market collapses during a recession? Obviously, at some point in the near future we will find out. The key point here is that fear of these adverse developments may constrain the severity of restrictive policy in the coming years.

The second condition for policy effectiveness is that changes in policy tools must be capable of causing significant change in the level of nominal aggregate demand. Several links between policy and aggregate demand have been seriously weakened since 1970. First, as noted, the degree of control exercised by the Fed over domestic interest rates and money and credit growth has declined substantially. Second, expansionary fiscal policy tends to produce capital outflows that raise interest rates, thus countering to some extent the intended thrust of the policy. Third, supply-side tax cuts ostensibly designed to raise the percentage of national income devoted to saving and investment have been spectacularly ineffective. The personal tax cuts of the 1980s have been accompanied by the lowest personal savings rates in postwar history. And the huge corporate tax cut in 1981 failed to stimulate investment spending. With a low profit rate, a stagnant national and international economy, excess capacity, and general uncertainty, corporations quite rationally chose to combine their tax cuts with corporate borrowing to finance massive speculation through mergers, acquisitions, stock buy-backs, and general casino action.

The final condition for policy effectiveness is that policy-induced changes in aggregate demand must have the desired effect on domestic economic objectives. The short-term problem is aggregate demand leakage. Inflation has not been a serious source of such leakage since 1982, though it could become one in the foreseeable future. The main problem in the mid-1980s has been import leakage, a problem that will continue to burden policy for many years.

However, it is the long-term problem—the link between increased aggregate demand and capital accumulation—that constitutes the most deeply rooted, intractable impediment to effective Keynesian regulation in the current period. In spite of all the Reagan-era tax breaks, the net rate of capital accumulation has been lower on average during the expansion of the 1980s than it was in the late 1970s, when it was lower than the rate of accumulation in the late 1960s and early 1970s. Indeed, at its peak year in 1985 real net investment was smaller than it had been in 1979.

*Keynesian macropolicy* seems powerless to rekindle accumulation because it *cannot remove all the institutional and structural, domestic and international impediments to sustained accumulation that developed in the 1970s and 1980s.* Keynesian regulatory mechanisms cannot change the institutional and structural determinants of the expected profit rate and they cannot restore stability and predictability to profit expectations. Nor can they recreate financial robustness by removing the debt burdens that restrict demand and threaten crisis in so many sectors of our economy and in so many nations of the world. They cannot even produce a low real interest rate.

Thus, we conclude that the Keynesian regulatory mechanism is bankrupt. No doubt policy can still be used to dampen short-term bursts of inflation or to generate short-term growth spurts, but the aggressive use of policy for an extended period in pursuit of either expansion or contraction seems out of the question. And the use of policy to recreate another era of stable prosperity by rekindling an accumulation boom is virtually impossible. The necessary conditions for the effective use of policy in pursuit of domestic objectives have been destroyed, not least of all by the internationalization of production and finance. We seem once again to be at the mercy of the anarchic forces of capitalist markets over which we have little control, just as we were in the 1930s before the creation of the Keynesian state.

## What Is To Be Done?

The new global economy is structurally biased against the interests of working people. The pressure on national governments to attract financial capital has raised real interest rates while concern with the balance of trade has led to generally restrictive macropolicy. With secularly high unemployment rates around the Western world, labor is perpetually in retreat and capital perpetually dominant. Moreover, inter-nation competition to attract real and financial capital has pressured national governments into deregulating their economies. In other words, we live in an era in which markets are global but regulatory mechanisms are national, class-biased, inherently inadequate, and crumbling under the onslaught of international and inter-nation competition.

So the question naturally arises: what is to be done? The analysis used here suggests the need for a regulatory system with more *direct public control* over the broad contours of the domestic economy than was granted to the Keynesian state. And the values and principles that motivate the analysis demand that any new regulatory mechanism be democratically constituted and controlled. It is obviously beyond the scope of this essay to discuss blueprints for a new system of economic regulation. Nevertheless, one thing seems clear. Unless the ultimate power to determine such key economic outcomes as the rate of unemployment, the distribution of income and wealth, the level and quality of social services, and the size and composition of investment is taken from the owners of capital and the dictatorship of the profit rate and placed in the public domain, our economic future will be bleak indeed.

The logic of this essay also suggests the need for more *autonomy* from the vicissitudes and irrational pressures of the international marketplace. Keynes was right when he argued in the 1930s and 1940s that *government controls over the movement of goods and, especially, money across the nation's borders are an essential precondition for effective national economic planning.* The internationalization of finance and production has made the need for such autonomy even more pressing today. In the absence of capital controls, any attempt to pursue genuine full employment or other progressive objectives will bring forth the wrath of the international capitalist class in the form of capital flight, a run on the currency, an assault on domestic financial markets, and rising interest rates. These developments will make it impossible to achieve our progressive goals.

Of course, the imposition of capital controls does not mean the elimination of international financial flows; it means, rather, their regulation. Under capital controls, the government has the authority to set the conditions under which money can lawfully enter and leave the country. For example, the government might permit unregulated *income* flows (such as interest payments, dividends, or profits), controlling only the investment and repatriation of the original capital itself. And it might allow capital to be repatriated some months after the government has been notified of the owner's intention to withdraw the funds, a time period that could be altered in length depending on conditions in financial markets.

Opponents of capital controls have questioned their practicality or their efficiency. One such argument is that capital controls would raise the cost to the United States of foreign borrowing because they reduce the liquidity of foreign-held assets. They probably would. But they could also help dramatically reduce our reliance on foreign capital because they would remove a powerful impediment to full employment and domestic financial market regulation. Under controls we could generate a much higher level of domestic saving and could channel these funds away from financial market and real estate speculation toward productive public and private investment. Another objection is that in today's complex telecommunications-based international financial casino, effective capital controls would be technically impossible to construct. The counter argument here is that the technical capability to monitor telecommunications and process vast quantities of data has itself undergone a revolution: the ability of the U.S. intelligence apparatus to perform such tasks is a case in point.

Finally, it should be noted that progressive activists have argued that support for capital and trade controls reflects an insular nationalist perspective, one that rejects solidarity with the economic and political struggles of working people around the globe. The fact that a regime of capital and trade controls might be supported by a national chauvinist political movement does not imply that a progressive internationalist economic and political agenda can do without them. Why should a reduction in the degree of control excercised by the international capitalist class over the economic destiny of the United States be harmful to the interests of working people in other countries? On the contrary, the imposition of capital and trade controls would make it possible for a new system of economic regulation to generate sustained full employment which, in turn, could help maintain a stable demand for imports and remove the material foundation for protectionist sentiment among U.S. workers.

The bottom line is this: capital mobility gives the wealthy classes around the globe veto power over the economic policies and priorities of every nation. No progressive, democratically controlled system of economic regulation can function effectively if it does not break that veto power through the imposition of capital controls.

## Notes

1. For the purpose of this analysis we abstract from the class-biased nature of actual policy formation and focus on the potential of the system to achieve its stated policy goals. Of course we recognize that in practice policy makers are generally uninterested in pursuing such a labor-empowering objective as sustained full employment and that they rarely muster much enthusiasm for progressive income or wealth redistribution.
2. We consider standard international policy objectives such as trade balance and a stable exchange rate to be constraints on the ability to attain domestic goals rather than as goals in and of themselves.
3. A second motivation for corporate investment is stressed in Marxian theory: fear. Intense competitive pressure can destroy profitability, threatening many companies with eventual bankruptcy. This can create an "invest or die" situation in which the only way to survive the competitive struggle is to substantially raise cost-cutting investment in the face of low or negative profits. However, sustained prosperity cannot be built through such "defensive" investment because the com-

bination of low profits and high investment results in mounting corporate debt burdens and because such investment raises unemployment and weakens real wage growth.

4. For a discussion of Keynes' less publicized, more radical views on macrotheory and macropolicy see my "Keynes and Capital Flight" in the March 1983 volume of the *Journal of Economic Literature*.

5. David Gordon helped popularize the idea that an articulated set of economic and political institutions and practices is required to sustain the rate of profit and the rate of capital accumulation. He coined the term "social structure of accumulation" to represent his particular version of this concept.

# Financial Instability and the Structure of the International Monetary System

## Gerald Epstein

### Introduction

In this essay I hope to contribute to an understanding of the current international monetary system and its implications for progressive economic restructuring. My starting point is an increasingly common view that the current international financial system, with its hypermobility of capital, represents a fundamentally new force in the world economy. According to this perspective, the international financial system has two central implications: first, it has led to extreme financial instability, represented most graphically by the world stock market crash of 1987. And second, where computer and satellite technology allow global financial markets to move massive sums of money in and out of countries at a moment's notice, international capital strike renders obsolete and utopian any hopes of national progressive restructuring.

The current international economic system *is* fundamentally new. However, its novelty is not due to international mobility of capital, per se, which, in fact, is not a new phenomenon. The current globalization of finance is rather similar in degree to that achieved in the late nineteenth and early twentieth century (see Zevin 1988). Considering the quality of computers in 1890, technology cannot be the determining factor. Rather, its uniqueness lies in the blend of high financial capital mobility with other central features of the current world economy, such as the absence of a hegemonic country, the existence of the welfare state, and the political independence and increasingly important economic role of many third world countries. In short, the key to understanding the current international financial system is the relative power of different nations and classes, and the nature of international financial competition.

I attempt to illustrate this point in the next section where I describe the structure and operations of two international monetary systems: the international gold standard and the Bretton Woods monetary system. I argue that their operations and collapse can be best understood by analyzing the structure of domestic and international competition and power, and focus, in particular, on the degree of control the hegemonic country exercised over the domestic and international monetary system. This control over the financial system was essential in two ways. First, it reduced the instability associated with uncontrolled finance. And second, it allowed the hegemon to reduce the burdens of running the system by helping the hegemon shift the costs of managing the system onto weak countries and classes within the hegemonic country. This reduced domestic class conflict and helped maintain a dominant coalition in favor of running the system. The systems broke down when the hegemonic power lost so much domestic and international power it could no longer stabilize finance and shift burdens. Financial and technological innovations play an important part in this story. But they must be understood as being induced by international competition, and as operating through their effects on the costs and benefits of maintaining the system and on the stability of the system as a whole.

In section three I describe the ways in which the current international monetary arrangements have contributed to international instability and stagnation. I argue that this instability and stagnation derive from the unique configuration of the current international system. One characteristic of the current system is that the controls over domestic and international financial markets that were so important in the 1950s and 1960s have broken down. These did not break down because of some technological imperative, or even because of a return to the normalcy of the early twentieth century. These regulations and controls broke down because of increasing competition and the stagnation of profitability in industrial sectors, which left governments vulnerable to pressure to deregulate what appeared to be a profitable and potentially competitive set of industries.

This de-regulation has lead to international capital mobility similar to that of the nineteenth century gold standard. However, the current system has a number of elements which make it quite different from that of the gold standard period. Specifically, first, the world economy now lacks a hegemonic country to manage the system; and second, most advanced capitalist countries now have welfare states and organized working classes to one degree or another which, in times of crisis, circumscribe capitalist prerogatives in the restructuring of economic relations. Finally, developing countries have become more politically independent and an important source of demand in the world economy. Thus, it is not as easy to shift the burdens of operating the system onto these countries without the effects coming home to roost.

This combination of factors—stagnation-induced financial de-regulation, loss of hegemony, and difficulties in burden shifting—has meant that the traditional tools of macroeconomic management no longer work well to protect profitability and maintain financial stability in the advanced capitalist countries.

In section four, I analyze current strategies for restructuring. Capitalists recognize the need for basic change. Different groupings of capitalists are simultaneously pursuing two strategies.[1] The first calls for a return to the gold standard structure of free international capital mobility, free trade, and most important, a dramatic reduction in the power of labor and the welfare state. As a substitute for British financial hegemony, the plan calls for a tripartite management of the system by the United States, Germany (or the European Monetary System), and Japan. This, they hope, will preserve free trade, financial integration, and profitability.

But the contradictions of these solutions are glaring. Financial deregulation is generating enormous instability and threatening free trade. International coordination is difficult at best. Labor, though weakened, will resist the dismantling of the welfare state. Thus the second plan is also being pursued. Preparations are being made to break up into trading and financial blocs—signaled by the agreements to eliminate barriers to trade and finance in Europe by 1992, by the U.S.-Canada free-trade agreement, and by Japanese overtures in the Pacific.

Progressive strategists, on the other hand, seem paralyzed by the inability to confront the issue of international financial integration. There is a tendency for left strategists to occupy one of two extremes. Either they assume that nothing can be done about international capital mobility, which breeds fatalism; or they ignore it, which breeds irrelevance. Needless to say, neither strategy will work. This analysis details the structural nature of the financial crisis and, it is hoped, lays some groundwork for evaluating progressive alternatives.

### Hegemonic Power, Financial Control and the Operations of International Monetary Systems

To understand the prospects for capitalist or progressive restructuring of the international monetary system, it is important to understand what allowed the previous monetary systems to flourish. Their survival depended crucially on power relations between nations, and between governments and national classes. Past international monetary systems have functioned when a dominant nation, Great Britain in the case of the gold standard, and the United States, in the case of Bretton Woods, had sufficient political and economic power relative to other nations and at home to ensure that the benefits to the powerful domestic classes of running the international system outweighed the costs. A central component of that strategy was the control of the domestic and international financial system. When the dynamics of economic growth undermined their power at home and abroad, domestic and international class conflict prevented the hegemonic country from managing the system.

#### International Gold Standard

Textbook renditions of the international gold standard portray it as an "automatic system." Countries running balance of payments deficits would lose gold which would lower their price level. This, in turn, would make their goods more competitive and reduce their balance of payments deficit. This process would continue until their payments were balanced. The opposite would result for a surplus country. This view implies that adjustment was symmetrical among surplus and deficit countries, and among all countries in the system, center and periphery.

It is now well known that the gold standard was far from automatic or symmetrical. The Bank of England orchestrated the system. Its ability to do so was dependent on its control over the domestic financial markets and on British dominance of highly integrated world financial markets, achieved through the central role of British banks in trade financing and the wide use of sterling in international transactions. The first allowed changes in the British discount rate, the rate the Bank of England charged its bank customers for loans, to cause changes in domestic interest rates. And the second allowed the increases in British interest rates to attract funds from around the globe.

If, for example, the United Kingdom was running balance of payments deficits it could raise its interest rate. The old saying was that a 6 percent discount rate could draw capital from the moon. That, in turn would increase interest rates in the London money market, eventually drawing money away from countries on the periphery. These peripheral countries would then be faced with balance of payments crises, high interest rates, recessions. The British economy, on the other hand, would not have to go through a wrenching recession or experience large increases in interest rates to resolve temporary balance of payments problems. Thus Britain was able to shift the burden of adjustment, and therefore the costs of maintaining the gold standard, largely onto other countries, particularly those in the periphery. Maintaining a domestic coalition in support of the gold standard was thus much easier.

The bank rate mechanism could work to maintain the gold standard only as long as Britain's balance of payments problems were temporary and as long as the Bank of England had control over the domestic money market; that is, as long as the underlying foundations of the system were strong. But as De Cecco (1974) has shown, in the latter part of the nineteenth century, those foundations were crumbling. International trade competition from Germany and the United States was undermining Britain's trade surplus. Britain was able to forestall serious balance of payments problems and maintain the gold standard only by turning more and more to the empire as a market for its exports. Equally important, it used its military and political control over the empire to insure that empire countries did not attempt to turn in their holdings of sterling earned as export surpluses, for gold. Britain's control over India was of central importance in this regard.

However, as economic competition from the United States and economic and military competition from Germany became more severe, even the empire was not enough to save Britain and the gold standard. In addition, the Bank of England was losing control over its domestic money market, thus making it more difficult for the bank to control domestic interest rates. The bank's control had been dependent on its special relation with the large London banks which dominated the market. As financial innovation led to greater competition from other banks, in London and outside, the bank's special relationship was no longer sufficient to give it control over the domestic money market, and therefore to make changes in the bank rate effective.

Thus the operations of the gold standard were not dependent on an automatic operation of the market or "rules of the game." Rather, the operation was dependent on the exercise of economic, political, and military power. The gold standard was dependent on British economic dominance over its main rivals, its ability to dominate peripheral countries and shift the burdens of adjustment to them through military/political means in the case of the empire and financial means in the case of others, and the ability of the Central Bank to dominate both domestic and highly integrated international financial markets.

## Bretton Woods System

As with the gold standard, the underlying structure of Bretton Woods is best studied by analyzing the domestic and international mechanisms of political and economic control rather than by studying the formal rules of the game. Indeed, as is little appreciated, the formal structure of the Bretton Woods system never really operated as the founders envisaged. European currencies were inconvertible until the late 1950s. As soon as they became convertible in the late 1950s, the dollar's position and the fixed exchange rate system became threatened by an excess of dollar liquidity relative to the U.S. gold stock. From that time forward, the Bretton Woods system of fixed exchange rates was maintained not by following "rules of the game" set forth in the Bretton Woods agreement, but by an elaborate set of negotiations between the United States and the other major industrial countries to prevent the system from collapsing.

The United States was able to maintain the system as long as its political and economic power were sufficient to shift most of the burdens of adjustment onto others, thereby enabling the pro-Bretton Woods coalition of multinational corporations and large multinational banks to maintain control. As the United States trade surplus deteriorated in the face of increased competition from Europe, Japan, and several other countries, it depended more and more on direct negotiations to maintain the system. One of the most important postwar steps in insulating U.S. gold reserves from external pressure was the explicit pledge by Germany, the largest surplus country during the period, not to use any of its dollars to buy U.S. gold. This promise was extracted after the United States threatened to reduce its troop levels in Germany in 1967 (Bergsten 1975; 31–32). The United States brought similar pressure on other countries dependent on U.S. military support, including Korea, Taiwan, and possibly Japan (ibid.).

But as the U.S. balance of payments deteriorated in the late 1960s under pressure from U.S. trade competitors and the expenditures on the Vietnam war, the United States government found it more difficult to shift the burdens of maintaining the fixed exchange rate system onto others within and outside the United States. Domestically oriented trade competing industries were developing strong animosity to the fixed exchange rate system which they believed were contributing to the loss of U.S. trade competitiveness (Bergsten 1975). And even stalwart allies of the Bretton Woods system, the multinational banks and corporations, were beginning to have serious doubts about the system. The U.S. Capital Controls program, started in the early 1960s and expanded during the decade, brought strong opposition from multinational corporations and banks who did not want their international expansion to be hindered by government regulations. Their political opposition was strong enough to render most of the controls ineffective, but the controls were costly enough to undermine support for the fixed exchange rate system.

Similarly, the Federal Reserve's control over the financial markets was declining as a result of increased international financial competition facing U.S. banks. The creation of the Eurodollar markets was allowing non-U.S. banks to begin competing for dollar deposits and loans in an unregulated environment. The ability of the Federal Reserve to control the creation of dollar credit, without greatly reducing the competitive position of U.S. banks, was thus greatly reduced. Unable to muster the political power to place effective controls on U.S. banks, the Fed was finding it increasingly difficult to protect the U.S. balance of payments through moderate changes in monetary policy. The greater the monetary tightness required, the more the burdens of adjustment would fall on the domestic economy, and the harder it would be to maintain the domestic coalition in favor of remaining on Bretton Woods. Credit crunches like those imposed in 1969 and 1970 dramatically undermined domestic support for the system. Underlying all these problems was the decline in productivity and profitability that began in the late 1960s. Bretton Woods was abandoned in 1971.

The key processes that led to the collapse of Bretton Woods were international trade and financial competition; domestic problems of profitability; and the dissipation of military and economic power in the attempt to maintain U.S. imperial interests, all of which undermined domestic support for the system of fixed exchange rates. Both systems, then, depended on the political and economic power to control the domestic and international financial systems and to shift the burdens of the system onto weaker countries and classes. The current international economic system has generated so much instability because, while it has succeeded in shifting a good deal of the burden onto third world countries and working people, no one has enough power over the domestic and international financial systems to ensure that those burdens do not come home to roost. And continuing problems of profitability virtually guarantee that there are plenty of burdens to go around.

## Instability, Stagnation, and the Current Structure of the International Financial System

The abandonment of Bretton Woods in 1971, and the move to floating exchange rates in 1973, led to a fifteen-year period of international monetary disorder. To understand the current international monetary system and the prospects for restructuring, it is useful to think of the international capitalist system as characterized by five problems which an international monetary system can ameliorate or intensify. I will refer to these as the "Marx problem," the "Keynes problem," the "Minsky problem," the "Kalecki problem," and the "Gramsci problem." The Marx problem is the problem of labor discipline; it concerns the ability of capitalists to ensure that labor works hard enough to maintain the profitability of production. The Keynes problem is the problem of effective demand; it concerns the ability of capitalists to find markets for their products. The Minsky problem is one of financial stability; it concerns the problems of instability in financial markets that can lead to bankruptcies, financial panics, debt deflations, and depressions. The Kalecki problem is the problem of competition; it concerns the ability of capitalists to maintain a high profit margin in the face of domestic and international rivals. And finally, the Gramsci problem concerns the necessity to form a political bloc which is coherent and cooperative enough to manage the economic and political system, since markets cannot manage themselves.[2]

International monetary systems are conducive to rapid capital accumulation when they help to solve these five problems on a world scale, and the systems contribute to instability and stagnation when they exacerbate them. On this score, the current international monetary system fails. To the extent it helps solve one problem, it does so only by exacerbating others.

Five characteristics of the current international financial system are particularly problematic in this regard. The first is the flexible exchange rate regime, which many hoped would solve the Kaleckian problems of competitiveness, but which has actually made them worse. The second is the international role of the dollar which, based as it is on the declining power of the United States in the world economy, contributes to Minskian financial instability. The third is the high degree of international capital mobility and financial innovation which has transformed the previous two problems into serious difficulties for accumulation and growth. The fourth is the third world debt situation, which was initially a solution to the Keynes problem in the 1970s, but is now a dominant Keynesian fetter on third world and world economic growth. The fifth is the military role of the United States in the world economy, which like the third world debt problem, solved the Keynes problem of effective demand by contributing to a huge U.S. import deficit in the 1980s, but which will soon become a major source of instability on the world economic scene as the United States attempts to reduce its dependence on foreign borrowing.

In the rest of this section I will describe how these factors have interacted to exacerbate one or more of these central problems of a capitalist economy.

### Exchange Rates

By the late 1960s there was a broad consensus within the mainstream of the economics profession that a flexible exchange rate system would provide more domestic autonomy for Keynesian demand management policies, particularly monetary policy, than a fixed exchange rate system allowed.

Moreover, most neoclassical economists believed that flexible exchange rates would operate so as to assure maximum efficiency in the allocation of resources among industries and countries according to the law of comparative advantage. Finally, the view was that flexible exchange rates would maximize the scope, political support, and benefits of free trade.

These views have turned out to be largely fallacious. The flexible exchange rate system instead has been associated with enormous instability. It has allowed large "disequilibria" in external balances—the huge current account deficit of the U.S. is a good example. It has fundamentally altered international competitiveness among industries and nations, and, if anything, has undermined domestic and international support for free trade. For example, the huge appreciation of the dollar between 1980 and 1985 cost the U.S. over a million manufacturing jobs and severely damaged U.S. manufacturing competitiveness in several industries (Branson and Love 1987). The resulting calls for protection from embattled U.S. industrialists sent shudders through the international multinational capitalist community.

Thus the flexible exchange rate regime has induced wild and destabilizing swings in exchange rates and competitiveness. This instability is rooted in the decline of U.S. hegemony, the role of the U.S. dollar, and the high degree of financial capital mobility.

## The International Role of the Dollar

An important destabilizing characteristic of the international scene is that the U.S. dollar has remained the dominant currency used in international financial transactions despite the relative decline of the U.S. productive economy in the world. At the end of 1984, the dollar's share of global official foreign exchange reserves was 65.8 percent (Horii 1986: 12). By contrast, the U.S. share of world manufacturing exports was about 14 percent. There is less and less demand for U.S. dollars for purposes of importing U.S. products. This means that the continued international use of the dollar depends increasingly on the financial returns, and political power, rather than on underlying productive activity of the United States. This increasing disjunction between the productive role of the United States and the continuing financial role of the dollar is one of the central elements of international financial instability plaguing the international monetary system.

Perhaps the best example of this instability is the dramatic halt to the U.S. economic expansion which occurred in 1979 with the rise to power of Paul Volcker as head of the Federal Reserve. By 1979, the exchange rate depreciation and inflation led to a full-fledged dollar crisis, with domestic and international banks and corporations flee-ing the dollar at unprecedented rates. With the dollar being the central international currency, this flight from the dollar threatened the entire international financial system. President Carter was forced to name Paul Volcker, a banker's banker, to head the Federal Re-serve. Under Volcker's guidance, the Federal Reserve began its dramatic monetary tightening to restore the international demand for U.S. dollars. The Fed did this by increasing the financial returns to holding dollars and the confidence in those returns, but at the cost of industrial destruction which undermined U.S. competitiveness even further.

The declining foundation for the role of the U.S. dollar continues to be a serious constraint on expansionary monetary policy. Since 1979, the Federal Reserve has avoided a dramatic loosening of U.S. monetary policy because of a fear of speculative attack on the dollar. At the same time, the dollar's international role has other important effects on the international economy. It gives other countries a stake in managing the exchange rate system and leads them to help sta-bilize the dollar. It has also allowed the United States to accumulate its large current account deficits.

*International Capital Mobility: Financial Globalization,*
*Innovation and De-regulation*

There has been a global explosion of financial transactions and innovations in the last decade. Several numbers give some ideas of the dimensions involved. The volume of foreign exchange trading alone is huge (estimates for 1986): in London, the daily transactions volume is $90 billion, in New York, $50 billion, Tokyo is close behind with $48 billion. If the contributions from other centers are added in, worldwide foreign exchange trade could be over $250 billion dollars a day, or more than $60 trillion per year. By contrast, the trading volume in New York was $5 billion in 1977, one-tenth the 1986 volume, and which is considerably less, even controlling for infla-tion. These exchanges dwarf the size of international trade transac-tions (Levich 1987: 8).

One aspect of this financial explosion is the "globalization" of money and finance: the ability of corporations, individuals, and governments to borrow, lend, and trade financial instruments in any of a number of currencies and locations around the globe. For example, the interpenetration of banking markets has proceeded at a rapid pace over the last decade and a half. The share of foreign assets and liabilities in domestic banks has doubled (or more than doubled) in many industrial countries, and has reached extremely high levels in some countries.

Another example of the internationalization of finance is the size of the Eurobond market relative to the size of the domestic U.S. bond market. Data show that whereas in 1970 there were virtually no international corporate bonds sold by U.S. corporations, in 1984 total international bond issues were greater than domestic ones. Thus major corporations have a global approach to raising finance. The "domestic" interest rate no longer captures the "cost of capital," and the ability of a domestic central bank to affect the cost of capital facing large corporations increasingly depends on its ability to affect the international cost of capital.

Not only have international financial markets become more global, but there has also been the explosive creation of new financial instruments or products (BIS 1986; OECD 1987). Many of these provide vehicles for corporations to speculate on changes in asset prices and values (for example, options and futures markets); others allow corporations to hedge risks; still others allow them to obtain credit to finance investment and speculation (e.g., takeovers, mergers and acquisitions).

Driving the creation of many of these instruments has been the attempts of commercial banks to maintain their profits and market shares in the face of dwindling demands for traditional bank loans and in the face of impaired capital positions to support such loans. The result has been the explosion of so-called securitization and off-balance sheet activities of banks. Securitization refers to the transformation of a credit instrument, for example a loan, into a marketable product which the bank can sell to other investors. A home mortgage is a good example. A bank lends money to someone to buy a house. It then takes the mortgage and sells it to an investor so that it doesn't have its money tied up. It can then use that money to finance someone else.

One of the central advantages of such activities for banks concerns their capital requirements. Regulators force banks to maintain a certain percentage of their assets as capital as a cushion in case borrowers default. With the soaring of third world loans, regulators became more insistent that banks adhere to and increase their capital cushions. In response, banks found ways to circumvent the capital requirements. They did this by so-called off-balance sheet activities. Banks are able to increase their income by selling, underwriting, or brokering instruments without having to hold capital to back up the transactions.

Neoclassical economists will typically argue that such innovations have arisen to reduce and spread risks. However, regulators are becoming increasingly fearful that they have had precisely the opposite effect (BIS 1986). First, banks do undertake risks when trading in such instruments, yet they have not provided increased capital to cover those risks. Second, securitization has greatly increased the interconnections among banks as the deals have become more and more complex. Thus, a default by one can have more and more reverberations throughout the financial system. Third, many of these instruments are so new, and the competitive rush to provide them so great, that the banks are likely to underprice and oversupply them, greatly increasing their credit risk. Finally, as more and more investment banks and non-banks get involved in these activities, and as the international connections become greater, who will be the lender of last resort becomes unclear.

Competitive pressures have led U.S. and other banks to place enormous pressure on regulators and governments to de-regulate so that they can "compete." With stagnant industrial sectors in many countries, the political and economic pressures on governments to comply has been enormous. The increased competition facing U.S. banks can be seen along a number of dimensions. First is competition from non-banks. Beginning in the early 1970s major U.S. corporations began reducing their reliance on banks for finance. Instead, they depended more on borrowing from each other. This attrition of the banks' best customers helps explain why U.S. banks lent so much to Latin American countries in the 1970s. Between 1981 and 1986, standard bank loans to corporate customers fell by half as a share of U.S. nonfinancial corporations' borrowing.

U.S. banks have also faced increasing competition from foreign banks. Indeed, over the last decade, U.S. banks have lost their position to the Japanese banks as the largest banks in the world. In 1969 U.S. banks held 33 percent of the assets of the world's largest banks, while the Japanese banks held only 17 percent. By 1986, however, U.S. banks held 12 percent while Japanese banks held almost 40 percent. (Salomon Brothers 1988: 6). This trend, which has been exacerbated by the devaluation of the dollar relative to the yen, was firmly established even as the dollar was rising.

## Third World Debt

I argued earlier that a central stabilizing factor in previous international monetary systems was the hegemon's ability to deflect burdens onto other countries. In the current period it has been harder to do that without the burdens coming home to roost. The third world debt crisis is the most important case in point.

In the 1970s a number of third world countries borrowed heavily from commercial banks, and thereby acted as an important source of world demand. In 1979, the tight monetary policy initiated by the Federal Reserve thrust a good deal of the burden of disinflation onto these debtor countries, driving down commodity prices on which many of them were so dependent for export earnings. While this policy helped restore confidence in the dollar and reduced the inflationary burdens on the U.S. and international financial system, it also generated a Minsky crisis where third world debtors could not service their debt. IMF-orchestrated austerity problems further shifted burdens to debtor countries (see Robert Wood's article in this volume).

## U.S. Debt Accumulation

The deregulation of financial activities, lowering of capital controls, the explosion of financial innovations, and the increased financial competition have allowed large accumulations of external debt, first by third world countries, and now by the United States. While this debt accumulation has allowed the United States to be a major source of effective demand in the world economy, eventually the domestic and international bases for continued borrowing will erode, and the outstanding U.S. debt is likely to become more a fetter on world growth than a support.

The limits of U.S. international debt accumulation are very difficult to predict. Some analysts suggest that the end is very near indeed. Others argue that the United States has a long way to go before it reaches domestic or international borrowing limits.

A casual look at some relevant trends would suggest that both groups have some evidence to support their positions. Table 1 presents data on the net creditor ( + ) or debtor ( − ) position as a percentage of the size of the economy (GNP) of the United States and several other countries at selected dates during the twentieth century. In support of the pessimists, the data suggest that the U.S. debtor position has grown rapidly, from a 4 percent net creditor position in 1980 to a 5 percent net debtor position by 1986, a change of 9 percentage points in just six years. And the U.S. debt continues to grow at a rapid pace.

On the optimists' side, the U.S. debt as a percentage of GNP is still much smaller than that of other countries currently and previously. Both Brazil's and Mexico's external debt is much greater as a percentage of the size of the economy, Japan's debt was 22 percent of its GNP in 1913, and if one goes back even further, the United States was a net debtor to the tune of 25 percent of GNP in 1873 (not shown).

In any case, sooner or later, the borrowing binge will stop. As recent research has shown, countries do not increase their borrowing indefinitely. Either dominant classes within borrower countries force an end to increased borrowing because of fear over reduced national independence and profitability; or lenders begin to ration borrowing countries because they eventually become poor credit risks (Epstein and Gintis 1988). The limits on U.S. debt accumulation implies that the United States will eventually become a source of Minskian instability and will stop acting as a source of world Keynesian demand.

*Table 1*
*Net International Investment Position/GNP*
*(percent, Net External Liabilities/GNP = − )*

|    | 1913   | 1935  | 1946  | 1962 | 1980   | 1986   |
|----|--------|-------|-------|------|--------|--------|
| US | − 5.6  | 23.8  | 11.6  | 9.0  | 4.0    | − 5.0  |
| UK | 204.0  | 132.0 | 8.0   | 4.8  | 7.0    | 21.0   |
| JP | − 22.0 | − 2.0 | − 1.0 | − .4 | 1.0    | 12.0   |
| BZ |        |       |       |      | − 25.7 | − 35.0 |
| MX |        |       |       |      | − 28.6 | − 53.2 |

*Source:* Consult author
US = United States; UK = United Kingdom; JP = Japan; BZ = Brazil; MX = Mexico
N.B. Brazil and Mexico figures do not include direct foreign investment.

## Implications

What are the implications of these trends for current strategies of economic restructuring? The first implication is that, as capitalists recognize, the current configuration of the international monetary system has made the standard tools of macroeconomic policy much less effective than they were several decades ago.

Yet one must be clear about the constraints facing monetary policy. It has become commonplace to argue that, given increasing financial instability, the central bank's only available monetary policy is to act as the lender of last resort. Thus, so the argument goes, the central bank can no longer pursue tight money. Yet, historically, the lender of last resort activities of the central bank have not been a substitute for contractionary policy. On the contrary, they have been a very important complement of contractionary policy. Contractionary monetary policy, designed to discipline labor and improve financial and nonfinancial profitability, has always potentially caused "unfortunate" side effects—increasing bankruptcy by financial institutions and others. The ability of the central bank to bail out selected financial institutions has made it possible, therefore, to discipline labor and maintain financial stability at the same time. To turn around an old phrase, it is the seat belt that allows the central bank to slam on the brakes.

The most recent example was the tight monetary policy by the United States starting in 1979. The ability of the Fed to bail out ailing financial institutions was a critical ingredient in its ability to discipline labor so severely and for so long. More recently, however, two constraints on the ability of the central bank to continue playing that role have emerged. First, increased financial fragility of many institutions means that the lender of last resort will have to do increasingly complicated mopping-up operations the next time the central bank needs to smash labor or reduce inflation. This increases the central bank's desires not to get back into that position and therefore its desire to keep a tight rein on money and credit.

The second factor is the flexible exchange rate system and speculation. Increasingly, tight monetary policy leads to large changes in exchange rates and loss of competitiveness. This creates huge problems for maintaining a tight money coalition and free trade at the same time, to which many corporate interests are firmly committed. Similarly, overly loose monetary policy can lead to speculative attacks against exchange rates and the need to tighten later, which leads to the difficulties just mentioned. Thus, recognizing that national activist macroeconomic policies are much less effective, capitalist governments are looking for new ways to restore profitability and stability.

One set of capitalist strategies is to move the world economy back toward the structure at the end of the nineteenth century. The elements of this strategy are to maintain a high degree of international financial integration; maintain and even expand the degree of free trade; return to a regime of relatively fixed exchange rates; and in the place of British hegemony, to have a tripartite management of the system by the United States, Germany, and Japan.

A move to fixed exchange rates eliminates the macroeconomic mechanism for solving the Keynes problem of effective demand and the Kalecki problem of competitiveness: now monetary and fiscal policy have to be directed toward maintaining the exchange rate rather than maintaining effective demand; and using exchange rate depreciations to achieve competitiveness will be greatly circumscribed. The solution proposed to both of these problems is to reduce what are euphemistically called "microeconomic rigidities." This really means reducing the power of labor unions directly and indirectly by eliminating state regulations. Capitalists hope that this policy will allow them to restructure production and lower wages to compete internationally and achieve increased effective demand through export-led growth. This strategy, it is hoped, will also help with the Marx problem by improving labor discipline.

To deal with Minskian problems of financial instability international coordination is again at the top of the agenda. Limited forms of internationally coordinated re-regulation are being implemented. One example is an international agreement to force banks to maintain capital balances on risky assets recently negotiated by advanced capitalist central banks. Some debt relief for third world countries, which essentially implies bailing out the banks, partially financed by taxpayers in industrial countries, is high on the international agenda. Apart from these relatively modest attempts at re-regulation, the general strategy is to maximize financial innovation and mobility.

The issue on which there is probably least agreement among strategists is how to deal with debt accumulation by the United States. It is well recognized that continued debt accumulation will lead to increased financial instability. But it is also recognized that if the United States reduces import demand a new engine for world economic growth must be found. Within the United States itself, corporations are adamantly opposed to increases in corporate taxes. Reductions in social spending in the United States and shifting military expenditures from the United States to Europe and Japan seems to be the emerging strategy.

The contradictions inherent in this program are many. The first is the Gramsci problem, the problem of political coherence. If the historical experience of the gold standard and the Bretton Woods systems tell us anything, they suggest that for an international monetary system to operate successfully, it must be able to forge a coherent set of policies to stabilize the international economic environment. Ad hoc measures for international economic cooperation are unlikely to survive the strains of the fiercely competitive major industrial countries, and the vicissitudes of electoral politics (Funabashi 1988). A world recession, in the face of continuing U.S. trade and budget deficits, will severely test tripartite management.

The capitalist program also pays too little heed to the Minsky problem of financial instability. While some restructuring of third world debt is likely, there is no strategy for dealing with the huge increase in corporate debt in most advanced capitalist countries, a significant portion of which is being used to finance mergers and acquisitions. Given the increased interpenetration of international financial institutions, the next recession will undoubtedly place extraordinary demands on international cooperation in lender of last resort activities for institutions whose nationality is highly complex. Debt has gone multinational, but the lender of last resort is still largely national.

The solution to the U.S. trade deficit and debt accumulation is also likely to be self-defeating. Drastic cuts in the U.S. government budget may actually make it more difficult for the United States to service its foreign debt. For as the United States has borrowed more and more, it has invested less and less (see Table 2). Further cuts in productive investment by the government and private sector would only exacerbate the debt servicing problems facing the United States, since its output will not grow as fast as its debt service.

Finally, attempts to reduce the power of labor and to roll back the welfare state will be contentious, to say the least. Its success depends on the degree to which workers and progressives generally can fight against these continuing corporate attacks. And, as I have tried to argue, it is political and economic power, not the technology of international financial markets, that will determine the outcome.

## Table 2
### Foreign Borrowing and Total Investment
### as a Percent of the U.S. Economy

|  | (1)<br>1969–73 | (2)<br>1974–80 | (3)<br>1981–86 | (4)<br>Change from<br>(2) to (3) |
|---|---|---|---|---|
| (in percent) |  |  |  |  |
| Foreign borrowing | 0 | 0 | 2.0 | 2.0 |
| Total investment | 7 | 5.4 | 4.2 | – 1.2 |
| Total investment (R&D) |  | 6.0* | 5.3 | – .7 |

*1975–80

*Definitions and Sources: Foreign Borrowing:* The U.S. Current Account Deficit in 1982 dollars, divided by the Net National Product in 1982 dollars; Council of Economic Advisors, *Economic Report of the President,* 1987, *Economic Indicators,* December 1987, and Department of Commerce, *Survey of Current Business,* November 1987. *Total Investment:* Net non-residential fixed investment, in 1982 dollars plus federal and state and local non-military net investment (excluding research and development), divided by Net National Product in 1982 dollars; *Economic Report of the President,* 1987, *Survey of Current Business,* July 1987 and Congressional Budget Office, "Trends in Public Investment," December 1987. *Total Investment* (R&D): Total investment plus non-military government and private research and development expenditures divided by net national product, all in 1982 dollars. These data were not available before 1975.

## Notes

1. Both of these plans might include significant government involvement in restructuring and competition policy. Thus, neither of these is laissez-faire.
2. I use these names as a shorthand for these problems, with the knowledge that one might disagree with attributing these particular concepts to these particular people. Indeed, one could argue that Marx, himself, identified all of these problems of capitalism.

## References

Bank for International Settlements. 1986. *Recent Innovations in International Banking* (The Cross Report).

Bergsten, C. Fred. 1975. *The Dilemmas of the Dollar.* New York: New York University Press.

Branson, W. and James Love. 1987. "The Real Exchange Rate and Employment In U.S. Manufacturing: State and Regional Results." *NBER Paper,* No.2435.

De Cecco, Marcello. 1974. *Money and Empire; The International Gold Standard, 1890–1914.* Oxford: Basil Blackwell.

Eichengreen, Barry, ed. 1985. *The Gold Standard in Theory and History*. New York: Methuen.

Epstein, Gerald and Herbert Gintis. 1988. "An Asset Balance Model of International Capital Market Equilibrium." University of Massachusetts at Amherst, Working Paper, No. 12.

Funabashi, Yoichi. 1988. *Managing the Dollar: From the Plaza to the Louvre*. Washington: Institute for International Economics.

Hawley, James P. 1987. *Dollars and Borders: U.S. Government Attempts to Restrict Capital Outflows, 1960–1980*, Armonk, NY: M. E. Sharpe.

Horii, Akinari. 1986. "The Evolution of Reserve Currency Diversifications." *BIS Economic Papers*. No. 18, December.

Levich, Richard M. 1987. "Financial Innovations in International Financial Markets." *NBER Working Paper*, No. 2277, June.

Lipsey, Robert E. and Irving B. Kravis. 1986. "The Competitiveness and Comparative Advantage of U.S. Multinationals, 1957–1983." *NBER Working Paper*, No. 2051.

OECD. 1987. *Asset and Liability Management by Banks*. Paris: OECD.

Salomon Brothers, Inc., 1988, "Domestic and International Bank Stock Investing: A Global Approach." New York: Salomon Brothers, Inc., Research Department, March.

Sweezy, Paul and Harry Magdoff. 1987. "International Cooperation: A Way Out?" *Monthly Review* (November): 1–19.

Wachtel, Howard M. 1986. *The Money Mandarins; The Making of a Supranational Economic Order*. New York: Pantheon.

Zevin, Robert. 1988. "Are World Financial Markets More Open? If So, Why and with What Effects?" Paper presented at the World Institute for Development Economic Research, Helsinki, Finland. July 4–6.

# Debt-Dependent Growth and Financial Innovation: Instability in the United States and Latin America

## *Robert Pollin*

Instability and change have characterized the financial operations of capitalist economies over the past twenty years. This is true both at the level of national economies and internationally. Moreover, instability in the financial sphere since the late 1960s has been closely interlinked with other major features of this phase of capitalist history—severe business-cycle downturns, long-term economic stagnation and the movement toward internationalization.

It is not difficult to identify some of the major features of contemporary financial change. Latin America experienced a boom in debt-dependent growth in the 1970s, which engendered the debt crisis of the 1980s and the tremendous mass hardship associated with the IMF austerity programs implemented to "resolve" the crisis. The U.S. economy also began a long period of debt-dependent growth beginning in the 1970s. This trend has continued, even accelerated, through the 1980s, though the October 1987 Wall Street crash made clear how fragile the U.S. financial system has become in the process. Moreover, in the aftermath of the crash, many U.S. observers began looking to Latin America for a "solution" to U.S. financial difficulties, arguing that Latin-style austerity was the necessary bitter pill the U.S. economy had to swallow to regain financial health.[1]

Parallel to and interacting with the emergence of debt-dependent growth has been the rapid integration of international financial markets. Again, many manifestations of this are apparent. They include the rise of the Eurodollar market; the centrality of Euromarket lenders in promoting Latin borrowing; and the increasing reliance on foreign savings in the United States as well—including a significant proportion from the indebted Latin countries—to finance its debt-dependent growth.

This essay has several aims. I argue that debt-dependent growth is the single most important proximate factor underlying the phenomenon of deepening financial instability in both the United States and Latin America. The analysis therefore tries to explain the sources of debt-dependent growth in Latin America and the U.S. Since these regions are moreover where problems of financial instability have emerged most dramatically within the first and third worlds, by focusing on them, I also am pursuing a broader purpose of trying to shed light on the general problem of international financial instability.

While there are great differences, which we need to identify, in the forces influencing financial change in the United States and Latin America, there are also crucial common elements. I try to show that in both regions, debt-dependent growth has been influenced by three basic factors: economic stagnation, financial innovation, and internationalization. The essay thus also tries to make clear the links between debt-dependent growth, stagnation, and financial innovation on an international scale. But the rise of debt-dependent growth and financial instability in the United States and Latin America is not simply a matter of parallel trends influenced by similar forces. In addition, the forces promoting financial change and instability in these regions have been interconnected and mutually reinforcing. I try to identify these interrelated influences.

Finally, the essay addresses the political issues surrounding financial change and instability. The conservative agenda here is straightforward. The spectacular failure of the International Monetary Fund's (IMF) mix of free market and austerity policies in Latin America has forced conservatives to flee to the high ground of "growth-oriented" free market policies. Both in Latin America and the United States, the thrust of these proposals is to pursue liberalization of the financial sphere within a general framework of dismantling controls on capitalist market forces. I argue that a serious alternative to this agenda must begin from an understanding of the interrelated problems of stagnation, internationalization, financial innovation, and debt dependency. I try to show that many left policy proposals have not been sufficiently grounded in such a framework, and the proposals, as a result, are inadequate. The essay thus closes with brief suggestions for formulating a more satisfactory left approach to financial policy issues.

*Instability and Change in the U.S. Financial Structure*

Since the mid-1960s, the major nonfinancial sectors of the U.S. economy—corporations, households, and the federal government—have increasingly relied on borrowing to support their expenditures.[2] Up until the mid-1960s, the percentage of GNP that was debt-financed was remarkably stable: the ratio of net new borrowing to GNP hovered at around 9 percent over each seventeen to eighteen-year long cycle between 1897 and 1966. Between 1967 and 1986, however, this figure rose to 14.6 percent, a 60 percent increase over the historical average. Nonfinancial corporations, households and the federal government have all participated in the uptrend in debt financing. The roots of this trend toward increasing debt dependency, as I argue below, are found in the long-term tendencies toward stagnation and internationalization.

### *Demand-Side Influences*

Stagnation of the U.S. economy since the mid-1960s has been apparent in high unemployment rates and declining real wages, in slower overall GNP growth and low-capacity utilization, and the downward trend of corporate profitability. This, to begin with, has engendered an increasing "necessitous" credit demand: in order to sustain expenditure growth in the face of declining revenues, households, corporations, and the federal government have become more dependent on borrowed funds. In addition, stagnation has encouraged the growth of "speculative" credit demand, as the lack of productive opportunities leads both private individuals and firms to seek profits through shifting assets rather than attempting to create new assets. Both necessitous and speculative borrowing have become increasingly prevalent within the private sector of the U.S. economy since the mid-1960s.

*Nonfinancial corporations.* For the corporate sector, the rise of necessitous debt financing is the result of stagnation in the real level of corporate profits and the decline in the average rate of corporate profitability. For our purposes here, we recognize the trend decline in profitability as an empirical fact, without linking our analysis to any particular explanation of the corporate profitability decline.

Because real profit levels were stagnating, this tended also to reduce the amount of internal funds corporations had available for investment. When internal funds fell, corporations were then faced with some combination of two alternatives: reduce expenditure levels to reflect the decline in internal funds, or increase borrowing to avoid having to reduce spending.

Most firms in this situation will probably try to pursue both alternatives partially. However, we observe empirically that firms have tended first to borrow more rather than cut expenditure levels. For firms to opt first to cut expenditures would require that they also slow the rate at which they can innovate and lower production costs. A firm's competitive position would thus weaken with a cut in expenditures: market dominance would be seized by those firms willing to make the requisite investments. Consistent with these competitive imperatives, the rate of corporate debt financing rose to partially fill the gap created by the decline in corporate internal funds.

The merger and takeover phenomenon can also be directly linked to the decline in corporate profitability. As average corporate profitability fell throughout the 1970s and early 1980s, corporate share prices declined as well, to a point substantially below the replacement cost of the corporations' physical assets. The ratio of firms' value on the stock market relative to the replacement cost of their physical assets thus fell to a postwar low by the early 1980s. It became cheaper, as a result, to acquire an existing firm's assets on the stock market than to invest in new assets. This created strong incentives for takeovers and, concomitantly, equal incentives for financial innovations such as "junk bonds" to finance takeover efforts—hence the rise of corporate speculative credit demand. Once these financial innovations were put in place, an additional, and ultimately the strongest single incentive for takeover activity also emerged: the huge profits available for the investment bankers, corporate executives, and inside traders engineering these arrangements. Between 1982 and 1987 the drive for such "promoters' profits" continued to encourage debt-financed takeovers and mergers, even though, as stock market values rose sharply over this period, firms' assets could no longer readily be acquired at bargain basement prices (Herman and Lowenstein 1986; DuBoff and Herman 1987).

*Households.* Speculative credit demand among U.S. households has been an important factor for a small minority of the wealthy. The low borrowing costs in the 1970s enabled these households to raise more funds to pursue speculative investments. Real estate was especially attractive to wealthy investors in the 1970s because it was a means of storing wealth that was not vulnerable to inflation-induced depreciations in value. And while borrowing costs rose in the 1980s, real income for the upper 10 percent of households also increased sharply, giving them the financial resources to continue borrowing heavily for speculative purposes. Thus in the 1980s, investments in financial assets joined real estate as a profitable way to store wealth, as real yields reached historic highs.

The majority of U.S. households, of course, do not invest in real estate or financial instruments. But they have increased their necessitous credit demand. Rising necessitous credit demand emerged as a result of the decline in real wages and family incomes, and the rise in housing costs since the early 1970s. From their peak in 1972 until 1985, real wages in the United States fell by 14.1 percent. In response to this (as well as to changing social conditions), women entered the labor force in increasing numbers, to provide many families with a second income. But because average wages continued to fall, even the growth of two-wage households has failed to maintain average family income levels—by 1985, real median family incomes had fallen by 4.9 percent from their 1973 peak. Even by 1987, after five years of cyclical expansion, median incomes were still below the 1973 peak. At the same time, the median cost of a new home rose by 7.4 percent over these years, and overall housing costs increased in real terms over this period by 8.6 percent. To a large extent, this rise was fueled by the speculative real estate investments of the wealthy. And because housing is the least flexible item in the family budget and thus the first claim on its income, these relative increases in housing have been particularly burdensome. Overall, as a result of stagnating or declining incomes and rising housing costs, average households have become increasingly debt-dependent as a way of trying to maintain their living standards.

*The Federal Government.* We have seen that corporations and households have increased their rates of debt financing both to avoid sharp reductions in their expenditure levels and to pursue speculative investment opportunities. To recognize this, however, does not itself explain why the aggregate rate of debt financing since the mid-1960s should have risen to its current historically unprecedented level. Certainly significant gaps between incomes and expenditure levels have existed in prior phases, as have waves of heavy financial speculation. Yet, as noted earlier, the aggregate debt financing ratio remained highly stable in these previous period.

To explain this unique situation we have to bring federal government borrowing into the analysis. Federal government borrowing has contributed to the unprecedented rise in aggregate debt financing in two crucial ways. First, since peacetime government deficit spending is a relatively new phenomenon, becoming a conscious policy instrument only in the 1960s, its emergence has tended to increase total debt financing simply because it is a large additional component of the aggregate figure. Of course, this is especially the case since 1980, with the onset of the Reagan administration's fiscal policy combining tax cuts for the wealthy with a military buildup.

The second, and even more fundamental contribution of government deficit spending has been its countercyclical impact. In earlier historical phases, the rise of debt financing has been checked and reversed when credit bubbles were burst by severe debt deflations and widespread defaults, which in turn forced sharply downward the economy's aggregate rate of debt financing. In the contemporary period, government deficit financing counteracts the debt deflation process by increasing the level of aggregate income in the short-run. As a result of this intervention, defaults can and do still occur in periods of cyclical decline, but not as severely as would have resulted without the government intervention. When the wave of defaults is avoided, the incipient debt-deflation is thwarted.

Thus, large-scale government debt financing acts to circumscribe the private economy's contradictionary tendencies.[3] However, in accomplishing this task, government debt financing also necessarily acts to nullify the debt deflation process as a financial regulator. In the absence of debt deflations, no automatic mechanism exists for discouraging the sustained growth in private debt financing. This is why, as a result of large-scale federal government debt financing recently, the U.S. economy has experienced an unprecedented rise in its aggregate rate of debt financing.

## Supply-Side Influences

The sustained growth in U.S. debt financing could only take place within financial markets that could generate a sufficient supply of credit to accommodate this growth. Financial markets have, of course, accommodated: the question is how such accommodation has been accomplished.

Mainstream economists generally contend that the growth in financial market-lending capacity comes from the expansive monetary policies of the Federal Reserve. In fact, the Fed's role in supporting lending growth since the mid-1960s has been secondary. The most important source of expansive lending in the United States has rather been the development of a wide range of innovative practices that greatly increased the ability of financial institutions to supply credit. Moreover, as we will see, the spread of innovations is what concatenated financial change on a global basis, and particularly between the United States and Latin America.

The profit motive, of course, is what has propelled financial institutions toward innovative practices. Given a positive interest spread and solvent customers, banks and other intermediaries make money by extending credit to the maximum extent. Innovation has allowed the intermediaries to increase their lending capacity independently of what Federal Reserve policy happens to be. The fact that innovation became a strong force in the postwar U.S. economy only in the 1960s does not mean that previously U.S. financial intermediaries were less concerned with profit. Rather, through the 1950s, the inherent innovating drive of financial institutions were suppressed by several factors, including the predominance of cautious financial attitudes engendered by the Depression experience; the stability of domestic prices and strength of the dollar in international markets, which reinforced status quo financial practices for U.S. institutions; and the highly liquid state of both financial and nonfinancial institutions after World War II, which meant both that credit supply was relatively abundant and demand relatively weak.

In the United States, the cumulative effect of several financial innovations allowed loans to be financed on a diminishing base of bank cash reserves—the reserve to loan ratio falling steadily from an average of 28 percent during the mid-1950s to 4.1 percent between 1980 and 1985. One such innovation was the creation of the Certificate of Deposit, a bank-issued financial instrument that was initially developed by former Citibank Chair Walter Wriston in 1961. These large, negotiable time deposits carry lower reserve requirements than traditional demand or time deposits, and thus permit a given supply of reserves to support more bank lending. Indeed, at present, domestic CD's of greater than eighteen months' maturity presently carry no reserve requirement at all.

Another, and for our purposes the most important, innovation was the development of interconnections between U.S. intermediaries and the Eurodollar market. U.S. involvement in the Eurodollar market expanded enormously in the late 1960s. This occurred because interest yields on CDs in the United States were limited by regulated ceiling interest rates. Because of inflationary pressures, nominal market rates on CDs rose above the ceiling rates. In response, U.S. lenders who would normally have purchased CDs chose rather to lend their funds within the unregulated Eurodollar market to obtain market yields. Intermediaries in the United States, in turn, would borrow back these funds from the Eurodollar market—both from their overseas branches and from unaffiliated institutions—to meet the demand for funds in the domestic market. In short, the Eurodollar market represented both an important source of cash reserves and also a means of circumventing the existing U.S. financial regulatory structure. As such, it was a major factor leading to the demise of the set of financial regulations established through the 1933 Glass-Steagall Act and similar subsequent measures.

Most broadly, the enormous growth of the Eurodollar market beginning in the late 1960s was the first major step in the development of an innovative and highly integrated global financial market. Assisted by advances in computers and telecommunication technology, financial innovation and integration spread throughout the major industrialized countries. Between 1970 and 1985, foreign banks' shares of total assets of national banking systems doubled in all the major industrial countries. Over this same period, CDs became legalized in France, Germany, and Japan, and similar instruments emerged elsewhere. The Bretton Woods fixed-exchange-rate system was an early victim of this changing international financial environment. In an international market that was inflationary, innovative, and rapidly integrating, the fixed-rate system was too rigid to be sustained. Bretton Woods' demise in turn permitted even more innovation and integration. By now, virtually no limits remain on what is both permissible and possible in international financial markets.

## The Impact of Financial Change for the United States and Latin America

For the international economy, the implications of the changing financial environment have appeared particularly clearly in the experiences of the United States and Latin America. Let me emphasize five points:

1. Global financial innovation and integration have minimized the possibility that the growth of U.S. federal budget deficits would "crowd out" private U.S. borrowers from financial markets (see

Pollin 1985). By now it is evident that loanable funds supply can increase to meet the demands of both the private sector and the government. Absent serious supply-side constraints, the federal deficit thus acts to *encourage* ("crowd in") private sector borrowing through the factors discussed above, i.e., increasing aggregate income in the short run and preventing the occurrence of full-scale debt deflations. The growth of innovative financial markets also explains how both public and private debt financing in the United States can concurrently reach unprecedented levels while the domestic private savings rate declines (Magdoff and Sweezy 1984).

2. Debt-dependent growth rendered the U.S. economy "financially fragile," that is, much less capable of withstanding the effects of shocks and business cycle downturns. This is because in cyclical downturns, all borrowers—including corporations, governments, and households—experience cash-flow declines They therefore become less able to service their debts and also sustain expenditure levels. To the extent that they continue servicing their debts, their purchasing power will fall sharply. The downturn thus becomes more severe as market demand contracts. If, alternatively, borrowers opt for default over continued debt servicing, this weakens the lending institutions that had financed debt-dependent growth. Assuming the lending institutions survive the rise in defaults, they still become less able and willing to extend new loans. The decline in loans then exacerbates the downturn further, precisely because growth had become heavily dependent on debt financing.

3. Global innovation and integration have weakened the ability of government policy to manage financial markets through traditional monetary and regulatory policies. Monetary policy is increasingly ineffective because, as the data on the ratio of reserves/loans cited above indicates, Federal Reserve policy interventions do not create significant constraints on the financial market's ability to generate loanable funds. Regulatory policies in the Glass-Steagall tradition are similarly ineffective because funds can relocate in countries free of such regulations and still be accessible throughout the global financial market. This does not mean that central bank policy and other government interventions have no impact. Considering the U.S. case, only Federal Reserve interventions prevented Depression-type financial collapses during the crises over Mexico in 1982, Continental Illinois in 1984, and the October 1987 Wall Street crash. But in these cases, the Fed acted not through its position as controller of bank reserves and the money supply but as lender of last resort. What the

Federal Reserve is increasingly unable to do is use open-market operations and its other fine-tuning instruments to affect financial market behavior.

4. The demise of Bretton Woods and development of the global Eurocurrency market, themselves products of the thrust toward financial innovation, in turn created the institutional framework that engendered the growth of Latin American lending in the early 1970s. Certainly other factors, especially the need to recycle OPEC surpluses, gave an upward jolt to the burst of Latin lending. But the institutional framework of an unregulated, globally integrated Eurocurrency market was the first necessary precondition.

5. Here a major link between financial change in the U.S. and Latin America emerges. It was because former Federal Reserve Chair Paul Volcker recognized in 1979 the ineffectiveness of monetary fine-tuning policies that he opted instead for a shock treatment to arrest inflation and the decline of the dollar. Volcker advertised the 1979 policy change as a move toward "monetarist" principles of maintaining a stable growth rate of banks' cash reserves. But the most important feature of the Federal Reserve's policy shift was the imposition of credit controls in March 1980. The controls included sharp increases in both reserve requirements and the discount rate as well as a "voluntary" program to limit credit growth. The result of these policies was that real GNP fell by a record 9.5 percent in the second quarter of 1980. Though the Federal Reserve lifted the controls in July 1980, they continued to pursue stringent reserve growth policies. This combination of policies, imposed within the context of an already fragile financial structure, produced the rise of real interest rates to historic highs, and, along with that, the long and severe recession of 1980–82.

The high interest rates and recession reverberated powerfully in Latin America. After nearly a decade of obtaining voluntary loans at low to negative real interest rates, the Federal Reserve shock treatment was devastating. Debt-servicing obligations rose sharply and export markets collapsed. This converted Mexico, the most heavily indebted Latin borrower at the time, into a "Ponzi" financial unit—a net debtor that has to increase involuntary borrowing just to meet interest payments. And while the Federal Reserve did stave off full-scale collapse through Volcker's bail-out package for Mexico, what is generally referred to as the Latin "debt crisis" really begins at this juncture. The crisis commences here not only because of Mexico's condition, but, more broadly because after Mexico's virtual default, international banks refused further voluntary lending throughout the region, converting other Latin debtors into Ponzi units as well.

## The Emergence of Debt-Dependent Growth in Latin America

The Latin American debt crisis, of course, was not simply the result of supply-side changes in financial markets. Rather, it emerged through the interconnections of these changes and the pressures for outward-oriented development policies. In this section, therefore, I consider the factors leading to the development of debt-dependent growth in Latin America (for a fuller discussion see Pollin and Alarcón 1988). I specifically focus on the experiences of Mexico, Argentina, and Brazil, Latin America's three largest and most heavily indebted economies.

### The Experience with Import-Substituting Industrialization

Pressures leading toward debt-dependent growth in Latin America are traceable to the demise of import-substitution industrialization policies. Such policies, in some form, were almost universally pursued in Latin America during the 1950s and 1960s; certainly they were enthusiastically embraced in Mexico, Brazil, and Argentina.

The overarching aim of import substituting policies in Latin America was to encourage the development of domestic manufacturing industries; these would "substitute" for the manufactured goods that were being imported to satisfy the demands of the Latin market. The policies were designed to operate within existing capitalist relations, but they nevertheless rejected the tenets of free trade and minimal government. High tariffs were imposed to discourage imported manufactures, while public investment and subsidies were used to directly support local manufacturing production. Dependency on foreign economies was thus supposed to diminish as domestic industrialization proceeded.

Import substituting policies were successful in meeting many of their aims. Mexico, Argentina, and Brazil did attain their most immediate goal of producing domestic substitutes for manufactured nonluxury consumption goods. In addition, these three countries all began to develop extensive backward linkages into capital goods production during the 1960s, and by the early 1970s, these sectors began exporting on the world market. GDP growth in these countries was also generally high over the 1950s and 1960s.

Despite this, import substitution policies proved unsustainable. The basic problem was that the Latin economies were never able to break their chronic and debilitating dependency on foreign capital, even though this was the explicit aim of the strategy. More specifically, the issue that import substitution policies could never adequately resolve was how the Latin economies could acquire a sufficient stock of capital goods to build domestic manufacturing capacity. In fact, almost all of this capital stock had to be obtained from foreign sources, either through imports or attracting multinational firms to invest in the region. This created several serious difficulties.

First, to the extent that capital goods were imported, it became necessary for the Latin economies to generate a sufficient supply of foreign exchange to pay for these imports. Exporting primary products—agricultural and mineral resources—was the only means available for the Latin economies to obtain the needed foreign exchange. Consequently, these economies' dependence on primary product exports increased. This clearly was an unintended and unwanted outcome, since a central feature of import substitution policies was to concentrate resources on building manufacturing capacity. The primary sector within this approach was drained of resources and allowed to stagnate.

Attracting foreign direct investment, the other chosen means of accumulating capital stock, was heavily promoted during the import substitution years, despite the nationalist rhetoric of the model. In Brazil, for example, multinational firms accounted for 44 percent of all domestic sales in 1965, while domestic private firms and state enterprises accounted for only 28 percent each (Maia Gomes 1986: 198). By 1972, the multinationals accounted for 50 percent of total manufacturing assets for both Brazil and Mexico (Evans and Gereffi 1982: 138).

The multinationals' primary purpose for locating in Latin America during this period was to leap over the Latin economies' protectionist walls, and thereby capture for themselves the benefits of protectionism within the local markets. They did not come to establish export platforms, and government policy did not encourage them to do so. Thus by the mid-1960s, exports of multinationals accounted for less than 2 percent of their local sales in both Mexico and Brazil (ibid.: 148). At the same time, the multinationals in Argentina, Brazil, and Mexico were essentially free to repatriate profits.

Since the multinationals repatriated profits to a substantial extent without contributing to exports, their presence produced a large drain on the Latin countries' current account. Reliance on the stagnant primary product sector for exports only reinforced the multinational-led bias toward current account deficits. The result of these factors was that the current account deficits were virtually permanent features of Brazil and Mexico's international profile from the early 1950s to the mid-1960s. The situation for Argentina was only slightly better.[4] It thus became apparent by the mid-1960s that import substituting policies could not overcome the constraints imposed by external deficits.

## Development Crises and Debt-Dependent Growth

The overriding question in Mexico, Argentina, and Brazil by the early 1970s was not whether new development approaches were necessary—this was agreed upon—but rather how the post-import substitution policies would address the problem of persistent current account deficits.

To begin with, the problems associated with closing persistent current account deficits were significantly worsened through the emergence of stagnation in the United States and other industrialized countries, as stagnation weakened export markets for Latin products. Within this framework, several alternatives were attempted. They reflected both the growing problems associated with stagnation and the contending class forces participating in the restructuring debate. Populist programs, attempting to inject redistributionist policies into the import-substitution framework emerged briefly in Argentina with the return of Juan Perón in 1973 and more seriously in Mexico under Luis Echeverría's "shared development" program. But both of these efforts were supplanted by right-wing initiatives—monetarism in Argentina after the 1974 military coup and an IMF-imposed austerity program in Mexico in early 1977. Mexico shifted directions again in 1978 after the discovery of large oil deposits. In Brazil an eclectic strategy was pursued, combining further efforts at import substitution with an aggressive export-promotion program and opposition to the IMF with unwavering allegiance to the prerogatives of domestic elites and foreign capital.

But the question as to whether any of the post-import substitution strategies could more successfully address the balance of payments constraint was never answered. This was because by the mid-1970s, global financial integration was growing apace, and in particular, international banks had become zealous loan merchants in Latin America and the Latin countries equally ardent recipients of funds. As a consequence, all development programs appeared sustainable since all were being financed by unprecedented credit infusions.

The funds were channeled in several directions, varying by country according to the specific character of the elite groups in power. Some of the loans, especially in Brazil, did go to develop productive capacity. But even in Brazil, huge sums were also squandered on wasteful construction projects (Tanzer 1984). In Mexico and Argentina, a substantial share of the funds left the domestic economies altogether through capital flight; in Brazil, where the government adhered to tight foreign exchange controls, this was less of a factor. Under Argentina's military dictatorship, military hardware purchases were another favored use of the foreign credits. But regardless of the purposes for which loans were channeled, all three countries' debt-led strategies collapsed in 1982 when, in the midst of the U.S. recession and after the August announcement by Mexico, further voluntary lending to the region ended.

## Uneven Effects of Debt Dependent Growth

The emergence of debt-dependent growth in the United States and Latin America share many common features. Most importantly, as we have seen, economic stagnation and global financial innovation/integration have exerted a powerful influence in both regions. At the same time, there are fundamental differences in the recent financial histories of the United States and the major Latin economies, both in the way debt dependency emerged in the 1970s and as financial change and instability have been experienced in the 1980s. It is important to identify these differences, as they show clearly how the processes of financial change and increasing instability have acted to exacerbate inequalities between the United States, still the world's strongest imperialist power, and the less developed Latin American economies.

To begin with, the impact of stagnation on the United States and Latin America has been quite distinct. In the United States, stagnation has been a direct cause of the rise of both necessitous and speculative credit demand in the private sector. Federal budget deficits also grew partially as a means of counteracting the economy's downward trend. Moreover, despite the growth of U.S debt financing over this period, stagnationist tendencies continued. In other words, the rise of debt financing in the United States has been associated with a weakening domestic economy.

The major Latin economies, as we have seen, clearly have been affected by stagnation in the United States and other industrialized economies, through the weakening of Latin export markets, the growth of innovative finance, and the effects of the 1982 recession. But debt-dependent growth in these economies was not associated with domestic stagnation at the aggregate level. Rather, Mexico, Brazil, and Argentina generally experienced rapid economic growth during the import substitution period. In Mexico and Brazil, strong growth continued, even accelerated, through the 1970s years of heavy borrowing, despite the massive amounts of funds squandered on capital flight and wasteful construction projects. Argentina is the exception here, but the failures of this economy in terms of aggregate GDP growth in the 1970s can be traced more to the particulars of the ultra-monetarist policy model than broader stagnationist forces.[5]

The overarching problem for these economies was not domestic stagnation but the persistent current-account deficits. To some extent of course, ruling classes in Mexico, Brazil, and Argentina were eager to borrow simply because the funds were there to be had at low real interest rates (what Wall Street guru Albert Wojnilower calls "the narcotic attraction of borrowing"). But they were also pushed to borrow because of their inability to balance their current accounts. In short, debt financing in Latin America was needed not to arrest long-term domestic decline, but rather to continue a development process that was unsustainable without heavy external support.

Both the U.S. and Latin financial structures became increasingly fragile through the years of debt-dependent growth. But it is clear, as a second major distinction, that the experiences in the two regions since the 1982 downturn have been dramatically different.

The U.S. economy has experienced several serious financial crises since 1982—the near collapse of Continental Illinois in 1984, the virtual failures of Ohio and Maryland S&Ls in 1985, and the 1987 stock market crash being only the most dramatic episodes. More broadly, annual bank failures have risen from 10 in 1982 to 184 in 1987 and the number of banks which the Federal Deposit Insurance Corporation classifies as "problem banks" has risen by a similar proportion. The behavior of the dollar has been highly erratic through these years as well. Despite all this, foreign savings continue to flow into the U.S. credit market at an unprecedented rate.[6] This flow of funds to the United States is not a measure of its own strong economic performance, but rather demonstrates that among financially fragile economies the U.S. remains powerful: it is still the largest economy and the dollar is still the most widely employed currency. Because of these flows, the U.S. has been able to avoid the severe austerity which would accompany any sharp reductions from current levels of debt financing.

In Latin America, on the other hand, new voluntary loans have been virtually nonexistent since 1982. In addition, most Latin economies, beset by inflation, currency instability, weak domestic markets and low real yields on financial assets, have experienced an acceleration of the capital flight that began in the 1970s. The impact of capital flight on the Latin economies since 1982 can hardly be understated. According to a careful study by David Felix and Juana Sánchez (1987), foreign assets held by Mexicans and Argentines as of 1985 *exceeded* those countries' level of foreign debt. For Brazil, Felix and Sánchez estimate that foreign assets constitute 34 percent of the country's foreign debt, a substantially lower but still significant figure. For Mexico and Argentina, Felix and Sánchez estimate that had only the 1985 *earnings* on foreign assets been repatriated, both countries "could have financed more than a doubling of their imports while still servicing their foreign debt and augmenting their foreign exchange reserves on their foreign assets" (1987:8). Clearly then, capital flight has been a major contributor to the harsh austerity experienced in Latin America since 1982, just as capital inflows to the United States—much of it coming from Latin America—has ameliorated financial instability here.[7]

A final important difference between the U.S. and the Latin economies is evident in the question of declining autonomy in financial policy matters. We have seen that global financial integration has eroded the ability of monetary and regulatory policies to successfully manipulate market forces. In the United States, however, several means of intervening in financial markets are still available, including fiscal policy, lender of last resort interventions, and occasional strong doses of 1980–82-type monetary stringency. Indeed, the impact of these U.S. policy instruments remain the single greatest influences in the global financial market. Moreover, the IMF and World Bank remain U.S.-dominated institutions.

For the Latin economies, the financial dependency which developed through the import substitution years always limited the capacity even of governments that were not mere imperial clients to pursue independent financial policies. But since 1982, conditions have worsened sharply. As long as the debt problem remains unresolved, financial policies depend on the U.S. economy, international banks, the IMF, and domestic capitalists who, through capital flight, vote with their checkbooks on government initiatives. The complete failure of the independent financial stabilization programs in Brazil (the "Cruzado plan") and Argentina (the "Austral plan") over 1985–86 demonstrated unequivocally the barriers these governments now face (MacEwan 1986; Pollin and Zepeda 1987).

## *Perspectives on Financial Stabilization Policies*

An interesting perspective on how financial change has affected the parameters for financial policy was recently offered by Walter Wriston, former chair of Citibank, who observed:

> Money only goes where it's wanted and only stays where it is well treated, and once you tie the world together, with telecommunications and information, the ball game is over. . . . It's a new world and the new concept of sovereignty is going to change. Politically, the new world is an integrated market in which nobody can get away with what they used to. You can't control what your people hear, you can't control the value of your currency, you can't control your capital flows. (Quoted in Frieden 1987: 114–15).

However one might evaluate this Wristonian perspective, one point must be conceded: as financial market forces have strengthened through innovation and integration, the terms of the debate over financial stabilization policies have shifted. More specifically, what has emerged is that financial stabilization proposals that claim to follow the market's logic have gained a fresh veneer of plausibility. This can be seen in debates both in the United States and Latin America.

In both regions, newly articulated free-market positions emphasize the need for deregulated financial institutions, unmanipulated exchange rates, and rules over discretion in central bank monetary policy. The arguments for such positions are embedded in a broader free market framework that also favors more incentives and fewer barriers for both foreign and domestic investment, lower taxes, and less public investment and government intervention. Proponents of this approach also invariably oppose concessions on Latin debt. According to their argument, once a favorable investment climate can be established through free market policies, both foreign and domestic capital would voluntarily flow back to the region (see Balassa et al. 1986 and Eisenbeis 1986).

To a large extent, the free-market proponents are easy to dismiss. For one thing, they are clearly wrong in their presumption that minimal government policies will be optimal, even for the capitalist class, whose interests they identify with overall social wellbeing.[8] Nevertheless, they have stumbled on two insights which are essential to recognize. First, their argument is correct that contemporary financial market forces have become increasingly powerful and that any serious policy initiative must take appropriate heed of these changes. They are also correct in seeking to embed their financial stabilization proposals within a broader restructuring scheme.

For the most part, liberal to left responses to free-market financial stabilization in both the United States and Latin contexts have not sufficiently assimilated these two points. Beyond supporting deep concessions on Latin debt, progressive policy formulations have centered around the reassertion of what I call "market inhibiting" financial regulations, including currency and capital controls, international coordination of interest and exchange rate policies, and, in the United States, limiting the independence of the Federal Reserve. The problem with such market-inhibiting policies is that they are too narrowly focused: they seek to reorient existing financial market forces, but do not take seriously enough the fact that market forces have substantially changed. More specifically, they do not attempt to develop their proposals within a comprehensive framework which addresses the interrelated problems of stagnation, internationalization, financial innovation and debt dependency.

Some examples of this type of left/liberal programmatic thinking include David Felix's suggestions (1985) for compulsory repatriation of Latin flight capital; proposals by Howard Wachtel (1986) and others for more international governmental coordination to limit exchange and interest fluctuations and to monitor the Eurodollar market; and strategies such as those of the Center for Popular Economics (1986) to bring the Federal Reserve under direct Congressional control and thereby expose the Fed to more popular pressures.

For those unwilling to accept the Wristonian policy ethos, these ideas carry some appeal. At the same time, as market-inhibiting proposals, they face the serious problem of bearing a close resemblance to the types of regulatory policies, such as the Bretton Woods system and the Glass-Steagall laws, that have been rendered ineffective, and even discredited, by contemporary financial developments.

The Wachtel proposal, for example, includes much of what already constitutes U.S. policy through the coordinated "G-7" efforts among industrialized economies to stabilize interest and exchange rates and the establishment of reserve requirements on the Eurodollar deposits of U.S.-affiliated banks. But no noticeable advances toward financial stabilization have emerged as a result of these policies' having been implemented. For Latin America, the Felix proposal for compulsory capital repatriation would be similarly ineffective because in an innovative financial market, premiums would be paid to those institutions able to protect the flight capital in defiance of the regulations. The only way new innovations to protect the flight capital could be avoided is if guarantees of a highly favorable investment climate for the returning capital were also firmly established—making peace, in other words, with the free market restructuring project.[9]

As an alternative to such limited market-inhibiting policies, the left should rather stress the need for a radical restructuring of financial market forces themselves. Otherwise, the restructuring debate is effectively ceded to free-market proponents. The two basic elements necessary for radical financial restructuring both in the United States and Latin America are social control over investment and redistribution downward of wealth and income: radical financial restructuring of financial markets, in other words, should be viewed as an element of a general program of radical social and political change.

To understand how such policies would be effective in stabilizing financial markets, one must recall the roots of debt dependency in the United States and Latin America. In the United States, redistributive policies such as mass public housing and full employment at decent wages would raise incomes and lower housing costs. This would then reduce households' necessitous demand for credit. Corporate necessitous borrowing could also fall if a public investment bank allocated credit to selected corporations through non-market criteria. If both household and corporate necessitous credit demand could be diminished, tax laws and other regulatory apparatus would be more capable of circumscribing speculative credit demand associated with both real estate and financial markets, as well as financial innovation broadly.

In Latin America, redistribution and social control over investment would give equitable industrialization policies an opportunity to succeed. Redistribution is needed to create sufficiently strong domestic markets to support internally driven growth. Democratic credit allocation could be used to advance the development of the nascent capital goods industries through promoting regional integration, eliminating the squandering of funds by domestic capitalists, and resisting the pressures to fashion policies to the specifications of transnational corporations.

These ideas, of course, are impractical within current political configurations, and practicality often constitutes a major brief in behalf of the left-liberal market-inhibiting policy approach. Wachtel, for example, stresses that his proposals are "eminently feasible and are compatible with the world's existing administrative and policy structures" (1986: 224). Insofar as his proposals could be implemented at present, Wachtel is clearly correct: indeed, as mentioned above, many of his proposals already constitute existing policy. But at the same time, his proposals are utterly impractical in that they have yielded no discernible improvements in current financial market conditions.

A concluding point needs to be raised on the issue of presenting "practical" proposals consistent with present political structures. At present, even though the ability of governments to influence financial markets through regulatory and monetary policy has diminished, this does not mean that governments are either neutral or marginal players in the present scene. Rather, as we have seen, debt-dependent growth in the United States has been sustained in the last instance only through the government's deficit-spending and lender-of-last-resort interventions. Such policies have prevented full-scale debt deflation and depression, and thus have permitted financial markets to continue profiting from speculative activities even as labor market incomes of American workers have declined. This is why Hyman Minsky (1988) recently called the recipients of capital income America's true "welfare queens." At present, in short, we have a system which has socialized the costs of financial speculation but privatized its gains. Similar conditions hold in Latin America, as the majority suffer harsh austerity while the wealthy continue to send their capital abroad. The job of the left is not to accept such arrangements as givens, merely seeking to ameliorate their effects. It is rather to fight for policies which take capitalists off the welfare rolls and promote financial stabilization within a broader framework of radical social change.

## *Notes*

I am indebted to Eduardo Zepeda for helping me formulate the broad outlines of this paper. I acknowledge the financial support of the University of California Riverside Committee on Research and Travel.

1. See, for example, the post-Nobel Prize interview with Robert Solow in the *Wall Street Journal* for 10/22/87, p. 40; and I.F. Stone, 1987, for pro-austerity statements by leading moderate to liberal analysts.
2. This section draws heavily on Pollin (1987), which is itself a survey article but which gives references to more detailed studies offering fuller empirical evidence as well as consideration of alternative perspectives.
3. It is also important to recognize that in several respects the tremendous growth of U.S. government budget deficits in the 1980s was also a *result* of stagnation. For example, upward trends for unemployment lowered income tax revenues and raised spending on transfer payments such as unemployment insurance and welfare. Additionally, the "taxpayers revolt" of the late 1970s and early 1980s, culminating in the large Reagan-era income tax cuts, represented an effort by primarily middle-income households to raise their take-home pay while their real pretax incomes were stagnant or falling. While the beneficiaries of the Reagan tax cuts were the rich rather than middle-income households, the origins of the revolt were broadly based.
4. The phenomenon of less developed countries experiencing persistent current account deficits is by no means confined to Latin America's import substitution period. Triffin (1968: ch. 1) describes a similar situation during the period of the nineteenth-century gold standard.
5. Moravic (1982) and Teitel and Thoumi (1986) present evidence on the growth of capital goods sectors in Mexico, Argentina, and Brazil and on export trends for these countries. These discussions are important for refuting the often expressed view that import substitution policies failed because of the inefficiencies that inevitably accompanied even these limited market-restraining policies. Two useful discussions on the Argentine experience with monetarism are Tokman (1984) and Teubal (1983).
6. For 1987, according to the Federal Reserve Board's Flow of Funds Accounts, foreign sources of funds constituted 16.6 percent of total U.S. credit market funds. However, the sharp rise in this ratio is not simply a phenomenon of the past few years. Rather, it ratcheted upward in the late 1960s in association with the growing link between U.S. finance and the Eurodollar market. The ratio has been highly pro-cyclical since then, and the current peak is not significantly higher than the 1971 figure of 15.4 percent. What is rather unique about the present situation is the combination of continued large savings inflows with the unprecedented increase in foreign direct investment.
7. Pastor (1987) is another careful study of the empirical dimensions and causes of Latin capital flight with somewhat lower estimates of Latin foreign asset holdings.

A problem related to capital flight is the growing "dollarization" of the Latin economies—the substitution of dollars for domestic currency in domestic transactions. The first serious treatment of this subject from a Marxist perspective is Zepeda (1988).

8. Japan is only the most obvious case where capitalist development has proceeded without any more than lipservice being paid to the precepts of free market economics. A recent casual observation made by Martin Bronfenbrenner, a leading mainstream economist who divides his time beween U.S. and Japanese academic institutions, is relevant here. Bronfenbrenner said that for the Japanese, capitalism does not mean free markets, but simply that the capitalist class runs things.

9. A fuller critique of Wachtel is MacEwan (1987). Pollin and Alarcón (1988) considers the Felix proposal at greater length and Pollin (1988) addresses the Center for Popular Economics' proposal for "democratizing the Fed."

## References

Balassa, B., G.M. Bueno, P.P. Kuczynski, and M.H. Simonsen. 1986. *Toward Renewed Economic Growth in Latin America.* Washington, DC: Institute For International Economics.

Center for Popular Economics. 1986. *The Economic Report of the People.* Boston, MA: South End Press.

DuBoff, R. and E. Herman. 1987. "The Promotional-Financial Dynamic of Merger Movements: A Historical Perspective." Unpublished paper presented at December American Economic Association meetings, Chicago, IL.

Eisenbeis, R.A. 1986. "Regulatory Policies and Financial Stability." In Federal Reserve Bank of Kansas City, *Debt, Financial Stability and Public Policy,* 107–37.

Evans, P. and G. Gereffi. 1982. "Foreign Investment and Dependent Development: Comparing Brazil and Mexico." in S.A. Hewlett and R.S. Weinert, *Brazil and Mexico: Patterns in Late Development.* Philadelphia: Institute for the Study of Human Issues.

Felix, D. 1985. "How to Resolve Latin America's Debt Crisis." *Challenge,* November/December, pp. 44–51.

——and J. Sánchez. 1987. "Capital Flight Aspects of the Latin American Debt Crisis." Working paper #106. Department of Economics, Washington University.

Frieden, J. 1987. *Banking on the Dollar: The Politics of American International Finance.* New York: Harper and Row.

Herman, E. and L. Lowenstein. 1986. "The Efficiency Effects of Hostile Takeovers." Working Paper #20, Center for Law and Economic Studies, Columbia University School of Law.

MacEwan, Arthur. 1986. "Latin America: Why Not Default?

*Monthly Review* 38, no. 4, pp. 1–13.

———. 1987. "Review of 'The Money Mandarins' " *Monthly Review* 39, no. 2, pp. 47–55.

Magdoff, Harry and Paul M. Sweezy. 1984. "The Federal Deficit: The Real Issues." *Monthly Review,* April. Reprinted in Magdoff and Sweezy, *Stagnation and the Financial Explosion.* New York: Monthly Review.

Maia Gomes, G. 1986. *The Roots of State Intervention in the Brazilian Economy.* New York: Praeger.

Minsky, H. 1988. The Crash of 1987: What Does it Mean?" *Against the Current,* May–June.

Moravic, M. 1982. "Exports of Latin American Manufactures to the Centres: Their Magnitude and Significance." *Cepal Review* 17, pp. 47–77.

Pastor, M. 1987. "Capital Flight and the Latin American Debt Crisis." Unpublished paper presented at December URPE/ASSA meetings, Chicago, IL.

Pollin, Robert. 1985: "Stability and Instability in the Debt/Income Relationship." *American Economic Review,* May, pp. 344–40.

———. 1987. "Structural Change and Increasing Instability in the U.S. Financial System." In Cherry et al., eds., *The Imperiled Economy.* New York: Union for Radical Political Economics, pp. 145–58.

———. 1988. "Should Congress Control the Federal Reserve?" *Dollars and Sense,* May.

———and D. Alarcón. 1988. "Debt Crisis, Accumulation Crisis and Economic Restructuring in Latin America." *International Review of Applied Economics,* June, pp. 127–154.

———and E. Zepeda. 1987. "Latin American Debt: The Choices Ahead." *Monthly Review,* February, pp. 1–16.

Stone, I.F. 1987. "Binge: End of A Profligate Era." *The Nation,* October 31.

Tanzer, Michael. 1984. "Stealing the Third World's Nonrenewable Resources: Lessons from Brazil." *Monthly Review,* April, pp. 25–36.

Teitel, S. and F. Thoumi. 1986. "From Import Substitution to Exports: The Manufacturing Export Experience of Argentina and Brazil." *Economic Development and Cultural Change,* April, pp. 455–90.

Teubal, M. 1983. "Argentina: The Crisis of Ultramonetarism." *Monthly Review,* February, pp. 18–26.

Tokman, V. 1984. "Global Monetarism and Destruction of Industry." *Cepal Review,* August, pp. 107–21.

Triffin, R. 1968. *Our International Monetary System: Yesterday, Today, and Tomorrow.* New York: Random House.

Wachtel, H. 1986. *The Money Mandarins: The Making of a Supranational Economic Order.* New York: Pantheon.

Zepeda, E. 1988. "Internationalization, Dollarization and the Roots of Mexico's Financial Crisis." Unpub. diss., Department of Economics, University of California-Riverside.

# Part II
# Reorganizing Production and Labor

# International Development and Industrial Restructuring: The Case of Garment and Electronics Industries in Southern California

## M. Patricia Fernández Kelly

### Introduction

Since the early 1960s, internationalization has been a major outgrowth of the crisis of competitiveness faced by investors seeking to improve their position in the domestic and world markets. This process has been portrayed primarily as an economic phenomenon characterized by the search for cheap labor to lower production costs. However, it is also political in that it represents a systemic shift away from the historical achievements of unions in advanced industrial countries and toward the tapping of pools of workers in third world areas where labor organizations are nonexistent or ineffectual. Internationalization is both a push for economic competitiveness and a thrust toward disciplining labor.

Research has focused mainly on the uneven effects of this process in Asia, Latin America, and even Africa. Yet, the impact of internationalization in advanced industrial countries is equally significant. In the United States capital flight, plant closings, and the erosion of traditional manufacturing have created spaces where new capital investments can be deployed to benefit from proximity to specialized markets, research and development centers and capital sources. Thus, internationalization is a two-pronged phenomenon which has altered the conditions for production and investment in less developed *and* in advanced industrial nations.

My purpose in this essay is twofold. First, I consider two recent approaches to internationalization and industrial restructuring in the United States. Second, I review preliminary findings concerning the reorganization of garment and electronics production in southern

California. The emphasis is on the employment of Hispanic women and the resurgence of "informal" labor arrangements as part of industries' efforts to regain competitiveness amid increasing globalization of the economy.

Garment and electronics manufacturing are good illustrations of these developments. First, both industries have been at the forefront of internationalization for more than two decades. Some early accounts predicted the rapid decline of domestic production in the two sectors as operations were transferred to overseas locations. Nevertheless, assembly work did not shrink over time, but was reorganized to provide greater flexibility and rapid response to specific markets. Thus, electronics manufacturers hire about the same number of direct production workers in the United States as do their counterparts in Asian export processing zones. Garment production, similarly, retains its priority in the United States as an employer of more workers than steel, auto manufacturing, and electronics combined.

Second, garment and electronics production have been depicted as two opposite poles in a developmental scale. The former has been characterized as a highly competitive industry with low wages and unsatisfactory working conditions that reflect an earlier stage in capitalist evolution. By contrast, electronics manufacture has been portrayed as a harbinger of post-industrialism—clean, enlightened in its management practices, and bountiful in its potential for revitalizing the economy,.

This overly polarized image of the two industries is erroneous. While there are important differences bettween the two, there are also some striking similarities. Both garment and electronics have histories characterized by rapid fluctuations in demand precipitated by seasonal cycles in the first case and by technological innovation and obsolescence in the second instance. Both sectors pay among the lowest wages to industrial workers in the United States and, as will be discussed below, they have also followed similar paths in adapting to foreign competition.

Third, and most important for the argument developed in this essay, both garment and electronics production are characterized by the presence of new working arrangements, particularly a strong shift toward subcontracting and, in varying degrees, a reliance upon industrial homework to supplement production in factories. The growing importance of both subcontracting and informal working arrangements is a vivid indicator of industrial restructuring in the

United States that parallels the process of economic internationalization.

Finally, garment and electronics hire mostly women in direct production. In southern California, between one-third and one-half of the women employed in the two sectors are native- and foreign-born Hispanics, primarily of Mexican ancestry. Many are undocumented aliens. Thus, ethnicity and gender have played important roles in the process of industrial restructuring in the United States.

The implications of these phenomena are still in question. However, they are part of the unique reality of contemporary production. My first task is to provide a contextual overview against which some of these trends may be assessed.

## *The New International Division of Labor and Deindustrialization*

Throughout the twentieth century several approaches to international development have vied for the attention of social scientists. Modernization theory, which flourished during the 1940s and 1950s, was succeeded by radical development approaches and the dependency school in the 1960s. The 1970s saw, in addition, the rise of world system analysis. All these perspectives differed in outlook and methodology, but they shared a common concern over the effects of capitalist development on third world countries. Recently that focus has expanded to address the repercussions of economic globalization in advanced industrial nations. Two bodies of literature are of particular importance in this respect. One focuses on the new international division of labor; the other addresses deindustrialization in developed countries.

According to students of the new international division of labor, the consolidation of multinational corporations after the end of World War II was followed by increased capital concentration, the explosion of computer technology, and the rise of new industrial powers such as Japan. Acute competition led investors to seek lower production costs by relocating manufacturing operations to low-wage areas of the world (Frobel, Heinrichs, and Kreye 1980; Nash and Fernández Kelly 1983; Sanderson 1985).

This process was viewed as the beginning of a new stage in capitalist development characterized by five features: (a) the unprecedented mobility of capital investments throughout the world; (b) the utilization of advanced technology to further the fragmentation of production and the deskilling of labor; (c) the centralization, in advanced industrial countries, of decision-making processes affecting production, combined with the dispersal of manufacturing to third world locations; (d) the resulting extension of proletarianization in less developed areas; and (e) the increasing reliance on women as providers of labor in direct production.

The emergence of a new international division of labor was assumed to express continuities and discontinuities vis-à-vis the past. Thus, the transfer of production to the third world was described as a prolongation of patterns of exploitation linking rich and poor countries. However, for the first time, the same process was seen as the cause of deindustrialization in advanced nations.

This theoretical model provided a new angle to study linkages between countries at various stages of development. It also offered a credible portrayal of technology as part and parcel of economic processes; it stressed the importance of the spatial reorganization of production, and assigned priority to gender as a key variable in industrial activity.

Nevertheless, many of the propositions advanced by this approach are crude oversimplifications. For example, the New International Division of Labor overstates the significance of "cheap labor" as the cause for the movement of capital. Thus, it anticipates a mechanical and continued migration of corporations to less developed areas. This has not yet occurred and it is not likely to occur in the future, partly because labor represents an increasingly smaller portion of the overall cost of production for many industries.

Moreover, the transfer of operations to overseas locations has had heterogeneous, not uniformly deleterious, effects in the third world. In some places it has resulted in higher standards of living, greater productivity per worker, and growing GNPs. In other cases it has paralleled rising inequality, dependence, and political violence. The ineluctable tendency toward proletarianization, forecasted by the proponents of the New International Division of Labor, is also cast in serious doubt when observing that export-oriented industrialization in the third world has incorporated a relatively small percentage of the labor force (ILO 1988). In Mexico, the country with the largest export-processing zone in the world, only 10 percent of all workers are employed in export-manufacturing. Moreover, export-oriented industrialization continues to flourish side by side with bloated service sectors and the so-called informal economy. Together with agriculture, these last two categories absorb most of the workers in the world (Portes and Walton, 1981).

Finally, the literature on the New International Division of Labor has not elaborated conceptual tools for understanding the movement of manufacturing operations to regions where labor is relatively costly by international standards, nor has it provided a satisfactory explanation for diverse patterns of competition among companies belonging to different industrial powers, or for the role of individual state policies in the process. Most important for the purposes of this discussion, the movement of manufacturing operations to third world locations is not leading to the total erosion of manufacturing in advanced industrial countries. It is to this question that I turn my attention now.

Since the late 1970s, an increasing number of scholars have addressed the effects of internationalization on advanced industrial centers, particularly Great Britain and the United States. (Bluestone and Harrison 1982). Their arguments have evolved along three lines: first, over the last two decades and a half there has been a series of plant closings and capital flight away from established industrial centers toward nonunionized, "right to work" states in the South and across borders to overseas locations. This is leading to the decline of basic industry and manufacturing employment.

Second, capital flight was precipitated by economic and political factors. As employers confronted demands for higher wages and improved working conditions they sought, in relocation, an avenue to expand profits and restrain unions.

Third, the growth of the service sector narrows alternatives for individual and collective improvement. The potential of services and advanced technology to recreate levels of prosperity and standards of living commensurate with those spurred by basic industry in the past is highly doubtful. On the average, employment in services provides smaller earnings and reduced job security when compared to traditional jobs in manufacturing.

As with the literature on the New International Division of Labor, writings on deindustrialization focus on broad tendencies and identify causal factors of a general character. In both cases, the growth of export-oriented operations in third world countries and the epidemic of plant closings in advanced industrial nations are explained as the result of the internal logic of capitalist accumulation.

However valid this final explanation may be, it does not aid our understanding of several important issues, such as the extent to which these phenomena are transitory or permanent, or whether they should be seen as part of a more complex restructuring of production. So far, the tendency is not toward an irreversible depletion of the industrial base in countries like the United States. It is true that millions of manufacturing jobs were lost in this nation during the 1970s, many as a result of migration to overseas locations. However, during the 1980s, manufacturing employment has actually expanded, although the rate of growth in the services has been greater.

It is also true that a large proportion of new service sector jobs in the U.S. provide alarmingly low earnings, lack of security, and few chances for promotion. Approximately two-thirds of all jobs created since the mid-1970s provide annual wages below $13,000 (Loveman and Tilly 1988). However, the service sector is highly diversified. Aggregate figures conceal a significant phenomenon: the steady growth of an affluent elite formed by professionals of all kinds, including financial experts, technological designers, and corporate administrators.

To explain these apparent contradictions, a new model is needed that incorporates some past theoretical contributions while at the same time providing an integrative view of capital and labor flows under current stages of international development. Scholars focusing on the spatial redistribution of production, international migration, and the changing nature of labor markets have made a start in this direction. Six of their findings are of special interest to my argument.

First, what is unique about the current stage of development is not the unidirectional movement of industry from the core to the periphery, but the particular circuits of labor and capital that have resulted from competition over time. Labor and capital migration across borders represent two complementary aspects of the same process. Investors choose to move operations to less developed nations for strategic reasons similar to those that lead them to employ immigrants in their home countries; the two are countervailing options. This explains why industries that have moved a sizable portion of their manufacturing operations to the third world are also likely to hire immigrants at home. Such immigrants often come from countries or regions that have experienced accelerated capitalist penetration in the past.

Second, in addition to attempting to lower production costs, investors are also seeking to redefine their relationship with labor

(Castells 1985; Sassen 1988). This redefinition includes avoiding the constraints placed upon employers by unions and government legislation. In this respect, the trend has been toward delegitimizing workers' organizations by portraying them as a dead weight stifling competitiveness and the free interaction of market forces. As a result, many unions have retrenched, made concessions in exchange for job security, and witnessed a decline in membership.

Third, technology has played a multifaceted role in this process by creating new tools for controlling production as well as labor. In some sectors (e.g., steel and auto manufacturing), automation has resulted in unprecedented levels of output with reduced workforces (Shaiken, 1985). In others (e.g., electronics) the availability of computer technology has allowed for the proliferation of small enterprises specializing in customized production for specialized markets. Yet in others (particularly the services), advanced technology is used to monitor the activities and productivity of workers. Thus, the effects of advanced technology have been uneven, creating new opportunites in certain sectors while tightening constraints upon workers, in others.

Fourth, the reallocation of capital, labor, and technological flows may be seen as elements of a more complex strategy, on the part of investors, to diversify production and gain a competitive edge. As a result, the trend is *not* toward a definitive transfer of manufacturing to less developed areas but rather, toward combining complementary or parallel operations by locating some in advanced industrial nations and others in developing countries. In general, standardized "bulk" manufacture requiring comparatively low levels of quality control has increasingly moved overseas. Production aimed at rapidly fluctuating opportunity markets or at markets with highly specialized requirements (e.g., defense) has tended to locate in advanced industrial centers.

Fifth, in advanced industrial foci, the diversification of production has been linked to the expansion of subcontracting, the proliferation of small specialized units of production, and the growth of informalization defined as operations which function outside or on the fringes of official labor and business legislation (Portes, Castells, and Benton, 1989). Such enterprises often rely upon labor provided by immigrants and refugees, many of whom are women.

Authors disagree about the magnitude and significance of the informal sector as part of the broader economy. Nevertheless, the point to stress here is that for many industries, subcontracting and informalization represent paths toward reducing costs, adjusting to markets, maintaining flexibility, and making production more predictable. In addition, informalization entails political elements of two types. On the one hand it diffuses the labor force making mobilization and militance more difficult. On the other hand, informalization represents a shift away from the state's protective and regulatory mission.

Sixth, this process of subcontracting and informalization has brought about the spatial recomposition of domestic production and changes in the class structure. Two tendencies are especially important in this respect. Large metropoles and old industrial centers affected by capital flight during the 1970s are now becoming preferred locations for corporate headquarters, financial networks, and in some cases research and development hubs. At the same time, the presence of growing numbers of professional and affluent technocrats in these neuralgic points has created demand for a myriad of labor-intensive operations in services and manufacturing where immigrants are often employed. Thus, the reorganization of industry is creating opportunities for new kinds of investment. It is also furthering class polarization and increasing inequalities in income distribution. Urban gentrification with its emphasis on boutiques, one-of-a-kind commodities, and culinary tourism has developed side by side with homelessness and poverty (Sassen 1988).

The complexity of these changes serves as an antidote for excessive generalizations. In the next two sections I examine specific processes taking place in the southern California garment and electronics industries.

### High Tech Production and Hispanic Women's Employment

One of the implications of the preceding discussion is that the present stage of capitalist development is characterized by industrial reorganization rather than decline. Another ramification is that the process of restructuring is affecting new as well as old industries. High-tech manufacturing aptly illustrates this point.

The electronics industry was at the forefront of internationalization from its inception. In the early 1960s, shortly after the invention of the integrated circuit, Fairchild, one of the oldest electronics producers, opened the first "offshore" semiconductor assembly plant in Hong Kong. By 1966, the same corporation had begun operations in South Korea. General Instruments moved micro-electronics production to Taiwan in 1964. And only a year later many other high-tech firms relocated to the U.S.-Mexican border (Siegel 1984). The next decade witnessed the incorporation of Singapore, Malaysia, and the Philippines into offshore manufacturing. During the late 1970s and 1980s, the Caribbean and even remote areas in South America have become locations for electronics production.

Despite their international proclivities, electronics firms have also provided growing employment for U.S. workers over the last two decades. Between 1967 and 1980, electronics component employment in this country grew at 2.4 percent a year. Between 1980 and 1987 there have been additional increases. At present, electronics production is the fastest growing industrial sector in the United States and it provides employment to more than one million people nationwide.

Southern California houses the largest cluster of electronics firms in the United States, having gradually superseded Santa Clara county—the so-called Silicon Valley—as a high-tech center. In 1968, there were only thirty electronics firms in Los Angeles, twelve in Orange county, and twenty in San Diego; by 1982, the numbers had risen to 579 in Los Angeles, 386 in Orange County, and 190 in San Diego. In 1987, Los Angeles contained the largest number of electronics companies in the nation while Orange county had become the fastest growing nucleus for electronics (U.S. Department of Commerce 1987).

Some large corporations in this sector employ thousands of skilled and semiskilled workers. However, the majority of electronics operations in the United States are small, and most of the work is labor intensive. For example, about 50 percent of the electronics firms in southern California hire fewer than twenty workers (U.S. Department of Commerce 1987).

What are some of the factors that explain the expansion and characteristics of electronics production in Los Angeles, Orange, and San Diego counties? Part of the answer to this question lies in broad economic processes taking place during the last two decades. In particular, the recession of the late 1970s and early 1980s led many companies to close down manufacturing facilities of various kinds and lay off thousands of workers. Between 16,000 and 30,000 jobs were directly lost to plant closing in Los Angeles in 1980. The vacuum created by these losses has been filled, to a large extent, by high-tech industries (Glassmeier, Hall, and Markusen 1985).

Firsthand interviews conducted by this author with a sample of 100 electronics firm executives in southern California indicate that, in addition to proximity to specialized markets, research and development centers, and good transportation, employers seek large, affordable labor pools and low unionization rates. Almost half of the firms in this sample responded that nearness to other similar companies (including potential customers and suppliers) was important for the selection of the firm's location. About 60 percent cited infrastructure as a key reason for their choice, and almost 40 percent acknowledged that the availability of large pools of unskilled and skilled labor was a significant factor in the selection of a site.

About 65 percent of direct production workers in these firms are women. More specifically, 44 percent of all direct production workers are Hispanic and almost 36 percent of them are female. A striking 30 to 40 percent of Hispanics working in direct production in electronics are immigrants. An additional 19 percent are foreign-born Asians, while blacks represent only 3 percent of the labor force in direct production in electronics.

The contrast between the level of incorporation of blacks and Hispanics in the electronics industry is noteworthy. Employers frankly state their preference for Hispanics, particularly the foreign-born, for direct production. These groups are perceived by employers as being more "diligent," "hard-working," and "loyal" than native-born Americans. To a large extent, the same generalizations are made about Asians.

These findings are consistent with research conducted in other industries (Cornelius, in press). The differential perceptions about Hispanics, Asians, and blacks raise questions about the relationship between capitalists and workers. Beyond discrimination, employers tend to shy away from blacks because "they tend to make too many demands," and "because they are too quick to claim rights and join unions."

The decision to locate in areas offering affordable labor is related to another cluster of characteristics, including type of production and the markets to which this production is directed. The evidence suggests that the bridge between these two aspects is customization. Customization, in turn, has been a palliative to foreign competition.

In spite of the concerns raised by unions and policymakers about the effect of imports on U.S. industrial activity, most employers in electronics do not see foreign competition as a major problem. Customized production provides a path for remaining profitable, even for small firms. More than half of all employers in southern California customize their manufactures in order to fulfill the needs of specialized markets. A large number of them cater to the defense industry.

Customization enhances competitiveness because it augments flexibility in production; yet flexibility can also be furthered through other means, such as increased subcontracting. More than half of all electronics firms in southern California subcontract with either domestic or foreign operations. Some of the overseas locations favored by electronics producers include Pacific Rim countries, such as Taiwan, Singapore, Malaysia, and the People's Republic of China and the U.S.-Mexico border.

Subcontracting is a mechanism with far-reaching implications for reshaping manufacturing processes. Few firm executives see offshore facilities in Mexico or Asia, or relations with affiliates and distributors throughout the world as a one-to-one substitute for production in the United States. Instead, offshore plants are viewed as part of a broader strategy of adaptation to fluctuating economic conditions. One company, for example, closed its front-edge semiconductor manufacturing operation in San Diego county in 1986 in order to become the American distributing arm of a subcontracted firm in the People's Republic of China. It also opened a distributing office in Singapore in order to channel part of the production of the Chinese operation into the Asian market. Finally, the same firm participated in arrangements that made it possible for a company in Escondido (also in San Diego county) to develop a custom-made piece of sophisticated equipment to be used in the Chinese operation. Twenty-five percent of the assembly workers in the Escondido plant are Hispanic.

This example captures a fact which is often neglected by the literature on the internationalization of production. Often, jobs lost in the United States as a result of plant closings are not the same as those that emerge in third world countries. Relocation can entail job redefinition through the introduction of new technology or further transformation of the labor process. Thus, while it is true that many U.S. jobs have migrated to overseas locations, they have also metamorphosed in their flight.

Other companies choose to combine foreign and domestic operations in order to maximize the probability of survival when economic conditions change. One manager stated: "Frankly, we opened our plant in Germany to have the flexibility; when the dollar gets more expensive—and it will—we'll transfer most of our direct production there. Right now it's cheaper to produce in California." Therefore, offshore operations and subcontracting in general are not favored only as a means to reduce production costs, but, perhaps primarily, as a way to ensure versatility, adapt to adverse conditions, and penetrate new markets.

For similar reasons, electronics companies display a surprising reliance on the intermittent use of homeworkers to adjust to fluctuations in demand. Homeworkers are utilized by over 10 percent of companies, although in some sub-areas this practice is particularly widespread. For example, in Kearny Mesa (San Diego county), an area characterized by a high concentration of electronics producers, up to 75 percent of companies make regular or periodic use of homeworkers.

Homework in electronics is legal in southern California. However, in the majority of cases, neither employers nor employees comply with the official requirement for certification and hour and wage records. Homework assembly and other subcontracted operations tend to fall outside the margins of legality. However, they also provide an opportunity for entrepreneurship and employment on the part of refugees, immigrants, and ethnic minorities. At least 30 percent of small electronics firms in southern California are owned or managed by South East Asian refugees and Hispanics. The same groups predominate among their workers (U.S. Department of Commerce 1987).

Small electronics firms are cited for violations of wage and hour regulations as frequently as garment factories. Employees are often paid in cash for overtime, and at regular rates instead of the time-and-a-half wages required by law. When demand peaks, employees in small electronics firms are allowed to take batches of components to their own homes, where they are processed at piece rates sometimes as low as 7 cents per unit. Unpaid family members often participate in home assembly. While the extension of homework and other forms of informal working arrangements in electronics are difficult to measure, observers characterize them as common phenomena at the lower end of the industrial hierarchy.

Homework in electronics and the proliferation of small enterprises belie, to some extent, the glittering public image of the industry but they also express the complexity of strategies used by firms to remain competitive. In fact, the electronics industry is made up of many layers. Some of these layers, including those formed by homeworkers, are concealed from aggregate figures and include manners of production which seem more appropriate in older than in newer industries.

Finally, the fact that the electronics industry is largely an employer of women underscores the importance of gender as a factor involved in the structuring of production. In this respect, electronics reflects national trends characterized by the unprecedented incorporation of married and unmarried females into the labor force.

The reasons behind the widespread hiring of women in electronics firms throughout the world have been studied since the mid-1970s (Fernández Kelly 1983). Most industrial promoters, government officials, and researchers agree that the jobs offered by that industry require keen eyesight and manual dexterity; characteristics commonly associated with women. However, a focus on them alone does not explain the low wages associated with women's employment, or the wage differentials that have historically distinguished men's from women's jobs. More likely, women are hired primarily because they can be easily replaced, paid comparatively low wages, and kept at bay with respect to wage demands and unionization drives. This is especially true for minority and immigrant women (Fernández Kelly and García 1988).

One of the conclusions that can be drawn from this analysis is that in its hiring practices, wage levels, and reliance on subcontracting, the electronics industry bears some similarities to garment manufacture. These similarities are not a coincidence. Rather, they are outcomes of similar constraints and alternatives faced by employers trying to retain a competitive position in the domestic and international markets.

## Garment Production and Informalization

The garment industry has been described as a declining sector which suffered grave losses when production was mainly transferred to Asia, the U.S.-Mexico border, and the Caribbean. However, this is a misleading picture. Garment production in general, and particularly in Los Angeles county, has expanded in the last decade thanks in large part to the existence of mechanisms that perpetuate the use of informal shops and homework. Nationwide, the garment industry includes approximately 24,000 firms employing about 2,000,000 people, with a $12 billion annual direct payroll. In addition, this sector indirectly employs 200,000 farmers involved in cotton and wool processing. Thus, the apparel industry is larger than the automotive, steel, and electronics industries combined, and, despite the setbacks of the last two decades, it continues to display notable resilience in the United States (International Ladies Garment Workers Union 1985).

Most garments sold in this country are manufactured domestically, with Los Angeles county second only to New York in apparel production. Approximately 46,219 women are employed as "textile, apparel, and furnishing machines operators" in that area. Almost 91 percent of these are minorities with 72 percent being Hispanic. Equivalent data for New York and Miami (the other areas with the fastest growing Hispanic populations) indicate similar trends in employment (U.S. Department of Commerce 1987).

The conclusion that restructuring rather than decline has characterized the recent history of the garment industry in southern California is confirmed by data showing that the total number of workers in the Los Angeles apparel industry rose from 51,719 in 1965 to 83,424 in 1982. The number of firms expanded and shrunk at different points during the same period (U.S. Department of Commerce 1982).

The survival of the garment industry is due to the proliferation of small firms since the mid-1970s. Of slightly more than three thousand registered apparel and textile manufacturers in Los Angeles county in 1986, 68 percent employed fewer than twenty workers with the majority of these hiring between one and four people. By contrast, there has been a notable reduction in the number of plants with between 100 and 499 employees. Operations with larger work forces have virtually disappeared.

These findings suggest that it is the lower stratum of garment production, characterized by the existence of small licensed or unlicensed garment shops, that is expanding. These are establishments where production is relatively unstable, where a large number of undocumented immigrant workers are found, and where wage and labor code infractions are frequent.

In other words, the expansion of informal operations within garment manufacture explains the resilience of the industry over the last decade. Interviews conducted by this author with government officials in agencies such as the Employment Development Department of Industrial Relations and the Wage and Hour Division of the U.S. Department of Labor further substantiate the impression that homework and other types of unregulated assembly in the garment industry have increased in the last five years.

The growth in the number of small garment operations must be seen as a symptom of deeper transformations affecting production. Informalization should not be regarded as a backward sector of the economy but as part and parcel of the adjustments caused by the most recent stage of capitalist development. First, there has been a fragmentation within the apparel industry characterized by the movement of manufacturers away from direct assembly. This has entailed a reduction in the number of vertically integrated firms and an increase in decentralization of the labor process. Large firms, which originally assembled their own products, are now mainly involved in the purchase of basic materials, design, cutting, and marketing. Sewing is invariably subcontracted out.

Second, many manufacturers combine domestic and international subcontracting, thus gaining access to different segments of the market. For example, the same firms may subcontract its "long-lead-time" standardized production to firms located in Asian export processing zones, while using the services of small domestic companies to penetrate opportunity markets demanding novelty products.

From the point of view of manufacturers, subcontracting offers the advantage of diversifying risks while allowing control over the volume of output. In addition, subcontracting reduces the costs of production by diffusing the need to maintain stable labor forces. Finally, the same process reduces the potential for unionization.

Third, the growth of subcontracting has accentuated the competitive features of the garment industry by allowing the entry of a growing number of firms, many of whom are short-lived and many of which operate outside government regulation. The fragmentation of garment production has created the need for quick adaptation, speed in production, and versatility on the part of subcontractors. This, in turn, has led to renewed violations of state and federal regulations.

Many small firms cannot survive the fluctuations of the market by operating legally, nor can they bear the costs accompanying state control. Thus, they tend to evade tax and licensing expenses. They are also likely to hire workers at peak seasons and then dismiss them when contracts end or demand for a particular product decreases. Positions in these shops are the lowest paying among all industrial jobs in the United States and offer few benefits. An example of this type of operation is home assembly, which in Los Angeles county accounts for up to one third of all garments manufactured.

Fourth, the expansion of subcontracting and homework has opened new opportunities for small businesses and created new categories of intermediaries. Start-up costs in the garment industry have always been comparatively low. Thus investment in this sector has historically attracted ethnic and immigrant entrepreneurs. About 40 percent of small garment manufacturers in southern California are Hispanic. Most of them are U.S.-born citizens with about one-third of them being foreign-born. Many of these small-business persons are women.

Finally, and somewhat paradoxically, the reorganization of garment production has had a positive impact upon Hispanic women's chances of becoming small independent subcontractors. Two mechanisms have been identified in this respect. First, the trend toward decentralization of the labor process and the attempt to lower production costs have led many employers to encourage women workers to open their own firms. Employers often lease out idle machinery to these women while providing them with some of the orders they obtain from larger manufacturers. Thus, a relatively large employer may sponsor the entrepreneurial activities of current and former employees who then become the owners of garment operations in leased commercial units located near the main firm. Each of these minuscule enterprises hires a few women, who tend to be undocumented Mexican immigrants. Work in these shops is irregular, production quotas vary significantly, and operatives are paid on a piece-rate basis.

These operations are among the most vulnerable in the entire subcontracting chain. Indeed, they can hardly be considered independent operations insofar as the women who manage them and their workers are directly dependent upon the parent firm. On the other hand, from the point of view of the main investor, sponsoring spin-off operations has distinct advantages; by encouraging employees to become independent subcontractors, they can discharge the costs associated with hiring and paying of benefits to workers, which would otherwise be their responsibility.

A second mechanism leading women to become entrepreneurs stems from broader contingencies and the characteristics of the family units to which they belong. For example, women with experience in the garment industry are often led to become managers or owners of small operations by a desire to maintain the living standards of their households. A typical illustration is that of two young undocumented immigrants from Mexico who received sewing equipment as a gift from a former employer retiring from business. As single mothers living together, these two women pooled their savings and started a small enterprise in Los Angeles.

The rationale behind Hispanic women's decisions to become entrepreneurs is not very different from the one that leads them to become involved in home assembly. In both cases, women aim at reconciling home-care responsibilities with financial need. However, the contradictions stemming from their involvement in non-remunerated and wage labor often place them at a disadvantage in terms of competitiveness and leverage vis-à-vis large contractors. Because these small operations function outside or on the fringes of legality, they are an easy target for periodic inspections, citations, and penalties assessed by state officials. Nonetheless, the measure of independence provided by entrepreneurial activity is cherished by these women. It may be one of the ironic consequences of industrial restructuring that niches are being created for the expression of women's potential as small-business persons.

### Conclusions

The argument developed in these pages offers an opportunity to consider several paths for future research and theoretical enhancement. First, this essay is based on the assumption that development is a key concept for understanding economic and political processes in advanced industrial countries as well as in the third world. Until recently, the literature on development overwhelmingly focused on the latter, perpetuating, as a result, false dichotomies that are difficult to sustain in the age of internationalization.

Second, the expansion of the global economy is giving rise to adaptive strategies that are more complex and internally diverse than often acknowledged by writings on the subject. Internationalization has not caused the permanent deindustrialization of developed countries and, with few exceptions, it has not transformed entire third world nations into export-oriented beachheads. Instead, there has been a process of industrial restructuring at both ends of the geopolitical spectrum, a transformation of the conditions for investment in various parts of the world, and a reorganization of the factors leading to class mobilization on the part of workers.

Finally, these processes are made doubly complex by the increasing targeting of women, immigrants, and refugees as providers of labor both in manufacturing and service sectors. The example of garment and electronics manufacturing shows that the outcome of these practices is highly contradictory. On one hand, the internationalization of production has diminished the potential of traditional workers' organizations. On the other hand, new class configurations and entrepreneurial options are emerging for vulnerable sectors of the working class. The two phenomena should force us to relinquish facile generalizations in favor of a more complex understanding of contemporary political reality.

## *Note*

This essay includes preliminary findings obtained as part of *A Collaborative Study of Hispanic Women in Garment and Electronics Industries* sponsored by the Ford and Tinker Foundations between 1984 and 1988. Special thanks are due to Dr. Bill Díaz for his continued encouragement and to Julia Sensenbrenner for her valuable suggestions.

## *References*

Bluestone, Barry and Bennett Harrison. 1982. *The Deindustrialization of America.* New York: Basic Books.

Castells, Manuel. 1985. *New Technologies, World Development, and Structural Transformation: The Trends and the Debate.* Report Prepared for the Committee for a Just World Peace, Abbaye de Royaumont Ile-de-France.

Cornelius, Wayne A., ed. In Press. *The Changing Role of Mexican Immigrants in the U.S. Economy.* La Jolla, CA: Center for U.S.-Mexican Studies, University of California, San Diego.

Fernández Kelly, M. Patricia. 1983. *For We Are Sold, I and My People: Women and Industry in Mexico's Frontier.* Albany: State University of New York Press.

———— and Anna M. Garcia. 1988. "Economic Restructuring in the United States: Hispanic Women in the Garment and Electronics Industries." In Gutek et al., eds. *Women and Work.*

Frobel, Folker, Jurgen Heinrichs, and Otto Kreye. 1980. *The New International Division of Labor.* New York: Cambridge University Press.

Glassmeier, A., P. Hall, and Anne Markusen. 1985. "Recent Evidence on High-Technology Industries' Spatial Tendencies: A Preliminary Investigation," Working Paper No. 417, Berkeley: University of California, Institute of Urban and Regional Development.

Gutek, Barbara, Ann H. Stromberg, and Laurie Larwood, eds. 1988. *Women and Work, An Annual Review, Volume 3*. New York: Sage Publications.

International Labour Organisation. 1988. *Economic and Social Effects of Multinational Enterprises in Export Processing Zones*. Geneva: ILO.

International Ladies Garment Workers' Union, Research Department. 1985. *Conditions in the Women's Garment Industry*. New York.

Loveman, Gary W., and Chris Tilly. 1988. "Good Jobs or Bad Jobs: What Does the U.S. Evidence Say?" Labour Market Analysis and Employment Planning Working Paper No. 22. International Labour Organization.

Nash, June, and M. Patricia Fernández Kelly, eds. 1983. *Women, Men, and the International Division of Labor*. Albany: State University of New York Press.

Portes, Alejandro, Manuel Castells, and Lauren Benton. 1989. *The Informal Economy: Studies in Advanced and Less Developed Countries*. Baltimore, MD: The Johns Hopkins University Press.

———— and John Walton. 1981. *Labor, Class, and the International System*. New York: Academic Press.

Sanderson, Steven. 1985. *The Americas in the New International Division of Labor*. New York: Holmes and Meier.

Sassen, Saskia. 1988. *The Mobility of Labor and Capital*. New York: Cambridge University Press.

Shaiken, Harley. 1985. *Work Transformed*. New York: Holt, Rinehart, and Winston.

Siegel, Leni. 1984. "Delicate Bonds: The Semiconductor Industry," Mountain View, CA: Pacific Studies Center.

U.S. Department of Commerce, Bureau of the Census. 1982. *County Business Patterns.*, Washington D.C.: Government Printing Office.

————. 1987. *County Business Patterns*. Washington D.C.: Government Printing Office.

# Divisions of Labor in Global Manufacturing: The Case of the Automobile Industry

## *Richard Child Hill*

According to theorists of the new international division of labor, sometimes also called "global Fordism," the division of labor in manufacturing is (1) increasingly subdivided into a number of partial operations which are (2) located at different industrial sites throughout the world according to (3) the most profitable combination of labor, capital, government subsidies, and transportation costs and (4) centrally coordinated through a headquarter's global strategy (Frobel, Heinrichs, and Kreye 1980).

In this view, the global factory emerges from a profit logic based upon economies of scale achieved through the mass production of standardized commodities by an increasingly deskilled workforce. Productivity increases are generated by annexing workers to single, routine operations. Labor control derives from management monopoly over knowledge of the production process, and wage costs are reduced by simplifying labor and pitting workers in different localities against one another. Today's "new" international division of labor—the unequal allocation of world labor and its products among various countries—is simply the extension of national "Fordist" regimes of "intensive" accumulation onto a global plane (Lipietz 1987).[1]

But is there so clear and obvious a capital logic which predicts the future development of industrial production on a world scale? The view taken here is that there is no one global trajectory of industrial transformation today. Over the past two decades Japanese corporations have come to organize the world's most competitive manufacturing systems on the basis of a logic that differs fundamentally from global Fordism. The challenge from Japan has forced enterprises, unions, and governments in Western capitalist societies to confront anew their own methods of industrial organization and the mechanisms through which production systems become mainsprings for economic development and change. Yet there is still considerable confusion over which changes should be encouraged and which resisted and little general agreement on what is at stake for whom.

This essay first reviews alternative strategies for organizing the international division of labor in auto manufacturing and shows how competitive pressures are leading transnational corporations to reorganize their industrial operations in ways that combine past alternatives into new global structures. It then discusses how the changing structure of global production poses development and employment issues for workers and communities in the United States and Japan.

## *Transnational Production Strategies*

Students of transnational corporations frequently draw a distinction between horizontal and vertical strategies for organizing international production (Porter 1986; Gilpin 1987: ch. 6). Corporations taking a horizontal, "company town" approach organize spatially concentrated and integrated manufacturing complexes at strategic regional points around the globe. As discussed in detail below, Japanese car manufacturers have excelled at organizing highly efficient, horizontally integrated, export-oriented manufacturing complexes. U.S. companies, on the other hand, have emphasized vertical production strategies. The vertical, "global factory" strategy divides the manufacturing process into multiple pieces, spreads the pieces over many regional locales, and coordinates relationships among the pieces from specialized centers of control.

Based upon the experience of England, the United States, and a few Western European nations, theorists of the new international division of labor have assumed that global factories emerge out of company towns in fixed temporal sequences determined economically by product and profit cycles (see, e.g., Vernon 1973; Markusen 1985). In this section I show that both competitive strategies are amply demonstratable in the current practices of transnational companies; the two strategies are therefore better viewed as alternative ways of organizing the division of labor in modern manufacturing. However, today's conditions of international economic competition and political rivalry are pressuring companies to adopt both production strategies. So I conclude this section by showing how transnational corporations are fitting the global factory and company town models, along with a third, cross penetration strategy, into a combined organizational pattern that may best characterize the future of global manufacturing.

## *The Global Factory*

The world car, built out of standarized parts and designed for production in all the world's markets, is the best single illustration of the "new" international division of labor in the world motor industry. Global sourcing of auto parts, the use of export platforms in third world countries to achieve price competitiveness in first world markets, also evidences a global factory division of labor.

Volkswagen illustrates a transnational auto company visibly committed to the world car, global factory concept. In a July 1987 interview for the trade journal *Automotive News,* VW-USA's vice-president for purchasing/logistics, Robert B. Chrysler, explained his company's global strategy: "What VW is truly striving for is a world car. We've talked about it for years and to do it, all of your designs have to be compatible worldwide. So we've gone back to a true German design."

What is VW's definition of a world car? According to Chrysler, "definitions vary" but at his company "we are looking at a basic design vehicle in many cases with even the same assembly sequence, where you could take a door out of the German press shop and put it on a VW made in the United States, Brazil, Mexico, or Brussels. The same would be true with any component parts. The point is to optimize our engineering resources and eliminate duplication around the world."

In its move toward the world car, VW has restructured its production and material control functions, historically attached to manufacturing, into a new area called purchasing/logistics. The aim, Chrysler explained, is to create a "unified posture on our supply base. What we try to do in sourcing is to go where VW has a manufacturing presence—where the company knows the suppliers and has educated them as to what VW wants. So we buy from Brazil because VW is a prominent car manufacturer there and we buy from Mexico because of VW's position there." At each of its major manufacturing facilities, VW puts together an international purchasing group to look into locally sourced components that can profitably be shipped to any part of the world where VW has a plant.[2]

In 1978, when VW-USA commenced production of the Rabbit at the Westmoreland, Pennsylvania, assembly plant, about two-thirds of the car's design was unique to the U.S. market and the company sourced heavily from U.S.-based suppliers. In 1984 VW began producing the Golf at the same Westmoreland plant, but by then it had reduced the number of U.S.-based suppliers from 650 to 250. Except for the special bumper systems and emissions controls required by U.S. law, the U.S. Golf was identical in design to the one VW was manufacturing in West Germany. Three years later, VW closed the Westmoreland plant entirely, choosing instead to rely on imports of finished vehicles from its subsidiary in Mexico.

## The Company Town

The company town model of the international division of labor has been theorized under the rubric of "flexible specialization" by Michael Piore and Charles Sabel (1984). Linked to a pre-Fordist craft heritage, flexible specialization is a post-Fordist model of industrial development which combines the advantages of craft flexibility with the most advanced information processing and telecommunication technology. Companies organized into flexible production systems possess the capacity to respond to economic problems and market uncertainties by continually reshaping productive processes through the rearrangement of component activities.

In striking contrast to the global factory, the company town production strategy concentrates labor and integrates manufacturing operations at points of final assembly. Company town profit logic is based upon innovations and efficiencies achieved through spatial agglomeration, flexible specialization, and just-in-time delivery logistics (Cusumano 1988). Productivity and savings are enhanced through just-in-time synchronization of delivery to the assembly line. Inventories, waste, plant size, and energy costs are considerably reduced. Corporate welfare programs and an "enterprise as community" ideology dampen labor strife. Rising wage costs are countered by reducing labor content through automated production methods and by a tiered wage system among regional suppliers based upon firm size and value added to the final product (Luria 1986).[3]

In one of the most comprehensive studies of the automobile industry to date, Altschuler et. al. (1984) conclude that the company town division of labor best mirrors the future of the world motor industry. Rejecting the world car model of the international division of labor, they argue instead:

> The new production technologies mean that the shift to low wage locations will not occur on the scale once expected. The markets of the developed countries are demanding precise, high quality production. Flexible manufacturing in combination with the redesign of products to gain its full benefits can provide this while sharply increasing labor productivity. These innovations have shifted the focus of thought about the future geography of production location from the less developed countries to the concentrated production of most components near the point of final assembly in the developed countries (1984; 249).

Toyota Motor Corporation, arguably the world's most successful auto manufacturer, has advanced the company town concept the farthest. Over 80 percent of Toyota's worldwide production capacity is concentrated in one satellite community, Toyota City, located on the periphery of Nagoya, Japan. As noted below, a key to Toyota's competitive success is the way the company has spatially organized and synchronized its many-layered production activities into a finely tuned regional system. Supportive local industrial policies also enabled Toyota Motor Corporation to strategically concentrate its headquarters, major production facilities, principal suppliers, and subcontractors in Toyota City and surrounding Aihi Prefecture. Among Toyota's 957 designated "major suppliers," 525 (55 percent) are headquartered within Aichi Prefecture.

On the model of welfare capitalism, social consumption in Toyota City is largely a Toyota Motor Corporation responsibility; so much so that Toyota has virtually curled a corporate finger around every facet of its employees' daily existence: jobs, housing, transportation, education, medical care, insurance, and leisure activities fall within the company's grasp.

## The Triad

The company town model of the international division of labor emphasizes the agglomeration of flexibly organized companies into integrated "manufacturing communities" (Friedman 1988). The global factory model emphasizes worldwide sourcing of standardized components for global mass production, increasingly through third world export enclaves. Neither model, however, sufficiently emphasizes another salient feature of global industrial organization:

*cross penetration* among producers in the advanced industrial regions of Western Europe, Japan, and North America. Cross penetration, the trajectory taken by most foreign direct manufacturing investment, is one mechanism underpinning the restructuring of global manufacturing today.

According to Kenichi Ohmae (1985), the competitive logic driving cross penetration among the advanced industrial nations is threefold. It is *political:* protectionist policies by governments in advanced industrial countries impel foreign direct investment inside each other's borders. It is *technological:* if companies wish to remain competitive in an era of rapid technological change, they must share costly research and development outlays and locate near sources of innovation for rapid adoption. It is *commercial:* the combined buying power of the "triad"—North America, Western Europe, and Japan—is required to realize economies of scale. The cultural expertise of a local partner also must be cultivated if a company is to respond effectively to national peculiarities in tastes and consumption habits. According to this conception of international manufacturing, to be a successful global competitor, every transnational corporation must be an "insider" in each triad region.

Cross penetration in the world motor industry is strikingly manifested in the massive "transplanting" of Japanese car production into North America. Eight Japanese car companies have put nearly $5 billion into the construction of ten assembly plants in the United States and Canada. By 1989, these Japanese transplants will be capable of producing 2.16 million cars and light trucks inside the North American market. Perhaps the most spectucular case of cross penetration in the world motor industry is the $500 million joint venture between General Motors and Toyota Motor Corporation to produce 250,000 subcompact cars annually in Fremont, California.

Japan's successful auto development strategy—protecting its domestic market against imports while exporting finished vehicles from a highly efficient, home-based manufacturing system—eventually led to many restrictive actions against its exports. To protect its overseas markets, Toyota, along with other Japanese automakers, found it necessary to invest directly in assembly and manufacturing facilities abroad. Toyota's investment in the Fremont venture was a good way to establish manufacturing operations in the United States at minimum cost. It was also an opportunity for a nationally organized producer to learn more about global strategy from the world's largest transnational auto manufacturer.

For General Motors, three strategic considerations were particularly important: product development, manufacturing expertise, and labor relations. GM wanted to build a profitable small car for the U.S. market and sought assistance from Toyota in small car design and "state of the art technology." GM also wanted to learn the Toyota production system first hand and Fremont gave it the opportunity to experiment with more flexible modes of organizing the labor process.

## Trilateralism

Are the global factory, the company town, and the triad tendencies in the international division of labor best viewed as singular, essentially separate corporate responses to specific competitive and political pressures or are they better viewed as interdependent parts of a progressively more coherent, overall global production strategy?

Kenichi Ohmae, extending the triad concept to encompass less developed regions of the world, offers one image of a global production strategy that combines all three models. He notes that, apart from their own interlinkages within the triad, each triad member has special market ties to a specific developing region. "Latin America is the United States' biggest trading partner except for Japan and Europe and vice versa. Southeast Asia is Japan's biggest trading partner except for the United States and Europe, and vice versa. Africa is the European Community's biggest trading partner except for Japan and the United States." Therefore, "the triad is [actually] four headed. Each . . . player participates in the three triad regions, plus one developing region to make four: Japan tapping Asia, the Europeans making use of traditional links in Africa and the Middle East; America selling to her continental neighbors" (1985: 122).

To put Ohmae's multidimensional conception of global organization in proper political perspective, I will call it the *trilateral* model of the international division of labor. In production-system terminology (discussed below), the trilateral model is based upon an intersecting, tri-regionally organized, tiered production system. The upper, higher value tiers of the production system are organized in concentrated, company town complexes in the wealthy triad core nations according to flexible specialization, just-in-time logistics, and corporate welfare principles. The lower value, middle-to-bottom tiers of the production system as well as the mass production of lower priced, standardized vehicles are spread among NICs and poorer nations in the periphery of each triad power according to a regional sourcing strategy.[4] Location is principally in Latin America for the North American transnational firms; in East and Southeast Asia for the Japanese multinationals; and in Africa and the Middle East for Western European global companies. Considerable cross penetration continues among the triad core powers.[5]

Today's most important variation on the trilateral theme is the growing interpenetration among North American and Japanese firms—known in Japan as the "Nichibei economy"—and the collaboration between Nichibei companies and governments in Asian and South American NICs to forge a transnational division of labor along the Pacific rim—the world's most dynamic economic region. The Nichibei-Pacific rim economy intertwines North American and Japanese poles of the triad into a transnational production system with its own specific characteristics.

Japanese car manufacturers—in order to keep their domestic and foreign plants profitable under conditions of the appreciated yen, in order to bypass U.S. export restrictions, and in order to protect against too large a U.S. trade imbalance—are now transfering lower value parts manufacturing and assembly operations to low-cost suppliers in Korea, Taiwan, Mexico, and other nations along the Pacific rim. The emerging Pacific rim division of labor is organized through a complicated set of joint production and ownership arrangements among Japanese, U.S., and NIC companies. Parts produced in Pacific rim NICs will be sent to assembly transplants in North America and to domestic operations in Japan.

The Ford/Mazda alliance provides a case study of the Nichibei–Pacific rim phenomenon. Ford owns 25 percent of Mazda (Japan's third largest car manufacturer) and in 1987 the two companies announced plans to standardize major parts of their new models in Japan, the United States, and Europe. They are also reorganizing their parts manufacturing bases in South Korea and Taiwan to ensure low-cost supply. By allying in this global factory fashion, Ford and Mazda expect to (1) reduce production costs without sacrificing each car model's design and performance; (2) stimulate technological improvements; and (3) gain the capacity to quickly shift parts supply bases in response to currency movements and trade barriers. At the same time, the alliance gives Ford access to Mazda's design and advanced flexible system production capabilities while allowing Mazda improved access to international markets for its parts and technology through Ford's worldwide distribution network.

Ford and Mazda are collaborating with Kia Motors in South Korea—Ford owns 10 percent and Mazda owns 8 percent of Kia—to manufacture a Mazda designed Festiva mini-car for export. Lio Ho, Ford's subsidiary in Taiwan, is manufacturing Mazda's GLC-based Tracer for export to Canada. Ford's Australian subsidiary is manufacturing a sporty derivative of Mazda's Tracer for export. Ford's subsidiary in Mexico is manufacturing Mazda designed engines for export to the United States and Canada. And in the United States, Mazda is manufacturing, according to flexible specialization principles, the compact MX6 and the Ford-designed Probe for the U.S. market and for export to Japan.

## Comparing Transnational Production Systems

This section will fill in the general, "macro" comparison of global divisions of labor in auto manufacturing rendered above with a more fine grained, historically specific "micro" comparison of Japanese and U.S. methods of organizing auto production. Comparisons will emphasize social and spatial dimensions of the two production systems: tiered specialization, social and spatial control, stratification, and uneven development. These dimensions of a production chain are variables which, by cohering in various configurations, form the alternative transnational production strategies surveyed above.

Divisions of labor in manufacturing occur within industrial production systems. Production system is a concept for viewing how labor processes and economic exchanges among firms are socially organized over space. A production system is a collection of operating units linked by technology and organization into the manufacture of final products. Firms become linked into production systems as they develop, manufacture, and market specific commodities. In the motor industry, production systems involve thousands of firms (including parents, subsidiaries, and subcontractors). These firms specialize in the production of a wider or more narrow range of parts (some 15,000 go into a car) or in a stage of the production process (for example, dashboard subassembly). Firms, ranging in size from enormous transnational companies to family workshops, are interlinked in value-added hierarchies which function over regional, national, and international space with varying degrees of logistical precision and efficiency.

Much has been written about differences between Japanese and

U.S. approaches to organizing manufacturing. Western analysts tend to highlight Japan's paternalistic social relations inside the large firm and corporatist political relationships among Japanese businesses and the state. But there is another distinctive feature to Japanese industrial organization: the way Japan's firms intertwine into industrial production systems through elaborate social and spatial divisions of labor. In fact, Japanese class and business relations look quite different when viewed from the angle of an industrial production system than when viewed from the interior of the big corporation.

During the 1950s and 1960s, Japanese manufacturing volume and output per model were too low to compete against U.S. mass production techniques. With Toyota in the lead, Japanese car manufacturers responded to U.S. global industrial hegemony by constructing a different kind of production system. The Japanese became masters at small-batch production—at manufacturing a variety of high-quality models at low volumes. U.S. mass production methods lowered costs by minimizing product diversity and maximizing economies of scale. Japanese production innovations, on the other hand, improved quality and productivity through greater flexibility in the deployment of equipment and labor, lower in-process inventories, and higher turnover rates. Over time, the higher product quality and productivity generated by Japanese flexible manufacturing methods translated into formidable global competitive power. By the early 1980s, Toyota and Nissan, insignificant companies in the 1950s, had become the world's second and third largest car makers (Cusumano 1985).

## Social Divisions of Labor

The production system of any one automaker includes assembly plants, other units operated by the automaker and its subsidiaries, suppliers of basic materials, subcontractors directly supplying sub-assemblies, parts, dies, engineering services, and a myriad of small and medium-sized forms indirectly involved in the production process through the supply of parts and services to the automakers' direct subcontractors. Production systems can be divided into production layers (as they are called in Japan) or tiers (as they tend to be called in the United States), and these interlinked layers make up a production chain among firms. Production layers are a major feature of all production systems that are incorporated into the final vehicle.

*Hierarchy.* U.S. parent automakers, in comparison to the Japanese, are more vertically integrated. For example, until recently General Motors internalized about 70 percent of the value of the auto production process in contrast to about 30 percent for Toyota. And since U.S. automakers had direct transactions with many more suppliers than did their Japanese corporate counterparts, there were fewer layers in the auto production systems organized by U.S. transnationals. But all this is changing. In response to Japanese competition, U.S. auto manufacturers are reducing vertical integration by outsourcing more components to subcontractors. Modular subassemblies, organized by independent suppliers, are forming tiers in a new production pryamid modeled explicitly on the Japanese system.

*Stratification.* A study by Japan's Ministry of International Trade and Industry (MITI) estimates that the average Japanese auto maker's production system comprises 171 first layer, 4,700 second layer, and 31,600 third layer subcontractors. Of the 13,430 auto parts makers in Japan in 1978, 80 percent employed less than twenty workers; almost one-third employed one to three workers (Sheard 1983; 53). Thus, Japan's auto production chain interlinks the most highly automated engine and final vehicle assembly plants in the world with crowded backyard workshops where families turn out small stampings on foot presses ten hours a day, six or seven days a week.

In the U.S. auto industry the pressure of international competition has led to an attack on traditional labor/management pattern-bargaining agreements. Pattern bargaining, which arose in the United States after World War II, calls for similar wage and benefit levels for comparably situated companies in an industry and often standard pay and benefits packages for all plants of the same company. In Japan, where there is less vertical integration and labor costs are steeply tiered, 25 percent of autoworkers get the premium, first-tier rate while 75 percent get a rate that is 20 to 70 percent lower. In the United States, in contrast, a much higher percentage of the value of a car is produced in companies paying premium wage rates.

*Social control.* Subcontractors in Japan's auto production system must accept strict conditions and controls as to price, quality, delivery, and transaction regulations. Toyota and Nissan, for example, have created a high degree of control over first-layer subcontractors. Many have been converted into partial subsidiaries. Parts suppliers thus become members of Toyota's or Nissan's "family" or "group" of subcontractors. For their part, subcontractors seek adoption by a

Toyota or Nissan parent to secure the benefits that go with stable markets, access to investment funds, stable supplies of good quality raw materials, technical and managerial guidance in plant layout, and so on.

It would be quite fallacious to view firms in Japan's auto production system as if they were independent actors engaging in market exchange relations with a major automaker. Rather it makes more sense to view each firm as a cog in a total production system organized around a transnational parent company. And that characterization increasingly applies to U.S. auto companies, too, as they decrease market coordination (by reducing short-term supplier contracts based upon competitive bidding) and bureaucratic control (by reducing vertical integration) in favor of more stable, long-term subcontracting relationships with their higher value parts suppliers.

## Spatial Divisions of Labor

Spatial organization and logistical coordination are also critical features of industrial production systems. What distinguishes Japan's auto production system in spatial terms is the way car manufacturers have adapted and amplified the classical Ford conveyor-belt system of factory production within plants to a regional production system tying together assembly plants and suppliers.

*Spatial control.* In Japanese auto production, spatial location and logistical coordination amount to systems of territorial control. Kanban, Japan's just-in-time delivery system, extends the design of space within the factory to the design of space between factories. Parent companies and their subcontractors are interconnected through a finely synchronized flow of parts carried by delivery trucks across regional transportation networks.

The *kanban* method originated with Toyota but now all automakers and most other major industrial companies use it. Kanban refers to a card that is attached to each pallet of parts that circulates between a subcontractor and automaker's plants. When an assembly worker takes the first part from a pallet, the card signals to the subcontractor to produce another pallet to replace the one being used. By requiring subcontractors to make frequent deliveries in small batches, kanban fosters a continuously self-adjusting order system. Although separated by physical space, the work rhythm of the subcontractor's production line is regulated by the auto assembler's line. The subcontractor, in effect, becomes a spatial extension of the parent. Subcontractors are also given a delivery schedule with instructions on amount and frequency of delivery. The order system plus the delivery schedule shift the responsibility and cost for maintaining a buffer level of stocks on to the subcontractor; and the reduction of overhead adds to the parent company's profits.

*Spatial Concentration.* Kanban operates between lower layers of the production system but it is most highly developed between automakers and their first-tier subcontractors. Kanban integrates the production lines of subcontractors with the parent firm and it promotes spatial concentration as subcontractors locate near the parent. Spatial proximity to the parent especially characterizes subcontractors who supply a large percent of their output to a specific automaker, who supply high-value components, or who supply bulky items. Just-in-time delivery in small batches requires close contact between parent and subcontractor; and spatial proximity further reduces transportation costs, minimizes possible disruption or delay in delivery, and allows for quick changes in delivery schedules. In general, the higher up the production chain, the more frequent the delivery, and the closer the proximity to the parent company.

*Uneven Development.* Japan's auto production system has traditionally concentrated in a few core urban-industrial areas in the sprawling Tokaido megalopolis: Tokyo, Yokohama, Nagoya, and to a lesser extent, Osaka. The production systems of individual Japanese automakers are even more locationally specific. The Toyota production system centers in Toyota City, on the periphery of Nagoya, and it is probably the most spatially concentrated in the world. Nissan centers on Tokyo-Yokohama, the principal trading center of Japan's machinery and engineering industries. Regional concentration derives in part from the intricate layering and tight, just-in-time coordination among firms in the Japanese auto production system.

The U.S. auto production system is considerably more dispersed and loosely controlled than the Japanese. During the expansionary, early post World War II period, U.S. automakers competed mostly against each other and seldom on the basis of production costs or prices. U.S. car companies built a system of dispersed assembly plants mainly to reduce the cost of shipping cars to growing markets in the South and West. The outlying assembly plants did not manufacture much; they mainly put together car parts produced somewhere else, usually in the core Great Lakes auto producing states: Michigan, Indiana, and Ohio. In this production system, assembly plants required immense logistical pipelines to keep supplied with metal stampings, engines, transmissions, cloth or vinyl for seats, windshields, radios, and the thousands of other items making up a car. Tens of thousands of people were required to manage that material flow, load and unload it, and inspect it for travel damage. Because the supply lines were easily disrupted, it was necessary to have big stockpiles in storage as security. In this "just-in-case" system, assembly plants were 50 percent warehouses, many people labored at logging inventory in and out, many parts were damaged or required recleaning necessitating more repair workers, and even more workers were needed just to gather and dispose of cardboard packaging. Plants grew to immense size to accommodate inventory storage and required enormous energy outlays for heat and light.

The Japanese, once they began selling cars in high volume in the United States, forced a change in the geography of U.S. auto production. Supply lines have been pulled in, several outlying assembly plants in the West and South have been closed. Manufacturing complexes rather than free-standing assembly plants are the order of the day. Parts are still shipped into manufacturing complexes but major supply points are usually within one-day truck driving distances. As U.S. companies reorganize their production system according to multiple tiering, subcontracting, and just-in-time principles, the center of manufacturing gravity is shifting from high-wage, North-Central industrial states bordering the Great Lakes to lower wage, less urban, and less unionized South-Central states (southern Ohio, Kentucky, Missouri, Tennessee).

## Transational Production: Social and Political Issues

The emerging trilateral production strategies pursued by U.S. and Japanese corporations pose critical development issues for industrial workers and manufacturing communities in Japan and North America. The spatial concentration and growth of enterprises knit together in production systems is what generates local employment and regional development. From the vantage point of auto workers and community residents, that which passes the benefits of industrial investment onto the local population as a higher standard of living is desirable. The preferred strategy is to maximize their locality's share of a production system's forward and backward linkages, high value-added intermediate goods, services, and components, and professional, technical, and scientific expertise. Therein lies the basis for a structured conflict between the development concerns of industrial communities in Japan and the United States and the current production strategies of Nichibei corporations.

## Japan

Thus far, the transnationalization of Japan's automobile industry has not led to the "hollowing out" of the nation's auto-dependent industrial regions. Nevertheless, deindustrialization remains a serious political issue in Japan. A recent survey of Japanese car companies estimated that a 2 million decline in motor vehicle exports to the United States could result in the loss of nearly half a million domestic jobs.

Toyota provides a case in point. Toyota's factories in Aichi Prefecture have remained busy thus far supplying engines and transmissions to the company's North American transplants. But as stiffening competition in the North American market has led to more U.S. plant closings and laid-off workers, the United Auto Workers and American supplier associations are challenging the low local content of Japanese transplants. To maintain access to the North American market, Toyota and other Japanese auto companies eventually will have to produce engines and transmissions in the United States and Canada.

Toyota's first tier, transplanted U.S. suppliers, is also under pressure to increase North American content. The Toyota group must either recruit more second-tier suppliers from Japan or increase their use of indigenous, North American companies. Either way, Aichi-based suppliers will lose export orders and face production cutbacks. And by channeling parts produced in Mexico and Asian NICs into its North American operations, Toyota is even further reducing business and jobs for lower tier, Aichi-based suppliers.

High-quality, low-cost parts produced by small and medium-sized subcontractors have underpinned Toyota's competitiveness in world markets. But the rising yen is eroding Toyota's protective commitments to its family of subcontractors. Smaller subcontractors, without technology attractive to the parent maker, are threatened with abandonment. While Toyota encourages its suppliers to invest overseas, the company does not provide financial assistance nor guarantee success in the North American market. Most small subcontractors do not have the resources to follow their parent abroad.

The rising yen is also forcing Japan's older, "sunset" industries—mining, shipbuilding, and steel—to further restructure and reduce employment. Japan's Ministry of Labor (1987) estimates that as many as 1.65 million workers may be forced to leave the manufacturing sector between 1986 and 1993. Although there are an estimated 900,000 surplus workers in Japan's manufacturing industries right now, mass layoffs have been avoided. Japanese steel companies have been able to avoid layoffs by deploying workers internally, dispatching workers to subsidiaries and suppliers, and asking older workers to retire early. But as the globalization of Japanese auto manufacturing proceeds, domestic demand for steel will decline, and steel companies will experience added pressure to lay off surplus workers.

Japan's industrial reorganization is also connected to a change in national development policy. Heretofore, the state has emphasized an export industrialization strategy in conjunction with an internal investment program to keep regional growth trajectories in balance. In June 1987, the government issued a Fourth Comprehensive National Development Program which neglected regional development schemes and emphasized instead the concentration of "postindustrial" service activities in Tokyo, Japan's exploding center of international finance. The state is encouraging Japanese auto corporations to source in East Asia and assemble in the North American market and is assisting a merger and consolidation movement among manufacturers. As unemployment in declining localities rises, and as wealth and income become more unequally distributed among regions and social groups, the social contract that has held postwar labor relations together in Japan (e.g., seniority-based wages, lifetime employment) may come under challenge.

## North America

The global trilateralization of production will likely accelerate rather than alter current directions of change in North American car manufacturing.

Most jobs in the auto industry are in parts production and there is a big shakeout underway in the U.S. auto supply industry as it moves toward the Japanese pattern of fewer and larger firms, arranged in tiers, under producers of complete subsystems. Value-added production pyramiding favors the larger, technologically more sophisticated partsmakers and engine service firms that cluster around final assembly sites. But Nichibei parts sourcing in Taiwan and Mexico will accentuate the competitive difficulties already facing smaller, lower tier, North American producers with less technical ability. The trend is clearly toward increasing concentration of capital and small business decline in the North American auto supply industry.

With profit rates in North American transplants running below domestic levels, and under pressure to increase North American content, Japanese automakers will likely continue their efforts to organize their North American production systems on the Japanese company town model. That means work conditions and wage structures, viewed by organized labor as protections won in the past, will continue to be "reinterpreted" and renegotiated in ways that often conflict with worker interests. Job classifications will be further reduced and a system of wage tiering corresponding to the value-added layering of activities in the auto production system will continue to emerge. The gap in wages and work conditions between auto workers making low-value components that can now be made efficiently by lower cost labor in Pacific rim countries and workers employed in upper tier, higher value, stamping, engine and transmission, and final assembly operations is also likely to grow.

Surplus capacity, plant closings, and reorganization in the auto production system will continue to have an uneven and frequently disastrous impact on North American communities in the U.S. Great Lakes region and Ontario, Canada. Dislocated workers and shrinking employment opportunities for new entrants into the labor force are disproportionately concentrated in older urban-industrial enclaves and disproportionately afflict inner-city minorities, particularly black males. The new, high technology, upper tier segments of the auto production chain—the "automation alleys"—arise elsewhere: in university towns and suburban greenbelts such as Ann Arbor and scenic Oakland County on the western and northwestern periphery of the Detroit region.

## Production Politics

Production systems give rise to constellations of social interests. Changing technologies and divisions of labor affect businesses, workers, communities, and governments in uneven and diverse ways. A politics of production is engendered which is as important in shaping the contours of industrial change as any logic to be found in the marketplace.

Governments have a stake in advancing net wealth and the standard of living of the citizenry residing within their borders. In the auto producing regions of Japan and North America, subnational governments have similar interests: they want to attract and retain high value-added activities and foster intraregional linkages among firms in their auto production systems. Government officials in both parts of the world are attempting to advance those objectives by making social investments in auto-supportive infrastructure, services, tax, and training subsidies.

State of Michigan officials, with a Japanese-style, corporatist model in mind, would like to bargain the conditions of transformation facing auto-linked businesses, labor, and communities by means of productivity coalitions: tripartite councils bringing together business, labor and government representatives. The objective is to prevent bitter acrimony between potential winners and losers from undermining the capacity of the state's industries to adapt to new international competitive conditions. Bargained trade-offs, for example, wages and work conditions for job security and more participation in production decisions, is the policy position many state officials in U.S. industrial regions are now advocating (Osborne 1988).

However, attempts at social accounting by auto-dependent regimes continue to be undermined by ferocious competition with other subnational governments for business investment and by the whipsawing strategies employed by transnational auto producers. Coherent, bargained development among the various social interests with stakes in the changing auto production system will continue to be subverted so long as governments are pressured to engage in beggar-thy-neighbor development strategies and high-priced bidding wars for new auto investment. The needs and concerns of the least protected and powerful are rarely represented in this bidding and bargaining game; indeed, it can truthfully be said that government policies in both Japan and North America have exacerbated uneven development and social inequalities linked to the current restructuring of the international division of labor. Channeling public investments into affluent centers of high finance, high technology, and high consumption while industrial towns and inner cities decay is hardly a blueprint for building progressive political coalitions.

## Conclusion

What lessons can we draw from the foregoing analysis? For one, the most serious national and regional development issues center upon the structure and functioning of global production systems.

This is as true for Great Lakes, Aichi Prefecture, or West Midlands governments attempting to prevent disinvestment from unraveling the production systems that underpin their regional economies as it is for development planners in Malaysia or the People's Republic of China who are attempting to build auto production systems from the bottom layers up.

Second, conceptions of the international Division of labor which focus exclusively on market exchange among economic sectors or upon bureaucratic arrangements internal to the transnational parent enterprise poorly describe the production chains that make up global manufacturing industries. Global production systems cross-cut economic sectors and mesh discrete enterprises into larger systems. Contrary to conventional wisdom, comparative advantage is based less upon the activities of individual firms than upon the structure of whole production systems. And how production systems interconnect oligopolistic and competitive sectors, primary and secondary labor forces, informal and formal activities, lifetime and temporary forms of employment is a critical theoretical and practical development issue.

Finally, it is better to characterize the organization of production systems as fluid rather than fixed and as offering a range of developmental possibilities. Past Japanese manufacturing experience, for example, suggests that efficient, relatively autonomous regional development strategies are *economically* feasible but only under propitious international *political* circumstances. Production systems do not evolve by accident, nor through some immanent logic of the market; they are consequences of social conflicts and shifting political alignments among companies, workers, communities, and governments as local and international circumstances change.

## Notes

1. According to Lipietz (1987), the Fordist labor process divides production into three levels: (1) conception, organization of methods and engineering; (2) skilled manufacturing work; and (3) unskilled assembly and execution. Fordist companies have invariably responded to profitability crises by spreading the production process over multiple pools of unevenly skilled, unevenly unionized, and unevenly paid workers, primarily within the boundaries of "national regimes of accumulation." Global Fordism expresses the same tendency, but through international expansion and reorganization, articulating the three levels of productive activity across different labor pools in different countries: levels 1 and 2 in the advanced industrial countries, levels 2 and 3 in the NICs, and level 3 in the even poorer, less industrialized nations.

2. Sourcing for the U.S.-assembled Golf came one-third from West Germany, one-third from the United States and one-third from Canada-Mexico-Brazil.
3. According to Piore and Sable (1984), flexible specialization can assume various socio-spatial forms: it can be the common basis for industrial districts with inter-firm community cohesion; it can be organized through family-like, federated enter-prises on the model of Japan's prewar Zaibatsu; and it is also compatible with solar firms and workshop factories—big companies organized internally as a collection of workshops governed by principles of welfare capitalism and close collaborative relationships with suppliers. All these forms share "limited entry," "bounded community," and "regional conglomeration."
4. Tomisawa (1986: 44) draws a distinction between two types of "industrial collab-oration" between Japan and the NICs: (a) "process differentiation collaboration" in which "automotive parts and intermediate products are supplied from NICs to Japan and the products are assembled in Japan"; and (b) "product differentiation collaboration" in which "NICs produce low-tech items while Japan specializes in high-tech products." The first is a division of labor within a transnational produc-tion system. The second is a division of labor between transnational production systems.
5. Trilateralism is a "base pattern" around which considerable variation occurs; it does not apply to all industries or all companies within the same industry. West Germany's Volkswagen, to note one exception, is more strongly linked to South America than to Africa or the Middle East.

## References

Altschuler, Alan, Martin Anderson, Daniel Jones, Daniel Roos, and James Womack. 1984. *The Future of the Automobile*. Cambridge: MIT Press.

Cusumano, Michael. 1985. *The Japanese Automobile Industry*. Cam-bridge: Harvard University Press.

————. 1988. *Manufacturing Innovation and Competitive Advan-tage: Reflections on the Japanese Automobile Industry*. Cam-bridge: Sloan School of Management.

Friedman, David. 1988. *The Misunderstood Miracle: Industrial De-velopment and Political Change in Japan*. Ithaca, NY: Cornell University Press.

Frobel, Folker, Jurgen Heinrichs, and Otto Kreye. 1980. *The New International Division of Labor*. Cambridge: Cambridge Univer-sity Press.

Gilpin, Robert. 1987. *The Political Economy of International Rela-tions*. Princeton, NJ: Princeton University Press.

Japan Ministry of Labor. 1987. *1987 White Paper*. Tokyo.

Lipietz, Alain. 1987. *Mirages and Miracles: The Crises of Global Fordism*. London: Verso.

Luria, Daniel D. 1986. "New Labor-Management Models from De-troit?" *Harvard Business Review* September-October.

Markusen, Ann. 1985. *Profit Cycles, Oligopoly and Regional Development*. Boston: MIT Press.

Ohmae, Kenichi. 1985. *Triad Power: The Coming Shape of Global Competition*. New York: MacMillan.

Osborne, David. 1988. *Laboratories in Democracy*. Cambridge: Harvard Business School Press.

Piore, Michael and Charles Sabel. 1984. *The Second Industrial Divide*. New York: Basic Books.

Porter, Michael, ed. 1986. *Competition in Global Industries*. Cambridge: Harvard Business School Press.

Sklar, Holly. 1980. *Trilateralism: The Trilateral Commission and Elite Planning for World Management*. Boston: South End Press.

Sheard, Paul. 1983. "Auto Production Systems in Japan: Organizational and Locational Features." *Australian Geographical Studies* 21 (April): 49–68.

Tomisawa, Konomi. 1986. *Japanese Auto Industry Moving into the USA: International Division of Labor Spirited by the Strong Yen* Tokyo: Long-Term Development Bank of Japan.

Vernon, Raymond. 1973. *Sovereignty at Bay*. New York: Basic Books.

# Bound by One Thread:
# The Restructuring of UK Clothing and Textile Multinationals

## *Diane Elson*

The biggest UK textile industry dispute in forty years galvanized the mill towns of Lancashire in the summer of 1988. Workers sought an improved pay offer from employers whose profits had recovered from their low point in the early 1980s. Ten to twelve thousand workers employed in spinning and weaving firms staged a series of one-day work stoppages, while more than 3,500 employed by Courtaulds, the largest UK multinational in the textile industry, went out on a ten-day strike.

Textile workers argued that their pay (basic wages of £78.61 for a 39-hour week) had fallen behind that in every other manufacturing industry; they claimed to be earning less than street sweepers. The workers sought an improvement in the increase of about 6.5 percent offered by the employers. The employers argued that competition from overseas, both from Europe and the third world, prevented them from offering more. The union pointed out that workers had cooperated in a massive rationalization and restructuring exercise, involving the loss of thousands of jobs in the early 1980s, which had restored profitability to the industry. Just previous to the strike, Courtaulds had announced pre-tax profits of £220.6 million, up 10 percent on the previous year.

After a five-week dispute, the workers gained a modest victory: the strike at Courtaulds was settled for a rise of 7 percent and a minimum pay level of £88.60 a week. However, the triumph was short lived. By the autumn a fresh round of closures was underway.

Courtaulds closed four mills in Lancashire with a loss of 670 jobs, arguing that the market for yarn in Europe had been weakened by imports from Turkey and Greece, overcapacity within Europe, and the indirect effect of increasing imports on the weaving industry. In addition, Courtaulds announced closure of two clothing factories in the northwest with a loss of 540 jobs. It is particularly significant that their chief customer was the large British retailer Marks and Spencer, which purchases around 20 percent of UK clothing output. Throughout the mid-1980s, Marks and Spencer had pursued a largely Buy British policy, arguing that this gave it better quality control and shorter delivery times (Elson 1988). According to the *Financial Times,* Courtaulds would continue to supply Marks and Spencer, but part of its supply would be sourced in the Far East. These cuts brought to about 2,000 the jobs shed by Courtaulds in the period April–November 1988.

The second largest British multinational in the textile and garment industry, Coats Viyella, reduced employment by 4,000 in 1988, chiefly in knitwear and wool textiles. The company was reported to be considering shipping knitting machinery to Turkey to produce there; and also considering using Turkey as a base to spin acrylic yarn for knitwear (*Financial Times,* September 23, 1988). The company was planning further rationalization of its clothing production, including an increase in overseas sourcing. Ten percent of its UK sales came from overseas sourcing in 1988. A sizeable export house had been purchased in Hong Kong, and it was planned to establish similar operations in other countries.

There is nothing surprising in all of this, the reader may feel. Surely, it is well known that textile and garment firms have been shedding jobs in developed countries and moving to developing countries in search of cheaper labor for at least a decade now?

However, while differentials in labor costs are a significant factor in restructuring textile and garment production, a closer examination shows that additional issues are also relevant (Elson 1988; 1989). The firms' internationalization strategies involve several other key factors: exchange rates, the structure of markets and the degree to which proximity to the market is important, and the changing organization of retailing. Furthermore, restructuring is not simply a matter of internationalizing the production process by transferring the more labor intensive activities to countries where labor costs are lower. It also involves changing the entire nature of "production systems," (as Richard Hill points out in this volume). Thus, companies' decisions to expand abroad are combined with decisions to restructure production at home, investing in new technologies and reorganizing the labor force.

Moreover, companies' decisions cannot be understood simply in terms of the production process. The firms are not, ultimately, in the business of making textiles and clothing, but in the business of making money. One of their options is to withdraw from production and concentrate more on marketing goods produced by others. Another is to sell off textile and clothing operations and buy into other industries. Nor is lowering the cost of making a better product the only competitive strategy. Companies may compete through acquisitions, taking over potential rivals and buying market-share. A full appreciation of restructuring thus needs to consider multinationals as circuits of productive capital, commodity capital, and financial capital. Restructuring may involve the internationalization of all these dimensions of capital as well as shifts of emphasis among them.[1]

This essay examines the strategies of three British multinationals in the textile and garment industry in the 1980s and the implications of these strategies for labor. The experience of these companies demonstrates that their strategies cannot be understood simply in terms of the relocation of labor-intensive parts of the production process to areas of cheaper labor.

The companies' strategies, however, cannot provide complete answers to the problems of capital: they may serve to strengthen the balance sheets of individual companies for short periods of time, but they contribute to the increasing volatility of the capitalist system as a whole. They may serve to weaken and demoralize labor in the developed countries to a considerable extent, but they may also provoke reorganization and new initiatives in the developed countries and the growth of an organized working class in the third world countries.

It is worth emphasizing the numbers of women workers in the textile and garment industry. In garment making the workforce is overwhelmingly female and is becoming more so with the introduction of new technology. What were traditionally jobs for skilled male craftsworkers in pattern-making, lay designing, and cutting are increasingly being undertaken by microprocessor-based systems operated by women. In textiles the gender balance has always been more even; and it is women, rather than men, who are being displaced by new technology. Nonetheless, textiles remains an industry with a large number of women workers.

The final section of the essay will briefly consider some of the ways in which labor has been responding to the strategies of the multinationals. There have been some efforts by labor to extend its solidarity across international boundaries, but such moves are in their infancy. In any case, an effective response to the strategies of multinationals must come at the social level, and, while the labor movement will be important, the community at large must be involved in limiting the prerogatives of capital. Though women workers are often seen as a particularly vulnerable section of labor, one of their strengths is an ability to see issues not only from a workplace perspective but also from the perspective of the wider community. Women's industrial struggles against multinationals have frequently involved mobilization of whole communities.

In developing any response to the actions of the multinationals, it is necessary to have a full picture of their strategies, and not rely on the overly simplified cheap labor explanation. Indeed, in the textile and garment industry there has not been a uniform process of plant closure. Both Courtaulds and Coats Viyella, for instance, have been investing heavily in new technology in the UK. Closures have been concentrated in plants with old technology. Moreover, in justifying their recent plant closures, the companies themselves focused on the issue of foreign exchange fluctuations, citing especially the increasing difficulties in producing profitably and competing from UK locations because of the weakening dollar. "Two years ago we identified an exchange rate of $1.60 as the point at which life would become difficult," the chairman of Courtaulds Textiles was quoted as saying (*Financial Times,* September 13, 1988). By the autumn of 1988 the pound had risen above $1.80. Most third world suppliers, particularly those in the Far East, price their textiles and clothing products in dollar terms. Thus as the dollar weakened, the cost in sterling of importing textile and garments into the UK from a wide range of countries, not just the United States, fell. The result was a surge in imports into the U.K., most of which was not produced by any sudden widening in labor costs between the UK and production sites in the third world but by the volatility of exchange rates.

## UK Textile and Clothing Multinationals

There are three major UK textile and garment multinationals: Courtaulds, Coats Viyella (both already mentioned), and Tootal, which is considerably smaller than the other two. Between them the three have a large share of textile and garment output and employment in the UK, for the UK textile and garment industry is more concentrated than that of other developed countries (OECD 1983: 26).

Courtaulds is one of the largest British companies and is a major multinational by world standards. It is involved in a very wide range of textile activities, including synthetic fibers, spinning, weaving, knitting, and garment-making. In addition, it has extensive and growing interests outside the industry in plastics, paints, packaging, and engineering and in wholesaling and retailing. It is the only one of the three to produce synthetic fibers.

In 1975, Courtaulds employed 124,000 people in the UK and 31,000 abroad, mainly in other developed countries such as France, the Republic of Ireland, West Germany, Sweden, Spain, Canada and the United States. It also had plant in South Africa. Just over a decade later, in 1986, UK employment was down to 46,000 and overseas employment to 19,000. Clothing factories had been set up in Portugal, Morocco, and Tunisia, and artificial fiber production in India in a joint venture with the Modi group. In 1988 the company divested its wood pulp interests in South Africa, selling them for a good price to a South African company.

Coats Viyella is the world's largest thread producer and also has extensive activities in yarns, fabrics and clothing, household furnishings, and retailing. It has existed in its present form only since January 1986, when it was formed by a merger between Coats Patons and Vantona Viyella to become Europe's leading company devoted to textiles and garments.

Coats Patons was a large multinational whose interests were mainly in thread production. In 1978 its worldwide employment was 66,000, of which 23,000 was in the UK and 42,000 overseas. Like Courtaulds it had plants in other European countries, in Australia and South Africa, and in North America. Unlike Courtaulds, in the 1970s Coats Patons also had extensive operations in the third world, with plants in Argentina, Brazil, Chile, Ecuador, Peru, and Venezuela, and with joint venture production in India. By 1983 Coats Patons had reduced its total workforce to 43,500, of which 15,200 were in the UK and 28,300 were overseas (ITGLWF 1984:11).

Vantona Viyella produced mainly household textiles and clothing in the UK. The logic of the merger that created Coats Viyella was said to be that it would enable Vantona Viyella to expand its export markets using Coats Patons' international thread sales network. The new company employed about 100,000 people in a network of 250 subsidiaries in more than thirty countries.

Although Coats Viyella employs more people than Courtaulds, its turnover and pre-tax profits are considerably smaller, about £1,760 million and £150 million respectively in 1988, as compared to about £2,420 million and £220 million for Courtaulds. This reflects the greater labor intensity of the product mix of Coats Viyella.

Tootal, the third UK textile and garment multinational, is considerably smaller than the two so far considered. Its turnover in 1988 was about £480 million and pre-tax profits about £40 million. Tootal's product mix is similar to that of Coats Viyella: sewing threads, fabrics, household textiles, and clothing are the main items. But Tootal has been moving out of the direct production of fabrics and clothing into the international sourcing and distribution of those goods.

In 1974, Tootal employed about 20,000 people in the UK, about 9,200 in its wholly owned overseas plants, and several thousand more in overseas joint ventures. The overseas plants were in Australia, Canada, West Germany, and the United States, and in Hong Kong, the Philippines, India, Indonesia, and South Africa. By 1984 UK employment was down to about 8,500 and overseas employment in wholly owned plants to about 6,300; employment in overseas associates, according to the Annual Report, was higher than either, at about 13,700. The company had opened thread mills in Malaysia and Sri Lanka and was planning a joint venture thread mill in China. By 1988 this mill was producing thread for both the Chinese market and for export to other Far Eastern markets; and a second Chinese mill was due to come on line in July 1989.[2]

## Restructuring Strategies

The three major multinationals in the U.K. textile and garment industry have all restructured their operations in a major way during the 1980s. All have made large cuts in their UK employment, particularly in the period 1979–82, which were years of disaster for the British textile industry. There was a recession in the British economy, and an appreciating pound made exports uncompetitive and sucked in imports. What Tootal complained of in its Annual Report, however, was not low-cost imports from the third world, but unfair competition from American firms which did not face such high energy costs and from German firms which had garments made up in Eastern Europe. In the period 1978–82, UK textile production and employment fell by one-third. Cotton textile production and employment were particularly hard hit. In mid-1978, 74,000 people were employed in this sector. By mid-1982 this had fallen to 43,000 (Economist Intelligence Unit 1983).

During this period at the end of the 1970s and beginning of the 1980s, one in four of the Courtaulds workforce was made redundant (Walsh 1987). Coats Viyella did not exist at that time, but its major components, Coats Patons and Vantona Viyella, both made substantial closures. Tootal closed three spinning mills and several fabric and clothing factories; its UK workforce fell from about 20,000 to about 10,000. Profits plummeted, and the industry was in deep crisis. Since that time, the profitability of the three multinationals has recovered, though their UK employment has continued to decline.

The strategies that restored profitability have certain similarities but also important differences of emphasis. A major component of Courtaulds strategy has been withdrawal from textiles and garments and an expansion of its other activities, particularly in paint and specialist chemicals. By 1988 textiles and fibers accounted for only about half of pre-tax profit; the other half came from wood pulp, chemicals and materials, coatings, and films and packaging. While some clothing factories have been set up in cheaper labor countries, such as Portugal, Morocco, and Tunisia, the other major component of the corporation's strategy has been investment in new technology in both spinning and garment production (Walsh 1987).

The main aim of the Courtaulds' investment in new technology has not been to reduce labor costs but to increase the flexibility of production. Instead of producing long runs of standardized products with long lead times between ordering and sale, the aim is to create production systems capable of producing short runs with short lead times and the ability to switch from one product to another with the minimum of "down-time." The growing importance of this aim reflects the competitive struggle to capture markets in a more slowly growing economic environment (see, in this context, the essay by MacEwan and Tabb, in this volume).

The process of investing in new technology to increase flexibility can be traced to the point of sale to the final customer. The introduction of "intelligent cash registers" and of computerized stock control systems means that it is possible for retailers to place short orders and use the cash registers to monitor what sells well and what sells badly. This information is fed into the stock control systems and only the high-selling lines are reordered. In a market which is growing more slowly as a result of the end of the long postwar boom in capital accumulation, this enables retailers to match supply more closely to demand and to try to stimulate more demand by offering a wider variety. Such retailing change is often presented as a mere response to an autonomous "fragmentation of taste," but the impetus for the fragmentation comes from competition among sellers. "Niche marketing" is a way of trying to make up for the fact that the market as a whole is not expanding rapidly and to reduce uncertainty and risk for the retailers. However, shorter orders increase the uncertainty faced by manufacturers. In order to compete for reorders, they need the capacity to respond quickly, the ability to produce a different variety without long and costly redesign and retooling.

In clothing, Courtaulds has invested in computerized systems for design, pattern-making, and laying and cutting. An example is a system that enables the user to design a garment on a mannequin in any style, color, fabric, or texture in just a few hours. Advanced computer graphics can give a life-like representation, showing the garment draping and hanging like the real thing (*Financial Times,* December 1, 1987).

More flexibility in clothing production creates more uncertainty downstream for producers of fabrics, fibers, and threads. Textile mills in their turn need more flexibility in the range of colors and grades of produce they can produce. To secure this Courtaulds has a £120 million program of investment in new technology scheduled for 1986–89 (Walsh 1987). The new technology is designed to facilitate the economic production of shorter runs of a wider range of products so that production can be much more closely matched to the fluctuating pattern of demand, and stockholding can be reduced.

The ultimate cost of this flexibility falls on labor, as the new equipment requires far fewer operators. A study of the introduction of new technology in a Courtaulds spinning mill in a town near Manchester found that employment would fall by more than half. The job losses would fall disproportionately on women: all the operations to be phased out are ones which predominantly affect women—speed frames, ring spinning, and winding. The union at the mill expected that in the future the workforce would be 85 percent male on higher pay and working in cleaner, more modern conditions (Walsh 1987). This was seen by management and union representatives as inevitable, given the character of the new technology which, it was argued, required shift work patterns and aptitudes which women could not supply. The unemployment generated would be one more factor contributing to the decline in the growth of final demand for textiles and clothing, a decline necessitating further attempts to capture demand through more frequent product changes. Hence the action of the individual company reinforces the overall volatility which that action—the introduction of new technology—was introduced to counteract.

Investment in new technology in the UK has also been central to the strategy of Coats Viyella, which remains much more dependent on the fortunes of the textile and garment industry than Courtaulds. Through the introduction of the latest open-ended spinning equipment, Coats Viyella hopes to produce cotton yarn as cheaply as its competitors do in the Far East. Formerly it took a workforce of 437 Lancashire millhands to produce 88,000 kilograms of yarn a week. After an investment of £6 million in new machinery, 108,000 kilograms a week is produced by only 274 workers in a mill that operates 168 hours a week, 50 weeks a year (*Financial Times,* March 23, 1988). The yarn is used to make home furnishings, and the new technology has enabled Coats Viyella to remain competitive in this sector. A recent review of likely trends in the textile industry in the 1990s offers support to this strategy, concluding, on the basis of some detailed cost comparisons: "If the primary textile industries of Western Europe were completely re-equipped with new machinery tomorrow, with no greater financial burden than they carry today, developing countries could not compete without subsidies on their exports." (Gilmartin 1987:86). However, this comparison does not seem to take account of very low cost countries just entering into the international market, notably China.

More important than the reduction in labor costs may be the fact that the new spinning equipment also offers greater flexibility through speeding up turnover and reducing requirements of working capital. It permits quicker delivery to the downstream operations and is being complemented by a £6.5 million modernization in weaving, a £2 million investment in color printing systems, and a £2.3 million investment in hemming factories. It is hoped to be able to link the reequipped home furnishings division direct to the customer through a computerized Interactive Sales Environment System. The idea is for Coats Viyella to be able to supply retailers with carpets and home furnishings made to specific orders from the customer.

The scheme, which is still being tested, uses computer terminals linked to a central computer at Coats Viyella, and it is aimed at cutting out expensive warehousing by both retailer and manufacturer (*The Observer,* October 22, 1987).

The advances of new technology are not so decisive in clothing. A recent comparison of the costs of manufacturing cotton shirts found that in 1985 costs in Hong Kong were 70 percent of costs in the UK and 64 percent of costs in West Germany (Gilmartin 1987:87). Such a cost differential may well outweigh the gain in flexibility achieved by producing in close proximity to the market. One commentator has suggested that British retailers are willing to pay up to 15 percent more for goods produced in Britain in order to avoid delivery uncertainties (*Daily Telegraph,* September 20, 1988). Beyond that, and they start considering overseas suppliers.

In clothing, if not in textiles, speed and flexibility can be achieved in labor intensive as well as in hi-tech ways, provided that design and quality control problems can be overcome. Thus as the dollar weakens, Marks and Spencer is reported to be reconsidering its Buy British policy and increasingly sourcing from overseas (*Daily Telegraph,* October 4, 1988).

Overseas sourcing of part of their range from the third world is another strategy open to multinationals in the clothing industry. It involves withdrawing from the manufacturing process in favor of supplying design and/or marketing services, and acting as a middleman between third world firms and first world retailers. Overseas sourcing represents an internationalization of marketing and distribution. In contrast to offshore processing, it represents an internationalization of the circuit of commodity capital rather than of the circuit of productive capital.[3] Withdrawal from manufacturing gives greater flexibility because capital is not tied up in equipment and turnover is generally faster. Risk can be shifted to the third world producers. Coats Viyella will certainly increase its overseas sourcing activities. From the knowledge that Coats Patons gained in its international thread production and marketing activities (Sinclair 1982), a computerized data base has been prepared of local textile and clothing firms worldwide. This will provide managers with instant access to information about suitable overseas sourcing of clothing.

Overseas sourcing has been taken much further by Tootal, which now describes itself not as a producer of thread, furnishings, and clothing, but as "a worldwide marketing, distribution, and sourcing business." This is something of an exaggeration because Tootal is still the world's second largest producer of thread, but certainly applies much more to its clothing and fabric activities. In 1988 about 55 percent of Tootal's British sales were sourced overseas, and it had established teams in Hong Kong and Singapore to match up local clothing firms with major European retailers. However, the company retains significant clothing operations in the UK, where it has invested in new technology for designing, pattern-making and laying and cutting, to enable it to respond rapidly to orders from retailers. It has expanded its UK subsidiary, Slimma, which produces "classic" up-market clothes for women, both own-label and for Marks and Spencer. By 1984 Slimma employed over 2,000 people, about a quarter of Tootal's UK employment, and accounted for one-third of Tootal's clothing sales.

Tootal is not interested in third world countries simply as sources of supply; it is also interested in their markets. Over half of Tootal's annual sales in 1988 were made outside Britain, and the expanding clothing industries of third world and southern Mediterranean countries were an important source of demand for its thread. However, it must be emphasized that Tootal also has extensive thread production and sales in North America, from which it derived almost one-third of pre-tax profits in 1987.

Access to markets was the original impetus for Tootal's overseas investments in both developed and developing countries. Thread mills were set up or acquired through takeover of existing producers in order to supply the local market. An example is the Allied Thread Company, which was established as a wholly owned subsidiary in the Philippines in 1953 as a way of getting over trade barriers erected by that country's government. It was a classic case of foreign investment to safeguard a market, induced by a policy of import substitution industrialization in the host country. In the 1970s there was further investment in thread production in Asia which, in the words of Tootal's chairman, "was geared to remaining in markets in newly emerging countries by setting up production units there" (*Financial Times,* June 11, 1984).

In the 1980s, Tootal's thread production and marketing were rationalized on a global basis. Instead of each mill supplying its local market, the headquarters of the newly set up Thread Division coordinated marketing and sourced thread from the company's global network of mills, according to current costs and capacities (*Financial Times,* September 30, 1988). Thus a large order from the growing clothing industry in Morocco was supplied not just from the UK plant, but also from Tootal operations in the United States and Malaysia.

Tootal's old spinning mills in the UK were closed in 1980 and production in the UK was concentrated in two modern mills located outside the traditional base of the textile industry in the northwest. China has now become a linch-pin of the company's international thread marketing operations. In 1988 Tootal's joint venture mill in Guangzhou (Canton) was reported to be supplying a quarter of the company's thread needs (*Financial Weekly,* April 28, 1988). A second mill is being built in Tianjin, in the north of China; and eventually 80 percent of Tootal's requirements for the Pacific Basin will be sourced in China. Labor costs in textile production in China are among the lowest in the world. A comparison of hourly labor costs in forty-eight countries in spring 1987 made by the management consultants Werner International puts China bottom but one. Only Indonesia had lower costs. Whereas costs in Hong Kong were 21 percent of U.S. costs, in China costs were only 2 percent of U.S. costs (Werner International 1987).

Of course, labor costs are not the only significant costs, and China may be weaker on factors such as quality, style, and services to customers. Tootal has dealt with such possibilities by splitting up the thread production process into separate parts. All yarn is produced up to the final twisting stage in China and then shipped via Hong Kong to be finished in mini-mills near to the customer. This gives flexibility in the color mix produced and enables a quick response to changes in the garment industry. Here is where the profits lie: 70 percent of the profit margin in thread comes from dying, winding and finishing stages. (*Financial Weekly,* October 30, 1986). It is in these final stages that Tootal is concentrating its investment in the UK and the U.S. In 1986, for example, a £7 million computer-controlled dyehouse was opened near Glasgow which will enable rapid production of non-standard colors at premium prices for the European market.

Most of Tootal's conventional fabric capacity in the UK was closed down in the early 1980s, though a few specialist lines survive, of which the most exotic is color printing "grey" cloth, imported from China, with batik designs and reexporting it to West Africa. The company turned from manufacturing to international fabric sourcing and distribution, drawing on suppliers in the Far East and India. It is now reported to be considering joint-venture fabric operations in China. Joint-venture production is something of a halfway house between operating wholly owned manufacturing facilities and acting as a marketing agent. It shifts some of the risk to the partner in the joint venture but is less flexible than marketing operations. However, marketing is only an option if reliable suppliers are available. Quality control is still a problem in the Chinese textile industry; hence the greater involvement of a joint venture is needed.

In the face of the weak dollar and the increase in imports into the UK in 1988, Tootal has been emphasizing its Far East operations: "The Far East is increasingly becoming a region of key strategic interest to the group. Tootal has a very long association with the region, particularly with China. At great cost we have achieved a major shift of production and sourcing to the Far East," said company chairman, John Crave. The latest venture is reported to be a $5 million sewing thread plant in South Korea, in partnership with a Korean firm, to serve the South Korean market. South Korea is no longer a "cheap labor" country: its hourly labor costs in textiles in 1987 were about ten times those of China, though still only about one-fifth of those in the United States, and one-quarter of those in the UK (Werner International 1987:202). More significant is its rapidly growing market.

## How Successful Has Restructuring Been?

During the mid-1980s profitability recovered and all three multinationals were widely described as having restructured successfully— from capital's point of view, that is. By autumn of 1988 there were growing doubts. Coats Viyella announced a £5 million fall in profits, and the value of its shares fell by 32 percent. Over the twelve months from October 1987 to October 1988, Coats Viyella shares fell by 47 percent relative to the market; and Courtaulds' shares fell by 30 percent. Tootal did somewhat better, its shares falling by only 18 percent.

All three had been adversely affected by a factor beyond the control of any individual firm: the instability in the international monetary system leading to volatile exchange rates. All three were vulnerable to take over bids in an international capital market in which firms preferred to spend their cash on acquisitions to buy market shares, rather than risk investing in new plant. There were rumors of takeover bids involving Coats Viyella and Tootal. Courtaulds was subject to a "dawn raid" on its shares in May 1988, apparently carried out on behalf of Australian entrepreneur Kerry

Packer. The *Financial Weekly* (May 5, 1988) commented: "That a company like Courtaulds—which is widely recognized as being well managed—should be 'put into play' by the tired old combination of anonymous stake building, vigorous churning of the market-makers and unbridled takeover rumors, is testimony to the market's myopia in the aftermath of the October crash."

Tootal appeared to many financial commentators to be in the best position, with its emphasis on international marketing and its sources of supply and markets in the one dynamic area left in the world capitalist economy, the Far East. But even this strategy is not without contradictions. The profitability of marketing depends ultimately on the growth and stability of the market, but this in turn depends on the growth and stability of the overall accumulation process. If all capitalists try to get out of production and into marketing and distribution, the result will be a zero-sum game in which the struggle for a given market will increase the volatility of the market. Sustained growth of demand requires that substantial investment in real productive assets be undertaken by a substantial number of capitalists.

One hope of the capitalists might be that the economies of the Far East will be sufficiently dynamic. But their smooth development cannot be taken for granted. For instance, rapid capital accumulation in South Korea has produced a large working class and a growing militancy in the labor movement. There were 3,000 strikes in a wave of unrest in August and September 1987 in which workers won average wage increases of nearly 18 percent. Workers are organizing and demanding recognition for independent trade unions to replace the pro-government "yellow" unions (*International Labour Reports,* No. 24, 1987; No. 27–28, 1988), and women textile and garment workers have been prominent in these struggles (*Asian Women Workers Newsletter,* various issues).

### Implications for Workers

The restructuring of the multinational textile industry has numerous implications for workers, and to fully examine those implications would go far beyond the scope of this essay. It will be useful, however, to briefly mention some key issues. The international activities of multinationals put pressure on workers in the companies' home bases, undermining their standard of living, their power, and their rights. At the same time, those activities open up new opportunities for international labor organization.[4]

At the official level there are the International Trade Secretariats which focus on linking unions within a specific industry. But these are not intended to mobilize or link up rank-and-file workers, and they are hampered by political divisions between communist and noncommunist-led unions. Direct links between workers have been fostered by union activists, supported by community research and resource organizations. Through such links messages of support and financial assistance have been sent to workers in dispute with the same multinational employer. Such links also facilitate exchange of information on company policies, bargaining tactics, health and safety standards, new technologies and trade union rights. These links are probably most advanced in industries dominated by a few multinationals, such as the auto industry (Humphrey 1988).

Third world workers often consider international links important in mobilizing opinion against repression of the labor movement by both their own governments and multinationals. For instance, support from groups of labor movement activists abroad has been helpful to women garment workers in the Sri Lankan Free Trade Zone. Women textile and garment workers in Asia are linked through networks of activists and communicate through channels such as the *Asian Women Workers' Newsletter,* produced by community groups in Hong Kong.

It must be recognized, however, that there are limits to international solidarity. One problem was pointed out by two British women garment workers who, aided by UK activists and their union, visited workers in the International Garments Manufacturing Company (IGMC) factory owned by Baird Textiles in the Bataan Export Processing Zone in the Philippines (see note 2). They expressed doubt about the possibility of effective international solidarity between Baird's workers in the UK and those in the Philippines because it was not even possible to generate effective solidarity among Baird's workers in different factories in the UK. "There is almost no contact between UK factories," they reported. "The managers encourage them to think they are still working for small firms, not a multinational corporation" (*International Labour Reports,* No. 27–28, 1988).

Nonetheless, it did prove possible for a useful exchange of information to take place between some of Baird's workers in the UK and in the Philippines on issues like health and safety, negotiating rights, and levels of pay. Groups of workers active in the labor movement in both countries were able to come to a better understanding of company structure and strategy. At least some British workers were able to overcome stereotypes of "docile Asian labor" as they found out about the struggle of workers in the Bataan Export Processing Zone and about the impressive level of organization there.

Such contacts, however, could not overcome the fundamental problem that the company has the initiative when it comes to choosing its production locations. Workers in both the Philippines and the UK said they were always told that management could get higher productivity, cheaper, elsewhere. In 1988 that threat was effectively used when IGMC announced it was closing down its plant in the Bataan Export Processing Zone and moving production to Indonesia, unless the Philippines workers agreed to new, worse terms and work practices, bypassing union organization. Despite a sit-in, the company was able to secure acceptance of its terms and refused to take back union activists (*International Labour Reports,* No. 27–28, 1988).

Controlling the multinationals requires action which can only be taken at the social level and is beyond the reach of shop floor activity. It requires the mobilization of community opinion and the enactment and enforcement of new legislation. Ultimately it requires that private property rights be superseded by community rights, exercised on behalf of the public rather than on behalf of shareholders. The labor movement will play a key role in that process, but consumers may also make an important contribution. The Green movement and the anti-apartheid movement have shown that consumers can be mobilized to take note of factors other than the price of the goods they buy, and to bring pressure to bear about side effects and conditions of production. Company concern about adverse consumer reaction is reported to have played a part in the partial success of Scottish women, who occupied the factory in which they made Lee jeans for the VF corporation, to prevent the loss of their jobs through closure (Elson and Pearson, eds. 1989).

In Manchester, a project is being set up to develop action on both the fronts discussed above. Under the title "The Labour Behind the Label - Women and the Internationalisation of the Textile and Garment Industry," the project will facilitate links between groups of women working in the industry in different countries and also educate and mobilize consumers to be concerned about the conditions of production of what they buy.[5] The project aims to develop an awareness among producers and consumers that, in the words of a Korean woman textile worker, "we are all bound by the same thread." The ultimate goal is to break those bonds and replace them by links of cooperation.

## Notes

1. The theoretical analysis underlying this approach is discussed in Jenkins (1984) and Elson (1986).
2. Smaller UK firms in the textile and clothing industry also have a few overseas plants. Baird Textiles in 1978 purchased 80 percent of the International Garments Manufacturing Company (IGMC), situated in the Bataan Export Processing Zone of the Philippines. The Bataan factory produced garments to designs sent from the UK, with machines from Japan, and materials from Hong Kong. Its products were exported, mainly to Britain. It should be noted that offshore processing, whereby garments are designed and cut out in one country, the pieces sent for making up in another country, and the finished garment re-imported into the first country, is not significant in the UK due to unfavorable UK tariff schedules.
3. The concept of circuits of capital is explained in Jenkins (1984) and Elson (1986).
4. This is discussed specifically in relation to women workers in several chapters of Elson and Pearson eds. (1989). A useful source of information on workers struggles in different countries and on-going attempts to construct international solidarity is *International Labor Reports*, available from P.O. Box 45, Stainborough, Barnsley, Yorkshire, S75 3EA, U.K.
5. For more information, contact the Textile and Garments Project, c/o Department of Sociology, University of Manchester, Manchester, M13 9PL, U.K.

## References

Economist Intelligence Unit 1983. *World Textile Trade and Production Trends,* Special Report No. 152. London: EIU.

Elson, Diane. 1986. "The New International Division of Labour in the Textile and Garment Industry: How Far Does the 'Babbage Principle' Explain It?" *International Journal of Sociology and Social Policy* 6, no. 2.

———. 1988. "Transnational Corporations in the New International Division of Labour: A Critique of 'Cheap Labour' Hypotheses." *Manchester Papers in Development* IV, no. 3.

———. 1989. "The Cutting Edge: Multinationals in Textiles and Clothing." In Elson and Pearson, eds., *Women's Employment and Multinationals in Europe*. London: Macmillan. 1989.

Elson, Diane and Ruth Pearson, eds. 1989. *Women's Employment and Multinationals in Europe*. London: Macmillan.

Gilmartin, Roger. 1987. "Textiles into the 1990s." *Textile Outlook International,* September.

International Textile, Garment and Leather Workers Federation. 1984. *Multinational Companies in the Textile, Garment and Leather Industries,* Brussels: ITGLWF.

Humphrey, John. 1988. "Internationalism." *International Labour Reports,* No. 27–28 and 29.

Jenkins, Rhys. 1984. "Divisions Over the International Division of Labour." *Capital and Class,* No. 22.

OECD. 1983. *Textile and Clothing Industries: Structural Problems and Policies in OECD Countries.* Paris: OECD.

Sinclair, Andrew. 1982. *Sewing It Up: Coats Patons Multinational Practices.* Edinburgh: Scottish Action and Education for Development.

Walsh, Jane. 1987. "Capital Restructuring and the British Textile Industry: A Case Study." Industrial Relations Unit, Warwick University.

Werner International. 1987. "Textile Labour Costs." *Textile Asia.* August.

# Capital Accumulation, Transformation of Agriculture, and the Agricultural Crisis: A Long-Term Perspective

## *Jean-Pierre Berlan*

The fortunes of agriculture in the United States have been closely tied to the fortunes of the world economy, and, as the world economy experienced its successful expansion in the 1950s and 1960s to be followed by crisis in the 1970s and 1980, so too has U.S. agriculture experienced a post-World War II era of rapid growth leading into the present crisis. Internationally, the current food and agricultural situation exhibits several problematic features: agricultural commodities cannot find markets and exporting countries are engaged in bitter fights for sales opportunities; farmers are on the brink of bankruptcy; the environment is in jeopardy; a large fraction of the population is ill-fed or underfed (some 14 percent even in the United States); and public health problems are being traced to major diet changes (particularly to the increasing consumption of animal fats). Overall, we are presented with the old paradox of too much food for the markets and too little food for the people.

Many economists and agricultural analysts explain the current state of affairs as the consequences of a cyclical process initiated in the early 1970s by contingent events, including the emergence of the Soviet Union as a large structural purchaser of grains, a succession of bad crops on a world scale, the vanishing of anchovies (an important feed supplement) from the Peruvian coast, and so on. Food shortages, then, led to high prices, high prices to high profits, high profits to increased production. In this boom, surging U.S. land values provided collateral on loans for investment in more land and new equipment. By 1985, the resulting debt burden on U.S. farmers was twice the debt of Latin American countries to the United States. Production overexpanded and was followed by an inevitable downturn, price collapse, and bankruptcies. In this view, the present crisis is its own cure—a new equilibrium will be reached if we only let the process of adjustment run its course through low prices, declining land values, bankruptcies, and land concentration. The only prerequisite to this adjustment, so the argument goes, is the removal of domestic and international fetters to market forces.

This cure and the diagnosis of the agricultural crisis as simply a consequence of cyclical and contingent factors rest on a crucial assumption, namely that there exists, somewhere, a favorable "equilibrium." However, while these short-run cyclical and contingent factors have been relevant, the current agricultural crisis is a part of something much larger. The short-run process has been grafted onto a fundamental historical transformation that has brought agriculture under the control of capital, and the success of capital has generated a permanent crisis of overproduction.

In this article, I will attempt to shed some light on this larger historical transformation in order to explain the forces underlying the present farm crisis. Although the issues are global, I will focus on the United States, now the vacillating keystone of the international system of agricultural production and trade.

## U.S. Agricultural Growth and Trade

Historically, U.S. agriculture has been made up of at least three distinct farming systems: slavery in the South, large-scale farming based on the use of an unlimited supply of migratory labor in the West, and a yeoman family farming system in the North Central and Plains States. An index aggregating the output of the three types of agriculture would yield somewhat blurred results. To deal more specifically with the family farm system, I have computed an index of grain production (wheat, corn, sorghum, oats, barley, buckwheat, rye, flaxseed, soybeans, sunflower) with the results shown in Figure 1 and Table 1.[1]

Figure 1 and Table 1 show that the growth of grain output in the United States has undergone three fairly distinct phases during the period from 1866 to 1982: First, from the Civil War to 1899, output grew rapidly, mainly due to the incorporation of new cropping land. Growth was especially rapid from the War until 1880—6.4 percent per year—but slowed to 2.5 percent per year in the 1880–99 period. Second, the era from 1899 to 1938 was one of "retardation of growth" (Barger and Landsberg 1942: 35) with output at a virtual

*Figure 1*
*Index of U.S. Grain Output, 1866-1988\**

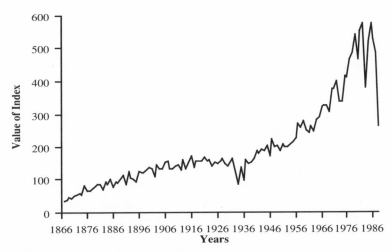

*Source*: U.S. Department of Commerce, Bureau of the Census, *Historical Statistics of the United States: Colonial Times to 1970*, and U.S. Department of Agriculture, *Agricultural Statistics*, various years.

\* The index is a Laspeyre index and includes: wheat, corn, sorghum, oats, barley, buckwheat rye, flaxseed, soybeans, and sunflowers.

standstill, that is, an average growth rate of 0.1 percent. However, this "retardation" period was itself made up of two subperiods: up through World War I, and partly stimulated by the war, production grew at 0.9 percent per year; between the wars, total output declined.[2] Third, the final period, 1939–82, shows an annual average yearly growth rate of 2.8 percent, accelerating to 5.0 percent during the boom decade of 1973–82.

Since 1982, U.S. agriculture has entered into a period of open crisis that departs from the preceding growth trend. In 1983, a large set-aside program was implemented to cut back production. The weather contributed further to holding down grains supply, as the corn and soybean crops were severely injured by drought. Similarly in 1988, drought came on top of a set-aside program that removed 80 million acres of cropland from production. Although the resulting rate of output decline during the mid-1980s was substantial, in-

*Table 1*
*Annual Rates of Growth of Grain Production*
*in the United States, 1866–1988*

| Period | Annual Percentage Rate of Growth |
|--------|----------------------------------|
| 1866–99 | 3.4 |
| 1866–80 | 6.4 |
| 1880–99 | 2.5 |
| 1899–1938 | 0.1 |
| 1988–1919 | 0.9 |
| 1919–38 | − 1.3 |
| 1938–1982 | 2.8 |
| 1938–73 | 2.4 |
| 1973–82 | 5.0 |
| (1982–88 | − 6.7)* |

*Source:* See Figure 1.
*The growth rate estimate for 1982–88 is not statistically significant because of the high variation in output and the small number of years.

stability was so great that no statistically significant trend can be established.

As for foreign trade, Figures 2 and 3 summarize its movement. At the turn of the century, the United States was a large exporter, but the country's position started to erode under the competition of Argentina, Australia, and Canada. After a short-lived spurt of exports of food and feed grain during World War I and its aftermath, the prewar trend of declining exports reasserted itself. At the end of the 1930s, the United States had become a marginal supplier of world markets. In 1940, only 2 percent of US cropland was cultivated for export. After World War II, exports again expanded, peaking at 39 percent of cropland use in 1980, but then decreasing in the following years.

The upturn of all the trend lines at the eve of World War II begs for an explanation. Why is it that capital accumulation, at a standstill during the 1930s, could proceed at a fairly rapid pace during the forty years or so that followed the war? Undoubtedly, many factors account for such a recovery: the war itself, the postwar economic recovery in Europe and Japan, "finely tuned" agricultural policies, trade liberalization, the rise in real incomes, the high price and income elasticity of meat consumption, the political and economic might of the US to shape favorable policies in Europe and elsewhere. However significant, these factors should be viewed as of secondary importance. The primary factor that must be examined is the profound structural transformation which laid the foundation for the postwar growth and for the shaping of the present world food system; that is, the primary factor is *the process of capital accumulation within agriculture itself.*

## Capital Accumulation and the Transformation of Agriculture

Beginning in 1920, the dominant problem of U.S. agriculture became overproduction (Johnson and Quance 1972). As shown in Figure 3, around the time of World War I, 27 percent of the harvested cropland went for horse feed and 73 percent for final consumption

*Figure 2*
*Share of World Exports of Cereal Grains,*
*U.S. and Other Regions, 1884-1986*

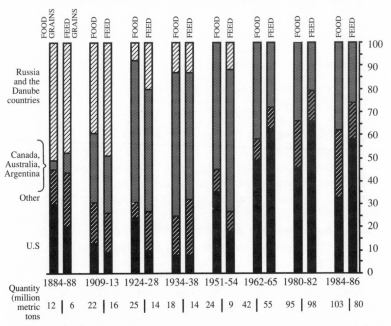

*Sources:* R. Stern, *World Grain Exports and Agricultural Policies of the United States*, Ph.D. Thesis, Columbia University, 1958; U.S. Department of Agriculture, *World Agricultural Trade*, 1957-65, Vol. 2; and F.A.O., *Statistics of International Trade*, various years.

*Figure 3*
*Uses of Harvested Cropland in the U.S.*
*1910-1986 (percentages of total)\**

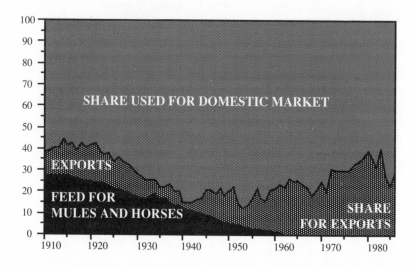

*Source*: U.S. Department of Agriculture, *Agricultural Statistics,* 1987, p. 300.

\* During these years, total acreage harvested varied, with a few exceptions, between 300 and 350 million acres; there is no trend.

(the latter including feed for non-farm draft animals). The replacement of draft animals by tractors thus increased by 37 percent (27/73) the potential final output, while urban motor transportation suppressed another important outlet for agriculture (city draft animals having absorbed some 6 percent of agricultural output). Since the oat crop, 20 percent of the corn crop, and a part of the hay crop were grown for horse feed, the decline of the number of horses triggered a rampant overproduction crisis in the 1920s that burst open in the 1930s (for all practical purposes horses had faded from the North Central states by 1945).

Thus, while the geographic frontier was closed by the turn of the century, a new frontier—a technological one—had opened a decade later. It was invisible since it ran through each farm. Huge amounts of cropland became free for final production and consumption. From the point of view of available food resources, the development of this new "frontier" was tantamount to the discovery and development of a whole new continent!

Motorization of agriculture greatly increased the capacity of U.S. agriculture to deliver production for final use at a time when the agricultural recovery of Europe decreased that area's demand for imports, and when Canada, Australia and Argentina were taking a larger share of world grain exports (Figure 2). The domestic market was unable to absorb this excess capacity since per capita food consumption changed marginally (Barger and Landsberg 1942: 141–89). In 1929, the underlying tendencies broke out: agricultural markets collapsed, entailing a severe and lasting overproduction crisis alleviated by the droughts of 1934 and 1936.

Power farming is portrayed as grand progress. From the point of view of capital accumulation, it certainly was. However, for farmers it also opened a Pandora's box, since oats as well as a part of the corn and hay crops became redundant. A farmer who had mechanized was confronted with two major "micro" problems, one of a technical nature and the other economic.

Technically, replacing oats required a new crop that would agronomically fit into a balanced rotation system, that is a legume (a species that fixes the nitrogen of the air into plant roots), to offset the decreasing volume of horse manure. The economic problem was a simple practical one: since cash was flowing out for cars, tractors, new machinery, parts, and gasoline, cash had to come in. The new crop had to be a cash crop.

This "simple practical" problem had profound implications. Up until roughly World War I, the economy of the corn-belt had been working to a large extent under a system of simple exchange, commodities for money for commodities. Production did not involve substantial market expenses: implements were simple and lasted a number of years; almost no commercial fertilizer was used on corn until the mid-1940s; horses worked for fifteen or twenty years (while tractors would wear out or become obsolete in seven); draft mares bred on a piece of pasture; repairs were handled by the farmer or a local craftsman. Land prices were still reasonable and debts low. "For a large number of farmers the production of agricultural commodities is not carried on as a means of making money, but rather as a mode of existence" (Barger and Landsberg 1942: 6).

Moreover, there was hardly any incentive for farmers to expand: horses had to rest; increasing the acreage of corn or the size of operations would entail the use of a second team of horses, the hiring of a driver, and the purchase of a new set of implements. "In the cultivation of the soil there is discernible scarcely any tendency toward that growth in the size of the entrepreneurial unit which has characterized other types of industry" (Barger and Landsberg 1942: 4). Briefly stated, there were virtually no economies of scale in corn-belt farming.

Automobiles were the first sign that the times were changing. In 1910, the six million plus farms had 50,000 automobiles; in 1920 there were 2.1 million; in 1930, 4.1 million. Farmers converted part of their large windfall World War I income—the net income of farm operators jumped from $4 billion in 1915 to $9 billion by 1918—into cars, tractors, and trucks. Few realized that the operating costs of these glittering wonders would drain their cash year after year and subvert the very sense of farming. Power farming then began to make money the driving force. It replaced simple exchange with the more complex and contradictory capitalist circuit of money-commodity-money, which makes sense only if the amount of money at the end of the circuit is larger than the amount at the beginning—that is, accumulation then becomes the aim of production.

Tractors created important economies of scale. They worked faster than horses, and they worked longer under more difficult conditions. They removed directly and indirectly the bottleneck of preparing the seedbed and cultivating corn. In Illinois one-third of the farms that had acquired a tractor in 1916 or 1917 were cropping a larger acreage in 1918 (Yerkes and Church 1918), and this at the very beginnings of the tractor age when machines left much to be desired.

Briefly stated, the tractor—and more generally power farming—simultaneously made capital accumulation necessary and possible: necessary by subverting the previous simple exchange relationship into a capitalist relationship; possible by creating economies of scale. Yet this process of capital accumulation generated a contradiction on a "macro" dimension, the contradiction of overproduction. Thus, the farmer who sought a crop to replace oats not only needed to provide a solution to the two "micro" problems noted above, but also had to solve the immense "macro" problem of overproduction.

## The Closing of the Technological Frontier

The solution to this knotty set of problems is now well known: soybeans. This legume plant, grown in limited quantity until the 1930s, now occupies as much land as corn. It was easily mechanized;

it brought in cash when processed into oil; and above all it made it possible to eat away the overproduction problem through its role in production of cheaper meat and animal products.

The primary task of transforming soybeans into a cash crop—creating a market for oils—was itself a rather complex task (Berlan, Bertrand and Lebas 1976). A first step was accomplished in 1928 when a group of co-ops and large companies (basically corn processors) offered to contract soybean production at a fixed price. Even though the quantities contracted were small, this move stands as a symbol of the emergence of agribusiness, the new powerful alliance between industrial capital and progressive (that is, large) farmers. A second step was the tariff protection of soybeans in 1930 (within the famous Smoot-Hawley tariff). The United States had previously imported but one staple, vegetable oils. Displacing foreign oils with domestic oils was an obvious demand from farmers and industrialists desperate for new outlets. The third step occurred in 1935, when the margarine manufacturers, under siege by farmers, agreed at a "Domestic Oils and Fats Conference" to use only *domestically* produced oils and fats. The result was dramatic: in 1931–35, soybean oil made up only 1 percent of margarine, but ten years later it was 39 percent.

Still, the early expansion of the soybean market would have had limited impact if additional uses had not been developed for the soybean meal. Meal (some 80 percent of the bean by weight) had to be a full commodity and not only a by-product. During the 1930s, experiment stations and the U.S. Department of Agriculture demonstrated that after a heat treatment this source of concentrated protein had near magical properties as animal feed. It greatly increased the ratio of meat to feed consumed and the meat was leaner. By the end of the 1930s, meal used as feed was worth more than oil, and in the postwar period the ever increasing market for meal was the driving force behind the expansion of soybean production, while the oil had to be dumped through various aid programs.

Thus, on the eve of World War II, the core of the new system of agricultural production and consumption based on a more "efficient" transformation of grain into meat and other animal products was well rooted in the land and in the minds of agricultural scientists. During the following decades, as the new system expanded first in the United States and then abroad, it grew in technological, economic and social sophistication, and the cost of meat began a historical decline. In the 1950s, the use of soybean meal and the development of sorghum in the Great Plains displaced small-scale fattening from midwest farms to huge feedlots west of the Mississippi. Beef consumption doubled between the 1950s and 1970s. Poultry production became concentrated in the southeastern states, where impoverished small farmers carried out the immediate production, under contracts with large, integrated poultry companies. Poultry consumption increased more than three-fold between 1940 and 1970.

The most important consequence of these changes was the formidable expansion of outlets for feed grains. Not only did soybean production for feed expand, but corn production for feed grew as well. Overproduction, then, for all practical purposes, was eaten away. It seemed that the threat of overproduction could be viewed as a contingent event which inspired agricultural policies could manage.

## New Agricultural Policies

The developments which had "solved" the overproduction crisis of the late 1920s and 1930s had also transformed the social relations of agriculture. The commercialization of agriculture and the shift from simple exchange to the money-commodity-money circuit of exchange, the emergence of power farming and the heavy reliance on purchased inputs, and the integration of grain farming into the feed-meat industry—all served to bring forth the full emergence of agribusiness, with industrial and financial capital thoroughly involved with and dominating agricultural production. This new mode of capital accumulation in U.S. agriculture, which had emerged out of the early overproduction crisis, set the stage on which new agricultural policies were put into effect. Ironically, these new policies would create the foundation for another overproduction crisis.

Effective pressure for policies of agricultural price stabilization grew from the needs of the emerging agribusiness complex. The important and prosperous farm machinery and tractor business had been brought to a standstill by the price collapse after World War I and was pummeled again by the price failures of the 1930s. These experiences had illustrated that the agricultural price system was too unreliable to shape a smooth path of capital accumulation, and consequently state intervention was necessary. If agribusiness was to grow, stability was essential, and "by the end of the 1920s the federal government was committed to the idea of accepting some responsibilities for farm prices" (Rasmussen 1960: 228).[3]

On the one hand, then, price stabilization policies evolved into a sophisticated system of state interventions to foster capital accumulation in an agribusiness complex—farming being a small but crucial segment—dominated by large industrial corporations and banks. A floor was set on agricultural prices to avoid a collapse which would have prevented the transformation of agriculture from getting off the ground. As a consequence, there has been an increasing use of industrial inputs and modern technology that have spectacularly increased yields and output.

On the other hand, the policies of fostering capital accumulation in agriculture have been threatened by the recurrent problem of overproduction that they continually recreate. Rising incomes and high income elasticities of demand for meat combined with falling prices and high price elasticities of demand to forestall the overproduction problem. Yet the expansion of consumption within the United States quickly proved insufficient. Thus, *the drive for foreign markets, the most conspicuous feature of U.S. agricultural policy, became a vital necessity* to manage the tendency of capital accumulation to break down under the stress of overproduction.

During World War II and in the immediate postwar years, agriculture found growing foreign markets (see Figures 2 and 3). When U.S. exports began to decline after the Korean War, the Foreign Trade and Assistance Act (PL 480) was enacted. This unique mixture of ostensible philanthropy and cynical pursuit of agribusiness interests proved a powerful tool to open new markets and shape the development of world agriculture.[4] In subsequent years, up to the early 1980s, U.S. exports continued to absorb a larger and larger share of agricultural production.

Briefly stated, during the decades up to the 1980s, the worldwide diffusion of the "wasteful" (as often stated) process of transforming cereal and high protein feed into meat held overproduction problems in check. Nonetheless, the overproduction pressures were maintained by the continual deepening of capital accumulation both in the United States and abroad. In the 1980s, the question is now whether the present crisis is simply a phase of a process leading into another dynamic equilibrium or the beginning of a new period of profound instability.

### Supply and Demand Imbalances

As long as international expansion increased outlets for U.S. agriculture at about the same rate as capital accumulation increased production, the tools of agricultural policy as they had been developed in the 1930s—particularly acreage restrictions—could control the temporary gaps between supply and demand. However, if longer-run supply and demand trends diverge, then traditional policy measures are likely to be insufficient. Some more basic structural changes, either in production or markets, would be needed to restore stability. Accordingly, to appraise the depths of the current crisis, it is necessary to examine the longer-run trends in supply and demand on a worldwide basis.

## Will Output Continue to Grow? How? Where?

With regard to supply, there is every reason to believe that output in the world economy will continue to grow substantially. Events in both Europe and Japan and technological developments which will affect production in the United States and throughout the world would all seem to augur considerable supply increases. Central factors include the following:

1. Although Europe is still a significant market for U.S. agricultural products, it is a shrinking market. More important, increasingly European agriculture is becoming a competitor, particularly in cereal grains. Europe's degree of agricultural self-sufficiency, including its self-sufficiency in oils, has steadily risen. In high-protein meal, however, Europe's rate of self-sufficiency is still minimal (around 20 percent, though increasing), and Europe remains the largest importer of U.S. soybeans. U.S. policymakers have placed considerable pressure on European governments to abandon the policies which give special advantages to their cereal producers. While the success of this pressure would expand grain markets for U.S. producers, for U.S. agriculture overall such success would produce a no-win situation. If cereal markets were lost to U.S. producers, European oil and protein production would shoot up and cut into those categories of U.S. exports.

2. Japan is still the best client for U.S. agricultural sales. It has little cropland (per capita, only one-tenth of that in the United States) and apparently no choice but to import food. Also, with the low level of meat consumption in Japan—thirteen pounds of beef per capita per year as compared to eighty in the U.S.—there would appear to be a virtually unlimited market for U.S. agricultural products.

There is, however, a problem with the idea that Japan's land scarcity makes it a dependent nation in world agriculture. For the last several decades, the main "factors" providing a dynamic to agricultural production have been financial capital and industrial inputs, such as machinery and especially chemicals. In recent years, Japanese capital has been using its financial and industrial capacities to develop agricultural production in countries such as Brazil, Indonesia, and Malaysia. Cheap land and cheap labor in these countries are used in conjunction with Japanese-made inputs to produce agricultural products that can then supply the Japanese market. In addition, when large infrastructure development is needed as a foundation for agricultural expansion (for example, roads, dams, ports), Japanese finance and Japanese inputs are available. This process has been emerging for some time. As early as the mid-1970s it was widely recognized that in the 1980s Japanese aid and investment programs in foreign countries would create an increase of several million tons of feed and oilseed grain on world markets and several hundred thousand tons of cotton. The larger share of these increases would be aimed at the Japanese market, and, consequently, U.S. producers, Japan's main suppliers, would be faced with difficult competition in any effort to increase their share of the Japanese market.

3. The major agricultural technological innovations which have been emerging in recent years, in the United States and elsewhere, have both enhanced the potential for production increases and have placed the whole process of change in agriculture more and more thoroughly under the control of large, agribusiness corporations. It has, of course, long been the case that the major technological changes in agriculture have originated in industry. The tractor, for example, was the product of the automobile industry, and chemical fertilizer production grew out of the production of explosives (and utilized factories built at government expense). In the present era, public agricultural research has led increasingly to an integrated system of production dominated by capital: "One of the major pathways leading to this result involved extensive research in plant and animal breeding. . . . The realization that the efficiency of transforming inputs into outputs depends on the characteristics of living organisms, and that these characteristics can be manipulated genetically, is the major theoretical contribution of scientific agricultural research to the process of technological change and to capital penetration [of agriculture]" (Lewontin and Berlan 1986).

These developments have paved the way for the concentration of agricultural innovation even more thoroughly in the hands of large-scale industry which is in a position to organize the creation of genetically new life forms and thus control the dispersion of agricultural change. These developments have made it possible to turn life into another factor of production. During the 1970s, petrochemical and pharmaceutical multinationals gained control of the world seed industry, and during the 1980s the living material of their operations has become a commodity by itself, produced and sold for profit. In a very short period, the patent authorities have moved from the long standing principle that "if it is living, it is not patentable" to the practice that living organisms—micro-organisms (1980), plants (1985), mammals (1987), and human tissues and cells (1988)—can be patented.

These technological changes and the industrial reorganization associated with them assure an accelerated movement toward a capital-using and high-yield agriculture. The constraints on change that existed because of the role and interests of small farmers are being swept aside. In short, the advance of technology is bringing farming more and more completely under the sway of capitalism and capital. Whatever the social costs, we can expect that agricultural supply will move rapidly upward.

## Will Outlets Expand?

There is little reason to expect an expansion of the demand for agricultural outputs that would keep pace with the increasing supply capacity. Inherent limits on price reductions in the production of meat, long-run general stagnation, and particular aspects of economic crisis all suggest that there will be no rapid growth of outlets for agricultural goods in the coming period:

1. The transformation of grains into meat provided a substantial outlet for agriculture while (a) meat production required large amounts of grain and (b) the improvement of the efficiency of grain-meat transformation allowed meat prices to fall, stimulating greater consumption. Now, however, the efficiency of the grain-to-meat transformation process has reached a point where further gains are limited. This is most clearly true for poultry, where the feed-efficiency ratio has dropped enormously—from 4 or 4.5 in the 1940s to 1.6—and is now dropping at a lower rate. Moreover, further gains in the grain-to-meat ratio are likely to translate into only minimal cost and price decreases because they now involve such large capital expenses. In any case, gains from productivity improvement are

mostly captured by the processing firms (or on the input side) and are not likely to translate into lower prices and greater consumption. Thus the period when increased productivity translated into (relative) price declines and increased consumption is over.

2. Sufficiently rapid expansion of incomes on a worldwide basis would offer an outlet for agricultural products, especially because in much of the world, meat consumption rises more than proportionally as income rises (that is to say, there is a high income elasticity for meat consumption). Of course the reality in the world economy is not rapid expansion but stagnation. Various other essays in this volume both describe and explain the prevailing stagnation, and there is no need to elaborate the argument here.

Suffice to note two particular related points. First, nowhere are the overproduction problems of the era more apparent than in agriculture. The obvious capacity of agriculture to expand production and the equally obvious unmet food needs of so much of the world's population make the overproduction contradiction particularly stark. Second, the overproduction problem in agriculture is closely associated with income inequality. There would, at least in the short to medium term, be no agricultural overproduction problem, in spite of general stagnation, if income distribution were moving in favor of the poor. Yet, in both the advanced countries, where conservative policies remain ascendant, and in the poor countries, where austerity programs are the watchword of the era, the trend appears to be toward greater inequality.

3. Of course, it is the poor countries that are often expected to provide the demand for agricultural goods in the coming period. The obvious need for food and the fact that in these countries the income elasticity of meat consumption is high, would seem to make them favorable outlets. Yet reality does not give much credence to these expectations. Aside from general stagnation, particular aspects of the current crisis in the third world make them poor potential outlets.

The debt situation in many countries is the most obvious obstacle to increased food demand. Between 1981 and 1987, for example, U.S. agricultural exports to Latin America fell from $6.4 billion to $3.7 billion. Mexico, by far the largest purchaser in Latin America of U.S. agricultural goods, had a 1987 debt service ratio of over 50 percent (that is, the amount due as interest and principal on the country's debt was more than 50 percent of export earnings). The other large Latin American purchasers of U.S. agricultural exports, Brazil and Venezuela, are also very large debtors, carrying debt service ratios in 1987 of 35 percent and 39 percent, respectively. In order to meet these obligations, the debtor countries are forced to raise exports, including food exports, and cut imports. Thus with debt service ratios at these levels, it would seem that these countries offer scant prospect for recovery of U.S. agricultural exports in the foreseeable future.

In oil-exporting third world countries, the outlook is no more favorable. As Tanzer points out elsewhere in this volume, the international oil industry has become "an unstable lottery," and, in spite of the experiences in the 1970s, there is no reason to expect long-run rising incomes in oil-exporting countries nor to expect that the income increases which do take place will be translated into food demand. Some oil exporters—Mexico in particular—are so far in debt that their oil revenues simply go to cover interest and principal payments. In the sparsely populated countries—Saudi Arabia is the clearest example—any rising oil income will have no noticeable impact on world food demand. In those countries with larger populations—such as Nigeria—even in the heyday of high oil prices the impact on per capita incomes and hence on food expenditures was small. Moreover, in virtually all the oil-exporting third world countries, the huge inequality of income distribution means that income increases have minimal impact on food demand.

4. Finally, the socialist countries are unlikely to greatly increase their imports of food or feedstuffs. Some, such as Poland, are virtually bankrupt, and others, while not in Poland's desperate situation, lack the export earnings which would allow substantial import growth. All have experienced a substantial slowdown in the rate of growth of income. Moreover, if these economic factors were not enough, political considerations make it unlikely that the U.S.S.R. will establish a long-run dependency on U.S. exports.

## The Costs of Balancing Out

A brief review of supply and demand trends thus indicates that, barring unexpected events such as a series of bad crop years (of which there have already been two in the 1980s), the agriculture supply and demand trend lines are diverging. The problem is especially serious because it has emerged at a time when the United States can no longer find solutions to economic difficulties by imposing policies on the world economy. However, when all is said and done, there will be a balance between supply and demand; this is an ex post facto necessity. How will this balance be established?

In answering this question, one should be skeptical about the present promises of the corporate and research establishment that bio-engineered "superior" micro-organisms, plants and animals, will make food cheap, increase effective demand and solve environmental problems. Whatever superiority these new plants and animals may have is *always in relation to a particular environment.* To express itself, genetic "superiority" requires more artificial growing conditions—that is, an increasing use of sophisticated inputs and, hence, further control of capital accumulation in agriculture by the agro-chemical industry. It will entail a drastic speed-up in the elimination of smaller farmers, in land concentration, and in the transformation into wasteland of large areas unable to compete on the terms imposed by this type of technological change. Indeed, in the present crisis, these changes are already underway in the United States and Europe. Thus, even under the very best of circumstances, any "progress" in dealing with the supply and demand imbalances by technological solutions will generate a host of social and environmental problems.

A direct attack on the problems resulting from the tendency for the growth of supply to outstrip the growth of demand will most likely involve a continuation, and perhaps intensification, of well known programs. The main thrusts of U.S. policy will be in attempts to establish more international outlets for agricultural surpluses and in further set-aside programs.

U.S. government efforts to regain some of the export shares lost during the period of the high-priced dollar in the early 1980s will continue. Examples include: huge subsidies to prop up exports, massive handouts of food aid to client states in the third world (Egypt is a case in point), attacks against Europe's Common Agricultural Policy, and pressure on Japan to consume more beef and import more food and feedstuffs. These actions, begun during the Reagan years, will surely continue in future administrations. It is, however, doubtful that they will accomplish anything more than moving around a surplus of worldwide dimensions.

With regard to set-aside programs, one new idea that may gain some success has been put forth by the agricultural research establishment: a set-aside of part of cropland in "ecological farm reservations." Accumulation would then proceed unabated in "efficient" farms on the best lands. Politically, such a scheme may gain appeal among that part of the population concerned with ecological issues. Also, with farmers aging and their political influence diminishing, they have declining ability to block programs which would override their interests. Still, for acreage restrictions to be effective, they will have to be massive.

The problem with these "solutions" is only partially that their success in terms of maintaining a supply-demand balance is questionable. More serious is that no programs for dealing with agriculture's problems, in the advanced countries or in the third world, departs from the socially costly and environmentally destructive mode of agriculture that ultimately threatens the very survival of the planet. The crisis of agriculture and food is far more than an "economic crisis" in the usual narrow sense of the term. It is one of the pillars in the foundation of the far larger environmental crisis.

In the United States alone, erosion endangers the carrying capacity of one half of the cropland, underground water is seriously overexploited, and pollutants accumulate along the food chain. During the period of high wheat prices in the 1970s, farmers in the United States and Canada tore out the hedges that had been established for decades in order to grow wheat "fence to fence"; their actions, however profitable, set the stage for future soil disasters.

Third World countries are caught up in a desperate and vicious process of destroying their natural resources simply to service debt and allow short-term survival. The destruction of forests—some 11 million hectares of forest disappear each year—already has catastrophic consequences, particularly when it comes to the tropical forests of Africa, Latin America, and Asia. The severity of the latest flooding of Bangladesh, for example, was in large part due to the deforestation of the Himalayas. In Africa, increased population, in the context of the existing inequalities, leads to the cropping of marginal land, further deforestation, and the spread of deserts. New disasters will be blamed on the whims of nature, in spite of the fact that perceptive agronomists have shown that these events are evidences of an *exploitative relationship among people and not between people and nature* (Dumont 1987 and 1988).

If we raise our eyes, we see that the air and the water and the life that inhabits them are in danger. The Mediterranean sea is dying if not dead. The ozone layer that protects the earth from deadly ultraviolet light is being destroyed. The buildup of carbon dioxide in the atmosphere may hold "unpleasant surprises in the greenhouse," according to the euphemism of *Nature,* and "there is now clear evidence that changes in the Earth's climate may be sudden rather than gradual" (Broecker 1987). Then we have acid rain and Chernobyl, while biologists lament the loss of tens of thousands of species every year.

There is an urgent necessity to bring accumulation under social control and to redirect scientific and technological efforts toward the satisfaction of social needs through methods that will take into account the finite character of our planet. The agricultural experience provides one part of the story, but the same is true in the rest of the economy. The agricultural crisis presents us with the danger that in efforts to find solutions to current difficulties governments and business will move even more rapidly toward "solutions" which are extremely dangerous, and only provide marginal relief in their own terms. Yet a crisis also provides opportunities to push the situation in new directions if people realize the existence of environmental limits and recognize that, ultimately, the irreversible damage being done to our people and our world are the only issues.

## Notes

1. See Pfeffer (1985) on the origins of the three systems of U.S. farm production. Since animal husbandry is based on grain, and beef, pork, and poultry products are corn and soybeans in a different form, an index of grain production is a reasonable proxy for total output, particularly since the 1930s. The published indices of final output are misleading because they do not include feedstuffs for draft animals. During the period 1920–39, in the North Central states horses were replaced by tractors. A stable volume of output for consumption was obtained with a declining use of agricultural inputs such as feed for draft animals. The rate of growth of an index of final production is then by construction higher than the one of an index of total production since the latter is the sum of the same final product plus a declining volume of intermediate agricultural inputs. Published indices of final production, then, overestimate growth and hide the underlying, fundamental trends.
2. There might be some dispute about the significance of the decline between the wars, since the drought years of 1934 and 1936 fall within the period. Yet these calamitous years, which wiped out almost half of the corn crop and a large chunk of the wheat crop, were a blessing since they restored the balance between supply and demand, a prerequisite for any economic recovery. No agricultural policymaker would have dared to do what the weather did.
3. Representatives of the emerging agribusiness complex were directly involved in formulating agricultural policies as the 1920s according to Schlesinger (1957) and Rasmussen (1960). Over the years there has been much lamenting that agricultural policies have consistently run contrary to their stated objectives of defending the family farm. Such concerns, however, miss the point, since the policies were designed not to save the family farm but to provide the stability for agribusiness-based accumulation.
4. It also served to support client states and to punish rebellious ones (Chile in the

early 1970s, for example), to draw the support of farmers for an imperial foreign policy, and to obfuscate the real objectives of food aid.

## References

Barger, Harold and Hans H. Landsberg. 1942. *American Agriculture, 1899–1939: A Study of Output, Employment and Productivity.* New York: National Bureau of Economic Research.

Berlan, Jean-Pierre, Jean-Pierre Bertrand and Laurence Lebas. 1976. *Le Complexe Soja des Etats-Unis.* Paris: Institut National de la Recherche Agronomique.

Broecker, Wallace S. 1987. "Unpleasant Surprises in the Greenhouse?" *Nature* 328, 9 July.

Dumont, Rene. 1988. "La survie de l'humanité en grand peril." *Le Monde Diplomatique,* October.

————. 1987. *Pour l'Afrique, J'accuse,* Paris: Collection Terre Humaine. Laffont.

Johnson, Glen L. and Leroy Quance. 1972. *The Overproduction Trap in U.S. Agriculture,* Washington, Resources for the Future. 1972.

Lewontin, Richard C. and Jean-Pierre Berlan. 1986. "Technology, Research and the Penetration of Capital: The Case of U.S. Agriculture." *Monthly Review* 38, no. 3, July–August.

Pfeffer, Max J. 1985. "Social Origins of Three Systems of Farm Production in the United States." *Rural Sociology* 48, no. 4.

Rasmussen, Wayne D. 1960. "The Agricultural Crisis of 1920–23 and the McNary-Haugenplan." In *Readings in the History of American Agriculture.* Champaign-Urbana: University of Illinois Press.

Schlesinger, Arthur M., Jr. 1957. *The Age of Roosevelt: Crisis of the Old Order, 1919–1933.* Boston: Houghton Mifflin.

Yerkes, Arnold P. and L.M. Church. 1918. "Tractor Experience in Illinois." *Farmer's Bulletin,* No. 963, June.

# Growing Instability
# in the International Oil Industry

## *Michael Tanzer*

### *Introduction*

Historically, the oil industry has always been both international and dependent upon state power. Thus, the overriding economic, political, and military forces which determine the balance of power among nation-states have generally been crucial in determining which companies and groups of national capital have controlled the world's oil resources and profits (Tanzer 1974: 38–53; Tanzer and Zorn 1985: 40–75). This essay will try to show how in recent years the growing fragmentation of power and instability in the overall international economy has manifested itself in the international oil industry—as both cause and effect.

In summary, the first half of the twentieth century has seen oil capital based in those countries victorious in the two major world wars emerge to dominate international oil. First, after World War I, there came Britain, followed by the United States and trailed by France, and after World War II the U.S. reigned supreme, trailed by Britain and a laggard France. (Insofar as the socialist countries were able to break out of the international system after the two world wars, they have been able to develop their own internal oil resources, and in recent years the Soviet Union even has become a significant player on world markets.)

Within the last twenty years, however, what was once a monopolistic industry *par excellence* has seen very serious fragmentation, basically paralleling the decline of U.S. hegemony in the late 1960s and early 1970s. The decisive upheaval stemmed from the events of the 1970–73 period, culminating in the 1973 Arab-Israeli War. It needs to be recalled that the Organization of Petroleum Exporting Countries (OPEC) was created in 1960, and in its first decade accomplished relatively little, except for stabilizing the per barrel revenues of its governments in a period of declining oil prices caused by intensifying competition among the companies.

Contrastingly, in the early 1970s the OPEC countries effectively achieved goals that had been the dreams of oil nationalists throughout the twentieth century. They wrested away from the companies the historic pillars of their control of the industry: their effective ownership of the country's crude oil, and the right to determine the price of the oil and the amounts to be produced. From the producing countries' viewpoint, it appeared as if the millennium had arrived, and twenty-five years early no less.

Now, however, some fifteen years after the great OPEC revolution, it is clear that while much was accomplished, much more was not. The international oil companies and their home governments, with their vast financial resources, control of refining and distribution facilities in oil importing countries as well as of crude oil production in non-OPEC countries, have been shown again to be cats with ninety-nine lives. The struggle of these conflicting and fragmented forces has turned the oil industry into an unstable lottery. On the upside it generates vast riches for the international oil companies and their financial institutions and home governments, and great wealth for the elites of the OPEC countries, and on the downside it spreads misery, despair, and bankruptcy for all but the largest of the wily oil company cats. This grim picture of enormously increased instability both interacts with and has considerable implications for the rest of the international economy.

## *The International Oil Companies*

As always, the best starting point for analysis is the international oil companies, since they interact directly with all the main players in the industry. Moreover, we live in an era when the major companies have undergone great structural upheavals under which various fractions of national capital have sought to wrest control from one another. In this sense, the weakening of managerial control that has accompanied both "privatization" of governmental oil enterprises and the assaults of large blocs of "raider capital" on major private oil companies has made the industry emblematic of the increased instability wracking the international capitalist system at the micro-level.

This corporate instability has clearly been a phenomenon of the 1980s, triggered by the events of the 1970s. Thus, for the golden period of U.S. hegemony following World War II (circa 1945–70) one could confidently (and sexistly) describe the international oil industry as dominated by the Anglo-American "Seven Sisters": five U.S. giants—Exxon, Mobil, Standard of California, Texaco, and Gulf Oil—and two British/Dutch firms—Royal Dutch/Shell and British Petroleum. As of 1970 these Big Seven, who controlled the world's low-cost crude oil in the Middle East and the rest of the third world, and all the further stages of refining and distribution, owned three-fifths of the capitalist world's crude oil (with one-third belonging to the rest of the major oil companies) and undoubtedly accounted for an even greater share of industry profits.

As a result of the OPEC upheavals of the 1970s, however, world crude oil ownership shifted dramatically, so that by 1981 the Big Seven owned only about one-fifth, the other multinational oil companies about the same, and the oil-producing countries now had three-fifths. It was this dramatic takeover by the producing countries that laid the basis for the optimism in the third world that it was now in a position to wrest the control and enormous profitability of oil away from the companies.

Indeed, in the 1970s the OPEC countries in aggregate fared extremely well, with the tenfold increase in oil prices catapulting their revenues from $14 billion in 1970 to a peak of $287 billion (in current dollars) in 1980 (*OPEC Annual Statistical Bulletin,* 1986, p. 6). At the same time, however, this did not spell the death knell of the oil companies, since their aggregate profits also increased handsomely, although not as dramatically: for the Big Five U.S. companies, profits increased from under $4 billion in 1972 to over $10 billion in 1983.

In the 1970s the principal reason for the international oil companies' profits to increase even though they lost control of ownership and high profits on OPEC oil was the greatly increased profitability on production of the oil they still owned in the industrial countries like the United States and the North Sea and in non-OPEC underdeveloped oil producing countries which had less bargaining power with the companies. Thus, for example, the tenfold increase in oil prices in the 1970s meant that profits on the companies' large Alaskan crude oil production leaped to almost $10 per barrel, compared to the 50 cents to $1.00 they had been making on OPEC crude oil production.

The real strength of the international oil companies compared to the OPEC countries was evidenced however in the 1980s, which have been a period of generally declining oil prices. For the OPEC countries, a combination of falling oil prices and declining production has caused a precipitous fall in revenues, from $287 billion in 1980 to $77 billion in 1986, with a rebound in 1987 to an estimated $90 billion (*Petroleum Intelligence Weekly,* December 7, 1987, p. 3.). Needless to say, this decline has played havoc with ambitious development plans started in the boom 1970s, as well as with standards of living.

The international oil companies, on the other hand, particularly the largest ones, have managed to weather the storm in much better fashion. For one thing, they continue to control the refining and distribution of oil, so that cuts in crude oil prices tend to increase their profits in these sectors. Similarly, reductions in crude oil prices lower the costs of feedstocks for their chemical operations, thereby increasing profitability. In other words, the companies are the beneficiaries of the lags and relative degrees of monopolization of markets that prevent a $1.00 per barrel reduction in crude oil prices from translating into a full $1.00 per barrel reduction in product prices.

Additionally, the companies have built up over the years large amounts of capital assets which they can depreciate and amortize for tax purposes, but which are only bookkeeping entries that do not detract from their true earnings—"cash flow," consisting of net profits after taxes plus depreciation and amortization. It is this cash flow which is the true measure of a company's economic power, since it can be utilized to pay dividends, to make new capital investments, to reduce debt, or to acquire other companies and assets which may be available at bargain-sale prices in depressed times. And what is remarkable about the largest oil companies as a group—particularly the Big Seven—is that in the 1980s they have been able to maintain their cash flow, which leaped in the 1970s, at a high plateau level, despite the crisis of the industry. (Thus, the Big Seven's cash flow in both 1980 and 1986 was the same $35 billion, even though their net profits dropped about 40 percent; this was completely offset by an 80 percent increase in depreciation and amortization.)

## Turbulence Among the Oil Companies

At the same time, as is typical in industry in depressed times, there has been a great deal of turbulence in the respective positions of the oil companies. At one extreme, we have the biggest and most diversified company, Exxon. Thus, while OPEC revenues fell by three-fourths in the 1980–86 period, Exxon's profits were down by only one-tenth, and cash flow actually increased in this period by almost one-fifth.

At the other extreme, Texaco's net profits slid as precipitously as OPEC revenues in the 1980s, from $2.3 billion in 1981 to $.7 billion in 1986. In fact, Texaco's declining profits in this period led it into its ill-fated 1984 attempt to add to U.S. crude oil reserves by buying up Getty Oil, for $10 billion. Unfortunately for Texaco, it snatched Getty at the last minute out of the hands of Pennzoil, and a Texas jury awarded a judgment to Pennzoil against Texaco of $11 billion. Texaco was even forced to take temporary refuge in bankruptcy and has been so weakened as to be highly vulnerable to dismemberment by Wall Street raiders.

The Texaco battle-royal is just the latest case in a series of take-overs which have shattered the once stable world of sovereign major oil companies. The trend began in the late 1970s, when the big oil companies were flush with increased profits from the OPEC price rises. At the same time, with everyone seeking to find new oil supplies in order to cash in on what seemed like a never-ending bonanza—many were predicting that $50 per barrel oil was just around the corner—the costs of exploration were also driven skyward. Thus, the companies found that it cost as much as $15–20 per barrel to discover new reserves, while buying up other oil companies could effectively provide proven reserves at $5–6 per barrel.

This trend toward exploring for oil on Wall Street was fueled, in addition, by the existence of large pools of speculative capital, which by threatening unfriendly takeovers of some companies drove these firms' managements to seek more acceptable (that is, oil industry) buyers. A further factor in the oil industry merger-mania was the virtual abandonment of antitrust enforcement under the Reagan administration after 1981.

Many of the largest oil companies were involved in such once unheard of takeovers. Shell Oil-U.S. started the trend when it purchased Belridge Oil of California; Shell-U.S. itself was then bought out by its 65-percent owner, Royal Dutch/Shell. As noted, Texaco bought Getty, while Occidental Petroleum was the winner in a bidding war for Cities Service. Finally, in the largest and most historically dramatic of the mergers, Standard Oil of California (now Chevron) paid more than $10 billion in 1984 to buy one of the hitherto untouchable Big Seven itself, Gulf Oil. All told, from 1979 to mid-1984, oil companies spent more than $35 billion to acquire each other (Tanzer and Zorn 1985: 38).

More recently, in 1987, British Petroleum continued the trend of non-U.S. oil companies taking advantage of a weak dollar by buying in, for $8 billion, the 45 percent share of Standard Oil of Ohio which it did not already own; this doubled BP's crude oil reserves and made it the third largest investor-owned oil company in the world. (At the same time, the Kuwaiti Investment Fund bought up 20 percent of BP's equity!) And Amoco, the fifth largest U.S. company, spent $4 billion largely to buy up bankrupt Dome Petroleum's enormous natural gas reserves in Canada. As a result partly of this takeover binge, by 1986 the Big Seven accounted for over nine-tenths of the profits of the twenty-five companies covered in *Value Line*'s integrated petroleum group (*Value Line Investment Survey,* January 8, 1988).

This dual trend toward concentration and upheaval was furthered by the disastrous collapse of the smaller independent oil companies, particularly in the U.S. Southwest. These companies, which were overwhelmingly oil producers, found themselves in the same predicament as OPEC countries as prices fell, and at the same time many of them were choking on the large amounts of debt that they had incurred to expand in the euphoric 1970s. In Texas, the key oil-producing state, the combination of a fall in prices in the 1980s of almost 75 percent to the 1986 low of $10 per barrel, along with a 15 percent drop in production, meant a disaster for the independents. A survey of 170 independent oil producers for the first half of 1986 showed total losses of $3.5 billion, with widespread layoffs, cuts in capital spending, and bankruptcy filings (*Petroleum Economist,* April 1987, p. 131). Note that in this same six-month period, the Big Five U.S. companies had profits of $5.5 billion.

In the U.S. the speculative disasters in oil were closely linked with similar disasters in other sectors. Thus, the Texas/Oklahoma oil boom and collapse gave rise to a parallel situation in real estate and in the banking systems which financed both sets of activities.

The turbulence in the international oil industry has also been manifested by a series of changes in reaction to what has widely been perceived as a new "competitive era," and which often go under the rubric of "restructuring." Thus, companies have been abandoning old businesses, reducing refining capacity, and in general seeking to become more efficient. While some part of restructuring has simply meant reshuffling businesses from one company to another, what has been almost universal is a drive to reduce employment and labor costs. Where once a job in a major international oil company such as Exxon had practically the security of one in the Civil Service, in the 1980s all this has changed. Thus, for example, from 1981 to 1985 Exxon lopped off almost 20 percent of its employees. Even more, in the 1982–86 period Mobil cut its employment by one-third. Ironically, one of the great fears of entrenched management has been that if "outsiders" take control of the company the insiders will lose their highly paid positions; this factor itself has created some of the turbulence in the industry as insiders seek to fend off restructuring by outsiders by taking preemptive restructuring steps themselves.

## Oil and the Industrial Countries

The 1970s boom period in oil prices was, in the short run, basically positive for the U.S. economy, particularly in its rivalry with Continental Europe and Japan, although it sowed the seeds for severe problems during the bust. The main negative for the U.S. economy was that its oil import bill increased enormously, according to the IMF *International Financial Statistics,* from $3 billion in 1970 to $77 billion in 1980, and as a share of imports rose from 7 percent to 30 percent. While the increased profits of the largely U.S. oil companies helped somewhat to offset this import drain, by and large these profits were not net additions to the U.S. economy, but were recycled from other sectors such as manufacturing.

On the positive side for the U.S. economy, since it imported a much smaller share of its oil and energy resources than Japan and continental Europe, the drain on its economy from the higher oil prices was relatively less. Moreover, since oil imports were universally paid for in dollars, there was a huge worldwide increase in the demand for dollars, which the United States alone could meet, in effect by printing money rather than shifting real resources. Further, with the dollar as the world's ultimate currency, the U.S. banking system could make huge profits in the area of "recycling" petrodollars earned by the OPEC countries. That this lucrative business could turn into a financial nightmare was not foreseen in the heady boom period.

For the United Kingdom, home of the other major oil companies, the most important effect of the 1970s oil boom was that it made possible the large-scale development of the high-cost oil reserves in the North Sea. This turned the United Kingdom from a major oil importer into a major oil exporter, which provided the Thatcher government with the revenues to help offset the losses stemming from its savage deindustrialization of Britain's traditional manufacturing export sector; similarly, North Sea oil could be used to help break the coal miners' strike in 1982 by providing a substitute energy source. Finally, as one of the hubs of the international monetary system, the City of London too benefitted greatly from the enormous increase in activity due to petrodollar recycling. In short, in the boom period the United Kingdom had all the benefits of being a combination of an oil exporter and a highly developed monetary center.

For Japan and continental Europe, the immediate impact of the oil boom was to hit them very hard because they were major oil importers. Thus, while in the 1960s they had increased their oil imports sharply to fuel their growing economies, the dangers of this dependency were masked by declining oil prices, so that in general during this period total oil imports were a manageable 10 to 15 percent of export earnings. In the 1970s, however, the chickens came home to roost with a vengeance, and oil imports as a percentage of total imports typically were 15 to 20 percent in France and Germany, 20 to 25 percent in Italy, and 30 to 35 percent in Japan (Tanzer and Zorn 1985: 74).

While the short-run impact was severe, including an initial rush by currency speculators to dump non-dollar currencies which forced Japan and continental Europe to borrow heavily to defend their currencies, gradually the problem was mitigated. The most important saving factors were the worldwide inflation as well as the rise in the value of the dollar which allowed these developed countries to increase the prices of their exports, and the large increase in their exports to the newly wealthy OPEC countries, particularly in the Middle East.

In summary then, we may say that the oil boom initially favored the United States and even more so Great Britain, while penalizing Japan and continental Europe. However, as we shall see now, during this period the seeds were sown for a much greater upheaval in the various countries, and particularly in their relative power positions, during the oil bust of the 1980s.

For the international economic system as a whole, the oil bust of the 1980s had serious destabilizing effects for virtually all of its important components. For the United States, particularly in the oil-producing center of the country, there was a chain-reaction collapse in oil revenues, exploration and development and employment, and real estate values, all of which contributed to toppling the regional banking structure. Additionally, the nation's whole banking system was badly hurt by the defaults and moratoriums and write-offs on third world debt, much of which had been built up by oil-exporters such as Mexico overreacting to the boom and going deeply into debt, and by oil-importers who had little other real choice but to borrow, at high interest rates, merely for the survival of their economies.

At the same time, while the oil price decline gave the United States some relief from its oil import bill, an important countervailing force was the reduction in the international demand for dollars. This in turn had several negative effects on the U.S. position. First, the decline in the dollar in the last few years meant that the United States had to export more real resources to pay for its imports. Second, as the U.S. dollar continued to decline in value, foreign investors were able to buy real assets in the United States at rock-bottom prices, and the previous post-World War II process by which the United States tried to gobble up the world began to unwind in the opposite direction. And while in classical economic theory, the continuing decline of the dollar eventually would lead to a reversal in the trade and investment flows, in the meantime the U.S. power position was greatly weakened. Moreover, with so much of the value of the dollar determined by speculation, not only on trade deficits but on the U.S. budget deficit, it is not at all clear that the classical forces will have sufficient time to come into operation before there is a series of speculative busts in the system.

Similarly, the United Kingdom was hurt by the bust since it no longer enjoyed the luxury of large oil export revenues to cushion its weakened manufacturing sector. And, now that it had built up an even larger financial sector to compete with its U.S. rivals, it was even more vulnerable to the growing instability in that area.

On the surface, Japan and Continental Europe were the main beneficiaries of the oil bust. As they were the largest oil importers, there was a sizable reduction in their import bills, so that according to IMF figures, by 1986, the year of lowest average prices, oil's share as a percentage of total imports had fallen to below 10 percent for France, Germany and Italy, and under 20 percent for Japan.[1]

Despite this superficially optimistic picture, however, all these countries were in a very tenuous position. For one thing, because of the dominance of the dollar in the international system, they were perforce locked to the health of the U.S. currency. Second, particularly in Japan, the liquidity in the domestic economy has fueled an enormously speculative economy, even more than in the United States, as price-earnings ratios averaged 50 to 60 (or four times the ratio in U.S.), and Japanese multinationals, like their U.S. competitors, were increasingly making their profits from financial speculation rather than goods production (*Barron's,* September 7, 1987, pp. 57–58). Indeed, to those who recall the events of the 1929 stock market crash, the Japanese government seems to have been given the same role as the titans of Wall Street in "not allowing" a crash, and if history is any judge, probably with the same lack of success.

## Third World Oil-Importing Countries

As is well-known, the third world oil-importing countries by and large were the major losers from the oil-price boom of the 1970s. While the industrial countries were generally able to offset the oil-price increases by raising the prices of their own manufactured commodity exports, the same option was not available for third world countries selling raw material commodities in highly competitive markets. It is true that the 1970s provided some benefits to these countries, but not nearly enough to offset the basic damage. For one thing, OPEC countries did provide some assistance to the poor oil importers—certainly at higher proportions of GNP than the Western industrial countries ever did—but this help was still but a fraction of the increased import costs. Another positive was that the greatly increased value of oil in the 1970s led to increased interest in exploration in these countries and a major shift in the terms and conditions of exploration and production agreements between the countries and the companies.

Presumably the slide in oil prices in the 1980s would have benefited the oil-importing countries considerably, but unfortunately it seems like the benefits may have come too late to have major positive effects. For one thing, the weakened bargaining power of these countries on oil exploration agreements in the face of a perceived glut of oil has given the companies the upper hand again, and contracts being offered are frequently back to the level of the late 1960s, if not worse. Moreover, the mountains of debt that many of these countries built up to pay in the 1970s for highly inflated oil and industrial country products has left them with interest and debt repayment problems that now dwarf the oil problem.

## *Privatization*

At the same time, as part of the enormous pressure generated by Western financial institutions on third world countries to repay their debts, there has been an unrelenting assault on the state oil enterprises in these countries. Ironically, while some of these have been among the most successful efforts made at long-run development, under the war cry of "efficiency," Western financial institutions like the World Bank and the IMF have been renewing their attempts to curb these state enterprises in favor of private enterprise—read foreign international oil companies.

An important example is that of Petrobras, the state oil company of Brazil. Despite the fact that, in the words of industry journal *Petroleum Economist,* "Petrobras, a fully integrated petroleum monopoly set up in 1951, has established an admirable track record in the development of offshore technology" and has singlehandedly cut reliance on oil imports by half, the state company has been starved for additional funds to meet Brazil's goal of oil self-sufficiency in the 1990s. Brazil, with its huge foreign debt, has been under pressure from foreign lenders to curb Petrobras, and in April 1987 the government cut its budget by almost 20 percent. As the head of Petrobras's engineering subsidiary noted, "We witness with astonishment what appears to be the liquidation of assets that have been painstakingly built over the years." Thus, the debt crisis has opened the door again for *Petroleum Economist*'s perennial argument that "considering Petrobras's worsening financial position, there is a case to be made for increased private sector participation in some of the multi-billion dollar projects that are essential for future energy self-sufficiency" (December 1987, pp. 438–40).

The case of Petrobras exemplifies one of the principal ways in which the oil sector intersects with major trends in international capitalism in general—namely in the headlong drive for weakening and/or destruction of public sectors all over the world, which is subsumed under the rubric of "privatization." In the United States there is little left to privatize in oil, although interestingly there are recent reports that a fifty-year goal of oil capital, namely, selling off the famous Strategic Petroleum Reserve of the Navy, is apparently resurfacing with bipartisan support in order to help curb the budget deficit. Similarly, in Canada there are plans afoot to sell off 10 to 20 percent of Canada's state oil company (*Petroleum Economist,* August 1987, p. 309).

But in Western Europe, which has a long tradition of state enterprise in the oil and energy sector, built up in the 1920s and 1930s, the drive is proceeding rapidly. The largest denationalizations took place in Great Britain, where the 1986 sale of British Gas "was the world's largest-ever stock flotation, drawing 4½ million applications with a total value of some £9 billion (ibid., January 1987, p. 11). Most recently, in late 1987, as noted, the British government sold off its remaining 32 percent of British Petroleum for over $12 billion.

Other governments in Western Europe are also taking first steps toward energy privatization. In October 1986 the French government sold 11 percent of the mammoth Elf state oil company, and plans to sell another 5 percent, cutting the government's holdings to about 50 percent. In Italy, where ENI maintains an extensive state presence in energy, pieces of the company are being sold off in such diverse areas as pipelaying and engineering, with chemicals next on the list. Similarly, the Spanish government recently sold off 38 percent of the state Gas y Electricidad utility and plans to sell up to half of its energy sector holding company, INH (ibid.).

What are the motives for this privatization drive? Nominally, we are told, "Budget pressures and widespread dissatisfaction with the performance of state-owned enterprises have led governments to seek greater efficiency by emphasising financial targets" (*Amex Bank Review,* December 1986, quoted in ibid.). In the real world of international capitalism, however, other less altruistic goals may be discerned.

At the longest-run ideological level, clearly conservative forces worldwide would like to drive a stake in the heart of public enterprises, especially successful ones, so as to minimize the threats to capitalism when the political pendulum swings. Aside from everything else, public enterprises were often set up as "yardsticks" for measuring what reasonable rates of prices and profits might be for the private sector, and this is certainly anathema to private capital. At the same time, privatization is often a golden opportunity for private capital to make both short-term and long-term profits. Where sales are of large blocs of stock, normally prices will be set at relatively low rates in order to insure the success of the sale, and the benefits from the sale will follow the highly skewed distribution of wealth in capitalist countries; just to make sure, preference is normally given for indigenous investors over foreigners. Moreover, in the long run, the present conservative political climate provides the ideal cover for private capital to get its hands on the future streams of profits from successful natural resource companies which otherwise would accrue in the public sector—and destroy a public sector that under a more progressive political climate might even compete with the international oil companies.

Spearheading the assault on third world oil-importing countries in favor of the private international oil companies, as usual, has been the World Bank. In the 1970s, the fear of an oil shortage and continually rising prices for the industrial countries forced the bank to reverse its historic policy of not giving loans and grants to governments of oil importing countries for oil exploration and development. Although the bank sought every opportunity to push its "expectation that relatively modest Bank financing would attract a much larger flow of investment from private sources" (Tanzer and Zorn 1985: 58), the overriding consideration of the need to weaken OPEC and increase the supply of non-OPEC oil reserves available to the Western industrial countries meant that the bank frequently loaned money to state oil companies, without private sector participation, and on favorable terms, for example, developing India's Bombay High oilfield.

Now, however, that there is a perceived "oil glut," the bank has returned to its historic policy of promoting the private sector with a vengeance. Today there are relatively few soft loans to state oil companies for oil exploration and development; what little soft money is available for the state sector is for gas development. This is quite acceptable to the private sector, since the oil companies are relatively less interested in gas for home consumption, and because the bank's loans give it a lever to push the governments not to subsidize gas prices, but to leave them to the free market.

## Where Do We Go From Here?

As regards the oil sector and its interrelations with the overall international economic system, obviously one of the most important questions is what the likely price of oil will be in the future, (as well as the volatility of that price). A survey of a dozen recent studies reflects the lack of consensus among "experts": price forecasts for the 1990–2000 period range from $10 per barrel to $50 per barrel (*Petroleum Economist,* September 1987, p. 326).

The inability to forecast oil prices with any degree of confidence is inherent in the basic fact that in the short to medium run at least there is normally an oversupply of crude oil in the ground. Thus, the issue is not physical availability of supplies, but the ability to control production. And today this is an overwhelmingly political issue, far more dependent, for example, on the nature of the ruling regime in Saudi Arabia than on its physical reserves (which are enormous). Thus one could construct a plausible scenario whereby a conservative religious takeover in that country, which would link it ideologically to Iran, could lead an anti-modernization, fundamentalist drive in the Persian Gulf to restrict production, with oil prices skyrocketing. On the other hand, another plausible scenario could see a collapse of real production in the international economy leading to such a drop in oil demand as to drive prices down even further. Indeed, one could see both sets of forces operating, with the price result virtually indeterminate.

What is more predictable is that the past boom and bust in the industry has already contributed to great fear and uncertainty about its future. The typical effect of this perceived increase in risk is to shorten the oil investor's "time horizon." And in an industry with a long time lag between initial investment and eventual profitability, this naturally led to a cut in productive investment in a major sector of the international economy.

In general, I believe this shortening of the oil investment time horizon has contributed significantly both to stagnation of real production and growth of financial speculation in the international economy as a whole. For one of the main attractions of financial speculation is that investments and profits take place within a relatively short time period. So, just as one of the motives of oil companies in acquiring other oil companies is to shorten the time period between investment and profit, similarly one of the purposes of the whole range of financial speculations also is to reduce this time period— options and futures are speculations in which the longest time period is usually one year, while program trading and arbitrage allow you to lock up profits within one hour!

In this sense the collapse of oil prices in the 1980s may have given a powerful push to worldwide stagnation and financial speculation, and thus helped contribute to the erosion of overall capitalist confidence which culminated in the October 1987 crash. Moreover, it is hard to envision how this loss of confidence in the oil industry can be readily overcome in the near to medium future. It is all well and good to know that oil exploration and development in the United States is profitable at $20–$25 per barrel, but potential investors, and lenders in particular, are going to need to have real confidence that such a level can be maintained over long periods of time. Thus, it seems safe to assume that the oil sector will be a powerful force to continue present trends in the overall international economy encompassing stagnant real production and a drive for higher profits through increasing financial activity and speculation.

Furthermore, takeovers and restructuring and increased concentration of assets among the biggest companies in the United States and United Kingdom are likely to continue apace. At the same time, as long as the dollar remains relatively weak, since the United States is viewed politically as the safest haven for international capital, there will be a strong temptation for foreign oil capital to buy up additional assets in the United States. But, one of the contradictions of the present world situation is that the United States, although weakened economically, is still the strongest military power in the capitalist world, and will not easily cede its resources to foreigners.

Thus, at some point we may see, and perhaps sooner rather than later, the pressures for protectionism and economic nationalism to defend U.S. assets grow far stronger, particularly after the Reagan ideologues are out of office. It is just this knowledge that the doors may swing closed, both for domestic and foreign takeovers, that may trigger a last burst of frenzied takeover activity in redividing the world oil pie. And we can be sure that such redivision and the attendant financial speculation will contribute to even further instability in the international economic system.

## Note

1. Figures for Germany and Japan include refined oil products also.

## References

Tanzer, Michael 1974. *The Energy Crisis: World Struggle for Power and Wealth*. New York: Monthly Review Press.
——— and Stephen Zorn. 1985. *Energy Update: Oil in the Late Twentieth Century*. New York: Monthly Review Press.

# Gender and the Global Economy

## *Lourdes Benería*

### *Introduction*

In recent years discussions about the economic and social condition of women across countries have increasingly focused on the internationalization of economic activity. These discussions have dealt with a variety of processes, such as the growing employment of women in industrial production, the effects of multinational investment on women's work, the participation of female labor in the unregulated sector of the economy, and the intensification of domestic work as the debt crisis in many third world countries lowers real wages and living standards for a large proportion of the population. Yet, much remains to be done, particularly in terms of thinking through the significance of these processes for designing policies and political actions that incorporate gender as a fundamental dimension.

Women's daily struggles, as will be argued in this essay, are taking on a global significance. This calls, as Núñez and Burbach (1987) have forcefully argued, for an internationalization of "popular struggles" going beyond traditional party politics and based on ties of solidarity among different groups. In fact, as women across the globe have so often repeated, traditional politics, and the left as part of it, have distinguished themselves for being both ignorant and unwilling to take up gender-related issues. Yet, if politics and social action do not seriously integrate gender in their objectives, the women's movement, at the different national and international levels, will act more on its own, and the power that springs from solidarity between political movements will be weakened.

In developing the foundation for effective action, meanwhile, we must be aware of the fact that the analysis needed to inform this work is still lacking. At the international level, and particularly since the publication of Boserup's *Woman's Role in Economic Development* in 1970, there has been a tendency to separate gender issues related to third world countries from those of the more industrialized world—thus the appearance of this new "field" called Women and Development. The theoretical framework and political implications behind it are far from being uniform and range from the liberal to the left. However, the tendency to view the subject as separate is quite common and runs parallel to that of viewing "development" as referring only to economic growth in third world countries.

The problem of this separation—in addition to the dangerous tendency to objectify third world women—is that, as the globalization of economic relations proceeds, the need to understand the role of gender from a global perspective emerges with greater intensity. Where are women located in the new international division of labor? Can we assume that women's labor force participation is increasing worldwide? As international capitalism expands, how are class and gender integrated in the face of a rapidly changing economic landscape? What are the major issues emerging with respect to how gender is used in the global economy? What is their social and political significance? Can generalizations be made given country and regional differences?.

This essay is an effort to analyze some of these global issues. It includes three parts. First, it will discuss whether a feminization of the international labor force is taking place. Second, it will analyze some specific gender issues within the international economy. Third, it will deal with the political significance of the globalization of these issues. Although we are not quite ready yet to give definite answers to many of the questions raised by this type of analysis, it is important to incorporate them into our understanding of global change. There is still much research to be done. In particular, statistical information is incomplete and often unreliable. But, most of all, generalizations at the level at which this analysis is presented are risky and need to be constantly qualified by the specificity of each country's experience.

*Is There a Feminization of the International Labor Force?*

There is no simple answer to the question of whether the international labor force is becoming feminized. First, at the general level, it is quite impossible to answer because of the many differences by region, country, and sector. Second, there are contradictory tendencies at work that need to be sorted out. Third, statistical information is still lacking and, in particular, cross-country comparisons are not easy to make. A more specific statistical problem is that of undercounting women's labor, which can lead to many distortions in analyzing this question.

To begin with the problem of undercounting, if we define the labor force in the widest possible sense—that is, including subsistence production and family workers—it is far from clear that a feminization of the labor force has taken place at the international level. Official statistics suggest that a process of feminization is taking place because subsistence and family labor, which concentrate a high proportion of women, have often been underestimated in labor force statistics (Benería 1984). Thus, if official statistics show that a majority of countries have experienced an increase in labor force participation rates for women, this increase might be misleading—to the extent that women have shifted from undercounted agricultural and household-centered productive activities (from subsistence and family labor) to more formalized and "visible" work. In this case, the statistically registered increase does not necessarily reflect a feminization of the labor force but a shift of women from the former to the latter type of activities.

Similarly, an increase in women's participation in the informal sector does not necessarily contribute to a feminization of the labor force if it represents a shift from the subsistence and undercounted sector. What it does represent is an increase in women's participation in income-earning activities. In the absence of reliable statistics, it is difficult to estimate the extent of this change.

In spite of statistical problems, there is a lot we *do* know. To begin with, many countries have registered an increase in women's labor force participation rates. For the more industrialized countries, this trend has been remarkable during the past twenty-five years. For example, for the majority of OECD countries, female participation rates had surpassed the 50 percent mark by the early 1980s. The increase has been significant even for a country such as Ireland where the government has pursued policies to encourage male rather than female employment (Pyle 1986). The pattern is less clear for third world countries. According to data from the International Labor Organization, the percentage of women in the labor force has increased for some countries but not for others, and no clear-cut pattern emerges when comparing the different regions. The major

*Table 1*
*Women's Participation in the Labor Force*
*Selected Countries and Years*
*(percentages)*

|        | Country     | Census year | % of Women workers who are wage workers |
|--------|-------------|-------------|------------------------------------------|
| **Africa** | Egypt       | 1947        | 34.0                                     |
|        |             | 1982        | 66.1                                     |
|        | Morocco     | 1952        | 12.2                                     |
|        |             | 1982        | 36.3                                     |
|        | Tunisia     | 1956        | 6.5                                      |
|        |             | 1975        | 37.0                                     |
| **Asia**   | Hong Kong   | 1966        | 80.8                                     |
|        |             | 1984        | 89.6                                     |
|        | Japan       | 1950        | 25.8                                     |
|        |             | 1984        | 54.0                                     |
|        | Korea       | 1955        | 4.3                                      |
|        |             | 1984        | 45.1                                     |
|        | Singapore   | 1947        | 16.6                                     |
|        |             | 1984        | 88.0                                     |
|        | Philippines | 1948        | 26.7                                     |
|        |             | 1985        | 40.5                                     |

*Source:* ILO, Yearbook of Labor Statistics, various years.

rise in women's employment has taken place in the industrial sector in which female employment increased by 56 percent between 1970 and 1980 (UNCTC/ILO, 1985). However, this growth has been very unevenly distributed, depending upon the pace of industrialization in each country. The rapidly industrializing middle income Asian countries, such as Hong Kong, South Korea and Singapore, have registered one of the largest increases in female industrial employment. This is a different pattern from the more industrialized Western countries where the absorption of women in the labor force has taken place predominantly in the service sector.

The registered increase in the proportion of women in the labor force reflects the much clearer trend that can be observed in most regions, namely, the feminization of *wage* labor. This process has taken place even in countries with a low percentage of women in the statistically registered labor force. As can be seen from Table 1, the proportion of women in the labor force that are wage workers increased considerably in the rapidly industrializing Asian countries (with a relatively high number of women in the labor force) as well as in countries such as Egypt, Morocco, and Tunisia (where female labor force participation rates are low). In other African countries, this pattern is less clear probably due to the predominance of women in the agricultural sector. In Latin America, despite the fact that most countries have registered an important increase in the percentage of women in the labor force, official statistics show that the proportion of women in wage labor has changed little (and in some cases it has decreased). This is probably due to the reverses in the pace of industrialization in the region, but it is also likely to hide the large proportion of women working as wage workers in the informal sector.

The increase in female wage labor in many countries reflects, first, a progressive process of proletarianization at a world scale and, second, a shift in the productive location of women workers. The changes are particularly visible in some areas, such as the export processing zones (EPZs) of many third world countries, which tend to represent the most "modern" sector of their economies. However, it is important to place this dynamic within the larger context of women's location in the economy. As can be seen in Table 2, the large majority of women in the third world are still engaged in agricultural work. This is the case for Asia, Africa, and the Middle East where 70 percent of women in the labor force are in agriculture. Latin America is the exception; the very low proportion of women in this sector and the high proportion in services, relative to other third world regions, is similar to that of the more industrialized Western countries. This reflects the traditionally higher concentration of men in Latin American agriculture but also the undercounting of women in the sector.

## *The Internationalization of Gender Issues*

In the uneven globalization of the world economy, gender issues take different forms and intensity. In this section, some of these issues are analyzed mostly from the perspective of women's work. They are given as an illustration of this unfolding process and without any pretense of providing an exhaustive list.

*Table 2*
*Distribution of the Labor Force by Sector and Region, 1980*
*(percentages)*

|                            | Men  | Women | Total |
|----------------------------|------|-------|-------|
| *Africa and the Middle East* |      |       |       |
| Agriculture                | 61.5 | 72.5  | 64.5  |
| Industry                   | 17.0 | 9.0   | 15.0  |
| Services                   | 21.5 | 18.5  | 20.5  |
| *Asia*                     |      |       |       |
| Agriculture                | 56.5 | 69.5  | 61.0  |
| Industry                   | 22.0 | 17.5  | 20.0  |
| Services                   | 21.5 | 13.0  | 19.0  |
| *Latin America*            |      |       |       |
| Agriculture                | 40.0 | 14.0  | 34.0  |
| Industry                   | 27.0 | 17.0  | 25.0  |
| Services                   | 33.0 | 69.0  | 41.0  |

*Source:* Calculated from Michael Hopkins, "Employment trends in developing countries, 1960–80 and beyond," *International Labor Review,* Geneva: ILO, July 1983: 461–78.

## Multinationals and women

In the recent literature on the new international division of labor, writings on the employment of women by transnational firms have been prominent. In particular, research has emphasized the high concentration of women in the EPZs of the world and in other areas, such as the U.S.-Mexico border, that have attracted large amounts of multinational investment in export-oriented, labor intensive production. This literature focuses mostly on third world countries and has tended to emphasize the exploitative and precarious conditions under which women tend to be employed (Safa, 1981; Nash and Fernández-Kelly, eds. 1983; Heyzer 1984).

Although this research has been very illuminating, its prominence has tended to exaggerate the importance of women's employment by multinational capital, particularly if judged from the relatively small proportion of direct female employment that it represents. Although there are few estimates and much more information is needed, the available figures indicate that direct multinational employment in third world countries may represent no more than two million women; this represents less than 1 percent of the female labor force in the third world and about 3 percent of total worldwide multinational employment. For the labor force as a whole, direct employment by multinational firms represents only about 0.5 percent (UNCTC/ILO 1985).

There are, however, reasons why this topic has been prominent in the literature. Although there is great variation from country to country, multinational investment and its employment of women is important, for example, in the newly industrialized countries (or NICs) and in areas of high concentration of international investment, such as the EPZs. In addition, the indirect effects of multinational employment of women need to be taken into consideration. Multinationals generate a multiplier effect through subcontracting chains, linking them with domestic firms of all sizes; women's employment is generated particularly in labor-intensive production. Thus, in a study of subcontracting firms, in Mexico City during 1981–82, it was found that the employment of women was on the increase among most of the firms studied; and that the proportion of women in the firm's labor force tended to be higher at the lower echelons of subcontracting (Benería and Roldán 1987). Although estimates of these indirect effects are lacking, the extent of their occurrence appears to be far reaching.

Another indirect effect of multinational capital is the setting of employment trends through a process by which domestic capital "discovers" or "accepts" women workers and an emulation effect takes place. Similarly, multinational employment tends to have a consumer effect by facilitating consumerist practices; this results not only from the relatively high level of wages paid by multinationals, as compared to national firms, but also from the integration of workers into the international consumer market that the process often entails.

For these reasons, and because multinational employment plays a leading role in the dynamics of the global economy, its effects on women's economic condition should not be underrated. However, it needs to be placed in its proper perspective: the large majority of women are not working with multinational capital but are found in agriculture and in the low-paying sectors of the labor market.

One result of the new employment of women in labor intensive production is that we can no longer emphatically state, as Boserup did for the 1960s, that "when larger industries gradually drive the home industries out of business, women lose their jobs. . . ." (Boserup 1970: 111). She also emphasized a tendency for women to be self-employed and in family-based industries. One of the reasons for this tendency, she argued, was what she called "employers' preference for male workers," that is, "the preferential recruitment of male labor to large-scale industries, which cannot violate the rules so easily as the smaller ones" (ibid.: 113). Similarly, she spoke of the prejudices involving the employment of women, such as "the fear that women might be exposed to a demoralizing influence in factory surroundings" (ibid.: 116). Although some of these gender-based prejudices are still at work twenty years later, important changes have taken place, particularly in terms of a greater acceptance of women's presence in the paid labor force and in the shift in employers' preference from men to women in some industrial production processes.

This preference-shift has been amply documented for the case of labor intensive, cheap labor, export processing industries associated with transnational capital (Frobel et al 1980; Hein 1986; House 1986) and also with national capital (Benería and Roldán 1987; Berik 1987). It is well known that the proportion of women in many of the world's export processing zones can be as high as 80–90 percent. In many cases, as Hein has typically argued for Mauritius, this amounts to the "emergence of an important new group of workers," the majority of whom are under twenty-five, single, and with a relatively high level of education. Hein found that the majority of women workers hired in Mauritius during the 1970s had completed or nearly completed primary school—in contrast with the pre-1972 situation in which they were over twenty-five, not single, and with very low levels of education. As the globalization of production moves from factory work to the "global office," as has already begun to happen, the new global worker is likely to have even higher levels of schooling.

## Women's Work and Wages

Lower wages for women have been widely documented across countries. Although the wage gap does not result simply from discriminatory practices, discrimination based on gender is universal, even though it may take different forms and vary from country to country. The principle of equal pay for equal work may have been adopted, at least in principle, in many countries, but pure wage discrimination is still openly practiced in some others.[1]

However, the most common cause for women's lower wages continues to be the high degree of occupational segregation or labor market segmentation between low-paid "female" jobs and better paid "male" jobs (Anker and Hein, 1986). This segregation can be observed across countries and has been widely documented. Yet,

*Table 3*

*Occupational Segregation: Selected Countries and Years*
*(percent of women in each category)*

| Occupation | Highest % and country | Lowest % and country |
|---|---|---|
| Professional, technical and related workers | 53.8 (Canada, 1986) | 3.9 (Bangladesh, 1983–4) |
| Administrative and managerial workers | 64.4 (Sweden, 1986) | 3.6 (Rep. Korea, 1986) |
| Clerical workers | 80.3 (United States, 1986) | 2.4 (Togo, 1981) |
| Sales Workers | 85.4 (Togo, 1981) | 22.8 (Costa Rica, 1984) |
| Agriculture, animal husbandry and forestry workers | 47.6 (Japan, 1986) | 6.2 (Chile, 1982) |
| Production related workers and laborers | 33.4 (Hong Kong, 1986) | 6.2 (Gambia, 1983) |
| Service workers | 73.3 (Austria, 1986) | 12.6 (Zambia, 1980) |

*Source:* ILO, Yearbook of Labor Statistics (1987)

what is considered to be a male or female job varies greatly from country to country. Boserup (1970: ch. 1) also emphasized this variation with respect to agricultural tasks and, as a result, emphasized that there is nothing "natural" about that sexual division of labor. Table 3 shows that the same type of argument can be used for occupations outside of agriculture whose male or female concentration is subject to a high degree of country variation. Yet, there is little variation in the fact that female occupations are paid less and that, when a male occupation becomes feminized, relative wages tend to decline.

Labor market segmentation is not only related to gender but to other factors such as race and ethnicity. The globalization of production increases the complexity of the interaction between these factors, given the possibility for capital to fragment the labor market and take advantage of these divisions at the international level. Yet this is an area of research that remains undeveloped.

Despite indications that segregation has been decreasing in recent years, even if slightly, in some industrialized countries (Beller 1984), it is still very high across countries (Anker and Hein 1985). The fact that it is a universal phenomenon found under different economic and political conditions indicates that it is not just a product of capitalist institutions and that its stubborness is likely to continue to be a source of gender differentiation under different economic regimes. Yet little has been done to deal with consequences of job segregation at the international level. Comparable worth policies have been discussed only in a handful of countries and implemented, in a piecemeal fashion, in even fewer. The very concept of equal pay for work of equal value, which developed because equal pay for equal work laws can hardly be implemented when men and women do different work, is practically unknown in many countries. In addition, the difficulty of implementing comparable worth policies and the opposition that they face from business and conservative circles do not allow much optimism for the immediate future. Worse still, continuous restructuring of labor hierarchies can undermine these policies: the current creation of new low paid jobs in industrialized economies provides numerous examples. This problem is intensified through the possibilities offered by international production where the global office is only the newest form threatening, for example, some of the successful comparable worth cases fought in the United States during the past decade.

Despite this not very optimistic outlook, the importance of continuously pointing out the existence of discriminatory practices and the effects of segregation on women's wages needs to be emphasized as these issues take on an international dimension. The existence of a large pool of female labor at a world scale is being used to deal with the pressures of international competition, profitability crises, and economic restructuring that characterize the current reorganization of production. The availability of cheap female labor has also been an instrumental factor in the export-led policies of third world countries shifting from previous import-substitution strategies.

The reasons for this new preference for women workers, as presented by different studies, are more complex than what is implied by the cheap labor argument and can be summarized as falling in three categories. First, women workers are assumed to facilitate *labor control and labor malleability* for a variety of reasons, such as their willingness to follow orders, their greater discipline, and other characteristics falling under the stereotype of docility. Whether these "gender traits" are real or assumed, they can be one of the reasons for this preference. Second, in some cases, women are hired for reasons having to do with *productivity,* when it is reported that women work better with small objects. This is the old nimble fingers argument which, in some cases, represents the recognition and use of skills that women have acquired through their gender socialization and work experience, as with the case of garment work. Third, women provide an important source of *flexible labor* through their predominance in temporary contracts as well as in part time and unstable work; this flexibility facilitates the maximum adjustment of labor supply to the requirements of and oscillations in labor demand. The importance of this adjustment is apparent for the peripheral, informalized labor processes, but it also applies to more formal types of work and has been an important factor in recent economic restructuring of industrialized countries.[2]

## Prostitution and Sex-related Tourism

A rather different illustration of a gender dimension in the global economy is the expansion of sex-related tourism, which has increased dramatically during the past decades in some countries. The cases of several Southeast Asia countries—South Korea, Thailand, and the Philippines in particular—are well known and raise similar issues. First, they illustrate the connection between the development of the international tourist industry and the rise of prostitution at the global level. Second, both sex-tourism and prostitution are stimulated by the growing internationalization of capital, as it expands the international business class (its primary client) and facilitates international traffic and exchange. Third, they are often connected with the existence of military activities and foreign military bases, as in the case of the Asian countries mentioned above. Fourth, although prostitution is an old business, what is new in these cases is its significant magnitude and economic significance as a source of foreign exchange and in the promotion of business ventures where government and corporate interests meet. In most of these countries, the state has taken a very active role to promote sex-related industries through tourist promotion, issuing of licenses, and international advertising.

Estimates of the size of this industry show very high numbers: 100,000 "hospitality girls" with licenses and health certificates from the Ministry of Labor and Employment in the Philippines in 1979; a similar number of prostitutes and 200,000 "masseuses" were estimated for Bangkok in 1977, and for Thailand as a whole the estimated number of prostitutes in 1981 ranged between 500,000 and 700,000 (Truong Than-Dam, 1983 and 1988). In relative terms, this figure for Bangkok alone amounts to 10 percent of female employment by multinationals. Estimates for South Korea and the Philippines also point to very high figures (Wood 1981; Aguilar 1987). Wages received by prostitutes and the cost of sex-related services in these countries are much lower than in the client countries. However, this is not to say that prostitution is just a matter of relative costs. In fact, it is a good illustration of the crossroads of race, gender, class and cultural differences, and of the complexities of their interaction in creating patterns of subordination and domination. As a woman who had worked on an island in the Philippines put it: "When the tourists started to come, the beach saw new hot-blooded men making it with brown girls . . . If you ask these blue-eyed men why they came here, they tell you that the girls serve them like kings in heaven with many docile feminine playmates" (O'Campo, 1987: 69).

And who are "the girls"? The great majority of course come from the poorest areas and households, such as the northern regions in Thailand (Phongpaichit 1980) and the marginal population of Manila slums (Aguilar 1987). What a perfect symbol this is of the connections between the pleasures of international jet-setting and the survival pains of everyday life in the global economy.

## Economic Crises and Women's Work

A final illustration of a gender dimension in the functioning of the global economy comes from the role of women in household adjustments to the austerity policies generated by the foreign debt crises in many third world countries. Recent studies of the impact of the debt crisis adjustment on household budgets describe the negative impact of these policies on the poor, particularly in Latin America and Africa (Cornia, Jolly, and Stewart, eds. 1987: vols 1 and 2). These studies illustrate how households survive under severe economic conditions and what kind of mechanisms they use to compensate for lower incomes and deteriorating access to resources. Thus, Cornia (vol. 1, ch. 4) has analyzed in detail the different ways in which households either use their available resources more efficiently or generate new ones in order to cope with critical conditions. These household responses range from changes in purchasing habits, food preparation, and consumption patterns to the incorporation of new household members in the labor force, increased production for own consumption, migration, and reliance on the extended family.

One missing element in this analysis is the role played by women. Yet, the nature of these coping mechanisms and the evidence emerging from new studies suggest that women play a very extensive role in dealing with the effects of the crisis. Food production, shopping, and household organization are mostly part of women's daily responsibilities. Likewise, the incorporation of *new* members in the labor force is likely to involve particularly women and the young, given their lower participation in paid production. Women also tend to be involved in coping strategies that shift household activities to more collective processes. Such is the case with the "comedores populares" in Lima or the "ollas comunes" in Bolivia (neighborhood-based communal kitchens) whose organization has given women a new, even if temporary and precarious, social function (Sara-Lafosse 1986).

How these processes are connected with the global economy is quite obvious. The significance of the debt as the latest form of surplus extraction from the third world and its connection with international financing and patterns of trade and investment imply that the daily troubles of a Bolivian miner's wife, for example, are part of any discussion of the global economy. As women across countries understand increasingly these mechanisms, their daily struggles take on a global significance. Given the universality of gender as an organizing principle, it should be central to our analysis and in designing policies and action.

### Evaluating Change and Action

Does the increasing visibility of women in the global economy represent a positive change for them? This is not a simple question to answer since there are contradictory factors at work. The debate on this subject, in fact, results in part from differences between countries and can hardly be resolved without paying attention to the specificity of each case. At a general level, there are those who think that, among working women as a whole, the emerging trends in the international economy have represented "a definite improvement in women's economic status," particularly in the industrial sector (Joekes 1987). However, given women's primary responsibility in reproductive activities and their concentration in household work, any evaluation of the overall situation needs to take this sphere into consideration.

This implies that it is useful to distinguish between at least two levels of analysis: one that focuses on gender asymmetries in the labor market and another that focuses on household and family relations. Thus, one way of posing this question is to ask whether gender is being "decomposed" or broken down as a result of global changes (Elson and Pearson 1981). Here, too, change is not unidimensional. The feminization of the labor force in some countries and the increasing participation of women in the global economy have been accompanied by a higher degree of labor force attachment and economic autonomy for the majority of women. This is the case for the more industrialized countries, and there is no reason to believe that the same is not the case for other regions.

The significance of this new labor force attachment and autonomy for women should be clear. Yet, the spectrum of new forms of gender "recomposition" and of subsequent discriminatory treatment for women workers, particularly under conditions of unstable employment and loss of jobs, has not disappeared. The loss of employment in the Malaysian computer chips industry in recent years provides an illustration of the precariousness of this attachment in some cases. It has been estimated that as many as 40,000 jobs have been lost due to shifting investment attracted by lower wages in other countries. The loss, which affected mostly young women, led the weekly *The Economist* (Jan. 31, 1987) to ask about what would happen to these young women: "Will, as the cynics say, the pretty ones become bar girls and the plain ones turn to Islam?" The sexism inherent in this quote illustrates the resistance of gender stereotypes to break down. It also illustrates the fragility of what otherwise could be considered a positive step toward gender equality.

Despite this type of retrogression, the acceptance of women as paid workers has clearly increased in most countries. The increase in women's employment and the higher degree of labor force attachment suggest the breaking down of gender stereotypes and a higher degree of gender equality. At the same time, this continues to coexist with other types of inequalities, such as those reflected in women's low pay and working conditions, and does not preclude the appearance of new ones.

At the household level, there are some indications of a new division of labor in which the number of hours that women spend in domestic work appears to have decreased in the high income countries, at the same time that men and women share domestic chores more equally (Blau and Ferber 1986). However, these changes are still not very significant and affect a small proportion of the population.

At the international level, and despite the caution needed regarding generalizations, the double burden for women workers appears to be a continuing universal phenomenon. Yet changes, difficult to capture and still in need of further research, may be taking place. Safa (1988), for example, argues: "Women's increased ability to contribute to family income may challenge traditional patriarchal authority and lead to more egalitarian family structures" (p. 25). This is particularly true, she writes, in countries such as Puerto Rico and the Dominican Republic where "women have become critical contributors to the household economy."

To sum up, the globalization of the economy presents gender dimensions that are contradictory. On the one hand, the feminization of employment implies an increase in women's income-producing activities, which might result in greater autonomy for women, in gender decomposition and a higher degree of equality between the sexes. On the other, these changes are based on inequalities that are likely to persist stubbornly precisely because they are instrumental in the current functioning of the global economy. In addition, gender inequalities continue to be tied to women's sexuality and role in reproduction, therefore implying that they will tend to persist unless these aspects are integrated in our analysis and search for solutions.

What kind of practical actions are possible in response to this developing situation? There are, to begin with, issues that can, at least in principle, be channeled through traditional progressive politics: trade union organizing that includes women's interests, enforcement of minimum wage levels, bargaining with the state for health care and reproductive rights, policies regarding maternity leaves, information about "best practices" across countries, day care, and working conditions affecting women in particular. As argued above, much needs to be done also to enforce, and in some countries introduce, equal pay for equal work legislation and to discuss and act upon the notion of comparable worth. To the extent that they are open to gender issues, progressive trade unions and political parties could channel such actions. To the extent that they are not, separate women's organizations are needed, as with the case of the Mexican Nineteenth of September Garment Workers Union, an independent union set up after the 1985 earthquake to take up the plight and survival issues of garment workers.

Likewise, survival issues can, in principle, be integrated in traditional politics. Yet, as in the case of the "comedores populares" in Lima, Peru, women involved have often found it difficult to have their interests clearly expressed and have complained of being used or not understood by organizations with little experience (or interest) in gender politics. In addition, there is a whole category of issues that are more difficult to integrate in traditional progressive politics, either because the left is reluctant or unwilling to take them up or because they do not clearly fall into what are considered important issues or normal channels of action. Particularly important are issues generally not viewed as clearly connected with class politics; the inability of the left to deal with such issues is notorious. It is no surprise, for example, that the most effective actions around international prostitution have been organized by feminist networks that tend not to raise fundamental questions about the class origin or class connections of international prostitution. To the extent that such connections exist, it is a loss both to the left and to feminist networks not to integrate gender and class issues.

Other examples include new emerging issues with a global dimension, such as the "export" of domestic workers from the poorer to the richer countries, and the exploitative conditions based on gender, class, and nationality that can be generated by the new reproductive technologies. We are hardly prepared to tackle these issues, but they are vivid examples of the new politics called for by Núñez and Burbach. For women, solidarity among different groups will be useful only to the extent that gender issues are given the fundamental role that they play.

## Notes

1. In Mauritius, minimum wage legislation allows an employer to pay a woman 57 percent of the minimum male wage during her first year of work (Hein, 1986). For Cyprus, House (1986) reports that employers openly admit to the practice of wage discrimination in a variety of jobs. However, where equal pay legislation has been introduced, wage discrimination is more difficult to document, even when it exists.
2. To illustrate with an example from the OECD countries, women's share of part-time employment in 1981 ranged from 63 percent in Greece to 93.8 percent in Germany (OECD, 1985). In addition, all indications point to an increasing use of part-time work as an important factor in current trends toward work flexibility.

## References

Aguilar, Delia. 1987. "Charting the Boundaries: Domestic Ideology in Filipino Women's Lives," Ph.D. dissertation, Union Graduate School.

Anker, Richard and Catharine Hein. eds. 1986: *Sex Inequalities in Urban Employment in the Third World*. New York: St. Martin's Press.

Beller, Andrea. 1984: "Trends in Occupational Segregation by Sex and Race." In B. Reskin, ed, *Sex Segregation in the Workplace*, Washington: National Academy Press: 11–26.

Benería, Lourdes. 1984. "Accounting for Women's Work." In L. Benería, ed., *Women and Development. The Sexual Division of Labor in Rural Societies*. New York: ILO/Praeger.

Benería, Lourdes and Martha Roldán. 1987. *The Crossroads of Class and Gender. Homework, Subcontracting and Household Dynamics in Mexico City*. Chicago: University of Chicago Press.

Berik, Gunseli. 1987. *Women Carpet Weavers in Rural Turkey: Patterns of Employment, Earnings and Status*. Geneva: ILO.

Blau, Francine and Marianne Ferber. 1986. *The Economics of Women, Men and Work*. Englewood Cliffs, NJ: Prentice-Hall.

Boserup, Ester. 1970. *Woman's Role in Economic Development*. New York: St. Martin's Press.

Cornia, Giovanni A., Richard Jolly, and Francis Stewart. 1987. *Adjustment with a Human Face*. New York: Oxford University Press.

Elson, Diane and Ruth Pearson. 1981. "The Subordination of Women and the Internationalization of Factory Production." In K. Young, C. Wolkowitz and R. McCullagh, eds., *Of Marriage and the Market*. London: CSE Books.

Frobel, Folker, Jurgen Heinrichs, and Otto Kreye. 1980. *The New International Division of Labor*. New York: Cambridge University Press.

Hein, Catharine. 1986. "The Feminization of Industrial Employment in Mauritius: A Case of Sex Segregation." In Anker and Hein eds., pp. 277–12.

Heyzer, Noeleen. 1984. "From Rural Subsistence to an Industrial Peripheral Work Force." In L. Benería, ed., *Women and Development. The Sexual Division of Labor in Rural Societies*, New York: Praeger.

House, William J. 1986. "The Status and Pay of Women in the Cyprus Labor Market." In Anker and Hein, eds., pp. 117–69.

Joekes, Susan P., 1987. *Women in the World Economy. An INSTRAW Study.* New York: Oxford University Press.

Nash, June and M. P. Fernández-Kelly. 1983. *Women, Men and the New International Division of Labor.* Albany, NY: State University Press.

Núñez, Orlando and Roger Burbach. 1986. *Democracia y Revolución en las Americas.* Managua: Editorial Vanguardia.

O'Campo, Martha. 1987. "Pornography and Prostitution in the Philippines." In L. Bell, ed., *Good Girls/Bad Girls,* Toronto: The Seal Press.

OECD. 1985. *The Integration of Women Into the Economy.* Paris: OECD.

Phonpaichit, P. 1980. "Rural Women of Thailand; From Peasant Girls to Bangkok Masseuses." Geneva: ILO, 198.

Pyle, Jeanne. 1986. "Export-Led Development and the Underemployment of Women: The Impact of Discriminatory Development Policy in the Republic of Ireland." Paper prepared for the ASA, 81st Annual Meeting, New York, August, 30–September 3.

Safa, Helen. 1981. "Runaway Shops and Female Employment; The Search for Cheap Labor," *Signs* 7, no. 2 (Winter): 418–33.

———. 1988. "Women and Industrialization in the Caribbean," in *Women, Employment and the Family,* edited by Sharon Stichter and Jane Parpart, forthcoming.

Sara-Lafosse, Violetta. 1986. "Communal Kitchens in the Low-Income Neighborhoods of Lima." In M. Schmink, J. Bruce and M. Kohn eds., *Learning About Women and Urban Services in Latin America and the Caribbean.* New York: The Population Council.

Truong Thanh-Dam. 1983. "The Dynamics of Sex-Tourism: The Case of Southeast Asia." *Development and Change,* 14, no. 4 (October): 533–53.

———. 1988. "Sex, Money and Morality. The Political Economy of Prostitution and Tourism in South East Asia." Doctoral dissertation, University of Amsterdam.

UNCTC/ILO. 1985. *Women Workers in Multinational Enterprises in Developing Countries.* Geneva: ILO.

Wood, Robert. 1981. "The Economics of Tourism." *Southeast Asia Chronicle,* no. 78, April.

# Capital Mobility, the Restructuring of Production, and the Politics of Labor

## William K. Tabb

In explaining why the workers in the advanced capitalist nations have not been the revolutionary force, the gravediggers of the system that Marx foresaw, radical thinkers since Engels have relied on versions of a labor aristocracy theory. Thus Paul Sweezy in an influential essay "Marx and the Proletariat" (1967), suggested that if the revolutionary moment of the early period of modern industry is missed, the proletariat tend to become less and less revolutionary as they become a highly internally diverse class less capable of a united consciousness. The better organized, better paid workers gain a stake in the continuity of existing social relations and are unlikely to welcome unpredictable system destabilization. In this regard E.P. Thompson (1978) speaks of the "imbrication of working class organization in the *status quo.*"

The contemporary period of global restructuring brings this accommodation into question. To those who judge any class response against an international workingmen's (and women's) association, the labor movement's efforts to respond to these developments are a hopeless disappointment. But things are happening which are of some importance and the developing trajectory offers some grounds for a limited optimism. At the same time, while there is increasing awareness of the problems posed for labor by the rapid internationalization of capital and labor markets, principled differences and just plain confusion exist as to what is to be done.

The perceptions of slow growth and a falling living standard, industrial and regional decline, and the loss of U.S. competitiveness have been presented in the popular media to suggest that unfair foreign competition and high U.S. wages create our economic problems. Convinced that if they hang on long enough things will get better, many workers can see no alternative to further concessions. Others see that plants close anyway, with moving expenses financed by wage concessions and the lower cost of production, courtesy of workers whose future bargaining power erodes with continued give-backs. They urge workers to just say no to concessions.

The trend toward weaker unions and relatively lower living standards for U.S. workers is unmistakable (Bluestone and Harrison 1988). So extreme have these changes been that they are forcing a rethinking of organized labor's post-World War II policies of accommodation to international capital, and have led to a search for alternative approaches on issues of foreign trade and investment, new modes of organizing based on appeals to gender equality and quality of work life, and new political coalition-building domestically and internationally. There is a lively struggle over labor's foreign policy and the broadening of the AFL-CIO's legislative agenda. A new progressive current, with new leadership, is emerging which advocates a more class-oriented militant unionism beyond, and in opposition to, business unionism and its traditional support of corporate liberalism.

The new current—which still lacks major influence—appreciates the need to institutionalize new structures of international solidarity and to devise new forms of trade union activity built around representation of workers employed in the same production system and those employed by the same transnational corporation, across job category and industry. While there is a tension between these two principles of grouping workers within union structures which will need to be worked out in practice, each corresponds to the reorganization of capital in this period of global restructuring. At the same time, the new current recognizes the centrality of political struggle within the individual nation-state as necessary to protect workers from absorbing the costs of dislocation brought on by the mobility of capital. Building broad political support for worker rights has become an important priority.

Strike activity and point of production organizing more generally have declined in effectiveness, leading the AFL-CIO bureaucracy to put their financial resources more heavily into campaign contributions and other efforts to buy friends in Washington. In this contest they were outspent. It can be argued, moreover, that the same money put into organizing the organized and politicizing the unionized as to their class interests would have paid higher dividends. Politicians like money but they fear and must respect the demands of highly conscious, well-organized groups who know what they want.

These lessons have provoked an internal struggle to put the "movement" back into the way labor operates. The possibility of stronger alliances with other progressive groups (women, blacks, environmentalists) and a less hostile relation to the Rainbow Coalition signal the emergence of a left-center alliance in opposition to the center-right corporate consensus that has ruled the house of labor. This consensus, however, is still dominant in a bureaucratically controlled federation which is deeply committed to accommodation. The revolution is not at hand, obviously. But these new developments do suggest that the period of American exceptionalism is coming to an end. Class politics is being transformed in this period of increased internationalization and relative deterioration of U.S. nation-state power. An increasingly pronounced ideological struggle within the U.S. labor movement is on the agenda, with a left social democratic and more militant class-conscious grouping facing reactionary and narrow business unionism.

The problems faced by the U.S. trade union movement are not unfamiliar to most readers and so are summarized briefly here before taking up the trade debate, and foreign policy aspects of trade with developing countries and the advanced capitalist nations. Finally, changing labor politics of the last decade or two are examined, as U.S. unions have struggled to develop reformist strategies to address their loss of power.

### The Global Economy: The Significant Trends

Most discussion of the internationalization process has focused on the relative decline of the U.S. economy in the global marketplace and the increased integration of the domestic into the international economy—the competitiveness issue. However, for American workers the issues are more direct—real wages and job security. The simplistic equation of competitiveness and profitability with worker standards of living masks the extent to which the interests of U.S.-based corporations diverge from those of their employees. Supply-side economics, with its tax "cuts" and work incentives, has left corporations richer and workers poorer (real average gross weekly earnings fell by 11.5 percent between the end of the Carter administration and the first quarter of 1988 and non-wage income rose almost three times as rapidly as payroll income). Rather than directly addressing this loss of worker purchasing power and the decline of labor's class strength, media discussion has focused on their alleged cause, loss of U.S. competitiveness.

In 1986, for the first time since World War II, the United States lost its position as the world's leading exporter, supplanted by West Germany, with Japan pressing closely from third place. Also in 1986, again for the first time, the United States ran a trade deficit in high-technology products. Each year the United States is responsible for designing a smaller proportion of the world's advanced technology and has lost ground in educational achievement, civilian research and innovation, and world market shares.

It is of course to be expected that the United States could not dominate the global economy as it had at the end of World War II, when Germany and Japan, France and England had to recover from war-time devastation. But the decline since the late 1960s represents more than just a catching up by some former imperial powers. Nor is the problem only one of the superdollar, the overrated currency of the early Reagan era. The weak dollar of the 1980s will encourage more foreign investment and partially reverse the trade balance, but a secular relative decline of U.S. economic power is unlikely to be stemmed so long as answers are sought in an open world economy in which American competitiveness is based primarily on reducing labor costs.

The context of global overcapacity has put pressure on unions to abandon industry-wide bargaining. This in many instances has created an enterprise unionism, pitting workers in different plants against each other. All labor has lost as pattern bargaining has eroded and semi-permanent recession levels of "natural" unemployment prevail. As workers are forced to pay capital more in tax and other concessions in hope that jobs will be created, income shares shift regressively and more power accrues to capital. The historically unprecedented shift in income to the very wealthy and loss of income to the bottom 60 percent of Americans in the 1980s has taken place in the context of rising real per capita GNP. Capital's increased share of GNP, and the decline in total labor compensation, as well as the rapid growth of the poverty population suggest an incipient set of both Keynesian and Marxian imbalances between investment and consumption, of overaccumulation, and a system-disturbing growth of fictitious capital. Worker purchasing power continues to decline, approximating average levels of a decade and a half earlier.

A message is being conveyed in the mainstream coverage of the labor movement that nothing can stop the continued decline of working-class standards: the corporate offensive is considered a necessary adjustment to international competitive pressures. And indeed, the aggressive class warfare of the past decade has taken its toll. In 1986, 14 percent of private sector workers were union members compared to 39 percent thirty years earlier. Private sector unionization rates are now at the pre-Wagner Act levels of the 1920s.

After two decades in which American capital extended better wages to the more powerful unions in exchange for class demobilization at home and support of cold war politics abroad, the ideological internationalization of transnational capital's operating premises by the dominant elements in the labor movement has created the preconditions for the deterioration of living and working conditions, as well as the political power, of the U.S. working class. The elements of this ideological hegemony include acceptance of cold war militarism, with attendant intervention in the third world to prop up local elites hospitable to foreign capital's dominance, and a military Keynesianism at home which privileges Sun Belt conservatism at the expense of social spending and social wage programs. In a period in which international solidarity is clearly a matter of labor self-interest, national chauvinism and a Ramboesque mindset hold many American workers in thrall. Yet the objective realities of the present moment sorely undermine the continued general acceptance of ruling-class ideology. Signs of such a potential reorientation are visible in the debates over trade and with regard to American labor's foreign policy.

## The Trade Debate

In the nineteenth century protectionism was strong even though labor was weak. This was because capital was overwhelmingly local, regional, or national. In the present period decisive fractions of capital are transnational in outlook and protectionism has lost its cross-class base of support.

In the current round, the free trade–free markets school wins all general debates against what Kevin Phillips has called "reactionary liberalism." The difficulty is that all change hurts someone, and at least since the time of Bastiat's Petition of the Candlemakers to the King against the Sun, there has been an acceptance of the view that special interest and nostalgia should not stand in the way of "progress," as defined by dominant fractions of capital.

If all that unions seem to be advocating is preserving yesterday's jobs and wages based on outmoded economic rents (which can no longer be extracted from oligopolies now facing global competition), then organized labor faces bleak prospects in Washington policy debates. Even when protection is achieved it is likely to buy time for corporations to amortize existing plants, to milk them and close them down or to fund automation and labor displacement. Rarely are job security and living standards of labor preserved.

The AFL-CIO top leadership is on the spot. Unlike some of its erstwhile friends who speak glibly of increasing factor mobility—physical relocation, retraining, and acceptance of downward mobility by once well-paid blue collar unionists—the trade union movement needs to deliver more for its members than an advocacy of competitive victory for U.S.-based corporations. Thus while labor can go part of the way on the competitiveness track, it cannot do so in the "make markets operate more smoothly" way that many liberal policy advisers are advocating.

Labor has learned that really free markets destroy unions and undermine working conditions and compensation standards. At the same time, while it is used to making deals with oligopolistic firms to obtain more for unionized workers (in exchange for giving up any claim to bargaining over technology and investment), it now finds capital is not interested. The erosion of a class opposition stance and of rank-and-file militance that could be mobilized by union leaders has meant AFL-CIO officials have little bargaining power with their corporate adversaries, or as much support as they would like from members who fear a sell-out even as they also desperately need strong unions to fight for them.

From a worker's viewpoint what is desired is a leveling up, not down, and a more inclusive definition of costs and benefits in economic decision-making. The real gains from trade should be measured net of adjustment costs, so that resulting unemployment, temporary and permanent, family breakups, and suicide, which can be demonstrated to result from new trade patterns, are costs counted before a final reckoning of the impact of trade can be established. Such "externalities" have never been included, nor will they ever be unless capital is forced to do so. Once the issue is put this way, the question is no longer one of trade but of serious changes for the American capitalist system.

Organized labor is moving slowly toward such an understanding of social cost accounting, and toward widening the terms of the trade debate to include the nature of economic relations more broadly. This expanding conceptualization of the trade issue is more than a mere intellectual exercise. The defeat of particular proposals in the legislative areas on the one side, and the lived experience of American workers on the other, inform organized labor's discussion of trade.

In what follows, four approaches to trade policy will be discussed. The first is the idea that foreigners have not played by the rules, that their governments subsidize exports to the United States while denying American producers access to their markets. This unfair-competition interpretation was embodied in efforts to compel a level playing field so that truly free trade could take place.

The very real difficulties in defining such rules, and the rejection of the approach in Congress, led to a second conceptual approach, embodied in the 1987 Gephardt Amendment which demanded more "balanced trade," on the assumption that those building up export surpluses with the United States should bring their trade balance back in line. While this amendment went down to defeat, the AFL-CIO has had more success in gaining congressional support for denying the benefits of specific trade privileges and aid to nations in which labor rights are not respected. This third approach, limiting trade with nations that violate such norms, makes jobs of U.S. workers more secure.

A fourth approach is the advocacy of industrial policy. This approach antedates the other three and is a creation of an earlier era, when it seemed politically possible to rebuild existing U.S. industries. As it turned out there was little support from any capitalists for industrial policy. There was opposition both from small business fearing a program that would raise their costs and their taxes without benefiting them and from transnational capital which saw its future in offshore outsourcing and so opposed domestic reindustrialization. Each of these four approaches will be taken up in turn.

In the early 1980s labor endorsed the Trade Remedies Reform Act, the so-called antitargeting bill. Introduced by Congressman Sam Gibbons, it provided for a countervailing duty when foreign governments subsidize their exports to this nation.[1] Congress rejected the proposed legislation, unwilling to move against "free trade." But even if this approach had been accepted it would not have been all that easy to identify when government programs extend "unfair" advantage to competitors. Each nation's tax policies are different. So are their environmental protection laws. In some nations, including the United States, employers pay health benefits as part of the direct cost of labor. In most advanced capitalist nations health care is paid by the state. Depreciation of capital equipment is treated differently under different nations' tax laws. Are these instances of "unfair" competition? There can be no "free market" outcome, short of abolishing government (and unions) altogether.

The next major round in the trade-industrial policy debate was in 1987, when Congressman Richard Gephardt introduced what became a famous amendment to the trade bill. It resolved some of the problems with previous approaches by forcing export surplus nations to adjust, but did not specify restrictions on particular products, and allowed trade balance to be restored by the surplus country importing more U.S. products. The legislation was not in fact protectionist in these regards (even if it was successfully so labeled). Under its provisions trade balance could be reestablished through a number of investment and sales combinations, including increased domestic consumption by export surplus nations (to stimulate global demand) and investment by surplus nations in debtor countries.

The advantage of such an approach over the level playing field chimera is that each nation is free to pursue its own strategy, constrained only by the need to bring its balance of trade into a very rough alignment. Attention can then be turned to ways to level up living standards. With free trade seen as harmful internationally (in the manner that free competition and free, unregulated labor, capital, and product markets are within nation-states), the way is open for international agreements which further labor reform, welfare state protections, and social control of investment. While the Gephardt Amendment was not discussed in these terms, labor's friends need to appreciate the ways in which negotiated trade is necessary and depends on surplus nations being forced to shoulder a significant share of adjustment costs as a step to further controls.

In the real world, the so-called protectionist trade bill of 1988, by the time it was signed by the president, was little more than a safety valve to relieve protectionist pressures and a gift to well-placed corporations, rather than anything likely to serve labor's interests. The nationalistic focus of the trade balance did not deal with issues which are crucial from a working-class viewpoint: control of capital, the prevention of costly "private decisions," and the rejection of the premise that corporations know what is best for the rest of us. These trade initiatives are motivated by concern over lost jobs of U.S. workers, not by class-conscious internationalism. But it is important to note that neither workers nor their leaders think in such international terms automatically. Rather, they are forced into broader awareness—an awareness that is currently being accelerated.

In 1983 President Reagan's Caribbean Basin Initiative was amended to require the president, in determining benefits, to consider "the degree to which workers in such countries are afforded reasonable workplace conditions and enjoy the right to organize and bargain collectively." Similar language and more specific requirements were written into the October 1984 renewal of the Generalized System of Preferences (granting developing nations duty-free access to U.S. markets), and in the 1985 renewal of the Overseas Private Investment Corporation (OPIC—the government agency that offers political risk insurance and other benefits to U.S. corporations investing abroad).

Such affirmations are nothing new. The International Labor Organization convention in 1919 committed signers to "endeavor to secure and maintain fair and humane conditions of labor for men, women, and children, both in their own countries and in all countries to which their commercial and industrial relations extended." The McKinley Tariff Act of 1890 banned products made by convict labor from entering the United States.

Some analysts suggest the reason such fine-sounding sentiments (supposedly binding on the nations signing these agreements) have not been enforced is that they are vague and nonoperational. However, the 1984 Trade and Tariff Act requires four internationally recognized standards which are most unambiguous and one which is perhaps open to interpretation but is hardly problematic. The first four are the right to free association, the right to organize and bargain collectively, and a prohibition against compulsory labor and the employment of children. The last, acceptable conditions of labor with respect to minimum wages, hours of work, and occupational health and safety, needs to be interpreted in terms of a particular nation's level of economic development, but this would hardly be a major obstacle if there was commitment in principle to its enforcement.

The issue of nonenforcement of these provisions has more to do

with power and class relations. Whether such demands are ineffective sops or steps toward effective organizing depends on whether
they are part of a broader organizing strategy targeting not only—or
even primarily—elite decisionmakers but a politically conscious internationalist workers movement.

When American labor inquires into the conditions under which
goods imported into the U.S. are produced—whether by child labor,
in a context where free trade unions are not permitted, and labor
activists are beaten, jailed, and killed—it is introducing an understanding that when commodities are purchased in the market they
embody specific social relations of domination and exploitation.
Where business interests stress that imports allow U.S. consumers
freedom of choice and lower prices (the advantages of free markets
and free trade) labor is beginning to articulate the costs of such free
enterprise and to contest the terms in which social relations are
understood. Making the linkage between labor repression in the
developing nations (a misleading euphemism to be sure) and the
decline of U.S. labor standards represents growth in class awareness
and is a major milestone in the decline of U.S. exceptionalism.

The stress on labor rights in the third world offers the occasion for
coalition-building among human rights activists, non-intervention
forces, and labor, putting pressure on the latter to rethink support for
"anticommunist" (i.e., antilabor, right-wing) dictatorships. That
labor won such progressive language in legislation designed primarily to aid U.S. overseas investments and the foreign sourcing of
goods should however be considered a mixed blessing at best. What
such legislation does after all is to facilitate capital's ability to move
about, playing workers against each other. Moreover, enforcement of
labor rights continues to be tempered by cold war assumptions
which the AFL-CIO has long endorsed and continues to support.

## AFL-CIO Foreign Policy

The AFL-CIO spends as much overseas as it does domestically.
Almost all of the money for its foreign operations comes from the
U.S. government. In 1987 the National Endowment for Democracy
(a "private institution" financed by annual appropriations from Con-
gress) contributed $4,814,371, the U.S. Agency for International
Development (a federal agency which works on occasion with the

CIA) $22,760,335 and the AFL-CIO itself a mere $662,000 to the budgets of the four regional institutes the AFL-CIO runs in Africa, Asia, Latin America, and Europe to instill "our" brand of trade unionism and to combat "their" influence. These funds are used to promote "business trade unionism and not ideological trade unionism," in the words of a report commissioned by the State Department in collaboration with the AFL-CIO and its African-American Labor Center. But of course labor's cold warriors have pursued ideological objectives of their own, objectives increasingly questioned by other unionists. For example, when the American Institute for Free Labor Development (AIFLD) tried recently to coopt the Coalition of Labor Union Women (CLUW) into founding "a hemispheric organization for trade union women," CLUW officers strongly opposed the plan. They pointed to the funding AIFLD received from the administration and its record of following Reagan administration foreign policy objectives. Without the cover of CLUW's respectability the project was shelved (Slaughter 1987:5).

The effort by right wingers to work openly, as in initiating regional meetings on labor's foreign policy and in numerous junkets for U.S. labor officials to see what U.S. labor is doing in Central America, may be a mistake. Greater visibility highlights what is being done in the name of unionized American workers and stimulates increasing opposition. Even the pressure for a public face of unity in the house of labor is less and less able to force "loyalty" on outspoken progressives. More and more U.S. workers make the connection between job loss and declining standards of living and U.S. support of right-wing governments around the world. Further, contact with Europeans in international coalitions against transnationals exposes them to a different point of view from the Kirkland orthodoxy. As labor's U.S. position deteriorates so does the ability of the AFL-CIO leadership to control unions elsewhere, or its own members, and to take steps to protect jobs, all of which implicitly bring into question its own foreign policy.

The AFL-CIO now places first on its agenda legislation that will "make the denial of internationally recognized worker rights an actionable practice under U.S. trade law. The U.S. should not permit free entry of goods produced in countries which refuse to respect basic worker rights" (Statement on Trade adopted by the AFL-CIO Executive Council, February 16, 1987). The desire to keep out low-wage imports has led the AFL-CIO to declare as unfair labor practices the very fundamentals of the authoritarian, export-oriented model the United States and its international corporations have encouraged and the labor federation has supported.

As noted above, when Congress voted an eight-year extension of the Generalized System of Preferences it directed the trade representative to make sure that beneficiaries adhere to the International Labor Organization's criteria for workers' rights. The AFL-CIO called for ending the preference for ten countries with the worst workers' rights records, naming Nicaragua, Romania, Paraguay, Chile, South Korea, Surinam, Taiwan, Guatamala, Haiti, and the Philippines. The federation detailed workers' rights violations in each of these countries and called for effective enforcement of the new laws. The Reagan administration *ended* special trade privileges for Nicaragua and Romania but *suspended* these for Paraguay. At the same time the U.S. special trade representative, Clayton Yeutter, said he would continue to *review* the workers' rights issue in Chile for yet another year. The other "free world" allies were not found to have violated international norms. The Reagan administration took no action against Baby Doc's Haiti or Marcos' Philippines until popular movements there were close to toppling these unpopular friends of America. Nonetheless, that the job loss and fair trade issues have been tied to acceptable labor standards has legitimated a progressive internationalism in the labor movement.[2]

It may well be that labor's cold warriors, cynical in their sophisticated understanding of the Reagan White House, knew the law would be enforced in just such a biased way and approved of the administration's actions. The tenor of their publications certainly confirms a right-wing consistency in outlook. The AFL-CIO continues to officially see communism, and not exploitation or even the anti-union policies of local dictators, as the central problem for workers and trade unions in less developed nations. The left has the more realistic and believable view of the social contradiction between the rich and powerful and the poor and oppressed, one that is not consistent with the official view of the third world as primarily a battlefield between East and West. The ascendancy of the Gorbachev policies further undermines hardliner credibility, as do the economic constraints on blank check expansion of the U.S. military and the official downgrading of the "Soviet threat."

Given the intense international competition and the pressures to be ever more mobile and flexible, especially in production location, capital has increased its bargaining power against workers who have ties of family, homeownership, and to local communities and nation-states. To protect their immediate economic situation, jobs, work-places, and the tax base of the jurisdictions in which they reside, the workers of the world need to unite. Defensive strategies to protect localized interests can be made effective by internationalist class-based alliances. All of this of course is far easier said than achieved in an era when capital's global reach taunts workers' lack of class connectedness.

There is increasing support for the sorts of controls over capitalist greed that have long been part of public discourse in Western Europe. Here too political leverage is possible which recognizes the common interest working people have in limiting antisocial behavior by capitalists. For example, prohibiting or taxing loans for specula-tion and unnecessary mergers, taxing foreign earnings of U.S.-based corporations, withdrawing preferential tax treatment for real estate loans (above some reasonable level for one home per family), and so on, are potential uses of the state to encourage socially desirable behavior. So is the demand for more spending on health, education, and welfare to increase the skills and life chances of U.S. workers in the context of full-employment policies.

The goals of progressive trade unions' industrial policy are the traditional ones of distributive justice, democratically accountable public intervention in the economy, economic growth which provides meaningful employment and income security, humane implementa-tion of technology, and quality of work issues from health and safety to self-actualizing work relations. Conceptually, such legislation of-fers protection of working-class interests. At the same time, suc-cessful control over capital's socially irresponsible "freedom" builds support for more direct forms of social control of investment and production. The issue is how labor would expect to attain them.

## *Changing Labor Politics*

In the 1970s, organized labor supported a national industrial pol-icy response to job loss. This approach was decisively defeated within the leadership not only as a result of the victory of Ronald Reagan, but also due to its rejection by such important figures as Charles Schultze and other Brookings Institution policy advisers, and, more basically, due to the lack of sufficient support from the diminished ranks of liberal corporatists in the business community and the Congress.

Since almost all schemes to make the United States more competitive again must place reliance on these same men and corporate institutions that have shown little willingness to be "partners" and "all work together" in the face of better profit opportunities elsewhere, one can be pessimistic. Working-class interests will not be protected by giving more power to a government beholden to these powerful interests. The cost to taxpayers, the relative distribution of benefits among workers, consumers, and corporations are all likely to favor the distribution of power, resources, and income even more to the corporate rich, at working people's expense. Given relative power relations it is easy to see labor's demand for industrial policy based on capital-labor cooperation as naive.

Industrial policy failed in the 1970s because working people in large numbers rejected it as not in their own interests. A program based on the needs of the minority of workers who are unionized manufacturing production workers is not a sufficiently broad-based program—especially so if other groups of workers perceive that it involves giveaways to monopolistic corporations and imposes real costs to them, via higher taxes and prices. If in the past much of the response of labor has been to try to protect the jobs in manufacturing by protecting and subsidizing companies, progressive unions increasingly are trying to broaden the struggle to raise wages in services, to organize the unorganized, to build coalitions around increasing the social wage for all working Americans, and to support labor struggles in the third world. Preventing unnecessary and socially costly plant closings would then be a part of a broad class program and not viewed by other workers as special interest protection. Such a broadened perspective can engender a more widespread internationalist consciousness that may prove historically important.

Labor might develop a strategy from combining elements of several recent struggles. First, a possible trajectory might develop from both an internationalist solidarity position implicit in the AFL-CIO's attack on labor policies of third world police states and emerging concepts of negotiated trade to limit devastating, sudden job losses from import penetration, and in such efforts as the auto union's proposal for domestic content legislation (which may appear prophetic in historical perspective). Second, competitive strategies that increase labor's power in its struggle with capital domestically might be combined with international agreements that build working-class unity across national borders. Strategies that require full employment, privilege domestic production and the provision of public goods, demand adjustment of trade surplus nations, rather than the deflationary biases of monetarist solutions, are cases in point. How far can worker-oriented reform be pushed?

It is hard to get "liberal" support for rules that impose social costs on corporations and limit capital's "freedom." If the full social cost of most capitalist activities had to be undone, or adequately compensated for, many would not be undertaken. Those that were carried out would no longer savage the working class. If labor seeks to move away from situations that pit workers against workers in other locations, or from a national competitiveness strategy aimed at helping both capital and labor within a given nation-state to what Michael Lebowitz (1987) was described as creating a "capitalist's dilemma" (in which capital is pitted against itself by rules of a new game established under labor's hegemony), we would not expect to see many smiling liberal capitalists talking about the virtues of "cooperation." But that is what a serious trade union movement must seek to achieve—adjustment based on putting the needs of working people first.

### The Prospects for U.S. Worker Solidarity

There is some indication that not only are material conditions educating workers but that the changing composition of the working class during global restructuring may be prompting a new unionism. The Hudson Institute, in a study commissioned by the Labor Department, "Workforce 2000," projects that native-born white males will account for only 15 percent of the entrants to the labor force by the year 2000. The rest will be nonwhite, female, or immigrant workers. Native white males in 1987 accounted for 47 percent of the workforce in this country. In little more than a decade the workforce will shake up the labor movement in ways that resemble the early twentieth-century impact of the then new immigrants.

While the Hudson Institute researchers see growing anti-immigrant feelings by nativist workers and greater hostility between Hispanics and blacks, a new class unity and militance is also possible. With manufacturing jobs continuing to decline as a share of GNP (Hudson projects to less than 17 percent in 2000 from 21 percent in 1985, and 30 percent in 1955) the wage distribution will continue to grow less equal because of the bipolar distribution of service sector wages offering a 1920s-like trend and class polarization (Johnston 1987). Within the United States the same divisions which exist internationally will be more obvious domestically. Much of the U.S. workforce will be drawn from the third world and its increasingly oppressive conditions will make economic justice the key social movement of the 1990s.

Given the growing Spanish-speaking workforce on the U.S. side of the border, ties of language and culture favor solidarity with the growing undocumented segment of the U.S. labor force and with workers in Latin America. Similar commonalities within various Asian and Caribbean communities in the United States have a parallel impact in creating an international worker consciousness. The emerging communities of solidarity may favor a labor movement more like that of the late nineteenth and early twentieth centuries than that of the immediate post-World War II period. Similarly, as labor organizes it will in time develop meaningful union structures including workers all over the world employed by the same transnational. There are signs that such structures are developing.

In April 1988 the first international labor conference on General Electric took place, bringing together union representatives from twenty nations to oppose "the transfer of work with the intention of exploiting working people and setting us one against the other" (*UE News,* April 22, 1988, p. 6). AFL-CIO President Lane Kirkland, in his remarks to the conference, recalled GE's "take-it-or-leave-it" bargaining (Boulwarism) and the 1969–70 strike unity which buried it. "Just as it once played a divide-and-conquer game against the unions of the CBC [Combined Bargaining Committee of GE and Westinghouse unions], GE now fosters rivalries among workers and labor movements of more than 50 countries. The unionists worked to build the same kind of unity on a global basis " (ibid., p. 7). We need to envision new "dual union" structures where workers are organized by industry and within a corporate coalition capable of united action against a common employer on a global scale.

While not a new phenomenon—World Company Councils have existed in the auto industry since 1966 and have been created in major industries—the goal of depriving transnationals of advantages from relocation by imposing uniform wages, working conditions, and labor protection to the maximal degree possible is central to the emergence of a real trade union internationalism. This need not be inconsistent with more immediate interests. It is useful to remember that the British trade unionists who played such a large role in the First International were concerned largely with preventing the importation of foreign strike-breakers. Similarly when the first international trade secretariats were established in the 1890s few workers saw these efforts to bring workers of the world together in anything but narrowly defensive terms.

The World Company Councils (of which some sixty-odd now exist) are not as effective as labor would like against the likes of Unilever or General Motors. The companies are able to play workers whose horizons and allegiances are fairly local against each other, forcing them to compete among themselves for jobs. Between workers of the core and those of the periphery attitudes of racism, national chauvinism, and patterns of unequal exchange are so strong as to lead Arghiri Emmanuel to speak of "the delusions of internationalism" (Emmanuel 1970). But these problems are not inherent in such organizations.

Discussion of labor tactics in relation to transnationals usually takes their conflict of interest as the starting point. But just as the class nature of the state can be consistent with a close collaboration between local political elites and the transnational corporation so some labor leaders may see accommodation with their firms against competitors (enterprises and workers based in other nations) as the best strategy to maximize their own interests. Just as the state should be seen as an arena of class struggle, an important venue for workers' organizations to make demands for the social control of capital, so within unions ideological struggle is ongoing, and in the present period favors those who challenge labor's accommodationist policies. This is not to say that the power of business unionism to discipline militants has faded, far from it, but rather that the payoff to rank-and-file workers from accepting class colloboration has substantially diminished. The struggle between accommodation and struggle approaches is ongoing in the labor movement.

With the intensified internationalization of capital and labor in recent decades has come increased awareness that the localism of particularistic struggles of working people can be meaningfully addressed only from an internationalist class understanding of the social forces at work. The tensions within a recomposed U.S. working class also offer opportunities for unity and revitalizing the labor movement as the instrumentality of oppressed and exploited groups based on mutual appreciation of racial and ethnic distinctiveness. The same is true of gender. The tension here is between patriarchal

business unionism and wider conceptions of working-class organization and invites coalition-building with progressive middle-class
strata.

The dynamics of labor organizing on a truer classwide basis also
generate pressure for a different kind of political action emphasis for
organized labor. Branded as a special interest, and thus marginalized
by the moderates grouped around the Democratic Leadership Conference, the progressive wing of the Democratic Party was ironically
saved from all but extinction by the daring campaign of Jesse Jackson. The Rainbow Coalition is the mobilization of the forces traditionally identified with an authentic left political presence—minority
groups, small farmers, industrial workers, the exploited masses. The
support Jackson has received from rank-and-file and progressive
officials has been an important challenge to the AFL-CIO leadership's preference for backing cold war-corporate welfare state-type
Democrats.

Jackson's formulation of the progressive agenda contrasts with the
mild, almost nonexistent way other leading Democrats discuss labor
issues. He has shown how seemingly isolated struggles by particular
groups involve the same enemies and system. Community has also
been an important focus for labor, as plant closings have spurred
anticorporate feelings and built support for "the new wave of social
legislation" that left activists have successfully been pushing within
the labor movement and in wider political arenas. The notion that
employees and their families, local communities, and others affected
by corporate decisions have a stakeholder claim on resource allocation extends the concept of production for use, not only simply for
exchange, into a struggle to redefine property rights (See Kusnet
1987).

There will also have to be a more significant opening to the
women's movement and to women as workers. Seventy-two percent
of all women between the ages of 20 and 44 work for wages, most in
gender-segregated employment. Many bear major responsibility for
caring for children, elderly parents, or spouses. Although half of all
women with children under age one are in the workforce, most have
no right to maternity leave. These workers need a solidarity from
unions that they have not been receiving. There are signs that this is
changing.

The awareness of declining living standards creates a large potential constituency both for a revitalized trade union movement and a

broad political movement for social change. This is not to say either will automatically appear. The objective conditions for such a pendulum swing are in place. We shall see if the 1990s resemble the 1930s and 1960s (but with a greater international solidarity this time around a real possibility. The workers of the world may be struggling for unity in ways that were unthinkable in earlier stages of capitalist development).

Economic restructuring is creating a recomposed working class and so also a trade union movement that will be as different from the current AFL-CIO as the emergent CIO was from the craft-oriented AFL. It will be more movement oriented and find its natural alliances in the other organizational representations of its members' identities—civil rights, feminist, nonintervention, and localist participatory new social movements. It will organize against its transnational employers across nation-state boundaries and be an integral part of a broader economic justice movement.

The three-way tension between the old-style business unionism, a top-down social democratic reformism of a liberal corporatist sort, and a more grass-roots, movement-oriented tendency will be played out against historical specifics of the instability and crises of global capitalism. It would be foolhardy to speculate specifically on how these forces will play out.

The burden of the argument being made here is that the bankruptcy of the cold war class collaboration business unionism that has been unable as well as unwilling to organize the broader working class is now clear. Unions are being pushed to relate in fundamentally new ways to capital and the state. Within the bad news of organized labor's decline and outmoded strategies is also to be found the possibility of new promise for its rebirth.

## Notes

1. The extent to which labor's political strength had declined is indicated by the modesty of this proposal compared to the effort by labor to protect U.S. jobs in the early 1970s, the Burke-Hartke bill which proposed less favorable tax treatment for foreign investment, presidential licensing of all direct foreign investment and technology transfers, guided by the criteria of domestic job impact, and other protectionist measures against global sourcing.
2. Lane Kirkland's warning that AFL-CIO members were to stay away from Washington demonstrations and rallies against U.S. Central America and South Africa policies did not stop labor's impressive participation on April 12, 1987.

## References

Bluestone, Barry and Bennett Harrison. 1988. *The Great U-Turn.* New York: Basic Books.

Emmanuel, Arghiri. 1970. "The Delusions of Internationalism." *Monthly Review,* February.

International Labor Rights Education and Research Fund. 1988. *Trade's Hidden Costs; Workers Rights in a Changing World Economy.* New York.

Johnston, William B. 1987. *Workforce 2000: Work and Workers for the 21st Century,* Indianapolis: Hudson Institute.

Kusnet, David. 1987. "A New Social Contract." *Multinational Monitor,* October.

Lebowitz, Michael. 1987. "Labor Strategies in a World of Capital." Paper presented to the Canadian Political Science Association. June 8.

Slaughter, Jane. 1987. "Plan for CLUW-AIFLD Project is Halted." *Labor Notes,* August.

Sweezy, Paul M. 1967. "Marx and the Proletariat." In *Modern Capitalism and Other Essays.* New York: Monthly Review Press.

Thompson, E. P. 1978. "The Peculiarities of the English." In *The Poverty of Theory and Other Essays."* New York: Monthly Review Press.

# Part III
# The Lasting Crisis: Constraints and Opportunities

# The Age of Restructuring

## John Bellamy Foster

Gone are the days when only the left argued that there were structural problems in the advanced capitalist economies. As a result of two decades of slow growth and increasing international instability "restructuring" has become a major establishment goal. Such restructuring from a capitalist perspective has come to mean: (1) lowering the break-even point of industry by driving down and dismantling rigid costs; (2) enhancing competitiveness through a dynamic technological process of creative destruction; and (3) developing the most cost-efficient international sourcing of raw materials and products. Moreover, structural adjustments of this kind, it is believed, are best accomplished by the market itself, which if given free rein will create the objective conditions for a more efficient capitalist order. "Any survey of the OECD literature," Joyce Kolko notes in *Restructuring the World Economy,* "reveals that the key themes are structural adjustment, restructuring, rigidities, deregulation, privatization, and the like" (1988:234).

It is this renewed faith in the rationalizing effect of market forces in the face of economic stagnation that has led to the recent gutting of government programs directed toward the needs of labor and the dispossessed, and to the deregulation of such industries as finance, telecommunications, and transport. Moreover, not content to rest with clearing away obstacles to so-called "objective restructuring" by the market, the powers that be have sought to give the whole process an added push, utilizing the tax system to redistribute income and wealth from the poor to the rich, and relying on the power of the state to promote "a weakened, restructured labor force with lowered expectations" in order to increase profits, wring out inflation, and "lessen downward wage inflexibility" (Rosenberg

1983:183–84). "The closest to a long-range subjective strategy for private capital," Kolko observes, "is its struggle against labor and it is now using the crisis to force new conditions in that relationship" (1988:180).

Capitalism is more than simply a class society, however; it is also a world system divided into national units. And in the 1980s economic stagnation and financial instability stretch clear across the capitalist world. Restructuring therefore extends into the realm of international competition as well. The goal of national restructuring to enhance national competitiveness is central to contemporary strategy, since it holds out the hope to each nation that it can grow at the expense of others, thereby quieting the class struggle within. Thus while liberal possessive individualists of the more conservative, right-wing variety stress class-based restructuring along the traditional laissez-faire lines normally preferred by capital, those of a slightly more progressive stamp, although seldom seriously questioning the former course, generally choose to place a certain degree of responsibility for the adjustment on capital and the state by focusing on the need for enhanced competition and creative destruction at home to create a "world-class economy" (see Thurow 1985). None of which prevents the dominant interests of the capitalist world from remaining all but unanimous in their conviction that restructuring of an especially forcible kind is needed in the underdeveloped third world to ensure "a level playing field" for all competitors.

The concept of "restructuring" is therefore part of a new abstract language of power obscuring the harsh reality of class and imperial struggle. Nevertheless, key categories in capital's armory are seldom mere disguises for a reality that lies underneath; they are also the means of organizing ruling-class initiatives. In this respect, the notion of free-market restructuring has the practical value of reducing the various levels of firm, class, and nation to a common logic of cost-competitiveness, thereby facilitating a desired form of change throughout the world economy.

This stepped-up implementation of capital's logic at every level of the world system has the long-term effect, however, of deepening the global impasse of the system. By adopting restructuring as its response to the slowdown of production, capital has not only created an immediate, conjunctural crisis associated with its assault on labor everywhere and in the third world in particular, but has also—as a result of its very success in weakening labor and the dependent periphery economically—aggravated the long-term, organic crisis of the system represented by stagnation and imperial instability. It is through this complex interfacing of the conjunctural and organic crises of the system that the strategic terrain of struggle in our time is being formed (Gramsci 1971:177–79). To discover this terrain we must explore in greater detail the interaction of restructuring with stagnation and imperial instability.

## Stagnation and Restructuring

Although orthodox economists seldom choose to emphasize the point, there can be little doubt that the U.S. economy has been stuck in a condition of stagnation for two decades. To quote from the Commission on Trade and Competitiveness appointed by New York Governor Mario Cuomo:

> The U.S. economy is still growing, but ever more slowly. In the 1960s the annual average GNP growth rate was 3.8 percent. In the 1970s, it fell to 2.8 percent. From 1980 through 1987 it slid even further to 2.2 percent. . . . The relative stagnation of the nation's economy can be seen in the degree to which industrial capacity is underutilized. . . . In 1966, the capacity utilization rate was 91 percent. As of January 1, 1988, the peak for the 1980s was less than 83 percent (1988:9–10).

The authors of the *Cuomo Commission Report* attribute these dismal statistics mainly to a loss of U.S. competitiveness and the emergence of a more competitive world economy in general rather than to any intrinsic difficulties of capitalism itself. Nevertheless, the same report notes later on that, "A study for the OECD showed that from the mid 1970s to the early 1980s, unemployment doubled in the advanced countries, and growth rates were cut in half" (ibid.: 37). Indeed, a recently released OECD report goes so far as to characterize this most recent period of development (1973–87) as one of "stagnation," and to criticize its own forecasts of the last fifteen years for continually overestimating future economic performance— which doesn't prevent the authors of this report from going on to provide a still rosier picture for the future predicated on a stepped-up restructuring program (1987:15 and 33).

The closest historical analogy to this situation is to be found in the Great Depression of the 1930s when high unemployment and slow growth dominated the economy for a decade. In 1938 unemployment in the United States, despite a long, slow recovery from the depression low of 1932, stood at 19 percent. What brought an end to this condition was not any natural recuperative power of the economic system itself—or meager efforts at New Deal spending—but rather the appearance of World War II in Europe and Asia. Taking on the role of "arsenal of democracy" from 1939 on, the United States was able to expand its GNP by two-thirds in only six years.

After World War II stagnation did not immediately return. Instead, the advanced capitalist economies experienced a quarter-century of rapid growth. From 1950 to 1973 "real GDP in the OECD area increased by an average of nearly 5 percent a year, two and a half times more rapidly than in the four preceding decades and approximately twice as rapidly" as in the 1973–87 period (ibid.: 18). Encouraged by this exceptional prosperity, most orthodox economists quickly concluded that capitalism had returned to its normal condition, and rather than worrying about stagnation they reverted to their usual function of providing ever more obscure ideological justifications for the established order.

Nevertheless, it is important to understand that the prosperity of these years had its basis not in the inherent workings of the accumulation process as such, but in the exceptional circumstances provided by certain self-limiting developmental factors. These special stimuli included: (1) the rebuilding of industries in Europe and Japan following the devastation of World War II; (2) the existence of consumer liquidity built up during the war; (3) major regional wars in Korea and Indochina; (4) the emergence of a "peacetime" arms industry; (5) the epoch-making industrializing effect of a second great wave of automobilization in the United States during the 1950s (which encompassed the expansion of the steel, glass, and rubber industries and the building of an interstate highway system), along with the rapid automobilization of Europe over the same period; (6) the development of a commercial airline industry, spurred by the wartime development of jet aircraft; (7) the creation of new markets in the third world as multinational corporations invaded every region of the globe; and (8) a vast ballooning of the world financial system. In addition, the existence of U.S. hegemony in the first two decades following the World War, while not in itself a developmental factor, provided a stable environment for capitalist expansion worldwide.

Each of these stimuli, however, turned out to be either directly self-limiting in character or was to result in a doubling-over of economic contradictions. The rebuilding of the war-devastated societies in Europe and Japan was completed, resulting in a slowing down of the growth rate of these economies as they returned to "business as usual." Consumer liquidity disappeared in rising mounds of consumer debt. Use of the U.S. war machine to battle revolutions throughout the globe came up against both the military limits of U.S. power and the political costs of its use, as manifested in the U.S. invasion of Vietnam and its subsequent defeat at the hands of the Vietnamese. Concentration of a large part of the economy on military output was to be of diminishing effectiveness in combating unemployment due to its capital intensive character; resulted in a contradiction-laden growth of the federal deficit; and increasingly appeared to carry long-term costs associated with the structuring of output toward non-reproductive "luxury goods." The wave of automobilization, along with the expansion of the aircraft industry, had essentially petered out by the late 1960s, entering a phase of simple reproduction. Multinational corporate expansion led to greater concentration of unabsorbed surplus capital in the core states as the outward expansion of the giant firms accelerated the return flow of capital to the center. And the hypertrophy of the world financial structure manifested itself in a global debt crisis that increasingly generated "hard landing" scenarios. By the beginning of the 1970s, moreover, it was apparent that undisputed U.S. hegemony was a thing of the past; in large part because of the massive outflow of dollars associated with a failed attempt to subjugate a small revolutionary peasant population half way around the globe (Magdoff 1982:3–5).

With the waning of these developmental factors—or the loss of their more positive effects—stagnation resurfaced as a major problem of the capitalist economy. And as conditions of slow growth and rising unemployment and excess capacity set in, the flight of capital from production, in a frantic search for "safe havens" in the realm of abstract money making, became an increasingly dominant feature of the system. Hence, it is no mere coincidence that the major international financial "trouble spots," as Magdoff and Sweezy observe, "emerged as stagnation spread throughout the capitalist world. Stagnation set the stage for the financial explosion as well as the heating up of competition in the face of global excess manufacturing capacity. . . . The tensions underneath broke out on the surface when growth slowed down, with a resulting increase in the virulence of nationalistic feelings" (Magdoff and Sweezy 1987b:18).

Looking over the history of the U.S. economy from the 1930s to the present therefore seems to offer *prima facie* evidence that stagnation has been more common than rapid growth. Moreover, the expansion that did take place during World War II and the years that immediately followed can be traced to developmental factors of a transitory historical character. In fact, we can go further *on theoretical grounds* to argue that stagnation, and not prosperity, is the normal state of the mature monopoly capitalist system.

Stagnation in this sense can be thought of as arising out of the whole pattern of capitalism's historical development. As Marx explained in the mid-nineteenth century,

> From day to day it . . . becomes clearer that the relations of production in which the bourgeoisie moves do not have a simple, uniform character but rather a dual one; that in the same relations in which wealth is produced, poverty is produced also; that in the same relations in which there is a development of the forces of production, there is also the development of a repressive force; that these relations produce bourgeois wealth, i.e. the wealth of the bourgeois class, only by continually annihilating the wealth of the individual members of this class and by producing an ever growing proletariat (Marx 1977: 798–99).

Marx labeled this "the absolute general law of capitalist accumulation," and it is this dual process of concentration and centralization of wealth at the top of society and creation of relative poverty at the bottom, which characterizes the long-run development of the system. Because of this, capitalism is continually threatened by an insufficiency of buying power among the mass of wage earners, who are frequently unable to purchase an adequate share of the growing mass of commodities that the system is capable of churning out. And insofar as added capitalist consumption or investment does not rush in to close the gap the result is a strong tendency toward economic crisis and stagnation.

Until the twentieth century, however, this contradiction did not act as a serious constraint on the system's operations. In its youth capitalism was blessed by seemingly endless possibilities for external and internal expansion. On the one hand, there was a vast noncapitalist frontier to conquer. On the other, there was the need to build up industry virtually from scratch. Furthermore, in the atomistically competitive capitalist order that existed in those times firms had little choice but to invest all of the economic surplus at their disposal as a means of mere survival. Hence, both new investment opportunities and the drive of capitalists to invest appeared then to be unlimited.

As capitalism aged, however, it transformed its historical environment in ways that tended to slow down the pace of its further advance. By the end of the nineteenth century the leading imperial powers had conquered most of the world's noncapitalist frontier. And as the noncapitalist environment was gradually incorporated into the world market, the system had to fall back more and more on its own internal resources and became increasingly constrained by its own contradictory logic. The search for new frontiers to conquer thus became an increasing source of anxiety for those who identified with the progress of the system. Indeed, the appearance of one revolutionary wave after another in the underdeveloped regions of the globe throughout the twentieth century meant that the geographical circle of capitalism, rather than continuing to expand, was actually beginning to contract.

Meanwhile, the process of industrialization had, by the early twentieth century, transformed the basic economic terrain upon which capitalism operated. Once the advanced capitalist states had all become highly industrialized—that is, had developed very efficient capital goods industries, capable of supplying at a moment's notice all the needs of the consumption goods sector, while maintaining considerable amounts of surplus capacity even during periods of prosperity—much of the demand for new plant and equipment associated with these initial phases of industrialization dropped off. Production could be maintained at a steady rate of growth through existing depreciation funds (which allowed for the replacement of worn-out productive capacity with ever more technologically advanced capital equipment), with very little if any new net investment. In the more mature capitalist environment that ensued, expansion of investment became increasingly geared to and dependent upon the expansion of consumption. For a system based on accumulation of capital, however, this meant an irreversible slowdown in the rate of growth (Sweezy 1981: 37–39).

These changes in the system's historical environment went hand in hand with certain modifications in the pattern of accumulation associated with the consolidation of monopoly capitalism early in the twentieth century. In the new regime of big business that replaced the atomistically competitive capitalism of Victorian times, new investment was no longer introduced automatically, as part of a life and death struggle of creative destruction, but was regulated and rationalized so as to preserve the profit margins of the large capitals. In the face of a deficiency in effective demand, monopolistic corporations generally cut back on output, employment and investment, rather than reducing prices (and hence profit margins), as would be the case in a freely competitive system. But demand difficulties become increasingly serious without an augmented rate of investment by monopoly capital itself, since the potential surplus product available to the giant corporations continues to rise relative to the total income of society as a whole. By maintaining high profit margins (and excessive rates of surplus value) modern monopolistic capital tends to induce a widening underemployment gap, holding down the rate of growth of the system and the proportion of potential surplus product realized. The result is a system characterized by slow growth and rising unemployment and excess capacity.

There is always the hope of course that new industries will enter in to solve the problem. Nevertheless, the shot-in-the-arm effect of new industries also diminished as capitalism aged. At the outset of the industrialization process, all industries represented new areas of commodity production, and had accelerated both the internal and external expansion of the system. But as capitalism evolved, the relative impact of new industries on the economy as a whole decreased. Such developments were increasingly confined to the system's margins rather than finding their location in its "central mechanism (Magdoff and Sweezy 1987a:6). Thus the impact of the computer and electronics revolution of the late twentieth century has had relatively few positive ramifications for the inner dynamic of the system when compared to the impact of the railroad in the nineteenth century or the automobile in the early part of this century. The railroad in the mid- to late nineteenth century directly accounted for about half of all capital investment. In contrast, the electronics industry, while enormously dynamic in its effect on product innovation, has hitherto played only a very marginal role with respect to the expansion of the overall market for new capital formation.

Stagnation is therefore deeply embedded in the process of capitalist development and can be considered the norm for a mature monopoly capitalist society. What this means is that: (1) contemporary economic history is best viewed in terms of the interaction of stagnation with the forces acting counter to it; and (2) this is not a symmetrical relationship, but one in which a powerful tendency toward stagnation is only partially and temporarily staved off through the effect of much weaker counter-tendencies of a self-limiting character (Magdoff and Sweezy 1987c: 23–24).

Two powerful counteracting forces are spurring the cyclical recovery that has been going on since early 1983. The first of these is an unprecedented peacetime military buildup financed through huge federal deficits. The second is the financial explosion. Nevertheless, the self-limiting character of these stimuli are more and more obvious. The stock market crash of October 19, 1987, when the Dow Jones Industrial Average plummeted 508 points in a single day, represented only the latest and most dramatic in a growing series of shocks to the system.

The spreading symptoms of this disease—if not the disease itself—have been witnessed with increasing anxiety by the powers that be. Gradually becoming convinced that there is a structural crisis, the attention of the leading establishment spokespeople, Magdoff and Sweezy explain,

> has been turning to the search for a way to restructure the U.S. economy in a radically new way. A typical example is the lead story in *Business Week* of November 16, [1987], less than a month after the [stock market] crash. *"It's time for America to wake up. The message is clear: Americans have spent too much, borrowed too much, and imported too much. Now it has to stop."* Although the hard edges of the purported remedies are smoothed over, the main thrust is clear: consumption has to be reduced. And to this end wages have to be held down and government spending on subsidies, welfare and social security programs lowered (Magdoff and Sweezy 1988: 12).

Of course the more perceptive observers understand that this makes no sense in terms of an economy already suffering from a crisis of underemployment and overcapacity. Nonetheless, the hope is held out that such restructuring can create the basis for a more competitive national economy that will be able to export the crisis to others by expanding exports and decreasing imports. The answer to the plight of the economy is therefore being sought in the outer transformation of capitalist society.

Yet one only has to step beyond one's own national boundaries to recognize how irrational such a strategy is when pursued by every country simultaneously. Indeed, further progress in the elimination of the gargantuan U.S. trade deficit, amounting to $153 billion in 1987, would inflict a serious blow on the capacity of debt-laden underdeveloped countries to service their debts. While those advanced capitalist countries that rely on a favorable trade balance, as a means of keeping mass unemployment and excess capacity partially in check, could easily be thrown into a deep depression as a result of a rapid reversal in the U.S. trade deficit.

*Imperialism and Restructuring*

The calamity—both existing and threatened—is greatest where the third world is concerned. Despite the much advertised expansion of South Korea, Taiwan, and a few other countries of East and Southeast Asia, the condition of most third world nations in the 1980s is best summed up as stagnation or depression on top of imperialist underdevelopment. The per capita GNP of Latin America in 1986 was nearly 8 percent below its level for 1980. From 1973–1985 per capita GNP in Sub-Saharan Africa dropped by 8.3 percent. In 1987 the World Bank reported that the ninety "developing countries" in its survey had experienced an average annual per capita growth of GNP of 1.5 percent in 1980–86 compared to 3.2 percent in 1973–80 and 3.9 percent in 1965–73 (International Labour Office 1987; World Bank 1987). The poorest countries are carrying the heaviest burden in the present world crisis of capitalism and are slipping further and further behind the advanced states, despite the stagnation of the latter. Moreover, it is the subaltern classes and not those who lord over them within these societies who are being forced to make "the necessary adjustments."

The way in which stagnation and the accompanying financial explosion has heaped additional burdens on the periphery can be seen in the evolution of the international debt crisis. Historically, third world countries entrapped in imperialism have had large deficits in their current account balances associated with outflows of interest, dividends, and other payments to foreign banks, corporations, insurance companies and owners of merchant fleets. Thus looking at the period 1968–73 (just prior to the first oil price shock), Latin American countries (excluding Cuba) showed a combined balance of payments deficit on current account of $21 billion (Magdoff 1982). This constant outward flow of tribute has meant that third world countries have been subject to frequent currency devaluations even during periods of relative stability in the world economy.

In the 1970s and 1980s stagnation in the center, together with the consequences of the oil price hikes, converted this normal condition of dependency into a full-scale disaster. During the Vietnam War the United States, taking advantage of the special role of the dollar as the preeminent international currency, financed its military aggression with growing federal budget and balance of payments deficits, resulting in a vast outflow of dollars abroad and the emergence of the Eurodollar market—a huge pool of international finance beyond the reach of any government's regulatory apparatus. This growth in world liquidity enormously expanded the base for international loan activity. Moreover, this was soon heightened by two other developments: (1) the burgeoning supply of financial capital in the center as stagnation set in and the demands of the "real economy" slowed down; and (2) the appearance of vast petrodollar surpluses that needed "recycling." The result of this expanded international liquidity base was the pushing of huge loans with high spreads onto underdeveloped countries.

Meanwhile, the faltering growth trend at the center was being experienced in the periphery as: (1) a general slowdown in world trade; (2) a shift in the terms of trade against the third world due to the drop in the relative prices of most primary commodities; and (3) the increased inaccessibility of center markets to third world products as a result of growing protectionism. Under these circumstances underdeveloped states seeking to maintain growth in the face of spreading stagnation, increasingly took on more debt simply to meet previous obligations. In 1972, 56 percent of the new debt taken on by Latin American states was required simply to cover previous debt service obligations; by 1981 this figure had risen to 75 percent. The "push" of loan capital from the center thus found its complement in a "pull" from the periphery, rooted in the entire pattern of dependent development (Ibid; MacEwan 1986: 184–200).

It would be too much to think that the financial creditors behind this system of international debt peonage failed altogether to see that trouble could arise in the future from this process. Nevertheless, the severity of the debt crisis that actually emerged was not anticipated by the dominant capitalist interests. Beginning in 1982—with Mexico's announcement that it was unable to cover the interest on its debt—this entire system entered a stage of full-blown and lasting crisis, imperiling already fragile third world economies and threatening to overwhelm the world financial structure with defaults on what now amounts to over $1 trillion in debt.

The proximate cause of the crisis was the metamorphosis of the slow growth of the late 1970s into the world recession of the early 1980s, accompanied by the skyrocketing of real interest rates. The sudden drop in export earnings, together with the quantum leap in debt payments resulting from the interest rate rise constituted the two edges of a scissors crisis of unprecedented severity that cut away the growth prospects of the debt-dependent states of the third world.

The interlocking global character of this crisis can be seen in the fact that the skyrocketing interest rates that had such disastrous consequences for the periphery could be traced to the following difficulties within the center of the system: (1) a growing demand for credit resulting from the heightened debt explosion of the early Reagan years; (2) the growth of policies aimed at fighting inflation by pushing up interest rates; and (3) an interest-rate war among the advanced capitalist states, as each country attempted to prevent a destabilizing flight of capital to other, higher interest-rate states. As always the chief sources of international economic distress could be traced to the center while its worst effects were felt in the periphery.

The depression experienced in Latin America and other parts of the third world in the 1980s led to the increased peripheralization of these countries as they fell further back into the traditional dependency trap. Moreover, "peripheralization," as Jackie Roddick says in *The Dance of the Millions,* "has been coupled with another process, restructuring, defined by the U.S. government, the IMF and the World Bank, as privatisation, deregulation and liberalisation" (Roddick 1988: 236). In its outer form this restructuring process is quite similar to what is taking place in the advanced capitalist countries. Still there is a big difference. "For restructuring in the LDCs," Joyce Kolko observes, "while also taking the form of the reactionary prescriptions in which it is applied in the OECD countries, is imperialist. . . . Being weaker and indebted, the LDCs have been more vulnerable to the implementation of the logical extremes of the new adjustment policies and ideology, represented above all by the IMF, than has so far been possible in the stronger countries" (Kolko 1988: 252).

Thus the IMF and the World Bank have demonstrated a growing desire to hand over more rope (that is, allow relatively favorable renegotiated payments) to those already dependent countries that are prepared to rearrange their economies along pure market lines. To quote Robert Pollin and Eduardo Zepeda:

> It has become apparent that Latin America's creditors—the international bankers and their allies in government lending institutions—have become willing to make small concessions in exchange for basic restructuring of the Latin economies. More specifically, they are calling for Latin American countries to become bastions of free-market capitalism, with minimal government, open borders for multinationals, and free trade serving as guiding precepts (Pollin and Zepeda 1987: 1–2).

What has kept this system in place—where popular forces have not managed to overthrow it—is the complicity of the governing classes (or class fractions) in third world states, backed up by armed forces, which often comes in the form of military intervention by the imperialist powers themselves. With respect to the 215 cases of U.S. threat or use of armed force between World War II and 1975, 185, including the Korean and Indochina wars, occurred in the periphery (Kolko 1988: 252). And numerous other instances have taken place since then. Yet, third world insurgencies have proven successful against the full might of capitalist society. And restructuring simply adds further credence to the idea that imperialism is ultimately its own undoing.

## Restructuring and Inter-Imperialist Rivalry

The instability of imperialism is not limited, however, to relations between center and periphery. It can also be seen in a sharp increase in inter-imperialist rivalry. Inequality among nations as well as classes is an essential aspect of the capitalist system without which it cannot function properly. And where there is not a clear hierarchy between states the result is growing international instability and the exacerbation of economic crisis tendencies. Over the long history of capitalism this problem of the international stratification of states has had its severest consequences when power struggles have broken out among the leading imperialist rivals during periods of hegemonic instability.

From this angle, it is possible to understand why the passing of British hegemony in the final quarter of the nineteenth century and the decades leading up to World War I, and the subsequent decline of U.S. hegemony in the Vietnam era, have carried such high costs for the world capitalist system. Without the hegemony of a particular state there is no "final arbiter" in the event of conflict among states, no international lender of last resort in the case of world liquidity crisis, and no basis for guaranteeing that certain "agreed upon" rules of international behavior will be followed. The consequence is growing international disorder as each individual state and multinational corporate actor manipulates the global market to press home some particular advantage, and as the sheer uncontrollability of the system magnifies. Both national in its foundations and international in its operations, world capitalism is constantly threatened by the instability of a center that does not hold (Kindleberger 1986: 288–305).

Thus the breakdown in the Bretton Woods dollar-based international currency regime in 1971—occurring at a time of renewed stagnation in the advanced capitalist states—marked the end of an era of relative stability associated with the American Imperium. And despite the continued primacy of the United States there is every reason to believe that the restoration of its former hegemonic position will remain beyond its grasp, while no other power is capable at present of filling the gap. The current period is therefore marked by increased jockeying for position among the advanced capitalist states, and by the ill-fated efforts of the United States to restore its lost hegemony by ever more drastic means—frequently carrying over into its role as global policeman.

Restructuring can only serve to worsen this problem of inter-imperialist rivalry. As each state makes its economy leaner and meaner to enlarge its own internally generated profits and export the crisis to others, the stress on the world economy intensifies, and international cooperation—always a dim possibility—becomes more remote. Hence, restructuring generates new inducements for the creation of international currency and trade blocs. Indeed, the enhanced economic integration of Europe planned for 1992 is widely perceived in the business community as an attempt to construct such a bloc.

### The Lasting Crisis

The earliest thinkers to confront the issue of what Marx labeled the absolute general law of capitalist accumulation thought that it was possible for capitalism, which had emerged in a tiny corner of the globe, to escape some of the limits of its internal dialectic by expanding outward into its external environment. The only way out for bourgeois society, Hegel argued, was external expansion: "This inner dialectic of civil society thus drives it—or at any rate drives a specific civil society—to push beyond its own limits and seek markets, and so its necessary means of subsistence, in other lands which are either deficient in the goods it has overproduced, or else generally backward in industry (Hegel 1952: 148–52; Harvey 1982: 413–15).

In contrast, Marx made it clear in his discussions of foreign trade and colonization that the hope that capitalism could depend on the expansion of foreign markets to solve its internal dilemmas was likely to prove illusory over the long run, since this simply "shifts the contradictions to a broader sphere, and gives them a wider orbit" (Marx 1978: 544).

Nevertheless, the Hegelian answer of solving the dilemmas of the system through external expansion persists. And given capitalism's history of imperial expansion, it is scarcely surprising that restructuring has become increasingly identified with outward transformation along geographical lines, and that this is frequently seen as the means whereby the system will restore its lost momentum of rapid growth. Such views stretch across the political spectrum. Thus even so important a Marxist thinker as David Harvey argues, with respect to "the continuous re-structuring of spatial configurations" under capitalism, "The more the forces of geographical inertia prevail, the deeper will the aggregate crises of capitalism become and more savage will switching crises [affecting place-specific capital and labor] have to be to restore the desired equilibirium." All of which compels him to decry that

> . . . a local alliance [in which labor plays a part] may act to conserve privileges already won, to sustain investment already made, to keep a local compromise intact, and to protect itself from the chill winds of spatial competition through import and export controls, foreign exchange controls and immigration laws. . . . The uneven geographical development of capitalism then assumes a form that is totally inconsistent with sustained accumulation either within the region or on a global scale (Harvey: 428–31).

This makes much more sense, however, if turned on its head. For if it is true, as Marx pointed out, that the growth of accumulation on a world scale only serves to give the developing crisis of capitalism a "wider orbit," and if we have reached the point where stagnation is endemic and unlikely to be reversed, it is easy to see that it does the system and a majority of the people within it little good to vacate local alliances completely in favor of the will-of-the-wisp of growth through the pursuit of comparative advantage. Indeed, if the foregoing analysis has taught us one thing above all it is that "the field of action" of Marx's absolute general law of capitalist accumulation is now the entire world; and that a recognition of the full implications of this, as reflected in stagnation and imperial instability, should guide current left strategy (Magdoff and Sweezy 1987c: 204). Radicals must therefore subject to strenuous criticism the prevailing wisdom that locally based defenses initiated by labor against global restructuring always serve to worsen the immediate crisis of the system and of the people who live within it, and to divide the working class along national and regional lines. Instead, "the spontaneous orientation of workers for protection," Michael Lebowitz has written, "is based upon the recognition that competition, within the confines of wage labor, is always part of the political economy of capital—but has no place in the political economy of the working class (Lebowitz 1986: 40).

To be sure, Harvey uses the above analysis to argue that since restructuring along geographical lines is an objective necessity for private capital—which in the long-run can find no spatial fix for its developing contradictions—there is little choice for labor but to accede to capital's requirements or abolish the system altogether. But such reasoning is inverted in the sense that it places the needs of capital first, and thus only serves to reinforce an unnecessary disjuncture between the subjective experience and practice of workers and the presumably objective needs of capital. The real cunning of history in our time lies in the fact that the straightforward struggle of labor against capital at every point along the line constitutes the only way to secure the objective economic environment in which people live and work, simply because it means placing limitations on the hegemony of private property itself.

History teaches us that the age of restructuring is a passing phase. Sooner or later a growing consciousness of the inability of the system to overcome stagnation by means of restructuring, and of the renewed links between oppressed peoples everywhere that are being forged by this very same restructuring process, is bound to take hold in the minds of working people throughout the world. And when this occurs—and international alliances are reestablished—the re-emergence of an effective resistance movement capable of recapturing the initiative in the genuine remaking of the world will again become possible.

### References

Cuomo Commission on Trade and Competitiveness. 1988. *The Cuomo Commission Report*. New York: Simon and Schuster.

Harvey, David. 1982. *The Limits to Capital*. Chicago: The University of Chicago Press.

Hegel, G.W.F. 1952. *The Philosophy of Right*. New York: Oxford University Press.

Gramsci, Antonio. 1971. *Selections from the Prison Notebooks.* New York: International Publishers.

International Labour Office. 1987. *World Labour Report,* 3. New York: Oxford University Press.

Kindleberger, Charles. 1986. *The World Economy in Depression, 1929–1939.* Berkeley: University of California Press.

Kolko, Joyce. 1988. *Restructuring the World Economy.* New York: Pantheon.

Lebowitz, Michael. 1986. "Capital Reinterpreted." *Monthly Review* 38, no. 2, June.

MacEwan, Arthur. 1986. "International Debt and Banking." *Science & Society,* Summer.

Magdoff, Harry. 1982. "International Economic Distress and the Third World," *Monthly Review* 33, no. 11, April.

—— and Paul M. Sweezy. 1987a. "Capitalism and the Distribution of Income and Wealth." *Monthly Review* 39, no. 5, October.

——. 1987b. "International Cooperation—A Way Out?" *Monthly Review* 39, no. 6, November.

——. 1987c. *Stagnation and the Financial Explosion.* New York: Monthly Review Press.

——. 1988. "The Stock Market Crash and its Aftermath," *Monthly Review* 39, no. 10, March.

Marx, Karl 1977. *Capital* Vol. I. New York: Vintage.

——1978. *Capital.* Vol. II. New York: Vintage.

Organisation for Economic Cooperation and Development. 1987. *Structural Adjustment and Economic Performance.* Paris: OECD.

Pollin, Robert and Eduardo Zepeda. 1987. "Latin American Debt." *Monthly Review,* 38, no. 9. February.

Roddick, Jackie. 1988. *The Dance of the Millions* (London: Latin American Bureau.

Rosenberg, Sam. 1983. "Reagan Social Policy and Labour Force Restructuring." *Cambridge Journal of Economics,* 7, no. 2, June.

Sweezy, Paul. 1981. *Four Lectures on Marxism.* New York: Monthly Review Press.

Thurow, Lester. 1985. *The Zero-Sum Solution: Building a World-Class American Economy.* New York: Simon and Schuster.

World Bank. 1987. *World Development Report.* New York: Oxford University Press.

# The International Monetary Fund and the World Bank in a Changing World Economy

## Robert E. Wood

As International Monetary Fund (IMF) and World Bank officials dispense their wisdom to the third world—more often than not as conditions for loans—they insist again and again that there is really no alternative to the policies they prescribe. Given international "realities," they argue with some justification, current policies are "unsustainable." Countries have no choice but to adjust.

What has long been evident to third world countries of practically every political coloring is that the IMF and the World Bank are not innocent observers of those realities. IMF and Bank officials often like to think of themselves as the proverbial messengers of bad news who unjustly bear the wrath of those who don't want to hear it. But this ignores the important role the two institutions play in creating those realities—particularly in their role in determining access to financing from other institutions. Overwhelmingly dominated by the United States and a few other advanced capitalist countries, the IMF and the World Bank are profoundly ideological institutions, even if they seek to identify their ideology with a combination of technical expertise and common sense.

The Bank's readiness—institutionalized in its constitution—to withhold loans for projects that might compete with private capital, and the demonstrated willingness of both institutions to cut off lending altogether to revolutionary regimes, have long attested to the severe constraints the IMF and World Bank impose on alternative development strategies. (Hayter 1971; Payer 1974 and 1982) If we assume, as Carlos Vilas argues elsewhere in this volume, that building socialism in most of the third world *requires* external financing, the importance of the ideological role of these institutions quickly becomes apparent.

Indeed, faced with the array of constraints built in at all levels of the world system, some on the left have come close to echoing the official view that there are no alternatives. Thus we find Andre Gunder Frank, on whose earlier revolutionary hopes many socialist critics, at least in the west, were weaned, concluding that:

> the usefulness of structuralist, dependence, and new dependence theories of underdevelopment as guides to policy seems to have been undermined by the world crisis of the 1970s. The original sin, inherited from a view of the world divided into parts, or at least the Achilles heel of these conceptions of dependence . . . has always been the implicit and sometimes explicit notion of some sort of "independent" alternative for the Third World. This theoretical alternative never existed in fact . . . not even through "socialist" revolutions as we have known them. . . . Independent national development in the Third World has proved to be a snare and a delusion; and self-reliance, collective or otherwise, is a myth that is supposed to hide this sad fact of life in the world capitalist system. . . . I see for the foreseeable future, the continued development of capitalism, economically aided and politically abetted by the participation and collaboration of the Third World and the "socialist" countries. (Frank 1982; 135, 143, 162)

It is certainly insufficient to counterpose a naive optimism against this kind of pessimism. Nor is it tenable to maintain a mechanistic faith in the third world's passage through capitalist development toward socialism. Yet if conflict and instability are the fundamental characteristics of the capitalist world economy, one should beware of generalizing from the obstacles and false starts of the moment. The "world economy" is not some given entity that exists apart from the actions of people and social institutions. It has been constructed in a particular way through political struggles and by the conscious efforts of governments and international agencies, and it will continue to be changed.

Certainly the view from within the IMF and World Bank is anything but sanguine. Virtually universal "adjustment" (the catchword at both institutions) across the third world has brought out the contradictions of the IMF/World Bank model of development in a manner much more evident than when only a few countries at a time were under their tutelage. The effort to contain the debt crisis by creating more debt has brought the crisis to the doors of the great institutions themselves. A sense of unease pervades both institutions. According to Percy Mistry, a top Bank adviser, "The bank is today a hesitant, unsure institution, focusing increasingly on activities it has demonstrated no particular competence in mastering" (*The Philadelphia Inquirer*, February 2, 1988, p. 11A). The IMF's managing director, Michel Camdessus, worries about "a growing sense of adjustment fatigue" among its third world clients (*New York Times*, February 1, 1988, p. D5). With both institutions taking in more money than they are handing out, both the policies they promote and the willingness of their clients to repay are increasingly threatened.

In a fundamental sense, the problems the IMF and World Bank face are a function of their success in realizing a certain vision of the world economy and of fostering a certain type of development within it. From their origins in the 1940s, both institutions have functioned as built-in systemic mechanisms of economic liberalization, opposing not only socialism but national capitalism as well, in favor of the progressive extension of international market forces. Their success is measured not only in the way those market forces reach today virtually everywhere in the third world, but also in the way the state socialist societies have been increasingly incorporated into the capitalist world system and into the two institutions themselves. China, Vietnam, Hungary, Romania, and Yugoslavia are now all members of the IMF and World Bank, and the Soviet Union has been sounding out membership as well for several years. While the prospect of Soviet membership has elicited a spate of attacks on the Bank and the Fund from the U.S. right, it seems inevitable that the membership of the two institutions will become within a few years almost universal, more-or-less synonymous with the roster of nation-states.

The outcome of these processes—an increasingly globalized international economy with a changing international division of labor, combined with the increasingly crucial roles played by the IMF and the World Bank—has led some observers to speculate that the two institutions represent the nucleus of a reorganization of the world system, away from U.S. hegemony and intercapitalist rivalry toward more systemic modes of rationalization, or generally what Karl Kautsky called "ultra-imperialism."

There is no question that the global recession and debt crisis of the 1980s have vastly expanded the roles of the two institutions, after a period in the 1970s when access to commercial bank loans at low real interest rates enabled a number of countries to avoid them. About eighty third world countries have signed high-conditionality agreements with the IMF since 1980, and the World Bank has aggressively widened its policy conditions through its structural adjustment lending.

Nonetheless, the future role of the Fund and the Bank remains uncertain. One reason for this is that both institutions exist at the sufferance of the United States and a few other capitalist countries, and the ruling classes in these societies are divided over the efficacy of multilateral institutions for achieving their interests. Definitions of national interests with respect to these institutions are still evolving, as are the bargains these key countries are prepared to strike with each other. Another reason involves the contradictions built into the strategies both institutions have promoted in the wake of global stagnation and debt crisis. The next section of this paper examines the degree to which the Fund and the Bank have come to play a "supranational" role, transcending the narrow interests of individual countries. The following two sections continue this exploration through an analysis of the institutional management of the debt crisis and the associated "adjustment" process, an analysis that highlights the heightening contradictions the Fund and the Bank find increasingly difficult to contain. A final section returns to the issue of constraint and contradiction in the world system.

## *Supranational Institutions?*

It is a common view that U.S. hegemony in the International Monetary Fund and the World Bank is becoming a relic of the past. Observers have cited the increased financial power of other advanced capitalist countries, especially Japan; the decline in ideological rigidity necessary to incorporate China and the Eastern European countries; the emerging collective influence of the third world; and the increased power of the institutions' professional staff. Are the IMF and World Bank becoming supranational institutions?

A move away from U.S. hegemony and toward a truly supranational role would have significant implications for the world economy as a whole and for progressive movements and states within it, but it is clear that a number of different possibilities are contained within the "supranationality" concept. A continuum of possible claims, from weak to strong, may be conceptualized as follows:

1. Supranationality could be defined essentially negatively as the lack of any single national hegemony, the relevant issue here being U.S. power. Control by a group of nations would not be ruled out, however.

2. A stronger definition of supranationality would assert substantial institutional autonomy, from either a single hegemon or a collective one. This autonomy would be manifested in the ability of the institution both to formulate policies and to implement them.

3. The strongest definition of supranationality would link the institutional autonomy of (2) to a concept of system logic or interest. In this case the institution would be seen functionally either as manifesting the unfolding logic of the system as a whole or at least rising above sectional interests to define a set of long-term interests of the overall system.

Each of these different meanings is embodied in claims found in the contemporary literature on the IMF and the Bank. There is some evidence for each, but overall, skepticism is in order with regard to (2) and (3), and the transition to (1), although underway, remains incomplete.

Evidence of continuing U.S. dominance in the World Bank is not hard to find. In the replenishment of the Bank's resources for 1988–90, the United States insisted both on lowering of its shares and at the same time on amending the Articles of Agreement to reduce the proportion of votes needed to veto any proposed further amendments, thereby preserving its effective veto. The U.S. continues to name the Bank's president, and to dictate policies for managing the debt crisis that are far more cautious than both the Bank's staff and most other members would prefer.

However, the most fundamental problem with seeing the IMF and World Bank as supranational institutions involves the limited nature of their jurisdiction. Despite the existence of a "scarce currency" clause in its Articles of Agreement aimed at countries with persistent international surpluses, the advanced capitalist countries are effectively insulated from IMF pressure. Both institutions are virtually irrelevant when it comes to both the domestic determination of national policies and negotiations over international concerns among the industrialized countries. The critical areas of trade and monetary relations are dealt with almost entirely outside the framework of the two institutions. The irrelevance of these institutions in these areas is in part attributable to government decisions, but it also reflects the rise of international finance capital that has, in Howard Wachtel's words, "overwhelmed public institutions that were designed for what now looks like a horse-and-buggy technological era (Wachtel 1986: 226).

Viewed from the third world, the IMF and World Bank loom considerably larger, although it is important not to overstate this. It is a moot point whether the changes commonly cited as evidence of the developing countries' growing influence—longer term IMF programs, the establishment of special, low-conditionality facilities to deal with various external shocks, the increased willingness of the World Bank to accommodate state-owned development finance corporations and industrial enterprises, and so on—have reflected increased third world power or rather simply the changing interests and perceptions of international capital and its major host states. The virtually complete collapse of third world efforts first to push for a "new international economic order" and then to get more limited "global negotiations" off the ground strongly suggests that any "supranational" interest defined by the IMF and World Bank is at best likely to constitute a common stance worked out by the major advanced capitalist countries. In this sense one might argue that trilateralism, which faded from the American political scene with such ignoble rapidity in the United States upon the election of Ronald Reagan, may have its one, but still tenuous, practical foothold in the IMF/World Bank system.

The next section explores this mix of continuing U.S. power and hesitant trilateralism in relationship to the debt crisis, the major preoccupation of both institutions since 1982. But first let us explore one way in which these institutions have moved toward a more systemic kind of supranational role.

The example is the creation, under World Bank auspices, of the Multilateral Investment Guarantee Agency (Miga), which was approved by the Bank's Board of Governors in 1985 and commenced operations in 1988. The concept behind Miga is to promote additional foreign investment flows to the third world by compensating for the limitations of both private sector and government agencies that provide political risk insurance for investments abroad. Private sector insurance of this type has been scarce and expensive. The operations of national agencies have tended to be hemmed in by a variety of politically defined restrictions, resulting in a patchwork of excluded investments. The U.S. agency Overseas Private Investment Corporation (OPIC), for example, is prohibited from insuring investments in countries without bilateral investment treaties with the U.S. (these include such important sites as Mexico, Venezuela, and Algeria); has country limits on the amount of coverage it will extend; and occasionally rejects applications on the basis of political pressures from competing domestic producers. The $5 billion insurance capacity of Miga has been designed to fill in the gaps left by the existing agencies. Miga is also likely to up the ante against expropriation or contract abrogation, for it claims subrogation rights—that is, it assumes the rights of any investors it indemnifies (*Finance and*

*Development,* December 1985, p. 54; *South,* February 1988, p. 83). This specter of direct conflict with the World Bank is likely to give such investments virtually untouchable status.

While the creation of Miga is not evidence of World Bank autonomy—indeed, its operational debut was delayed significantly by the slowness of ratification in the United States and the United Kingdom—it does represent an attempt to identify a systemic objective and use the Bank to overcome the limitations of existing market-based and national programs, and in this sense can be seen as a step toward a more supranational role. The historical shift of policy-oriented program lending out of bilateral aid programs, where it was concentrated in the 1960s and early 1970s, into the IMF and the World Bank, can likewise be seen as a trend in the supranational direction. Fully one-half of World Bank lending is now nonproject lending.

## Debt Crisis Management

The debt crisis has given the IMF and the World Bank a new prominence, as both institutions have been recruited by creditor banks and governments to play central roles in managing the crisis. While controversy has tended to focus on the details of conditionality, the most significant aspect of their involvement has been the generally unstated, taken-for-granted assumption that third world debt can and must be paid. Within both institutions there is widespread staff dissent from this assumption, but U.S. dominance has kept any mention of generalized debt relief off the official agenda. As syndicated economics columnist Hobart Rowen puts it: "Conable's World Bank seems frozen in a time warp, waiting for an official Treasury nod that it's OK to mention debt relief (*Philadelphia Enquirer,* February 2, 1988, p 11A).

A full analysis of the management of the debt crisis by the IMF and World Bank is beyond the scope of this paper (but see Wood 1986 and 1988). Both institutions have instituted a number of changes which, while significant, have fallen short of any fundamental change: the IMF's mobilization of "concerted" commercial lending linked to its agreements; "enhanced surveillance" to provide backup for multi-year rescheduling agreements (MYRAs); the expansion of contingency financing mechanisms to cover interest rate gyrations and the estabishment of the Structural Adjustment Facility (SAF) and then the Enhanced Structural Adjustment Facility (ESAF) within the IMF; within the World Bank, new forms of cofinancing and investment insurance; accelerated disbursement; increased structural adjustment and sector lending; an expanded role in coordinating the aid of other donors; the establishment of a Special Facility for Sub-Saharan Africa; a temporary suspension of country debt ceilings so as to allow the Bank to pump new money into the major debtors, and so on. In addition, both institutions have taken a number of steps to coordinate their activities, including the first formal establishment of "cross-conditionality" in the policy framework papers required for SAF and ESAF loans.

In a sense, the success of the IMF and World Bank in managing what supporters and critics alike have called a "debt containment strategy" has been nothing less than extraordinary. Not a single country has yet repudiated a single penny of debt.[1] In every case where individual countries have fallen behind in their debt service payments or have imposed unilateral moratoria, they have reiterated their commitment to pay in the long run. Despite the rhetoric of defiance at conferences in Cartagena, Havana, Harare, and elsewhere, no debtors' cartel has emerged. And most extraordinarily, despite close to 200 debt restructuring agreements since 1980, third world countries have consistently paid out more in debt service each year than before the advent of the crisis—over $100 billion annually—resulting in net transfers to the advanced capitalist societies of about $40 billion each year in 1987 and 1988.[2] And this at a time when declines in the terms of trade have resulted in a loss of an additional $100 billion a year in export revenues for the third world as a whole.

A different standard of success involves the efforts of the IMF and the Bank to use the debt crisis to reorient the economies of the third world in a fundamental way. For many third world countries there has been a tragic irony in this—the debt to commercial banks they incurred in the 1970s to escape IMF discipline led them back to the IMF in the 1980s in a weaker bargaining position than ever. By early 1984, with sixty-seven high-conditionality agreements signed with third world countries since 1980, the IMF Managing Director could proudly assert: "Adjustment is now virtually universal. . . . Never before has there been such an extensive yet convergent adjustment effort." (*IMF Survey,* February 23, 1987, p. 50). World Bank and IMF officials particularly stressed the new openness to foreign capital and private sector development.

The Bank's critics from the right haven't been impressed, continuing to attack the Bank as a "socialistic" institution. Left critics, on the other hand, have tended to take the IMF and Bank more at their own word. Robert Pollin and Eduardo Zepeda, for example assert that Latin American economies have become "increasingly privatized" under IMF tutelage, and similar assertions are found in much of the recent left literature (Pollin and Zepeda, 1987: 4).[3]

There is no question that the IMF and World Bank have brought about significant policy shifts in a number of countries. But evidence to date of long-term, fundamental restructuring remains very limited. Laws and regulations governing foreign investment have been widely eased in favor of the investors, yet the level of new foreign investment remains low, and substantial divestment by multinational corporations has occurred in some countries. Debt-equity schemes have been promoted by the World Bank's private sector-oriented affiliate, the International Finance Corporation (IFC), but popular opposition and government concerns about their inflationary effects have resulted in strict limitations and/or suspensions in a number of the seemingly most promising countries. Privatization has become a kind of buzz word everywhere, but a recent World Bank report finds very little of it outside of Chile and Bangladesh, and where it has occurred, it has generally involved informal "reprivatization" of small state enterprises that had originally been private. (Berg and Shirley 1987: 4–5) In the agricultural sector, countries have generally preferred to raise producer prices than to dismantle marketing boards and state enterprises providing inputs, as desired by the World Bank. In fact, the World Bank has been notably unsuccessful in getting the major debtor countries to accept structural adjustment loans at all.

Indeed, what we see increasingly is a kind of dialectical relationship between market-oriented reforms and increased state intervention along the lines suggested by Arthur MacEwan. MacEwan argued that "the evolution of the debt crisis appears likely to force more direct state intervention in the economy, both in the periphery and in the center . . . Governments will be forced to extend their direct interventions in the economy to limit the havoc and disruption that the market would otherwise breed." MacEwan concluded:

> It seems likely that the ideological proclivities of IMF advisors, of the U.S. government, and of free market conservatives in Latin America will not be a match for the realities of the situation. The need for

stability—a need which these groups share with all of the elites within Latin America—is likely to prevail. (MacEwan, 1986: 207)

This dynamic is likely to be hastened by the debt crisis of the IMF and World Bank themselves. Historically, the main sanction against debt repudiation or default was the potential denial of access to new lending, a threat made particularly plausible with the rise of syndicated lending, cross-default clauses, and the institutionalization of rescheduling procedures in the London Club. After the virtual collapse of commercial lending to the third world after 1982, the Baker Plan sought to resuscitate the promise of renewed commercial lending, but again it has not been forthcoming. What then has kept debtors paying? The key incentive has been the promise of positive net transfers of *official* lending from the World Bank, the IMF, and other multilateral and bilateral agencies. But as Table 1 shows, a key development in the past few years has been the precipitous decline in positive transfers, as debt service to these official institutions has overtaken new lending, in much the same way it did with the commercial banks a few years earlier.

Table 1 shows that the IMF has been a major importer of capital from the third world since 1986. In fact, the IMF data understate this, because they do not include the various charges and fees (in effect, interest) paid on outstanding drawings, which came to almost $3 billion in fiscal year 1987. (IMF *Annual Report,* 1987, p. 138) While the IMF emphasizes that such "perverse flows" are a cyclical phenomenon, its schedule of repurchases shows a continuing high level at least through 1991. Furthermore, a substantial part of its new lending through its two new outlets, the Structural Adjustment and Enhanced Structural Adjustment Facilities, is simply in effect drawing out the terms of existing debt held by low-income countries.

Turning to the World Bank, we see that net transfer from its hard loan window, the IBRD, which accounted for over three-quarters of World Bank disbursements in fiscal year 1988, fell precipitously between 1985 and 1986, from a positive transfer of $2,182 million to a negative transfer of $276 million. Negative transfer increased to $547 million in fiscal year 1987 and then jumped to $3.3 billion in 1988. (World Bank, *Annual Report* 1988.)[4] The Bank's other affiliate, the IFC, also received more in interest on its loans and dividends on its investments than it disbursed in new loans and investments. Through 1987 it was only the IDA, whose lending is limited to low-income countries, that made overall net transfers from the World Bank

*Table 1*

**Net Transfers to Developing Countries (Disbursements minus principal repayments, interest, and fees) for Selected Official Creditors, 1982–87 ($ billions)**

| Creditor | 1982 | 1983 | 1984 | 1985 | 1986 | 1987 |
|---|---|---|---|---|---|---|
| IMF* | 6.845 | 11.331 | 5.125 | 0.406 | −2.112 | −5.418 |
| World Bank** | | | | | | |
| IBRD | 2.226 | 1.964 | 2.800 | 2.182 | −0.276 | −0.547 |
| IDA | 1.918 | 2.408 | 2.287 | 2.205 | 2.208 | 2.682 |
| IBRD/IDA | 4.144 | 4.372 | 5.087 | 4.387 | 1.932 | 2.135 |
| IFC | 0.040 | −0.018 | −0.022 | −0.010 | −0.009 | −0.114 |
| IDB** | 0.669 | 0.632 | 1.109 | 0.868 | 0.300 | −0.295 |
| ADB** | 0.420 | 0.503 | 0.513 | 0.421 | 0.237 | 0.121 |
| Bilateral | | | | | | |
| Agencies | 5.856 | 5.432 | 3.909 | −1.272 | −1.250 | −2.095 |
| All Official | | | | | | |
| Creditors | 14.504 | 12.563 | 11.820 | 5.568 | 4.431 | 0.892 |

Sources: *IMF Survey,* June 15, 1987, p. 178; *IMF Survey,* February 8, 1988, p. 45; World Bank, *Annual Report* 1982–1987; International Finance Corporation, *Annual Report* 1982–1987; Inter-American Development Bank, *Annual Report* 1982–1987; Asian Development Bank, *Annual Report* 1982–1987; World Bank, *World Debt Tables, 1988–89 ed., vol. I. Analysis and Summary Tables* (Washington, D.C., 1989), p. 3.
*Net use of credit (does not include interest payments or fees)
**Fiscal year

Key:  IMF    International Monetary Fund
      IBRD   International Bank for Reconstruction and Development
      IDA    International Development Association
      IFC    International Finance Corporation
      IDB    Inter-American Development Bank
      ADB    Asian Development Bank

positive. But these steadily declined from $5,087 million in 1984 to $2,135 million in 1987. Then, in fiscal year 1988, net transfer from the IBRD/IDA combined was negative for the first time in the bank's history: minus $421 million. The World Bank no longer offset capital outflows due to private loans and investments; it now had become a direct net appropriator of the economic surplus of the third world.

While the IBRD is the most extreme case among the multilateral institutions, Table 1 shows that both the Inter-American Development ment Bank (IDB) and the Asian Development Bank (ADB), by far the two most important regional institutions, moved rapidly toward negative transfers in these years as well. Net transfers from the IDB became negative in 1987. While ADB net transfers remained positive overall in 1987, well over one-third of the ADB's recipients repaid more to the bank than they received in new disbursements. (Asian Development Bank *Annual Report 1987*, p. 138). Net transfers from all official creditors combined fell steadily from $14.5 billion in 1982 to $892 million in 1987.

To the degree that the promise of positive transfers from official lending has constituted the main incentive for countries to service their debts or reschedule them according to regime rules, these data suggest an emerging crisis for the hitherto successful debt containment strategy of the Bank and IMF. They also threaten to undermine the financial stability, and therefore also the political underpinnings, of the two institutions.[5] At the end of fiscal year 1988, arrears came to $2.7 billion for the IMF and $712 million for the World Bank (IMF *Annual Report 1988*, p. 57; World Bank *Annual Report 1988*, pp. 173, 191).

Refusing to contemplate rescheduling or debt relief, both institutions have looked to capital increases to preserve their influence and creditworthiness. After resisting for some time, the United States finally gave a go-ahead for a capital increase for the Bank at the IMF/World Bank meetings in September 1987, which was subsequently set at $74.8 billion. However, the United States so far has blocked a new IMF quota increase, even though the Fund's staff and Managing Director desire one. A proposed capital increase for the Inter-American Development Bank has been stymied by the United States' insistence that such a capital increase be tied to internal changes that would give the United States an effective veto over IDB lending. The former IDB president resigned in 1987 over the issue, and reaching accommodation with the United States has so far eluded the new president, Enrique Iglesias.

Accumulation of new debt to service old debt has been the linchpin of the containment strategy, and under it third world debt has almost doubled since 1980, reaching an estimated $1.3 trillion in 1988, as indicated in Table 2. Indeed, so wedded has the World Bank been to this strategy that when growth of new debt slowed slightly in 1986 and 1987, a World Bank official expressed despair rather than joy: "The fact that debt did not increase much. . . . is not a good thing in these current circumstances," (*New York Times*, February 21, 1987, p. 35).

*Table 2*
*Developing Country Debt and Financial Flows, 1982–88*
*($ billions)*

|                          | 1982 | 1983 | 1984 | 1985 | 1986 | 1987 | 1988 |
|--------------------------|------|------|------|------|------|------|------|
| *All Developing Countries** |      |      |      |      |      |      |      |
| Total External Debt      | 831  | 894  | 933  | 1051 | 1152 | 1281 | 1320 |
| *DRS Countries Only*** |      |      |      |      |      |      |      |
| Total External Debt      | 752  | 816  | 852  | 962  | 1053 | 1170 | 1200 |
| Long-Term Debt           | 562  | 645  | 687  | 794  | 894  | 996  | 1020 |
| Official Sources         | 203  | 226  | 238  | 305  | 364  | 437  | 450  |
| Private Sources          | 359  | 419  | 449  | 489  | 530  | 559  | 570  |
| Short-term Debt          | 169  | 140  | 132  | 131  | 119  | 133  | 140  |
| Use of IMF Credit        | 21   | 31   | 33   | 38   | 40   | 40   | 40   |
| New Disbursements***     | 117  | 97   | 92   | 89   | 88   | 87   | 88   |
| Debt Service***          | 99   | 93   | 102  | 112  | 117  | 125  | 131  |
| Interest                 | 49   | 47   | 53   | 56   | 55   | 54   | 59   |
| Principal Repayment      | 50   | 46   | 49   | 56   | 62   | 71   | 72   |
| Net Transfers***         | 18   | 5    | −10  | −23  | −29  | −38  | −43  |

*Source:* World Bank, *World Debt Tables, 1988–89 ed., Vol. 1. Analysis and Summary Tables* (Washington, D.C., 1989), pp. x, xii.
*Does not include high income oil-exporters
**109 countries participating in the World Bank's Debtor Reporting System.
***Grants and short-term debt flows not included.

## Adjustment, Growth, and Distribution

The redirection of the third world's foreign exchange, to the point that the third world is a net exporter of capital, has inevitably had devastating effects on investment and growth. But long before debt service acquired its current prominence, critics of the IMF were arguing that the IMF consistently misdiagnosed the real sources of the balance of payments problems developing countries have, and that the standard panopoly of IMF remedies served only to deepen the crisis, plunging countries into recession and lowering growth rates in the long run. (Dell 1982)

The IMF has gone to considerable lengths in recent years to refute this "growth-oriented critique," with rather unspectacular results. Its most recent study, which reviewed a wide range of previous studies, observed that the best cross-national studies, which combined a range of demand-management and supply-side variables

found that the rate of growth declined in a number of countries during the course of a program, but this result was matched by a number of cases where the growth rate in fact rose. Once the influence of all relevant policies on the growth rate is recognized, there is no clear presumption that Fund-supported adjustment programs adversely affect growth. (Khan and Knight 1986: 32)

An earlier Fund study of IMF programs between 1971–80 had likewise concluded that:

> program countries . . . exhibited only marginal changes in their growth rates of real GDP and consumption—changes that were not significantly different from those experienced by non-oil developing countries in general. . . . Thus, considering the group of program countries in the aggregate, the costs associated with the external adjustment effort appear to have been less severe than has sometimes been suggested by participants in the controversy on Fund conditionality. (Donavan 1982: 197)

While IMF officials have cited these findings as vindication against the growth-oriented critiques, they hardly support their repeated assertion that IMF-sponsored adjustment and growth go hand in hand. They are really quite extraordinary admissions of failure.

While the effects of IMF stabilization programs on gross measures of growth are not unimportant, focusing narrowly on growth neglects the more fundamental issue of how these programs affect class relations and the *nature* of development. In an unusually comprehensive study of 18 Latin American countries between 1965–1981, Manuel Pastor Jr. concurs with IMF defenders that "Fund programs have no consistent impact on growth." But Pastor goes on to analyze the distributional impact of IMF-supported programs, and here he concludes that: "the single most consistent effect the IMF seems to have is the redistribution of income away from workers" (1987: 258). He suggests that this results both from "the economic framework of the IMF" and from the need to secure the cooperation of local elites, which involves "sparing them the costs of adjustment" (ibid.: 253).

Faced with "IMF riots" and growing criticism of the distributional impact of its policies, the IMF has responded in two ways. On the one hand, it denies responsibility: "Changes in income distribution as such are not a performance criterion in adjustment programs . . . the authorities have discretion in seeking to achieve any politically acceptable distribution of income." (Sisson 1986: 33) IMF Managing Director Michel Camdessus reiterates: "the specification of policies bearing on the distribution of the adjustment burden must rest with the country itself. It does not form part of Fund conditionality. Nor should it" (*IMF Survey,* May 30, 1988).

On the other hand, the IMF has commissioned several largely

*hypothetical* analyses of the effects of Fund programs on the poor. These studies combine factual inaccuracy with incredible political naïveté. For example, a 1988 Fund study asserts that IMF monetary policies help the poor by reducing inflation. Apart from failing to demonstrate that the poor are indeed major beneficiaries of reduced inflation, the assertion ignores Pastor's finding that countries with Fund-supported programs had *higher* inflation than countries without them. Similarly, the study asserts that the shift of capital resources to the private sector "may also benefit the poor by increasing the supply of loanable funds available to them," a virtually laughable conclusion in most Fund-supported contexts. Pastor's rigorous empirical findings, supported by a great deal of case study evidence, refute the Fund's pollyannish speculations (Heller et al. 1988).

The toll of this kind of adjustment and debt crisis management, with all of its ramifications on the world economy, has been almost beyond telling. In the four years after Mexico's near-default in 1982, average incomes dropped in 22 of 25 Latin American countries, and in 31 of 46 Sub-Saharan African countries. Per capita incomes in much of Africa are back to what they were in 1960, and in much of Latin America, back to the mid-1970s. Long-term positive trends in health and education have been reversed, as per capita expenditures have fallen to levels one-quarter to one-half of what they were a decade ago. (Huang and Nicholas, 1987: 22) Reduced demand for imports from the industrialized countries have imposed substantial costs on them as well; already by 1984 it was estimated that the debt crisis had cost over half a million U.S. workers their jobs, and UNCTAD estimates that one-quarter of the current U.S. trade deficit stems from the third world debt crisis.

The actions of the IMF and World Bank have both reflected and buttressed the dominant power of finance capital in the world economy. Through these institutions finance capital has insulated itself from the market forces it celebrates ideologically, at the cost of becoming an enormous drag on development in both the core and the periphery. (Pfister and Suter, 1987)

## Conclusion: Constraint and Contradiction

One of the most striking features of the contemporary global crisis has been the uniformity of response among third world countries. As we have seen, no country has repudiated its debt or deliberately provoked a declaration of default. And where variation has occurred—basically in testing the limits of default—it has tended (1) to be temporary (the list of "resisters" constantly changes) and (2) to reflect no consistent relation to obvious class or political factors (resisting regimes have had very different social bases and political complexions). No matter how important the variation in class structures, state institutions, and social movements may be, it has not produced very much variation in national responses to the crises of debt or to, for that matter, the World Bank and IMF. And further, as Joyce Kolko's *Restructuring the World Economy* demonstrates, practically the whole world has been caught up in a common restructuring project. (Kolko, 1988)

The point here is not the dominance of "external" over "internal" factors, but rather the need to recognize the existence of near total interpenetration of the various levels of the world system. It won't do to conceptualize the World Bank and the IMF as all-powerful, external forces shoving their agendas down the throats of the united oppressed of the third world, but neither is it adequate to explain the power of these institutions entirely in terms of the complicity of comprador classes. They are constitutive of each other, and they are part of an increasingly globalized and asymmetrically interdependent world economy.

That this system constrains the viability of alternative forms of development—based on equality, human needs, and social justice—more severely than most of us on the left originally realized seems, in the 1980s, a foregone conclusion. Yet the contradictions of the current era, epitomized by the roles of the World Bank and IMF as direct appropriators of capital from the Third World, are undermining these constraints just as the need for alternatives becomes more evident than ever. As we move from historical analysis of the World Bank and the IMF to practical political stances towards them, much depends on what we believe is achievable within and against the constraints of the capitalist world system. Gramsci's prescription of an optimism of the will to counterbalance the pessimism of the intellect finds a real challenge here.

## Notes

1. Whether defaults can be said to have occurred is more complicated. As one account puts it: "Every debtor country which has had to reschedule its debts since

the crisis of 1982 has already defaulted on the terms of its original obligations, though the formal acknowledgment of that default has so far been largely postponed." (Lever and Huhne, 1986: 91). It is up to the banks to declare default, and in fact the first and only declaration so far involved North Korea in August 1987. North Korea immediately protested the designation and came to terms with its creditors.

2. Debt data are estimates and are constantly revised, but the World Bank's are probably as complete as any. (World Bank 1989: xii).

3. For recent attacks from the right, see James Bovard, "Behind the Words at the World Bank," *Wall Street Journal,* September 30, 1985; Patrick Buchanan, "Break the bank before its breaks us," *Philadelphia Inquirer,* December 29, 1987, p. 8A; Nicholas N. Eberstadt, "How Creditworthy is the World Bank?" *New York Times,* March 1, 1988, p. A23.

4. Negative net transfer to current borrowers was about $2 billion.

5. This had not gone unnoticed within these institutions. World Bank senior financial advisor Percy Mistry, in a paper for the Bank's president in April 1987, wrote: "Institutions like the World Bank and IDB are building up large portfolios in high-risk countries and their capital ratios, in contrast to commercial banks, have been rapidly deteriorating. In the absence of swift commencement of negotiations on augmenting their capital, these institutions are being placed by shareholders in a position of increasing financial jeopardy and instability." (Mistry, 1987: v)

## References

Berg, Elliot and Mary M. Shirley. 1987. *Divestiture in Developing Countries.* World Bank Discussion Paper #11.

Dell, Sidney. 1982. "Stabilization: The Political Economy of Overkill." *World Development* 10, no. 8, August.

Donavan, Donald J. 1982. "Macroeconomic Performance and Adjustment Under Fund-Supported Programs: The Experience of the Seventies." *IMF Staff Papers* 29.

"The Multilateral Investment Guarantee Agency: an Update." *Finance and Development* 22, no. 4, December 1985.

Frank, Andre Gunder. 1982. "Crisis of Ideology and Ideology of Crisis." In Samir Amin et al, *Dynamics of Global Crisis.* New York: Monthly Review Press.

Hayter, Teresa. 1971. *Aid as Imperialism.* Harmondsworth: Penguin Books.

Heller, Peter S. et al. 1988. *The Implications of Fund-Supported Adjustment Programs for Poverty: Experiences in Selected Countries.* International Monetary Fund, Occasional Paper #58.

Huang, Yukon and Peter Nicholas. 1987. "The Social Costs of Adjustment." *Finance and Development* 24, no. 2.

Khan, Moshin S. and Malcolm D. Knight. 1986. "Do Fund-supported adjustment programs retard growth?" *Finance and Development* 23, no. 1, March.

Kolko, Joyce. 1988. *Restructuring the World Economy.* New York: Pantheon.

Lever, Harold and Christopher Huhne. 1986. *Debt and Danger: The World Financial Crisis.* Boston/New York: Atlantic Monthly Press.

MacEwan, Arthur. 1986. "International Debt and Banking: Rising Instability within the General Crisis." *Science & Society* 50, no. 2, Summer.

Mistry, Percy. 1987. "Third World Debt: Beyond the Baker Plan." *The Banker* 137, September.

Pastor, Manuel. 1987. "The Effects of IMF Programs in the Third World: Debate and Evidence from Latin America." *World Development* 15, no. 2.

Payer, Cheryl. 1974. *The Debt Trap: The International Monetary Fund and the Third World.* New York: Monthly Review Press.

———. 1982. *The World Bank: A Critical Analysis.* New York: Monthly Review Press.

Pfister, Ulrich and Christian Suter. 1987. "International Financial Relations as Part of the World System." *International Studies Quarterly* 31, no. 3, September.

Pollin, Robert and Eduardo Zepeda. 1987. "Latin American Debt: the Choice Ahead." *Monthly Review* 38, no. 9, February.

Sisson, Charles A. 1986. "Fund-supported programs and income distribution in LDCs." *Finance and Development* 23, no. 1, March.

Wachtel, Howard M. 1986. *The Money Mandarins: the Making of a New Supranational Economic Order.* New York: Pantheon.

Wood, Robert E. 1986. *From Marshall Plan to Debt Crisis: Foreign Aid and Development Choices in the World Economy.* Berkeley and Los Angeles: University of California Press.

———. 1988. "Debt Crisis Update: 1988." *Socialist Review* no. 88/3 (July–September).

World Bank. 1989. *World Debt Tables, 1988–89, Vol. I, Analysis and Summary Tables.* Washington: World Bank.

# International Constraints on Progressive Change in Peripheral Societies: The Case of Nicaragua

## Carlos M. Vilas

Generally speaking, the great changes that have taken place in the international economy during the last several decades have not brought much good news for most of the world's poor countries. The structures of power and of international economic organization have changed substantially, but most of the countries in the periphery of the international capitalist system remain in a weak and dependent position. Accordingly, the options for progressive change are limited and the constraints on development are severe.

Among the advanced countries—in the "core" of the international system—there has been a rapid process of internal differentiation since World War II. Japan and West Germany have advanced in relation to the United States, which no longer holds the position of unchallenged leadership in international capitalism. A growing proportion of the world's trade and capital movement takes place among the developed capitalist countries, as opposed to between them and the economies of the periphery. In addition, a small group of relatively developed centrally planned economies have appeared on the scene—the Soviet Union, the German Democratic Republic (GDR), Czechoslovakia.

Rapid change in the "core" has been accompanied by increasing marginalization of the "periphery." Of course, there has been some significant differentiation in the periphery, as a "new industrialization" has taken place in some areas and agribusiness has also seen some significant advances. Nevertheless, most peripheral economies have been bypassed by these transformations, which, in any case, have had a greater impact on the national accounts of certain countries than upon social conditions. Similarly, the oil-price changes of the 1970s and early 1980s had little positive impact upon conditions of most of the economies or on the lives of most of the people in the third world.

Remaining tied and subordinate to the economies of the central capitalist powers, countries of the periphery moreover have been adversely affected by recent instability in the advanced nations. Slow growth in Europe and the United States has curtailed the markets for their exports, and they have been caught amid the gyrations of currency values. While there may have been a retreat of direct U.S. political influence from some areas, this has frequently been balanced by an increase of U.S. pressure in those areas traditionally more subject to U.S. control.

Almost two dozen countries of the periphery have attempted a deep socioeconomic and political transformation with a socialist orientation. Yet very few have been able to surmount backwardness and underdevelopment, and even fewer have advanced effectively on the road to socialism.

The goal of this essay is to gain a better sense of the sorts of changes that are possible in the small, backward economies of the periphery. Facing the constraints imposed by the international system, such countries have special problems in attempting to bring about development through a dramatic process of socioeconomic and political change. We can derive some insights on the process and its difficulties by taking the recent experience of Nicaragua as a particularly graphic example.

The central argument of this essay is that the principal characteristics of the agroexport economies of the third world make high levels of economic activity and efficiency unthinkable during the initial stage of a revolutionary transformation. In the revolutionary period, many of the limitations and tensions of the old regime are aggravated by both economic and extra-economic factors. The contradiction between accumulation and distribution—or between development and social justice—is exacerbated, even in comparison to the prerevolutionary situation. Only with access to broad and very flexible foreign cooperation can these countries overcome the difficulties of this first stage and initiate a more autonomous trajectory of development with greater social justice.

## Small, Backward, and Peripheral Economies

The small, backward, and peripheral economies characteristic of the majority of the countries of the third world are fundamentally agrarian—in terms of their productive activities, their links to the international economy, and the spatial distribution of their populations. Relying heavily on agricultural exports, these economies have a subordinate connection to the world market.

Large-scale national or foreign ownership predominates in the agroexport sector, and productivity levels are superior to the national average. This relatively modern activity is linked—sometimes through direct ownership, sometimes through marketing arrangements—to monopolistic transnational organizational structures. Alongside and connected to the agroexport sector, other domestic activity tends to be petty commodity production for the domestic market. This petty commodity sector operates under conditions of technological backwardness, with limited or nonexistent access to modern investment conditions, and with marginal, low-yield lands. Small-scale family production units predominate—peasant farms and, in the cities, artisan workshops; these units are labor intensive and have low levels of output per worker.

Nonetheless, the relatively backward petty commodity sector provides important support for the agroexport sector. The surplus it generates is transferred to the modern sector through commercial connections—the prices and conditions of purchasing inputs and the sale of final product. Moreover, the backward sector generates the labor force that the agroexport sector absorbs on a partial or seasonal basis; this permits the labor force to be reproduced at low cost to the modern capitalist sector. The reproduction of a cheap labor force is of course reinforced by extra-economic structures of compulsion—absence of effective labor legislation, prohibition or repression of unions, and so on.

The limited size of these economies determines their marginal weight in the international system, and their high degree of openness aggravates the restrictions produced by their small size. Their marginal position in the international economy means that they function basically as price takers for the commodities they export. An expansion of output and export revenues would be induced by either an increase in export prices or a drop in the prices of imported inputs. These two factors, however, are not affected by any policies or actions taken within the agroexport economies themselves. A third factor which could lead to expansion would be an increase in productivity. Here, however, the abundant supply of a cheap labor force—or one made cheap by extra-economic compulsion—restricts any significant investment in technological advancement which would raise labor productivity.

The small agroexport economies are also adversely affected by a real deterioration in their terms of trade, a phenomenon which hits in a double way. Directly, the deterioration of the terms of trade causes a rise in internal costs. Indirectly, it brings about difficulties by creating a deficit in the current balance of payments. In both cases, the most accessible remedy is to reduce domestic costs of production through increased control over the labor force and the subsequent reduction of labor costs. As a consequence, the repressive character of the regime is increased.

## The Options of the Revolution

In small agroexport economies, revolutionary governments tend to approach development strategies in terms of a choice between continued reliance on agroexports and a new emphasis on production for the domestic market. However, the viability of each option is limited.

The limitations that the agroexport strategy long experienced before the revolution are aggravated after its triumph. In the revolutionary period, improved living conditions for the workers and increased prices for peasant outputs raise the costs of production of agroexport commodities over the costs of competing commodities in the international market. Furthermore, the management of an agroexport economy requires resources and capabilities that are concentrated in the social groups displaced from power, many of whose members emigrate from the country because of the revolution. Foreign governments and the enterprises, both domestic and foreign, that operate in the international market are also capable of hindering the external articulation of the economy in question—to say nothing of the long-run tendency of international prices of primary products to fall. The problems do not disappear when for a variety of reasons elements of the old dominant groups form part of the revolutionary alliance. Then promotion of an agroexport strategy tends to aggravate the conflicts within that alliance.

The option of stressing production for the domestic market, while less vulnerable to external factors, is no less complex. The backward, even primitive, character of the technologies that predominate in petty commodity production limits any substantial medium-term increase in the surplus. Also, the capacity to generate savings is limited, since consumption levels in the domestic market are usually very low. It becomes necessary to rely on labor-intensive production techniques, but even then there exists a need for imported inputs that requires the generation of convertible foreign currencies. Further-more, because the productive structure is broken up into myriad small family units, there are complex needs for regulation and con-trol—especially when the there are severe limitations on the avail-ability of investment resources. Regulation and control, however, can raise the problem of the efficacy of incentives.

Finally, there is an integrated option, combining agroexports and a new emphasis on the domestic market through the development of some kind of industrial processing of primary resources. Although this integrated strategy is presented as one that can overcome the limitations and contradictions of the other two, it can end up ac-cumulating the problems of both and thus neutralizing the potentials of each. This is also the option that may involve the greatest level of internal conflict, in that it generally implies a coexistence within the revolutionary bloc of classes and groups that benefit from and are harmed by the partial strategies it aims to integrate.

Regardless of the particular strategy adopted after the revolution, the very process of revolutionary social change presents several potential problems for any economic advancement. As already men-tioned, to the degree that the agroexport program depends on the international competitiveness of the country's labor force—which in turn depends on maintaining low labor costs through economic and extra-economic measures—the revolutionary transformation of po-litical relations hinders the continuation of that program. Improving the living and working conditions of the direct producers and de-veloping social security and education programs all raise incomes and reduce the economic compulsion on the labor force. Likewise, giving land to the peasants through agrarian reform shifts the labor force away from agroexports. Developing union organizations and labor legislation and, in general, changing the institutional and politi-cal conditions eliminate the extra-economic compulsion on the labor force. Moreover, changing the correlation of social forces in the political arena and within enterprises discourages investment by the local bourgeoisie—including those elements that could be integrated into the revolutionary alliance.

Policies oriented toward satisfying the demands of the popular classes increase the cost of reproducing the labor force, raising production costs in the export sector and causing export profits and incomes to fall. This fall is accentuated by the immediate impact of changes in ownership and management of farms and factories in the export sector—through confiscations, nationalizations, and inter-ventions. Foreign pressures, through blockades, embargos, and the like, carry the process a step further. With the decline in export revenues, import capacity is in turn reduced. Production levels are then reduced because of the heavy reliance on foreign inputs, spare parts, and the like.

Additionally, the reduction of export revenues accentuates the tension between productive and infrastructure investments on the one hand, and the expansion of social programs on the other. The pressure of these programs on the country's fiscal capacity then grows, reinforcing inflationary tendencies and contributing to a greater deterioration of the official exchange rate (which falls further and further behind the real exchange rate).

In summary, a double set of tensions accumulates: between the necessities of accumulation and the necessities of improving consumption levels and social services; and between the need to keep the maladjustments of the external balance under control and the revolutionary commitment to socioeconomic transformation. Agroexports can no longer generate the surplus needed for accumulation, and the internal market is still in no condition to accomplish this task. A disengagement from the international economy may take place, but it is not the disengagement called for by strategies which emphasize the internal market; instead of providing the basis for strength, this disengagement is, ironically, often the result of weakness. The counterrevolutionary war, which constitutes the most common scenario of revolutionary transformation in the era of imperialism, severely increases all these tensions (see Vilas 1988).

## The Need for External Assistance

The economic problems that appear after the triumph of the revolution, the contradictions and tensions, are not likely to be overcome without substantial external assistance. Here the thesis of this essay is clear: only through access to broad, flexible, and cheap external cooperation can revolution in small, backward, and peripheral economies overcome the early stage of difficulties and transform itself into a positive transition to socialism.

In very general terms, revolutionary regimes need foreign cooperation because the rhythm and conditions for constituting the new political and the new economic orders are out of phase. A popular revolution—socialist, populist, or one of national liberation—is above all a political revolution. Gaps always exist, however, between the taking of political power by the revolutionary forces and the various other tasks of the revolution, such as creating a new and efficient institutional system, designing new power relations, or achieving socioeconomic transformation.

The popular revolutions in the periphery face an inverse situation to that confronted by the bourgeois revolutions of modern Europe. In the latter case, the development of the new economic order came before and in fact sustained the rise of the bourgeoisie to political power. The bourgeoisie was the socially dominant class before it became the politically dominant class. Society and the economy were "revolutionized" first and political power afterward. In contrast, a popular revolution is, to a certain extent, a new political order in search of a new economic order. The popular classes first become the politically dominant class, and the old economic order is destroyed more rapidly than its replacement is constructed. Without help from the countries with more advanced economies, the viability of the socioeconomic transformation is questionable.

Can it be stated, as a consequence, that the situation of these economies is practically the same as that of any underdeveloped country, revolutionary or not? I do not think so. Foreign cooperation and access to resources from specialized international bodies and the agencies of the more developed countries is problematic, to say the least, for revolutionary regimes. At equal levels of development, and confronting equally complex economic problems, it is always much more difficult for a revolutionary regime to gain access to these bodies than it is for a nonrevolutionary regime to do so. The United States government regularly blocks the funds and lines of cooperation of the multilateral organizations in order to aggravate the economic hardships of revolutionary regimes.

Recognition of such difficulties begs the first of two major sets of questions regarding the need for external cooperation: will external resources be available? From what sources? On what terms and under what conditions? Where is help to be found? In what magnitudes? And at what prices? The second set of questions concerns internal aspects of the revolutionary regime: will it be able to use the foreign support effectively? What sort of development strategies and policies are appropriate? How can foreign cooperation be used productively?

## *The Economic Strategy of the Sandinista Revolution*

The economic strategy of the Sandinista National Liberation Front (FSLN) established agroexports as the sector in which the foundation of the accumulation process would have to be developed. The choice of this option was a result of the coincidence of two currents present at the center of the revolutionary alliance. On the one hand, a conception prevailed in the FSLN that the development of productive forces and accumulation for the purpose of profound social transformation required large, modern, capital-intensive production units, relying on salaried labor and competitive at an international level. These units could be found in the agroexport sector, and many of them formerly belonged to Somocista capital. On the other hand, some groups of professionals from the more traditional elite families of the country, who opposed Somocismo and who were tied professionally to the more modern sectors of agroexport capitalism, saw in the dictatorship a corrupt and irrational system that undercut the country's access to more advanced levels of development. After 1979 these groups came to play a decisive role in the apparatus of the revolutionary state and, in particular, in economic planning and management.

With the assets confiscated from the Somocistas, a state sector was created that took charge of foreign trade, the financial system, and important portions of transport, production, and domestic commerce. An ambitious public investment program had as its objective the development of the productive forces in the agroexport sector. The program attempted to reinsert the sector into international trade by diversifying exports, incorporating greater value added, and winning new markets in the third world and socialist bloc. A broad agrarian reform drastically reduced the power of the old landed oligarchy: almost 75 percent of the land they held before the revolution passed to cooperatives and small and medium-sized peasants or was converted to state farms.

During 1980 and 1981 Nicaragua enjoyed ample external assistance, receiving nearly $1.5 billion in foreign loans and grants. In this context, the agroexport strategy initially attained positive results. Production was reactivated, the basic demands of the population were satisfied, social and educational services were expanded, and big investment projects were begun. In general, production for the domestic market recuperated more rapidly than that for export, but the expansion of consumption demand was still greater than the expansion of production. Nonetheless, imports of foodstuffs managed to close the gap and kept internal prices under control.

Starting in 1982, the first maladjustments began to appear: a deceleration of economic activity, a fall in export income, and growing foreign indebtedness. The situation became more acute by 1983:

an overmonetarization of the economy, a takeoff of the black market and speculative activity, an acceleration of inflationary tendencies, and a rapid fall of workers' real incomes. Various factors interceded to produce these results, which I have noted in detail elsewhere (Vilas 1987); for the sake of space they will be noted only briefly here:

First, there was a reduction of private capitalist investment, basically as a response to the new political environment.

Second, the public investment program matured very slowly. It was hindered by its intensive use of technologies with which there was little previous experience, its complex administrative demands, its heavy financial needs, and the unsatisfactory quality of feasibility studies.

Third, export income dropped. As compared to 1980, export income (in current dollars) was 11 percent higher in each of the three succeeding years and then an average of 23 percent less in the 1984–86 period (30 percent less than in the 1981–83 period).

Fourth, foreign funds were blocked as a result of U.S. government pressure on the multilateral credit organizations and on some European governments. In these circumstances, Nicaragua had to turn to bilateral accords with more rigid and onerous conditions (for figures and analysis see Conroy 1987 and Kornbluh 1987: ch. 2).

Fifth, beginning in 1983, the war of aggression launched by the U.S. government generated increased tensions. The direct and indirect damages of this war on the Nicaraguan economy have been estimated at around $3.6 billion. Damages include the physical destruction of assets, the displacement of approximately 25 percent of the economically active population into defense activities, the dedication of half of the government budget to this same end, an increased federal deficit, the acceleration of inflation, and so on.

The combined fiscal and foreign trade deficits and the daily increase in the gap between the official exchange rate and the real exchange relationship led to a growing overmonetarization of the economy and rising inflation. Exchange activity became detached from production activity, leading to a transfer of money capital out of the country or toward speculative endeavors. The shift of private capital away from production was also encouraged by the reduced efficiency of the state policy and control mechanisms: for example, providing dollar incentives for private investment and making state loans available at negative real interest rates. The dramatic acceleration of inflationary tendencies, nourished by these state actions, encouraged a run of liquid assets over to the dollar; the currency of the country whose government was the military aggressor became an investment of privileged profitability.

In February 1985, an adjustment program was adopted to reinforce the position of government revenues, redesign investment programs toward more modest goals, and reduce the fiscal deficit. Instead, the program detonated an acceleration of inflationary tendencies, a deterioration of basic goods supplies, a strengthening of speculative pressures, and a more acute deterioration of workers' real incomes. A reduction in the fiscal deficit did occur—from almost 25 percent of the GDP in 1984, to 23 percent in 1985 and 17 percent in 1986. Yet with defense spending taking up a larger and larger share of the government budget, the improvements in the deficit came only at the cost of curtailing activity in the productive sector, thus exacerbating downward pressure on the economy.

The ratio of foreign trade (exports plus imports) to GDP fell from 0.66 in the 1980–81 period to 0.49 in 1986, much more by the reduction of exports (two-thirds) than by the reduction of imports (one-third). At the same time that the volume of foreign trade was reduced, the country experienced an important transformation in the direction of its foreign trade away from U.S. markets. Of course, this transformation was accelerated by the commercial embargo decreed by the U.S. government in May 1985.

During 1987, the military situation worsened as the U.S. government increased its financing of the counterrevolutionary groups, and the disarticulation and disarray of the Nicaraguan economy was consequently aggravated. Exports, despite a slight improvement, continued to constitute only about half of the value they had attained at the beginning of the decade. The general lack of economic control became more severe. Speculative activity and activity in the parallel—or "black"—markets spread to almost all parts of the economy. Even government institutions, in order to keep functioning, turned to the parallel markets for necessities. There was an increase in the amount of exchange which took place in dollars, leading to runs on the dollar and a sharp increase in the value of the dollar relative to the Nicaraguan cordoba. Inflation passed the 1000 percent per year level. The real value of salaries, which already in 1986 had fallen dramatically, was reduced to a merely symbolic concept—from a level of 100 in 1980 to a level of 11 by the end of 1987. Foreign indebtedness grew by a third with respect to the previous year. Lack of maintenance, obsolescence, and other problems aggravated the limitations of the entire physical infrastructure, affecting transport, communications, electrical energy, and other activities. The general deterioration of basic social services—education and health—was also evident.

Nicaragua thus entered into the Central American peace plan negotiation process in a condition of extreme economic vulnerability. Facing this not very encouraging panorama, the revolutionary government in February 1988 implemented a monetary reform aimed at reducing the hyperliquidity of the economy and curtailing speculative activities, structuring a new system of relative prices, fixing a new exchange rate, and reducing drastically the state apparatus and public employment. Simultaneously, it began direct negotiations with the counterrevolutionary groups, attempting to reach a definitive cease-fire agreement. The recent nature of all these events makes it inadvisable to advance conclusions regarding them at this time.

## External Cooperation

Nicaragua's political, military, and economic relations with the U.S.S.R., Cuba, and other COMECON countries constitute one of the central themes in the attack against the Sandinista Popular Revolution by the U.S. government and the internal opposition. Nicaragua is presented as the beachhead of Soviet-Cuban penetration on the Latin American mainland. The reiteration of the argument and the difficulties of access to systematic information on this theme have contributed to an exaggerated image of the magnitude and reach of socialist cooperation with the efforts of socioeconomic transformation in Nicaragua. Revolutionary rhetoric has also contributed to this image.

The cooperation of the socialist countries with Nicaragua covers two fundamental areas: military and economic. Here I will comment only on the second, which includes credits and loans, donations, cooperative projects, and commercial relations.

Various studies have been done that indicate that the magnitude of the economic cooperation with Nicaragua by the socialist countries is more limited than is generally thought (Acciaris 1984; Berrios 1985; and Berrios and Edelman 1985) The most important aspect of such cooperation is commercial exchange, which provides prices and general terms advantageous to Nicaragua and which allows Nicaragua to maintain a systematic favorable balance in the commercial accounts with the socialist countries. In this sense the socialist countries seem to be functioning mainly as markets for Nicaraguan exports, which have otherwise faced growing closure of traditional markets—particularly in the United States. Assistance in terms of supplying imports has been relatively less important, excepting in the notable case of petroleum since 1985. In more recent years, however—not covered in the cited studies—COMECON countries have come to play a larger role in the supply of machinery and equipment and of primary and intermediary materials. During 1987, imports from socialist countries represented more than half the total of Nicaragua's imports.

The credits conceded to Nicaragua involve bilateral relations, and they are tied to financing of exports from the lender country. Donations have been directed to solving urgent problems, including, in some instances, the need for freely convertible foreign exchange.

Several important public investment projects count on COM-ECON cooperation; they are oriented almost entirely to strengthening and diversifying the export sector. Some of these, however, have met with difficulties. The construction of a deep-water port in the Atlantic, with Bulgarian technical assistance, is currently suspended and Bulgarian cooperation has ended. The gigantic "Victoria de Julio" sugar refinery, which had important Cuban assistance and funding, has been plagued by profitability problems because of the downward movement of international sugar prices; this project was, in fact, one of the most controversial investments of the revolutionary government. The start of the textile combine in the city of Estelí, based on cooperation from the German Democratic Republic and Czechoslovakia, was recently suspended due to the reduction in public sector activities associated with the February 1988 monetary and administrative reforms. Other projects, such as some ambitious irrigation plans and the production of vegetables for canning and export, offer better prospects, although in general the execution has been much slower than originally planned.

It is difficult to quantify the total value of economic cooperation received by Nicaragua from the socialist countries. Referring directly to the U.S.S.R., an FSLN source cited a figure of $2 billion for the 1980–87 period, or an average of $250 million per year (*Barricada,* November 7, 1987). The three-year U.S.S.R.-Nicaragua cooperation agreement signed at the beginning of January 1988 involves 210 million rubles per year, equivalent to some $294 million annually (*Barricada,* January 16, 1988).

An obstacle to greater assistance levels seems to rest in the lack of a system of medium-range and long-range planning that would allow Nicaragua to introduce its needs in COMECON's five-year plans. With the exception of the already mentioned three-year agreement with the U.S.S.R., Nicaragua's accords with socialist countries are renewed on an annual basis. At the same time, one of the most beneficial aspects of socialist cooperation for Nicaragua is precisely its emergency character, which has permitted the country to get around numerous bottlenecks. Perhaps the best illustration is the Cuban ship that supplies petroleum and basic consumer goods to the city of Puerto Cabezas on the Atlantic coast every three months. The help of socialist countries still seems more like a fire brigade than a body of enginners teaching people to construct fireproof buildings.

Nonetheless, if we add together the $2 billion that has come from the U.S.S.R., the amounts of cooperation estimated to have come from the other socialist countries, the funds coming from the rest of the world, it can be conjectured that the total amount of external cooperation received by Nicaragua between 1980 and 1987 was between $4.5 and $5 billion. The $5 billion figure works out to an average of some $625 million a year or $1.7 million per day.

Within the context of a small country like Nicaragua with a population of some 3.5 million people and an annual per capita income of less than $800 the aid that has been received since the triumph of the Sandinistas appears considerable. Nonetheless, when measured against the economic undertakings of the revolutionary regime and in the face of the considerable obstacles that have emerged, even this large amount of aid has limited impact.

In particular, the harmful effect of the counterrevolutionary war on the country's infrastructure, productive apparatus, and natural resources has been very large. Moreover, the war has a first claim on the country's manpower and administrative and organizational resources. While these negative impacts of the war would be difficult to quantify, it could be easily argued that they have been substantially larger than the positive impact of the aid. Also, it is important to recognize that Nicaragua has lacked the internal institutional capabilities that could transform the aid into economic development. Planning systems, well-defined economic strategies and policies, informational resources, an efficient state administrative apparatus—all such institutions in Nicaragua are in their infancy.

It seems clear, then, that if Nicaragua is going to achieve a social transformation of any magnitude there will be a continuing need for extensive external assistance. That assistance will be most effective if the necessarily long-term need is well recognized.

Finally, beyond the question of aid but closely connected to it, there is the issue of the impact of broad cooperation by the socialist countries with Nicaragua upon the matrix of relations between the United States and the Soviet Union. The efforts at transformation and development of the economies of the capitalist periphery are certainly inscribed within the overall North-South problematic, but also within the East-West problematic. The East-West issue becomes especially important when the peripheral economies strengthen their relations with the community of socialist countries. With respect to the United States, a constant of its foreign policy toward Central America and the Caribbean has been to view its relations with the area as a dimension or chapter of its policy toward extracontinental third parties—Great Britain first, Spain later, Germany even later, and the Soviet Union currently. As for the Soviet Union, it is evident that Central America does not form the central part of its main international concerns.

From this perspective, while the viability of revolutionary processes in small, backward, and peripheral countries will be affected by the correlation of forces between the superpowers and the projection of their strategic interests in the different regions of the third world, these countries cannot rely on fortuitous international developments. Their success ultimately depends on their own internal conditions and on their capacity to overcome the limitations that the international system lays out.

## References

Acciaris, Ricardo. 1984. "Nicaragua-Pays socialista: Vers la consolidation des liens economiques?" *Problèmes d'Amérique Latine* 74.

Berrīos, Rubēn. 1985. "Economic Relations between Nicaragua and the Socialist Countries." Washington, DC: Woodrow Wilson International Center for Scholars, mimeo.

Berríos, Rubén and Marc Edelman. 1985. "Hacía la diversificación de la dependencía: Los vínculos económicos de Nicaragua con los países socialistas." *Comercio Exterior* 35, no. 10 (October).

Conroy, Mike. 1987. "Economic Aggression as an Instrument of Low-Intensity Warfare." In Thomas Walker, ed., *Reagan Versus the Sandinistas: The Undeclared War on Nicaragua*. Boulder, CO: Westview Press.

Kornbluh, Peter. 1987. *Nicaragua: The Price of Intervention: Reagan's War Against the Sandinistas*. Washington, DC: Institute for Policy Studies.

Vilas, Carlos M. 1987. "Troubles Everywhere: An Economic Perspective on the Sandinista Revolution." In Rose Spalding, ed., *The Political Economy of Revolutionary Nicaragua*. Boston: Allen and Unwin.

———. 1988. War and Revolution in Nicaragua." *The Socialist Register* New York: Monthly Review Press.

# Restructuring of the World Economy and Its Political Implications for the Third World

## Clive Y. Thomas

My task is to examine the political implications for the third world of the present restructuring of the world economy. As the former is contingent on the latter, the first step will be to identify the nature of the restructuring process, which accordingly is presented in a condensed form in the first two sections of this essay. The political implications are examined in greater detail in later sections.

### The World Economy in Transition

Soon after World War II, the world economy entered a long upswing in economic activity which ended in the early 1970s. The upswing coincided with the ascendancy of the transnational corporations and the peaking of U.S. hegemony. The persistence after 1970 of major disproportions in global production and consumption, falls in rates of profitability in many major sectors, the decline of U.S. hegemony, and the emergence of a new trilateral system anchored in Europe, Japan, and the United States are viewed by many on the left as evidence of the final eruption of an underlying structural crisis long in the making. The restructuring of the world economy now in process is, then, capitalism's attempt to adjust to this structural crisis.

My own assessment is somewhat different. In my view, the 1970s marked the emergence of a *fundamental disjuncture* in the development of the capitalist world economy. The process of restructuring which is taking place is in effect a *process of transition* to a qualitatively different world economy. The period since the 1970s, therefore, must be viewed as one producing epic changes, no less significant or revolutionary in their implications than those which occurred during the first Industrial Revolution. The substantial expansion of technical production possibilities does not, however, mean that the world economy will take full advantage of the new opportunities, that maximum growth will be realized, or that a sustained and dramatic increase in living standards of the broad masses of people will occur. As in previous instances, these developments would depend on the balance of political and social forces.

As in other periods of fundamental change, the line of causality is exceedingly complex. No single set of factors is solely or even mainly responsible for the change. It is only by means of a thorough historical-social analysis that intelligible order can be imposed on the various manifestations of this transition. The best I can do here is to identify certain phenomena which, when taken as a concatenation of simultaneous events occurring in a highly compressed time frame, illustrate the fundamental nature of the changes taking place. In summary form, these include the following developments.

1. There has been a rapid "delinking" of primary production from industrial growth. This is particularly marked in the relation of industrial output to material input, yielding what scientists have described as "an end of the age of materials." This process undermines virtually all schools of economic thought, for, based on historical experience, these have all posited a close nexus between industrial expansion (translated as growth in the "center") and growth in primary output, employment, and incomes (translated as growth in the "periphery"). It is significant that despite rapid delinking, at the end of 1987 three-quarters of the countries of the periphery still depended on primary exports to generate three-quarters or more of their export income.

2. Consequent on the above and despite the emergence of the so-called NICs (newly industrialized countries), the "periphery" as a group has been unable to alter its deprived status in the global distribution of income and wealth. Indeed, the data show for the "periphery" a restricted share in global trade and investment and a continuation of transactions among countries of the "center" as the major locus of growth in the global economy. Thus the famous "marginalization of the periphery" evident during the long wave of expansion has continued, conforming to the capitalist pattern of uneven growth between countries and uneven distribution of the benefits and costs of economic activity.

3. Over the past decade, in the center countries employment

expansion has become "delinked" from industrial and manufacturing growth. This phenomenon has been much commented upon and used as evidence of basic alterations in the production structure of the center.

4. The developments listed above are related to the unprecedented explosion of scientific and technological innovations and their rapid application to economic activity over the past two decades. The three major foci of these changes are in biotechnology, information technology, and new materials technology. The scientific community itself, and not only outside commentators, refers to these changes as "quantum" leaps.

5. An explosion of services has occurred, reaching the point where goods which enter world trade are regarded as "composite commodities" that embrace both the goods themselves and the services involved in their production and distribution. The growth in composite commodities has been accompanied by the unprecedented tradeability of services, reflecting their new technological character. The speed of these changes has led some observers to predict that within two decades world trade in services may well exceed world trade in goods.

6. This explosive development is particularly marked in the area of financial services, where, paradoxically, it poses a real threat of "delinking" financial markets from their ultimate foundation in accumulation and production. This development is partly responsible for such phenomena as the dramatic third world indebtedness, the U.S. deficits, an increasing disregard of fundamental solvency in the marketplace, and the speculative preoccupation with cash flows and liquidity.

7. The differentiation in both the center and the periphery, which commenced during the long upswing in economic growth, has continued in the present phase. The process is reflected in the rising positions of West Germany, Japan, and the Asian and Latin American NICs. However, differentiation in the periphery, despite the rise of the NICs, still only produces conflict in the so-called secondary structures of opportunity of the world economy. Conflict in the center remains primary, in that it poses direct threats to the bases of control and stability in the world system. Although epochal changes are underway, there is as yet no evidence of a break in the line of domination-subordination in the center-periphery system.

8. The transitional character of the period has produced a "new protectionism." Of course, protectionism is not an aberrant feature

of capitalism signifying deviant behavior from a free-trade norm. Historically, it has been endemic, varying in its intensity as structural changes in the world economy have emerged. In periods of revolutionary transition such as the present, it emerges as a "rational" response to the "irrationality" of market disruption. The need to control economic adjustment and social dislocation explains the unprecedented innovations in the techniques of protection; the focused application of these to the export of manufactures from the NICs; the dominant role protection has played since the early 1970s in the explosion of agricultural output in the center; and the retreat of all major actors in the global economy from the liberal ideal of multilateralism, and the consequent proliferation of segmented circuits of international trade—for example, CBI, CARIBCAN, the European Community, and the Canada-U.S. free-trade arrangement.

9. Based as it is on fundamental changes, the "new protectionism" is also linked to two other emerging phenomena. One is the prevalence of spontaneous distortions in market activity across all countries, evidenced in the rise of counter-trade, the informalization of work, "capital flight" from the periphery to the center, and the growth of illicit activities around the globe. The other is the increasing need, on the part of major powers, for global cooperation as a prerequisite to national economic management. This need, however, has to contend with the competitive-destructive character of capitalism and the continuous pressures to secure national advantages.

## Some Global Social Repercussions

A fundamental transformation of capitalism such as I have hypothesized is a historical process, encompassing social relations as well as economic and technical relations. The very revolutionary character of the period, however, makes it difficult to determine with any precision the socio-political changes which are unfolding. For present purposes, what is especially difficult to determine is whether just a higher stage of capitalist organization will emerge at the end of the period, or whether a comparable transformation in the socio-political sphere will occur, so that capitalist society itself is transcended. There is no certainty that the revolution in productive forces will outstrip the social potential of capitalist relations, thereby raising qualitatively the revolutionary potential of this period.

Based on historical evidence and observation of a wide variety of social systems, my judgment is that there is an as yet unexhausted vitality in contemporary capitalism. Commentators who speak of the present era as the "highest" or "final" stage of capitalist evolution, or invoke imminent third world revolution, are being either excessively reductionist in their application of Marxism or overly speculative. One of the most salutary lessons of this century is provided, by and large, by the flexibility and adaptability which the capitalist ruling classes have displayed.

I do not underrate the expansionist-stagnatory rhythms of capitalist growth or the major social disruptions which a market economy periodically produces. What I seek to emphasize is the dual character of capitalist response to crisis: the constant revolutionizing of production through application of the latest scientific, technical, and organizational innovations; *and* a "willingness" under pressure to resort to reform as a means of preempting revolutionary challenges. The former is clearly evident in the current transition (as I have outlined it above). Therefore, it is only a failure to reform which can pose the "ultimate" threat of capitalist disintegration. Social revolution can take place only when the practical scope for political, ideological, and social engineering and manipulation is exhausted, or when the dominated classes and social groups refuse to accept reform. Neither occurrence, however, is imminent.

The one caveat to this judgment lies in the area of our immediate concern. The emerging capitalists in the periphery are, *as a social class*, underdeveloped in comparison to their counterpart in the center. In spite of the emergence of some "vibrant" business elites and the increasing sophistication of some state classes, I believe that at this stage peripheral capitalists are incapable of seeing their class project in terms of the need for historic reforms. To most of these ruling groups, reform is anathema. Also, the capitalist classes in the periphery generally rely on the exploitation of economic rents through strategic control of assets instead of pushing a constant revolution in productive techniques. Consequently, while the working class in the periphery is far less developed "as a class" than its counterpart in the center, and therefore in some formulations has less revolutionary potential, the even more underdeveloped character of its capitalist class, and the backward undemocratic forms of political relations which prevail, make the periphery as a whole more susceptible to revolutionary upheaval at this conjuncture.

Whether the ruling classes of the periphery would yield to the pressures for a so-called bourgeois-democratic transformation or whether they would resist and thereby encourage the social momentum in favor of anti-imperialist, anticapitalist movements emerges as a central political issue of this period. As I shall argue in the next section, the vital test of these possibilities may well be the capability of the periphery's ruling classes to embrace political democracy as a *necessary form* at this historical juncture. Before turning to this argument, it is important to highlight some of the more general social-political developments associated with the transitional character of the period. These are:

1. The contradictory effects of the transition—particularly the emergence of economic difficulties and altered national positions in the world order—have given rise to strident assaults on the state as an agent of social change. This is a major development, since in the previous period of long upswing in economic activity there was an increasing "centrality" of the state in capitalist growth and expansion. Presently, however, the state is widely viewed as an obstacle to economic progress, and the radical right has been able to achieve three major political gains in recent years: a successful assault on the welfare state in the center; a concerted move toward widespread deregulation and increased market emphasis in the periphery; and a considerably reduced expectation that the state should be guarantor of basic needs or play a major role ensuring equity.

2. The result of this retreat of the state has been a worsening income distribution in many countries, especially in the countries of the south. The transition therefore has not removed the capitalist dynamic of inequality in the distribution of gains and losses. It has entrenched it in new forms.

3. In the center, changed attitudes toward the state, combined with inflation, increased unemployment, and changing structures of employment, have aided the demise of the principal working-class organizations, the trade unions. This is connected to major changes in the character of work, which some analysts on the left view as significant as those in the transition from early manufacturing to large-scale industry and later to Taylorism.

4. The features listed so far are linked to a highly charged atmosphere of ideological debate on development strategy in the periphery. Here two very stereotyped models are counterposed to each other, although in practice neither has been pursued in anything close to its pure form. On the one hand, there is the model of unrestrained market forces and private enterprise as the key to

successful development. In this model, export diversification is counterposed to import substitution, with the latter portrayed as an inefficient state-directed process. The private-sector-versus-public-sector issue is presented as a zero-sum game, where one sector can grow only at the expense of the other. On the other hand, there is the model which stresses autarky, or the "delinking" of the periphery from the capitalist world economy as a *necessary,* if not sufficient, condition for "real" development.

5. Development of information technology has reached a point where all shades of opinion comment on the unprecedented degree of "villagization" of the global economy. The most striking consequence is the growing hold of the consumerist culture of the West. Indeed, the only significant area of self-conscious rejection of this trend is located in present-day Islamic appeals. The transition therefore is strongly associated, both as cause and effect, with a historically unprecedented global homogenization of consumption goods, services, finance, and even the institutions and instruments of economic management.

6. On a global scale, the contradictory development of bureaucracy in the face of ideological assaults on the state is another noteworthy feature of the transition. This development includes, first, a burgeoning growth of corruption, which has reached such staggering proportions that some social scientists see it as an "independent productive factor." A second factor is the growing informalization of wide areas of economic activity across the globe: it is estimated that as much as one-third of the labor force in the OECD countries operates substantially in the informal sectors. A third factor is the unprecedented impact of the international bureaucracy on the national management of economic systems in the periphery (the IMF/IBRD syndrome).

7. Armaments expenditures, now in excess of $1,000 billion annually, have become a major consideration during the transition. The growth of military spending is being fueled partly by the rapid changes in science and technology. Military capability often operates as an independent influence in the determination of the lines of hegemony in the global system. Thus the substantially reduced status of the United States as an economic power exists alongside its military preeminence, allowing it to sustain a hegemonic capability beyond its economic capability.

Before leaving this point we should be reminded of the extent to which the development of global productive potential has led to a *pari pasu* development of the destructive forces. The coming of "socialism" in the twentieth century has not brought with it the much-anticipated decline in war between countries, not even within the grouping of socialist countries. The threat of global annihilation which the present technology has unleashed has created a historically unique situation in which peace—or at least the absence of war—among the major states is a *necessary condition* for the survival of humankind.

## Political Implications for the Third World

Although there are common characteristics in the socioeconomic structures of third world countries, the differentiation that has taken place since the early 1970s makes it extremely difficult to generalize about the political implications of the current transition. Nonetheless, general propositions in social theory are both possible and useful. In the current period some general understanding of developments in the third world is especially important. The character of peripheral societies has made them an arena of recurring conflict. One of the defining features of the periphery has been the special nature of its *external* integration, and, as this external integration has affected internal structures, numerous impediments to development have emerged. The appearance of the NICs has brought some changes. Yet for the periphery as a whole, development along the lines of the NICs, while it cannot be proved *a priori* impossible, certainly cannot occur without disrupting existing structures of international and class relationships. The impediments to development remain, and the epic character of the changes I have described will add to these impediments. Consequently, we can expect intensifying conflicts between social classes and between nations. The transitional character of the period therefore simultaneously offers *both* new opportunities and the prospect of an intensification of national vulnerabilities.

## Revolution, Reform, and the Status Quo

The pivotal issue to consider is whether the leading classes in the states and economies of the periphery have the capacity to lead these countries through the transition, or whether the willingness and capacity of the "revolutionary classes" to revolt will be enhanced by the dislocations and vulnerabilities introduced in the transition period. If the leading classes are able to seize the opportunities inherent in the restructuring, then revolutionary prospects in the third world will be, in general, reduced. If they are unable to do so, then new bases of social conflict will be created.

The fundamental political issue thus becomes one of determining whether *reform* or *social revolution* lies ahead in the periphery, and not, as it is frequently posed, whether the future holds *social revolution* or continuation of the status quo. "Reform" as used here is a broad category, implying a variety of forms and reflecting the variety of actual circumstances. It is also not confined to any notion of a particular uniformity of political and social arrangements. Precisely, however, because it embraces such variety, it becomes necessary to devise a "test" or "social barometer" of the reform capability of the present leading classes. I believe that the best test may well be their ability to superintend the development of the political forms and behavioral styles of representative democracy—in other words, to promote what some on the left disparagingly call the bourgeois-democratic transformation of the state and political relations and, in some contexts, even to introduce certain elements of social democracy. The corollary of this is that the revolutionary capability of the masses is best measured by the extent to which their objective circumstances can be fused with an ideology, consciousness, and forms of organization which secure the "bourgeois-democratic" transformation and, at the same time, link it to the ideals of economic and social justice. The controversial implication of this argument is that in order to advance the positions of the masses in the periphery, socialist aims should not be counterposed to political democracy.[1]

The course of reform or revolution in the third world during the current transition is in part a political, or "subjective," issue. The movement of events, however, is significantly affected by the material, or "objective," circumstances. One matter of paramount importance is whether or not the economic structure of peripheral countries will allow them as a group to benefit from the new scientific and technological revolution. These economies in general are still characterized by multistructured and heterogeneous production forms. The absence of capitalist modernization coexists with the tendency for the leading classes to appropriate the surplus in the form of rents, and not through the constant search for self-expanding value by changes of techniques in a production-for-profit process. In this situation, the social position of the masses is especially weak.

Also, the structure of the classes and social groups in the periphery continues to pose certain difficulties. Reflecting its early phase of formation, the class structure is generally weaker, more fluid, and more complex than its counterpart in the center. The multistructured and heterogeneous production forms both shape and limit the scope for class formation.

Consequently, we come to the important matter of the impact of the various class forces on the state and political relations. In the present context, the state is less the object of conquest by the leading economic class and more the instrument by which the leading "state classes" seek to consolidate their economic and social ascendancy. Since World War II, the state in the periphery has become a developmentalist state. It has played the leading role in shaping development strategy and in owning and managing productive enterprises. State economic policies in the third world are, as I have written elsewhere, fundamentally characterized by the deliberate intention to use the state apparatus "as a principal instrument of developing a strong class formation, capable of assuming the responsibility of raising the level of development of the productive forces." The carrying out of this intention results in two very important characteristics of the developmentalist state: "one is the well-known instability and easy susceptibility to very narrow changes in alignments among the petty-bourgeois elements which presently dominate the state machinery. The other is its illusory appearance of being *independent*, i.e., in effect beyond class" (Thomas 1974: 87).

It is important to recognize that in the recent postcolonial societies of Africa, Asia, and the Caribbean, despite serious weaknesses, the state is more politically legitimate than its predecessor, the colonial state. In effect, a qualitative shift in political structure has taken place since independence, in part as a result of the expansion of the state into the economic, social, and ideological domains, and in part due to the growth of mass politics (Thomas, 1984: 54).[2] In older independent parts of the periphery, such as in Latin America, for example, long struggles against local tyranny and repression have ensured a similar legitimation of the state even though, more often than not, it has been in the control of antipopular groups and classes.

Questions about the state and politics in the periphery have to be posed in relation to two dominant tendencies within the ruling circles of the center, particularly the United States. One is that despite the support these groups have given to local dictatorships, their hope is that bourgeois-democratic forms of rule could be instituted. Reform movements in the periphery are therefore likely to be supported where vital strategic interests are not challenged. The other tendency is that the present ascendancy of the "radical right" has encouraged the retreat of the state in the periphery from its developmentalist-interventionist mode.

## State Classes

The rise of the state property sector in the periphery and the accompanying interventionist modes of the state have been linked to the growth of "state classes." This phenomenon was very noticeable during the long boom after World War II. In predicting their capacity to engage in reform, we need to take account of certain features of these classes. One is that despite frequent claims to "socialist and people-oriented development," their styles of rule have had a common aura of "bureaucratic development," which in turn has been a rich medium for perpetuating the variety of forms of rent-appropriation that distinguish these societies. This observation does not gainsay the historically progressive role played by these classes in creating a state property sector, orienting resource mobilization to long-run commercial profitability, and seeking to create a viable industrial sector. However, recognition of a historically progressive role should not be confused with giving political support to the leading elements of the state and society.

The historically progressive role of the state classes *does* come into doubt when we consider the future and evaluate their capacity to lead the reform process which will be necessary. Their styles of rule have invariably reinforced prevailing social hierarchies and the pervasiveness of privilege. With the tendency for economic development to require some form of state sanction, it has also promoted clientelist relations and given advantage to those who have "access." As a consequence, the autonomy of social groups is considerably reduced and with it the scope for the development of class consciousness. As Elsenhans notes, "the moment resource allocation . . . becomes dependent on personal relations . . . open communication is endangered. The moment access to further power is based on an insight into relationships of alliance and rivalry within state classes, only such information will be sought which will promote one's own power" (1987: 87). Elsenhans goes on to point out that when connections acquire great importance, a mode of behavior emerges which "guards over the entire economic and social situation as a private sphere, [which] makes the formation of an alliance based on similar economic and social situations difficult" (ibid.).

The study of early capitalist development in Europe and elsewhere suggests that the class (or classes) which superintends democratization is always best positioned to preempt most of the benefits for itself. In theory, therefore, while political democracy in the periphery can be achieved and sustained only through intense mass struggles, the risk of its appropriation by the present leading classes exists. This reinforces the need for the masses to fuse the struggles against imperialism and for socioeconomic justice with that for political democracy. For the masses, which are largely excluded from economic and political control over their lives, political democracy represents a *necessary* advance in the long-run pursuit of their objective interests. It is, however, a two-edged sword insofar as the leading classes may be able, in some circumstances, to direct the process to serve their class project.

## *Retreat and Disinvolvement of the Developmental State*

As I have stated, the magnitude of the current changes in the world economy is such that the perpetuation of existing patterns of political domination in the third world is not possible. Attempts to sustain the status quo would lead inexorably to socioeconomic degeneration and civil war on a wide scale. I think that this is the way significant factions of the ruling circles in the center countries see the situation, and therefore they may exercise leverage in the direction of political and social reforms in the periphery. When we consider the options of reform or social revolution, the former appears the more likely. This judgment is based on the expectation that the leading classes would—either on their own initiative or through leverage—move toward reform. Thus I have argued the importance of political democracy over the next period.

These issues are implicit in the debates which dominate the recent left literature on politics and the state in the third world. I refer here especially to the thesis of "disinvolvement" or "retreat" of the developmental state.[3] The literature has posed several important questions. Is the retreat a generalized one affecting all major dimensions of state activity? Or is it confined to a few specific areas, such as the state property sector and the provision of basic needs? Is the retreat fundamental (that is, real) or is it tactical (that is, short-run, reversible, and illusory)? Do its causes lie within the third world? Or is it part of a worldwide process? How far is it reinforced by global bureaucracies such as the IMF-World Bank group? To what extent is the phenomenon ideological?

There is such a rich variety of situations occurring that all these questions can be answered negatively and affirmatively at the same time. Thus there is clearly some universality in the tendency to "retreat," as is readily apparent in its simultaneous occurrence across a wide range of countries and social systems. There are also situations in which the local context is primary, making them far removed from a simple mechanical enforcement of external pressures. There have also been instances where the process has been reversed, the tactical element is clear, and the formal retreat has served to mask intensified forms of informal control.

Beyond revealing that the phenomenon is exceedingly complex, this inquiry on "the retreat of the state" allows three major conclusions which are important here. First, the existing variation reflects a genuine search for modes of state activity which would promote development without putting at risk the social and political power of the ruling classes. What is occurring, therefore, is a real exercise in reform as distinct from gimmickry. Its main stimulus is the public sector's weakness, which has emerged over the past two decades. State enterprises in the third world exhibit, for example, low managerial efficiency, limited flexibility, and slow adaptability to new technologies. Consequently, certain demands have become reasonable and rational, among them strengthening the market mechanism in the national economy; greater decentralization and accountability for state enterprises; and a widening of opportunities for individual incentives at all levels of the society.

Confusion has arisen because the radical right seized on these weaknesses well before they were even conceded by the left and has used them to denounce all government as bad government. The success this has brought right-wing forces in the center countries has encouraged them to try to impose a similar ideological outlook in the periphery. This offensive has been aided by the acceleration of state reform in the socialist countries of East Europe and China; the radical right has highlighted this as further evidence of state failure. While this ideological offensive confuses, it should not be allowed to mask the real internal imperatives for reform of the state productive sector in the periphery.

The second conclusion, therefore, is that much in the retreat of the state may be "ideological," in the sense that it affects the style of politics rather more than the actual impact of the state on the economic processes. In the debates on economic policy, we find calls for more private initiatives, and it is presumed that the state will lead the process of its own disinvolvement! Since it is hard to imagine a state doing any such thing of its own volition, other considerations must apply. One which immediately springs to mind is that we may be witnessing efforts to alter the *direction* of state activity, and not in fact a movement to liquidate the centrality of its "economic function." Another is that this shift in direction may well be paralleled with more openly *activist roles for the state in the process of economic concentration and the further hierarchization of economic and social relations.* Already measures have been taken to reduce the role of the state in providing welfare, basic needs, unemployment relief, and so on. This legitimizes the social and economic inequality of capitalism under the guise of disinvolvement. State failure as a generalized phenomenon is therefore being used to discredit all state efforts aimed at redressing class inequalities. It is imperative for their own interests that the revolutionary classes in the periphery do not permit this shift or derailment of the state's role in securing economic and social justice.

The third conclusion is that it would be wrong to pose the state-society problematic as a zero-sum game. If the retreat or disinvolvement of the state genuinely reflects a strengthening of civil society in relation to the state, then this would be conducive to political reform and the long-run enhancement of both state and society. A strengthened civil society places limits on the scope for arbitrary political actions, reduces reliance on commandist forms of political rule, encourages the autonomy of groups, and reduces the significance of clientelist relations in social life.

In concluding this section, it should be noted that there exist in all contemporary societies a necessary interdependence and complementarity between state and market. How this interdependence and complementarity are regulated is a political matter, resolvable only by the balance of political interests in the society; and there is, therefore, no *a priori* determination of the ideal state-market relation. The process of political reform in the periphery is therefore best seen as a process of reconstitution of the state's economic function and the manner of its insertion into the system of material production in the national and world economy.

## The Illusion of Democratization?

The significance I attribute to the role of political democracy in the present period of global restructuring is not only controversial. It is also directly contradicted by the thesis which asserts that the process of democratization is illusory, that it is merely a repetition of a familiar pattern of deception of the masses. This deception, it is argued, will lead to a return to the political status quo which existed before the present movement in favor of democratization. The thesis is most strongly advanced in the case of Latin America, where the states have been independent for a long time and where patterns of advance and retreat have been observed historically. Thus it has been pointed out that the 1950s and early 1960s were touted as the "twilight of the tyrants" and "the age of democracy" in Latin America. However, by the 1970s even countries with relatively strong democratic traditions—for example, Uruguay and Chile—had become military dictatorships. Presently we are witnessing yet again the "twilight of the tyrants" as they are being removed from Haiti, Argentina, Uruguay, Peru, Bolivia, and, further afield, the Philippines. The process, however, is said to be little more than what Nef calls a "recycling of an old economic, social and political crisis under a new set of labels" (1987: 8). What will emerge in the future is "a limited and restricted democracy where large sections of the population . . . are purposely excluded from acceptable political debate" (ibid.).

The thesis points out that the military in these countries is expected to secure this arrangement, and that in the last analysis the arbiter of the process is the U.S. establishment. Political regimes which emerge after "electoral victories" will be expected to superintend the resolution of the current economic impasse. However, as they pursue the seemingly invariable policies of wage restraint, cuts in social expenditures, and so on, these governments will become unpopular. In the wake of the protests that are expected to follow, they will turn to the military to preserve law and order. The U.S. establishment will accede to this development, if only for strategic anti-socialist reasons. A new cycle of instability, repression, and dictatorial rule will emerge. The illusion of democratization will then be apparent. In this thesis, the leading classes in the periphery do not want and do not think it is in their interests to advance democratization in a genuine way.

While plausible, this scenario is unlikely because of the deep-seated nature of the economic impasse which I have outlined. These countries are not faced with just another capitalist crisis, but, as I have argued, with a profound process of qualitative change in the development of the productive forces of global capitalism. The old forms of rule are not compatible with the scientific, technological, and social forces that hae been unleashed. Information technology provides one broad example, feeding the emergence of a global consciousness of acceptable norms of citizenship.

The "illusory thesis" is also weak because it views democratization only from the top, as a maneuver of the ruling classes. The thesis basically ignores the extent to which democratization is in fact the product of struggles by the masses to gain control of their lives. These struggles may indeed be coopted. There is no guarantee this will not occur. Ultimately, however, these struggle are *the real source of the democratization drives in the periphery*. If democratization did not really have its source in mass struggles, the ruling classes would not pay it any serious attention.

My argument on the pivotal importance of political democracy to the future of the third world is not based on illusions about the many real and admitted shortcomings of political democracy. It is for this reason that the epithet "bourgeois democracy" has been coined. Nor is it based on any illusions about the dangers of cooptation. Indeed, my prediction is that cooptation is the most likely prospect in the development of politics and the state in the periphery. After all, historically, when the ruling classes in the center were forced to accede to democratization, they embraced the process in ways designed to limit both popular forms of democracy and egalitarian social change. Yet because political democracy is compatible with capitalist inequalities does not mean it is unimportant.

The great danger which lies ahead is that in the periphery social democracy may preempt the appeal of socialism, scientific and democratic, much as it has in the center. If this were to occur, it would surely prolong the main essentials of the capitalist world order. It would make the state in the periphery more capable and efficient, thereby enhancing the capacity of its leading classes to benefit from the extensions of capitalist relations and the reduction of patronage, clientelism, and rent appropriation. Objectively, however, such an eventuality would also mean an improvement of the present status of the masses in the periphery—a status in which authoritarian and coercive rule is widespread, where civil society is weak in relation to the state, where people as citizens have been unable to consolidate substantial rights.

It is for these reasons that I have stressed that a socialist response must be inherently democratic, in every sense of the term. It cannot view democracy as tactical and left authoritarianism as a viable state form. A socialist response must fuse the ideals of democracy with resistance to dictatorial rule. Socialism must be viewed not as the antithesis of political democracy, but rather as transcending political democracy, and, by removing social and economic inequalities, making democracy real. In this way progressive forces may begin to build vital class alliances and thus overcome the limited development and weakness of the worker-peasant class in the periphery.

## Notes

1. Unfortunately, the left in the periphery, and elsewhere, faces an acute crisis of ideology and has done little to mobilize social forces on the recognition of their own interests. This is nowhere better revealed than in the handling of the very problematic I have identified here. It is precisely for this reason that I have addressed the matter more fully elsewhere; see Thomas (1984). This source also contains a definition and elaboration of the meaning of "political democracy" as applied in the argument here.
2. As I have noted, "While it is true that in many of these societies the mass politics of the nationalist movement is rapidly transformed into state control of popular mass organizations, it is also true that in the first phase of the transfer of power to the local state the level of mass politics is sufficiently striking as to constitute a key feature of political relations" (Thomas 1984:54).
3. A review of relevant research results is provided by Roberts (1987). See the articles published along with that of Roberts and in the preceding issue of the *IDS Bulletin;* see also Evans et al. (1985).

## References

Elsenhans, Hartmut. 1987. "Dependencia, Underdevelopment and the Third World State." *Law and State* 36.

Evans, Peter B. et al. 1985. *Bringing the State Back In*. Cambridge: Cambridge University Press.

Nef, John. 1987. "The Illusion of Redemocratization in Latin America." *International Viewpoints* (York University), March 2.

Roberts, Hush. 1987. "Politics in Command." *IDS Bulletin* 18, no. 4 (October).

Thomas, Clive Y. 1974. *Dependence and Transformation.* New York: Monthly Review Press.

—————. 1984. *The Rise of the Authoritarian State in Peripheral Societies,* New York and London: Monthly Review Press/Heinemmann.

# A New Stage of Capitalism Ahead?

## *Harry Magdoff*

Historical memory has a way of playing tricks with our understanding of the present. As World War II drew to a close, what was uppermost in the thinking about the postwar world was the Great Depression and the likelihood of a return to stagnation and mass unemployment. That memory became dimmer and dimmer the more the postwar wave of economic expansion took hold. In its stead came a vision of prosperity without end: a secular boom that might go on for a hundred years, if not longer. Nevertheless, the boom began to weaken at the end of the 1960s; world capitalism has been losing steam ever since, with the centers of world capitalism turning from fully employed to increasingly seriously underemployed economies. Yet even after almost two decades of stagnation, the aura of the successful early postwar decades persists, reinforced by the buoyant, ballooning sphere of international finance and speculation. Thus, in radical as well as conservative circles the belief prevails that the years of slowdown and extensive unemployment are only an interlude, that somehow or other the secular boom will before long reassert itself. This is implicitly assumed when ruling classes defend their austerity programs, which they argue are needed to clear the way for a resumption of vigorous growth.

To be sure, confidence in the future needs something more to lean on than remembrance of things past. For some, optimism flows from statistical analyses of long waves—the sort of logic used by speculators in the stock market. Others pin their expectations on technological innovations still to come. Meanwhile, a more visible development has spurred the imagination of the international business community—the progress being made toward the final removal by 1992 of all national barriers to the free flow of workers, capital, goods, and services within the European Community. A single, homogenized market of over 300 million customers with an anticipated gross domestic product of $2.7 trillion, it is believed, will provide the countries of the Common Market with the chance to break out of slow growth. Economic acceleration of such a large market could in turn become the engine of growth for the rest of the capitalist world.

Underpinning the euphoria associated with the approaching new stage of economic unification are two preconceptions: (1) absolute faith in the effectiveness of the free market, from which it follows that the freer the market the stronger the economic expansion; and (2) in keeping with that presumption, the belief that the satisfactory growth rate of the European Community in the 1960s was due to the reduction in restraints of trade brought about by the 1957 Treaty of Rome that set up the Common Market. Hence, the elimination of still more barriers to cross-border movements—such as the flow of capital and migration of labor—should provide a more substantial and lasting stimulus than that of 1957.

Although trust in the market as regulator of the economy is a hallowed dogma of capitalism, the degree of confidence in its effectiveness changes from time to time, often influenced by the changing phases of the business cycle. Faith in the market as the cure-all for economic difficulties, however, has reached a new high in recent years. This is perhaps not too surprising in view of the degree to which the advanced capitalist world has been and continues to be propped up by an ever-expanding volume of debt and speculation. The more the debt-cum-speculation balloon is inflated, the more threatening does interference by government regulators become, lest the balloon burst. Not only are central bankers and other officials restrained from interfering (except to rescue near-bankrupt large banks and giant corporations), they are impelled to deregulate further in order to ease strains and overcome potential breaking points associated with financial excesses. In addition, the new stage of globalization creates added urgency for the lifting of barriers, especially in the financial sphere. Today's international capital markets not only limit the freedom of action of national authorities in domestic affairs (for example, in such areas as interest-rate levels and control of capital flows), they have also become so big and complex that there is no alternative to dependence (domestically and internationally) on the price mechanism and the market. Thus, although the moves to greater market freedom in the age of Reagan and Thatcher may appear to be purely a matter of ideology, they have in fact been emerging in response to real problems. By the same token, they are not solutions but palliatives that lead to other and still more complex problems, not the least of which is the resulting increase in fragility of the entire financial system.

## Stagnation and Growth

The main point that needs to be emphasized is that the persistence of slow growth, mass unemployment, and excess capacity in key industries has little to do with more or less freedom of movement of goods and capital. The basic cause (or causes) of the stagnation that set in during the early 1970s is ignored by those who see looming on the horizon a new and durable economic upsurge. Deeply buried in such optimism is an implicit assumption that a healthy, long-term growth rate is built into a capitalist economy, in other words that there is an automatic tendency for a level of investment to be maintained that is sufficient to provide a high level of employment and income. Neither theory nor history supports such a supposition.

It is of course possible to design models that show a capitalist economy pursuing a steady upward trend. But to be consistent these mathematical structures are built on severely restricted assumptions which differ greatly from the real world. Thus, these models assume long-run stability in the interaction of such basic variables as levels of investment, profit rates, and capital/output ratios, whereas in reality these all fluctuate more or less independently in response to technological change, competition among capitals, class struggle, and so on. The most significant study of the uniform growth-rate model and its inner contradictions was made by Michal Kalecki in his *Theory of Economic Dynamics*. Kalecki's analysis leads to the conclusion that "long-run development is not inherent in the capitalist economy," and that "specific 'development factors' are required to sustain a long-run upward movement" (1968:161).

In a sense, this analysis of long-term trends was Kalecki's interpretation of Marx's well-known statement that "the real barrier to capitalist production is capital itself." Given a sufficient initial boost, investment feeds upon itself. New investment increases profits, and the improved profit prospects stimulate still more investment. This process, however, eventually comes up against a barrier in the overexpansion of capacity relative to effective demand. When this happens, investment contracts, profits decline, and the overall growth rate slows down or turns negative. This is the reason why specific development factors are needed to overcome barriers to the continued growth of capitalist production.

Turning from theory to history, we find that during the last 200 years long waves of especially rapid and sustained growth are initiated by one or more of the following factors: (1) the adoption and spread of major technological innovations—the kinds that require massive capital investment, new kinds of infrastructure, relocation of population, and so forth; (2) development of new markets by capitalist penetration of the periphery, as a result either of colonial expansion or the acquisition of spheres of influence; (3) preparing for and waging wars; and (4) rebuilding in the aftermath of wars.

To an important extent all of these factors were influential at the end of World War II, along with a fifth important stimulus provided by the hegemony of the United States over the imperialist world. The fact that *all* of these stimuli came together in a relatively short period provided the momentum for one of the longest booms in the history of capitalism. A brief review of these developments should help to develop our case.

First, the reconstruction of war-devastated areas in Western Europe and Japan required a concentrated mobilization of material resources, labor, and capital investment. Severe obstacles had of course to be overcome before this process could begin. In the United States the initial postwar push came much easier, since there was no devastation and the war economy itself prepared the way. During the war automobile production and residential construction for civilian use were prohibited in order to conserve raw materials and productive facilities for armaments needed to conduct a global war. Because of the absence of consumer durable goods and wartime wage/price controls, debts were paid off, workers accumulated savings, and capitalists stashed away profits in liquid form. The combination of deferred demand and the financial means to satisfy it provided the initial propulsive force for a new wave of prosperity in the United States.

Second, a new source of growth emerged in Western Europe and Japan with the spread of the mass use of private cars. Even in the United States, which had built up a mass-production car industry in the 1920s, the spread of the automobile also left its mark on the postwar era as a much larger percentage of the population became owners. The proliferation of autos boosted investment in road-building and greatly stimulated demand for housing, shopping malls, and other services to accommodate a shift in population to the suburbs.

Third, technological innovations generated by military demand provided the basis for new industries such as high-speed jet planes, improved means of communication, computers, and a wide range of electronic equipment and devices.

Fourth, beginning with the Korean war, the United States committed itself to the construction and maintenance of a huge new military machine. This produced a major new set of industries engaged in the mass manufacture of military equipment. In addition, U.S. procurement during the Korean war gave a crucial impulse to the rise of the German and Japanese economies.

Fifth, the assumption by the United States of hegemony over the capitalist world provided a degree of stability in the war-torn advanced capitalist countries and led to the establishment of international institutions facilitating and financing economic growth. The framework was the straddling of the globe by U.S. military bases. Apart from the advantages this gave to the United States in acquiring cooperating allies and keeping the periphery within the imperialist network, the dollars spent abroad for the maintenance of armed forces and bases supplied foreign currency to the host countries with which they were able to expand their imports and investments. The Marshall Plan and subsequent aid programs supported the creation of U.S. clients and protectorates, thus facilitating the spread of U.S.-based multinational firms. The Bretton Woods agreements, by making the dollar "as good as gold," triggered the inundation of international money markets with dollars, which in turn furnished the liquidity for the growth of world trade. The World Bank and the International Monetary Fund, also created by the Bretton Woods Agreements, contributed their part by supplying funds for infrastructural projects, and by providing the means for disciplining third world countries.

All of the above-listed stimulative factors ultimately either came to an end, or their influence greatly diminished. Just as the conjunction of the props led to expansion, so the sequential lessening of their influence paved the way for the onset of stagnation. This can be seen as we briefly review what happened to each one of the stimuli.

(1) The rebuilding of war-devastated countries has long been completed. The stimulation provided by the war-created pent-up demand in the United States ended by the early 1950s.

(2) The rate of growth in the demand for automobiles has drastically shrunk—a normal development in growth industries. In the early stages, the rate of increase in demand is very steep, inducing an accelerating growth of productive capacity. But as the existing market is increasingly satisfied, demand slows down to meet primarily replacement needs and population growth. With this the profit potential in expanding capacity evaporates, as do the secondary stimulative effects.

(3) The impact of the major postwar technological innovations has largely petered out. Technological change of course continues at a rapid pace, but the new innovations have not been the kind that have widespread enough effects to reactivate substantial economic growth.

(4) The arms build-up continues to sustain at least the U.S. economy. Yet its impact is nowhere near that of the earlier build-up. In contrast to the rise in military spending in the 1950s and 1960s, it is heavily concentrated on sophisticated technology that does not require as much new investment in manufacturing capacity.

(5) The U.S. empire has been shrinking. Three changes account for this. First, the defeat of the United States in the Vietnam war undermined its leadership role. Second, the rise of competing powers in Western Europe and Japan diminished U.S. industrial and economic predominance. Indeed, the very build-up of industrial capacity throughout the capitalist world during the boom years engendered a huge amount of excess capacity relative to demand, notably in steel, shipbuilding, autos, textiles, and petrochemicals. Third, the flood of U.S. dollars into world markets, associated with the global operations of the U.S. military machine and the international spread of its multinational corporations and banks, eventually led to a weakening of the dollar's privileged position. In the heyday of U.S. imperialism, the growing dollar float outside the United States provided liquidity for the rapid expansion of world trade. But with the breakdown in 1971 of the Bretton Woods agreement on gold-dollar convertibility, the dollar became extremely volatile and a medium for heavy speculation in foreign exchange markets.

This diagnosis is obviously far from exhaustive, but it should suffice to identify the fundamental reasons for the long postwar boom and the subsequent protracted stagnation. It is true that the lowering of tariffs under GATT and the establishment of the Common Market contributed to the exceptional increase in international trade, and hence to economic expansion, in the postwar period. But it did so at a time when a unique combination of special development factors had already launched a powerful long-run upward movement. When these development factors lost their momentum, so did world trade. It follows that expecting 1992 to become the prelude to the kind of boom that came after 1957 is putting the cart before the horse. Further freeing of markets is not, nor has it ever been by itself, a sufficient stimulus: at most it can serve as an auxiliary, never an independent, force determining an economy's growth rate.

Nor is there anything in sight that seems likely to inject new vigor into the global capitalist system. War used to be an answer, but history seems to have played a nasty trick on capitalism by depriving it of this trump card. Nor are there lush opportunities in the third world. Markets in debt-burdened countries have shrunk as the IMF and the lending bankers forced a reduction of their imports. And the few newly industrializing countries have become competitors in slow-growing export trade.

Nevertheless hope springs eternal in the form of confidence in the limitless potential of science and technology. Much of this is based on what the future may bring—a future that may take years or decades before new discoveries reach commercial practicality. But even when they do, they may not be of the sort needed to re-start the engine of growth. In this respect, the investment experience in the United States as shown in Tables 1 and 2 is highly instructive. The period depicted is one of recovery from a rather severe business cycle downturn in the early 1980s. Normally, capital investment rises strongly during the recovery phase of the cycle. And so it did this time too, though not more so than in previous upturns. But this time it took place in the midst of the so-called information revolution— proclaimed by many as the new industrial revolution.

Indeed, as expected, this area has been growing at a furious pace. As can be seen in Table 1, investment in information-processing equipment doubled between 1982 and 1987. Yet it is equally significant that apart from this growth area, investment in machinery and equipment increased by no more than 15 percent during a five-year recovery period. And even that was because of investment in transportation equipment (including the rental car business), not productive capacity as such. If we turn our attention to the area of traditional production capacity (lines 2 and 4 of Table 1), we see that the increase was less than 6 percent, and most of that was due to purchases of furniture and fixtures for distribution and other service establishments. Clearly, although the new technology contributed to

*Table 1*

*Investment in Machinery and Equipment by U.S. Business Firms*
*(in billions of 1982 dollars)*

| Type | 1982 | 1985 | 1987 |
|---|---|---|---|
| Information processing and related equipment[a] | 66.6 | 119.3 | 139.4 |
| Industrial equipment[b] | 59.3 | 64.6 | 61.4 |
| Transportation and related equipment[c] | 42.5 | 61.5 | 59.1 |
| Other equipment[d] | 55.1 | 58.6 | 59.7 |
| Total | 223.4 | 304.0 | 319.6 |

*Source: Survey of Current Business,* July 1986 and July 1987.

[a]Primarily computing, accounting, and office machinery, and communications equipment.

[b]Metalworking machinery, special industry equipment, materials handling equipment, etc.

[c]Trucks, buses, autos, airplanes, etc.

[d]Farm machinery, construction machinery, furniture and fixtures, etc.

the recovery, it was not able to offset the sluggish pace of other investment areas. Despite the fact that these innovations have been spreading like wildfire, they have nevertheless failed to spark a new boom.

The story told in Table 2—investment in non-residential structures—is an even starker reflection of stagnation. The decline in total investment was due to one special factor: the termination of oil exploration and development after the price of oil fell. If we abstract from that type of speculative investment, there is an insignificant rise of 2 percent from 1982 to 1987. It should also be noted that investment in industrial plants *decreased* by 30 percent—the sort of decline that one would expect in a severe depression but is now occurring in a cyclical upswing. On the other hand, what sustained investment in nonresidential construction (other than for oil and gas) was growth in office buildings, shopping centers, hotels, and the like.

The investment pattern revealed in these two tables is not new. It is typical of the 1970s and 1980s as a whole, an important distinguishing feature of the stage of stagnation in contrast with the preceding boom (Magdoff and Sweezy 1987:50-58). This does not mean, however, that there has been any let-up in technological innovation during the last two decades. Whole new areas have been blossoming in electronics, lasers, communication, biotechnology, with much more being promised in reports from scientific laboratories. What has to be emphasized is that miraculous scientific and technological innovations do not necessarily produce miraculous growth rates for the economy as a whole. In this respect, the characteristic innovations of recent years bear no resemblance to the great landmark innovations, such as the steam engine, the railroad, and the automobile in earlier times.

## Soaring Finance

The real growth miracle in the stagnation decades, and particularly in the 1980s, has been in the area of finance, as exemplified by the rise of global stock and bond market trading, soaring speculation in all forms of futures, the mad rush to buy and sell whole companies, and the spread of transnational banking. In fact, what has prevented the stagnating economies from performing much worse during this period has been the explosion of debt and speculation throughout the capitalist system.

One aspect of the changes taking place is seen in Table 3. The third line of the table presents the volume of bank credit extended by the leading private banks across national borders. Accompanying this measure of the international banking market are the data for gross domestic product and foreign trade of the capitalist world. The most obvious aspect of this table is the speed with which the international banking market has expanded. In 1964 it amounted to a little over one percent of the world's gross domestic product. At that level, the function of international banking was to facilitate the international flow of goods and services. By 1972, on the other hand, the activities

*Table 2*
*Investment in Non-residential Structures in the United States*
*(in billions of 1982 dollars)*

| Type | 1982 | 1985 | 1987 |
|------|------|------|------|
| Industrial | 17.3 | 15.0 | 12.2 |
| Commercial | 37.5 | 53.3 | 46.3 |
| Public utilities[a] | 28.3 | 25.1 | 25.7 |
| Oil and gas exploration and wells | 37.8 | 33.3 | 17.5 |
| All other[b] | 22.4 | 22.8 | 23.8 |
| Total | 143.3 | 149.5 | 125.5 |

*Source: Survey of Current Business,* July 1986 and July 1987.
[a] Electric light and power, gas, telephone, and railways.
[b] Religious structures, hospitals, hotels, recreational buildings, farm structures, etc.

## Table 3
### International Banking, Economic Activity, and International Trade

| | Amount (billions of dollars at current prices and exchange rates) | | | | |
| --- | --- | --- | --- | --- | --- |
| | 1964 | 1972 | 1980 | 1983 | 1985 |
| Gross Domestic Product World except Eastern Europe | 1,605 | 3,336 | 10,172 | 10,140 | 12,825 |
| International trade in goods and services World except Eastern Europe | 188 | 463 | 2,150 | 1,986 | 2,190 |
| International banking activity | 20 | 208 | 1,559 | 2,253 | 2,598 |

*Source:* Ralph C. Bryant, *International Financial Intermediation* (Washington, D.C.: The Brookings Institution, 1987), p. 22. The statistics on gross domestic product and trade come from International Monetary Fund records. The data on international trade are totals of exports of goods and services for all countries other than Eastern Europe. The international banking series is constructed by Morgan Guaranty Trust Company of New York as a measure of the gross size of the international banking market; it covers bank credit extended across national borders and includes redepositing among the reporting banks.

of this kind of banking went far beyond such service usefulness, amounting to 45 percent of world trade. It then kept on growing by leaps and bounds, despite the slowing up of world production and trade, so that by 1985 international banking activity eventually exceeded world trade.

The explanation of this burgeoning of international banking is that it supplies the wherewithal for, and participates in, the ever higher levels of debt, speculation, and financial capital flows across national borders. The staggering amounts of money involved can be judged from an example of only one area of speculation: the New York investment banking firm of Morgan Stanley estimates that "an average of $420 billion crossed the world's foreign exchanges *each day* in 1987, of which more than 90 percent represented financial transactions unrelated to trade or investment" (*Forbes*, August 22, 1988; emphasis added).

There is a logical connection, in my view, between the lagging levels of real investment and this latest stage of finance. In the absence of new development factors sufficient to produce buoyant growth rates, profit opportunities for investment in productive capacity are strictly limited. At the same time, as long as economic activity holds at a relatively high level, profits continue to accumulate. As a result, the big players in the capitalist game in Western Europe, Japan, and the United States sit on growing mountains of cash. And with this, the energies of the players shift to profit-making by buying and selling in financial markets.

It is against this background that 1992 needs to be considered. There is little reason to support the expectation that a unified internal market in the European Community will give Europe a chance to break out of slow growth. The more realistic prospect is that it will, in the words of a *Wall Street Journal* report, become "a battleground for the world's major corporations" (December 29, 1988). In the era of monopoly capital, the strategy of giants in industry, commerce, and finance is to consolidate their control, be it over raw materials, productive capacity, or market share. When markets are sluggish and investment opportunities scarce, the thrust toward tighter control intensifies, ever more so when a new field of battle opens up.

These observations are not based on idle guesswork. Battle lines started to be drawn as soon as it became clear that the opening up in 1992 was actually underway. Table 4 tells part of the story. Notice the stability of the volume of U.S. direct investment in the European Community in 1982–84. Then in just three years there is an increase of 75 percent. (This increase is exaggerated because of the increase in the valuation of foreign assets to reflect the decline in the interna-

*Table 4*
*U.S. Direct Investment in European Community*
*(stock of investment in billions of dollars)*

| | |
|---|---|
| 1982 | 71.7 |
| 1983 | 70.2 |
| 1984 | 69.7 |
| 1985 | 82.1 |
| 1986 | 98.5 |
| 1987 | 122.2 |

*Source: Survey of Current Business,* August 1986 and August 1988. The data for 1982 to 1985 cover the ten member countries of the European Community in those years. The data for 1986 and 1987 include in addition the investment position of the two new members—Spain and Portugal. This difference does not effect the overall picture, since the increase in investment in these two countries was less than $2 billion between 1985 and 1987.

tional value of the dollar. This accounting adjustment, however, is only part of the story. Stagnation in Europe has for a long time put a damper on the growth of U.S. investment. A sharp investment upturn began in 1985, reflecting not only the anticipation of intensified competition but also the possibility of new tariff walls being erected around the European Community.)

European giants have also been actively engaged in the mergers and acquisitions game not only in Europe but in the United States as well, as both a defensive and an offensive weapon. Meanwhile within Europe, banks, brokers, and insurers have been merging and making alliances, as described in *Business Week*:

> In the past 18 months, some 400 banks and finance firms across Europe have merged, taken stakes in one another, or cooked up joint marketing ventures to sell stocks, mutual funds, insurance, and other financial instruments. These alliances are both helping strengthen the institutions at home and giving many a leg up in becoming global rivals to the behemoths of Japan, the United States, and Switzerland, who are firing up their own European campaigns. (December 12, 1988)

What is too often neglected in discussions of this period is the question of what will happen to the working class as a result of the scramble for control. A sign of what may be in store is already to be found in the way investment has been moving to Spain and Portugal to take advantage of lower wage levels. Freeing the flow of capital may well speed up the shift of production to lower labor-cost regions. Factories that decide not to move will be motivated to reduce labor costs by modernization that will eliminate jobs. Both of these developments create a real threat to the working classes of nations already burdened by mass unemployment.

Above all, it is important to recognize that the more a country gets involved in the international economy, the more difficult it becomes to escape the impact of external developments. This is generally true, but it is even more so during a period of stagnation. For with sluggish or no growth, the relative advance of one nation usually comes at the expense of others. The likelihood of this being the case is even greater when all barriers to the movement of goods and money are removed. For then capital will flow freely and rapidly between nations in response to balance-of-payments strains, exchange-rate fluctuations, and interest-rate differentials. That in turn will severely restrict the ability of affected nations to pursue progressive strategies, with policy options narrowed down to a choice among austerity programs that press down on wages and social benefits.

As far as industrial and financial corporations are concerned, what they are looking for in the removal of barriers to the flow of capital and trade is a "level playing field" on which they can fight their battles. But what will be level about the field as far as the working class is concerned? Will the freedom of movement of capital include freedom to depress living standards for the sake of competitive advantage? This is the challenge the working class faces.

In the false hope that market unification will open the path to vigorous growth and expanding employment opportunities, lies hidden a tendency to underestimate the burdens on the masses that are all too likely to result. It is still three years to 1992, but not a bit too soon for the working-class movements of Europe, separately and collectively, to begin planning their responses to this potentially devastating threat.

## References

Kalecki, Michal. 1968. *Theory of Economic Dynamics.* New York: Monthly Review Press.

Magdoff, Harry and Paul Sweezy. 1987. "Supply-Side Theory and Capital Investment." In Harry Magdoff and Paul Sweezy, *Stagnation and the Financial Explosion.* New York: Monthly Review Press.

# Contributors

Lourdes Benería is Professor of City and Regional Planning and Women's Studies at Cornell University. Her most recent book, written with Martha Roldán, is *Crossroads of Class and Gender: Homework, Subcontracting and Household Dynamics in Mexico City.*

Jean-Pierre Berlan is Directeur de Recherche at the Institut National de la Recherche Agronomique (Aix-en-Provence) and at the Centre de Recherche sur les Dynamiques et Politiques Economiques et l'Economie des Resources in the Faculté des Sciences Economiques de l'Université Aix-Marseille II.

James Crotty teaches economics at the University of Massachusetts-Amherst. He works in the areas of Marxian crisis theory and macroeconomic theory and policy. His current research focuses on the role of financial markets in accumulation and crisis.

Diane Elson teaches in the Department of Economics, University of Manchester. She is a member of the editorial board of *New Left Review* and is active in the movement to promote links between women in first and third world countries.

Gerald Epstein teaches economics at the University of Massachusetts-Amherst and is a staff economist at the Center for Popular Economics.

M. Patricia Fernández Kelly is Associate Professor of Sociology and a Research Scientist in the Institute for Policy Studies at Johns Hopkins University. She is the author of *For We Are Sold, I and My People: Women and Industry in Mexico's Frontier.*

John Bellamy Foster teaches sociology and political economy at the University of Oregon. He is author of *The Theory of Monopoly Capitalism* and co-editor, with Henryk Szlajfer, of *The Faltering Economy: The Problem of Accumulation Under Monopoly Capitalism*.

Richard Child Hill is Professor of Sociology and Urban Affairs at Michigan State University. He is co-author of *Detroit: Race and Uneven Development*. His current research focuses on comparative study of the social and political impact of industrial restructuring in the United States, Great Britain, and Japan.

Arthur MacEwan teaches economics at the University of Massachusetts-Boston and is a member of the editorial collective of *Dollars & Sense* magazine.

Harry Magdoff is co-editor of *Monthly Review*. His books include *The Age of Imperialism, Imperialism: From Colonial Times to the Present*, and, most recently, with Paul M. Sweezy, *The Irreversible Crisis*.

Morris H. Morley teaches politics at Macquarie University (Australia). He is the author of *Imperial State and Revolution: the United States and Cuba, 1952–1986*.

James F. Petras is Professor of Sociology at the State University of New York, Binghamton. Among his most recent books are *Latin America: Bankers, Generals, and the Struggle for Social Justice* and *The U.S. and Latin America: Sacrificing Dictators to Save the State*.

Robert Pollin teaches economics at the University of California, Riverside. His work deals with money and banking, international affairs, and macroeconomics. He is a member of the national steering committee of the Union for Radical Political Economics.

Hugo Radice is Lecturer in Economics at the University of Leeds. His work focuses on multinational firms and the political economy of Eastern Europe. He is a founding member of the Conference of Socialist Economists and is currently on the editorial board of the *Review of Radical Political Economics*.

William K. Tabb is Professor of Economics at Queens College and Professor of Sociology at the Graduate Center of the City University of New York.

Michael Tanzer is President of Tanzer Economic Associates, Inc., a New York-based consulting firm specializing on energy and mineral issues. His most recent book is *Energy Update: Oil in the Late Twentieth Century.*

Clive Y. Thomas, a Guyanese economist, is Professor and Director of the Institute of Development Studies at the University of Guyana. His books include *The Poor and the Powerless: Economic Policy and Change in the Caribbean, The Rise of the Authoritarian State in Peripheral Societies,* and *Plantations, Peasants and State.*

Carlos M. Vilas, an Argentinian political scientist, has worked in Nicaragua since 1980, first in the Ministry of Planning and then in the Centro de Investigaciones y Documentación de la Costa Atlántica. He is the author of *The Sandinista Revolution: National Liberation and Social Transformation in Central America.*

Robert E. Wood teaches sociology at Rutgers University, Camden. He is the author of *From Marshall Plan to Debt Crisis: Foreign Aid and Development in the World Economy.*

# Index

16, 350, 360–61; trade with Eastern
Europe, 51–52
Exchange rates, 88–91, 95, 138–39, 190,
199–200. *See also* International monetary systems
Exports. *See* Trade; U.S. exports
Exxon. *See* "Seven Sisters"

Federal Reserve Bank: and Bretton
Woods system, 107; decline in degree
of control, 96, 129–31; and growth in
financial market-lending capacity, 126–
27; and interest rates and credit availability, 84–85; and Latin American financial instability, 130–31; and third
world debt, 114; under Paul Volcker,
11, 82, 93, 111, 130
Financial innovations, 126–28, 130
Financial instability and international
monetary systems, 101–19; and capital
mobility, 101; and economic restructuring decisions, 116–18. *See also*
Debt-dependent growth; International
monetary systems; Latin American financial instability; U.S. financial markets
Financial instruments: creation of new,
112–13; investments in, 125
Financial markets: and debt-dependent
growth, 121; "delinking," 333; and Eurodollar market, 128; restructuring of,
12; unregulated, 66, 86–87, 103. *See
also* Eurodollar market; Stagnation;
Speculation; U.S. financial markets
Fixed exchange rates, 117. *See also* Bretton Woods monetary system
Flexible exchange rates: expectations,
109–10; and instability and stagnation,
108–9; and international capital mobility, 111–14; and international role of
the dollar, 110–11; and third world
debt, 114; and U.S. debt, 114–15
Foreign capital: third world dependency
on, 132; U.S. dependency on, 35, 85,
94, 95
Foreign exchange reserves: dollar's share
of, 110; and flexible exchange rates,
111–12; German, Japanese, and U.S.
share of, 56
France, privatization in, 236
Free market policies, 281–82, 350–51;
and debt-dependency, 122, 137–38;
and financial stabilization, 138–39; and
flexible exchange rates, 110; and pro

tectionism, 58; and U.S.-Canada
agreement, 103. *See also* Trade debate
Garment industry, characteristics of,
148–49; in Los Angeles county, 159–63
Gender and the international economy,
241–56; and comparable worth issue,
250; and economic crises, 252–53; and
feminization of international labor
force, 242–45; and gender-based prejudices, 247–48; impact of changes on
women, 253–56; and internationalization of gender issues, 245; and multinationals, 246–48; and new international division of labor, 149–51, 163–
64; and new technology in British textile industry, 189, 194–95; and prostitution, 250–52; and wages, 248–51. *See
also* Women workers
General Motors, 171–72, 176
Gephardt Amendment, 265, 266
Global factory, 166–67
Globalist-nationalist debate, 9, 65–69;
and "British decline," 64–65; and crisis in international economy, 24–26;
and financial instability, 101–19; and
program for left, 78–80
"Gramsci problem," 108, 109, 118
Great Britain: capitalist development,
28–29; debt as percentage of GNP,
115; denationalizations, 236; and dominance of international gold standard
monetary system, 104–6; economic
effects of oil prices, 232, 233–34;
effects of internationalization on, 151–
52. *See also* British capitalism;
Thatcher government
Great Depression, 83, 283–84
Growth rates: and expectations of new
stage of capitalism, 351–57; factors
effecting, 352–57; and IMF stabilization programs, 310–12; for the OECD,
283; U.S. agriculture, 206–7, 208
Gulf Oil. *See* "Seven Sisters"

Hispanic women, employment in U.S.,
148, 149, 156, 160, 162–63
Homeworkers, 158–59, 161–62
Horizontal production strategies, 167–68
Household labor, changes in, 253–55
Housing costs, 89, 125

IMF, 25, 29; austerity programs, and U.S.
economy, 121–22; and Brazil, 133; and
global recession and debt crisis, 14–